1,519 ALL-NATURAL ALL-AMAZING

GARDENING SECRETS

⊰ HOW DOES YOUR ⊱
GARDEN GROW?

Ever since the first human decided it would be a better idea to grow a useful plant in a convenient place than to trek through the forest to find it, gardeners have been coming up with ingenious ways to help plants prosper. As this process of discovery and innovation has continued into the modern age, gardeners have learned—often by accident—that simple solutions to common garden problems can often be found in their kitchen cabinets and recycling bins. From spritzing slugs with leftover coffee to capturing pesky flies and yellow jackets with simple soda-bottle traps, this book brings together hundreds of tried-and-true ways to grow a better garden naturally—without resorting to costly chemicals.

Yet the best pleasures of gardening don't revolve around problems and solutions. Rather, there is much pure joy to be found in exploring new ideas, new plants, and creative ways to use them to make your yard more beautiful and productive. Whether you're creating a new landscape or improving an old one, this book will provide the kind

of guidance you might get from a wise teacher on topics such as growing greener grass or lacing your landscape with delicious, easy-to-grow fruits, herbs, and vegetables. The starting point is always a natural one, because when you garden in partnership with nature, plans and projects tend to turn out well, with less struggle and more fun.

INSPIRED IDEAS

The more time you spend in a garden, the more you find that there are always new things to discover. You will never hear experienced gardeners say that they know everything they need to know, because the closer you look, the more you learn. For example, the simple act of gathering a bouquet of blossoms and bringing it indoors often leads to amazing revelations about the intricate structure of flowers you thought you knew well. Even soil improvement can become a source of ongoing fascination as you watch

kitchen trimmings change into rich, crumbly compost or observe the earthworm population boom that happens as you enrich vegetable plots and flowerbeds with organic matter.

Gardeners are curious by nature, so many of the tips here provide information you can use to transform inspired ideas into workable plans. Are there ways to keep beloved shade trees, yet still be able to grow interesting plants? How can you grow enough basil to satisfy your craving for its delicious flavor and aroma? Turning your garden dreams into reality is easy if you have good information topped off with your own imagination.

PRACTICAL AND PRETTY

Gardeners constantly pursue two goals—nurturing beautiful and productive plants and doing it in ways that don't require a lot of time and energy. Some of gardeners' most satisfying moments happen when pretty and practical come together, which is one of the goals of this book. For example, it's great to grow sun-ripened tomatoes but even better when you use a water-saving rain barrel to keep the plants supplied with moisture. You have to prune your roses anyway, so why not use the thorny branches to keep your neighbor's cat from claiming bathroom privileges in your newly seeded beds?

Money is a practical aspect of gardening, too, so there are many tips here to make your efforts more economical. From winterizing roses with fall leaves to using good old vinegar to get rid of weeds in the crevices of your front walkway, many of the tips in this book will show you how you can make do quite nicely with things you already have on hand. When necessary purchases do come up, you'll be a better shopper if you understand what the numbers on the bag of fertilizer mean or how to tell a superior plant from a substandard one.

FINDING YOUR WAY

No two gardens are alike, so this book begins with practical guidance on getting to know your site better, followed by a feast of ideas for planning a better garden or designing a better landscape. Climate is a crucial factor because successful gardening hinges in large part on growing plants that suit the site and season in which they are grown. If you have trouble envisioning your garden from a plant's point of view, the tips and information in Part One will green up your thinking in no time.

Part Two takes an in-depth look at hundreds of plants—from peonies to pines. Whether you have your heart set on growing nutritious vegetables or fragrant herbs or filling pots and window boxes with beautiful flowers, you will find a treasure trove of great tips for growing your favorite plants. Need some new ideas? Why not enrich your landscape with the dramatic texture of ornamental grasses or the constancy of stately evergreens? When it comes to neat things to do with plants, the possibilities are endless.

Part Three explores the practical side of gardening, from how to choose the best tools for digging or pruning to the best ways to turn thin sand or compacted clay into fertile, loamy soil. There are tips for unlocking the mysteries of seeds and great ways to multiply your plants using simple propagation techniques.

Wherever you want to go with your garden, this book is ready to take you there. It will be a wonderful journey. Ready to get started?

—*The Editors*

CONTENTS

❧ Part One ❧
Creating Your Garden

❧ Part Two ❧
Caring for Your Plants

❧ Part Three ☙

Maintaining Your Garden

Creating Your Garden

GARDEN PLANNING AND DESIGN

SPECIAL GARDENS

If you would be happy for a
week, take a wife;
If you would be happy for a
month, kill your pig;
But if you would be happy all
your life, plant a garden.

—*Chinese proverb*

GARDEN PLANNING
AND DESIGN

A landscape is always a work in progress, but it need not always feel like work. Instead, view your landscape as a canvas that reflects the best things nature can do in that particular site, as interpreted through your own creativity and personal tastes.

Where to begin? Spend some time getting to know your yard from both a plant and people point of view. Become familiar with patterns of sun and shade and consider the many views that can be improved or created. If there is little to see when you look out your favorite windows, you may quickly find great spots for colorful flowerbeds. A yard that lacks excitement when seen from the street may instantly benefit from the addition of shapely shrubs or other architectural plants.

There are practical matters to consider, too, such as defining boundaries and making sure that your landscape plans don't interfere with underground utilities. Yet the most practical matter of all is what you want your landscape to do for you and your family. At its best, a landscape provides space for recreation and relaxation and maintains its handsome good looks without constant maintenance. Use the ideas and tips in this chapter to plan the landscape of your dreams.

❧ Home Landscaping

EACH GARDEN HAS A DISTINCT micro-climate brought about by the topography of the land, the locations of buildings, the proximity of a body of water, wind patterns, and similar factors. If you take this microclimate into account when planning your garden, you'll be able to expose your plants to the site's advantages and protect them from its disadvantages. You'll also save time, money, and energy by working with the microclimate instead of trying to combat it.

BASIC CONSIDERATIONS

Divide by three. Think of your yard as having three distinct parts: public spaces, such as the front yard and driveway; private spaces, including patios, swimming pools, and children's play areas; and utility spaces for items like garbage cans and firewood. Public areas should appear neat and organized, while private spaces allow for unlimited creative expression. Be practical when making plans for utility areas.

Make a plan. Take a pencil and paper outdoors and sketch out buildings, sun positions, shade patterns, slopes, and other features. Or take snapshots as a substitute for a hand-drawn plan.

Match your style to your personal tastes. If you enjoy working in your yard and eating what

you grow, a vegetable and herb garden should be a priority. If you love flowers, a perennial bed or rock garden will provide hours of blissful distraction. Busy weekend gardeners often are most satisfied with container plants, small beds of annuals, and a well-tended patch of lawn.

Marry the landscape and house. One of the keys to an attractive landscape is to ease the transition between the "built" and the "natural" environments by combining plants and structural elements. Plant shrubs near your house's foundation to mask the base, and use shapely small trees to visually pull out the front corners. Use colorful containers or beautiful accent shrubs near entryways, or consider letting a climber run up a porch post. Stick with flower colors that flatter your house in the front and explore other hues in the backyard's private spaces.

Take it slow. If you've just moved to a new or neglected property, don't plunge in right away. Instead, let the site grow on you. Take time to develop your plan and get acquainted with your yard. If it's an older yard, you may be surprised to find treasures already growing there. In new yards, look at the plants that seem to be doing especially well in other neighborhood landscapes and envision how they might look if you used them in your own yard.

Telltale signs. Analyze your site to recognize subtle differences that may have big implications for plants. Observe which plants are blown about by wind and which stay still—the latter may indicate protected spots for growing marginally hardy plants. Watch where snow melts first and where it lingers. Note where soil dries quickly and where it remains waterlogged. Variations in soil temperature and moisture mean the difference between a plant that merely survives and one that thrives.

LIGHT AND SHADE

Getting acquainted with the way sun and shade affect various parts of your yard is fundamental to developing a sound landscape plan. Here are the main patterns to track in your yard's unique location, along with tips for using the sun's path to give plants exactly what they need.

In summer, the sun rises and sets slightly north of an east-west line. The north side of a structure

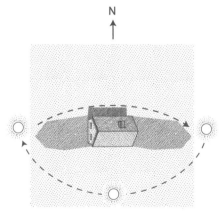

that lies east to west will be in shade at midday and receive weak light in the early morning and late afternoon. East-facing locations will get bright morning sun followed by afternoon shade, while those facing south and west will get enough sun to please full-sun plants.

In winter, the sun rises and sets well to the south of the east-west line, casting long shadows on the north side of the house. This limits the kinds of

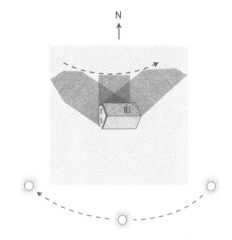

plants and trees that will do well in that part of your yard. Winter light is more subdued to eastern exposures than to areas that face south or west.

Morning light, afternoon shade. Grow plants that are vulnerable to sun damage on the eastern side of your house or other structure, since morning light is gentler than that of midday or afternoon.

Save space for sun seekers. Reserve western exposures for drought- and heat-tolerant specimens that require abundant sun.

Push winter hardiness. If a plant is only marginally hardy in your area, it has a better chance of survival if placed by a wall facing south or southeast. In winter, it will stay warm and be sheltered from cold winds, yet benefit from morning sun.

Protect fruit trees that flower early, such as peaches and cherries, from late-spring frosts by planting them on the north side of the house or on a north-facing slope. This will help delay the trees' blossoming until the danger of frost has passed.

Another delaying tactic. Site plants that blossom in winter or early spring, such as witch hazel, camellia, and hellebore, where they will receive no direct morning sun. Delayed exposure to light will allow the buds to thaw out gradually and risk less damage if they're nipped by frost overnight.

Garden in shade. Most yards are subject to some shade, which is both a blessing and a curse. Instead of trying to eliminate or modify it or trying to grow sun-loving plants, raise an attractive, diverse garden of shade lovers. They often have bolder and more colorful foliage than sun plants. When stocked with shade-tolerant plants, a shady area is often the most inviting part of the landscape on a hot summer day.

Compensate for competition. If your shade plants share their root space with trees, you'll need to give them extra fertilizer and water—especially during a drought. The greedy tree roots will rob the plants of needed nutrients and moisture.

Prevent rot. Shaded areas stay damp longer than sunny ones and can become breeding grounds for diseases. Amend the soil so that it's very well drained and let it dry between waterings. Promote air circulation by giving plants plenty of elbow room. Clean up diseased foliage and autumn debris promptly.

Forget grass. Lawngrasses won't grow in the deep shade beneath densely branched trees. Furnish your shade garden's floor with a shade-tolerant groundcover, groups of ferns, moss, or attractive year-round mulch instead.

Prune low branches from trees to make your shade garden feel a little lighter and brighter—or remove selected higher branches to thin the canopy. Even shade-tolerant plants grow best when they get plenty of filtered light.

Plants with variegated leaves or light-colored blooms will help infuse your shady nook with contrast and light. Try variegated hostas, white caladiums, and impatiens that bloom white or light pink.

Light-colored stepping stones are yet another way to make a sun-bereft area more appealing. Or pave pathways with light-colored mulch, such as beige pea gravel.

Brighten up walls and fences in shady areas. Paint them white or light gray so they reflect more light into those sun-deprived areas.

Add a mirror. The reflected light from a mirror hung on a wall or fence will dance amidst the light and shadows of a shady garden, adding interest as well as light.

SIZE AND SHAPE

In a very small garden, different levels not only add interest, they give you more space for planting. Instead of letting a lawn take up most of the yard, create terraced levels, including steps where you can cluster some pots, and rockeries against low walls. Use containers of all kinds to increase your planting area.

Make your backyard look bigger by planting shrubs at the far end. This will disguise the length of a short lot by obscuring the boundary.

Avoid the tunnel effect. In addition to a curved path, broaden the look of a narrow yard with spreading or broad, rounded shapes. Let a winding path meander into the distance and stagger plantings on each side so they are

balanced but not truly symmetrical. Soften the linear lines of walls or fences with climbing plants. Also install focal points, such as a small pool or pergola, to draw the eye horizontally.

Long, narrow yard? Avoid anything that encourages the eye to focus on the far end. Instead of running a long, straight path down the garden's length, use stepping stones in a curved line. Or place a trellis at right angles to the side boundaries partway down the garden and add decorative foliage plants.

Emphasize entryways. Grow flowerbeds, shapely shrubs, and use attractive containers to dress-up entryways. Other landscape problems are easily overlooked if your entryways are attractive and inviting.

On sloping ground, plan to have winding paths and steps, which are both convenient and interesting. These handsome elements will make your maintenance work easier, and your garden will look more varied.

Difficult corners can be filled with a large, bushy evergreen or a small tree, which has bark that's attractive in winter.

End isolation. If your house is at the top of a slope, don't isolate it further by surrounding it with a bare lawn. Plant shrubs and perennials on at least two sides to unite the house with the garden and to soften the harshness of the setting.

꧁ Creating Flowerbeds

BESIDES BEAUTIFYING THE YARD, flowerbeds can serve many purposes. Accent your front door by flanking it with beds of bright flowers, or hide the base of a chain-link fence with them. You can also use strategically placed beds to direct foot traffic or dramatize a turn in a walkway. Long-blooming annuals are often the most dependable sources of color in flowerbeds, and they are invaluable for tying together the intermittent bloom times of perennials and shrubs.

FLOWERBED BASICS

Consider style. Take the architecture of your house into account when designing a new bed so that both work in harmony. A Georgian-style or ultramodern house, for example, might look best with straight-edged, formal beds. A saltbox or ranch-style house would be enhanced by naturalistic beds in the cottage-garden tradition.

Bigger isn't better. "Praise large gardens, plant small ones," says a wise Chinese proverb. A small, well-designed bed with beautiful color combinations and interesting specimens can be just as attractive and satisfying as a large one—and easier to manage, too. Plan the size of your flowerbed according to what suits

your property and to the time you can devote to maintaining it.

Tie together trees with a curved bed planted with small shade-tolerant shrubs and spring-flowering bulbs. If low maintenance is your goal, fill the bed with spreading groundcover plants.

Stake a bed. For uniform straight edges, mark the boundaries of a new bed with stakes and string before digging in with a spade or edger. For a curved bed, mark the contours with a piece of garden hose—it's flexible enough to assume any shape, yet stable enough to stay put.

In an island bed surrounded by lawn or paths on all sides, place the tallest plants in the center, then use increasingly shorter plants as you move toward the edges. For a naturalistic effect, offset the center of the island slightly and accent it with a blooming shrub or small, flowering tree.

Try high-contrast color combinations. Formal beds in front yards often look best when color combos sing with clarity, such as yellow and blue, red and white, or orange and purple.

Consider flower shape. In addition to color and bloom time, pick plants by the forms of their flowers. Many flowers have flat, daisy-shaped blossoms, which look livelier in the company of others with varying shapes and forms, from spikes and saucers to trumpets and bells. A mix of contrasting and complementary shapes will add interest to the bed.

Try one color. Working with a single color, such as white or yellow, can be fun. Include a collection of annuals and perennials that bloom in slightly different hues and feature different forms and sizes. The effect can be amazing.

Look at the leaves. Because there will be times when blooms are sparse, take into account the form, size, and color of the plant's foliage. Annuals with showy foliage, such as dusty miller, coleus, Persian shield, and ornamental sweet potato vine, do a good job of unifying the diversified plantings of bright bloomers.

WORKING WITH ARCHITECTURAL PLANTS

Plants come in unlimited shapes and sizes, which you can use to great advantage. Think of your garden as an architect would a building—as a three-dimensional structure with line, scale, and texture—and then use plants as the building blocks. For the framework, you can choose from a vast array of "architectural plants"—hardy specimens with well-defined silhouettes that lend durable and dramatic form to the landscape in all seasons.

Plant selection. Good architectural plants include trees, shrubs, and ornamental grasses, which come in myriad shapes depending on the growth habit of the stems and foliage.

Practical uses. Whether alone or in a group, distinctly sculptural plants can establish a boundary, minimize a defect, or provide an accent.

Setting a mood. Architectural plants can also set a tone: A symmetrical evergreen hedge, for example, lends a formal look, while a well-placed weeping cherry sets a more relaxed mood.

Creative effects. Plant shapes can be used to achieve a variety of effects, too. In general, vertical forms, such as pyramids, columns, and upright ovals, are eye-catchers, drawing the design of the garden skyward. Horizontal forms, including spreading and

umbrella shapes, act as anchors, linking the garden to ground level.

Combining shapes. Perhaps the most challenging—and rewarding—aspect of plant architecture is combining different shapes into a compatible grouping. Pairing strongly divergent profiles, such as a soaring pyramid and prostrate "fan," makes for dynamic contrast, whereas pairing related shapes, such as an egg and a globe or an umbrella and a bowl, results in a soft, harmonious design. When you begin looking at plants as architectural elements, you'll find yourself seeing your landscape—and those of your neighbors—in a whole new way!

Plan for the full season. Choose a variety of flowering ornamentals. Many bulbs provide early spring color, while perennials change the garden's look from week to week. Annuals are steady performers, adding enduring color and filling in while hardy plants mature; because they last only one season, annuals also let you experiment with different schemes.

Discourage invasive plants, such as St. John's wort, periwinkle, potentilla, or pachysandra from spreading beyond their beds. Dig a narrow trench and drive flat tiles, slates, or roofing shingles—lined up side by side—vertically into the ground to from a barrier.

Build a bermed bed. If your land is flat, you can vary the terrain by building berms, or mounds of soil. Either raise the whole bed on one berm or make several to highlight various plant groupings.

Another way to add height to a flowerbed is to accent the bed with climbers. You will get quick coverage on a trellis with fast-growing annual vines, such as morning glory, sweet pea, or scarlet runner bean.

Before planting shrubs in a new bed, do a dry run to see how you like their colors and textures when they're placed in a group. Simply place them—still in their pots—in the desired locations, then stand back and take a critical look. If the arrangement doesn't appeal to you, it's very easy to change your plan before you plant the shrubs.

BORDERS

A bed backed by a wall, hedge, or fence is the ideal setting for a border. A border can be described best as a bed that comes forward from the backdrop, with the plants in the bed arranged in decreasing height from back to front. This design gives an unobstructed view of all the plants and lets each one receive sun. But be flexible: the occasional short plant tucked behind a tall one may provide appealing texture and make the bed more beautiful.

Plant in drifts instead of straight rows. Group large plants in threes and smaller ones in fives or sevens. Odd numbers of plants look more natural than even-numbered groupings. Only a specimen plant used as a special accent should be planted singly.

Use a simple color scheme. Plan for a long season of bloom, but limit your color choices to three main colors, such as pink, yellow, and blue or red, white, and blue. Include neutral white bloomers or plants with gray foliage to help offset potential clashes.

Add an edge. Just as a border includes a backdrop, it also needs a defined front edge to provide a sense of containment. In addition to small, mound-forming plants, include a hard edge if the border adjoins lawn. Edging materials made from concrete, plastic, or composite wood are efficient but can be costly. You'll save by choosing natural stones, brick pavers, or recycled brick instead.

Create a rustic trellis border. For a charming, old-fashioned border, use this simple and inexpensive technique. Insert sturdy 12- to 16-inch (30- to 41-cm) wood stakes every 6 inches (15 cm) along the edge of your border. Then interlace the uprights with pliable vines or willow stems to create a lattice. The resulting trellis makes an especially complementary background and support for old-fashioned climbers, runner beans, strawberries, and herbs.

FOUNDATION PLANTINGS

Most landscapes include foundation shrubs for a good reason. In addition to masking the base of the house, they limit the splashing of mud by heavy rain, provide some protection from extreme cold and heat, and frame the view when you look out your windows. Here are some guidelines for fine-tuning your foundation beds.

Emphasize evergreens, which provide year-round color and structure. Include deciduous shrubs that feature remarkable texture or colorful flowers.

Be size wise. Foundation shrubs should grow only as tall as the lowest edges of windows. Replace overgrown shrubs with dwarf varieties that fit their space better. Corner shrubs can be taller but should reach only two-thirds of the way to the eaves of the house. Oversized corner shrubs tend to make a house look small.

High windows? Stack foundation shrubs in two layers, which will provide more visual depth.

Stretch a low foundation by keeping shrubs very short and designing a bed that pulls forward into the yard. The effect will be much more harmonious than if you use taller plants.

BOUNDARY MARKERS

A fence is a good way to enhance the privacy of your backyard, but in the front yard, fences are often neither practical nor permissible. Instead, you can define boundaries with flowerbeds, hedges, intermittent shrubs, or mixed plantings of shrubs and trees. Dense evergreen hedges require ongoing maintenance, but other types of boundary plantings need little care to keep them in good condition.

Multiuse hedges. Whether they're comprised of meticulously clipped evergreens or made up of a diverse collection of deciduous shrubs, hedges provide structure and a sense of permanence in the garden. They are practical for screening a deck or patio for privacy and buffering traffic noise and wind. They can frame a pretty vista or block an unsightly view. They can also mark property lines, define intimate garden "rooms," add dimension to a flat expanse, or be sculpted into topiary.

No hedges in front. Planting a hedge of shrubs or trees across the front of your house hides it from view, which can create security problems and reduce the value of your home. Although the privacy created by a row of plants may seem enticing, it comes at a cost.

Create peace and quiet. Planting a dense, wide evergreen hedge on a mound of soil, or berm, can help block noise if a side of your yard borders a busy street. Some open hedges may also create their own "white noise" as wind passes through the branches and rustles the leaves.

Need a windbreak? You can minimize the damaging effects of wind by installing a barrier of hardy trees or shrubs. Site the windbreak so that prevailing winds hit it broadside. The distance between the windbreak and the area to be protected should be 10 times the plants' height; for example, place a 5-foot (1.5-meter) hedge 50 feet (15 meters) away. Set plants in staggered rows; evergreens, such as fir, pine, and spruce, or dense deciduous plants, such as viburnum, abelia, and forsythia, are good choices.

❦ Watch Out!

Property boundaries often include utility right-of-ways, where pipes or lines may be buried. Before digging, check your property plat or call local utilities if you need help locating underground lines.

Try a tapestry hedge. Be adventurous in designing your living wall by using different plants or species that are compatible both aesthetically and culturally. The resulting "tapestry hedge" will add visual interest and let you use more of your favorite plants to provide blooms or attract wildlife. Ornamental grasses combined with evergreen and deciduous shrubs create a beautiful, all-season tapestry hedge.

Time pruning. Prune deciduous hedges in the winter or just after they've flowered. Prune evergreen hedges in spring, early summer, or fall. In cold climates, all hedges need to be pruned early enough so that any new growth will have time to harden off to prevent winter injury.

Prune those hedges. An effective tall hedge takes a long time to establish, and regular pruning is necessary to create dense growth. Don't allow plants to grow tall and lanky at the expense of density; otherwise, you'll end up with a thin and useless hedge. Limit the height of an evergreen hedge to no more than 6 feet (2 meters), or you'll need a ladder to prune it. If you want more height, use trees instead.

Use conifers. Conifers create handsome, dense hedges. Shape hemlocks, arborvitae, and yews by clipping the young sprouts, leaving ¾ inch to 2 inches (2 to 5 cm) of new growth. Or you can prune them lightly for a more natural look. Pines can also be hedged; prune them by removing one-half to two-thirds of candle growth (new shoots with growth buds) with pruners in late spring or early summer. Most conifers perform best as a hedge when maintained in a roughly pyramidal shape, with the base wider than the top. Prune the plants slowly and carefully, stepping back every now and then to gauge your progress.

Separate your vegetable garden from the yard and protect it from animals by growing a hedge of thorny fruits, such as blackberries.

Support them on a trellis around the perimeter. For extra color, interplant the brambles with morning glories, scarlet runner beans, sunflowers, or other climbing vines and tall annuals.

Discourage intruders. Use a thorny hedge as a barrier against dogs, opossums, and other uninvited visitors. Among the most unwelcoming plants are barberry, pyracantha, hawthorn, shrub roses, holly, and hardy orange. When planted beneath windows, thorny plants can discourage burglars, too.

MAINTAINING BEDS

Tending to the needs of vigorous flowers is often a joy, but even the most lovingly planted flowers cannot simply grow themselves. Keep a close eye on your beds to spot problems with pests or diseases early, and pull out plants that simply fail to grow. Feed plants that appear small or pale with water-soluble fertilizer and provide extra water for thirsty specimens during long hot spells. Each time you visit your flowerbeds, pull any weeds and remove spent flowers.

Don't forget to mulch. Protect roots, suppress weeds, and prevent soil from splashing up onto your flowers by covering the bed with 2 to 3 inches (5 to 8 cm) of attractive mulch, such as shredded bark, cocoa hulls, or pine needles.

Watch your step. If your soil is heavy, wet, or sticky, lay down wooden planks to kneel onto when tending flowers; you'll avoid compressing soil around roots. In broad beds, install stone or concrete stepping stones.

Prolong blooming by deadheading; if you keep plants from setting seed, they will produce more flowers. When buds are visible along the stem, cut or pinch off the spent blooms just above the buds. When there are no buds on the stem, cut back to the base.

Save your favorites. To let a few nonhybrid flowers develop mature seeds, leave old blossoms on the plants until they begin to shatter. Store your collected seeds in a cool, dry place and plant them the following year. Some flowers, such as cleome, Johnny jump-up, and melampodium, reseed themselves with little help.

✿ Understanding Zones

DO YOU KNOW WHAT ZONE you live in? You should, because the plant hardiness zone you live in is one of the most important factors affecting which plants will survive and thrive in your garden. These climate zones were mapped by the U.S. Department of Agriculture to help gardeners and farmers select the most hardy plants and crops. The zones are based on the average coldest temperature for each region.

The 11 hardiness zones reflect North America's enormous climate diversity. The USDA divides the continent into separate zones. At one extreme is the near-Artic zone 1, found mostly in Canada and Alaska, where winter temperatures drop to below -50°F (-46°C). At the other end is tropical zone 11, found mostly in Florida's southernmost tip and Hawaii, where it rarely dips below 40°F (4°C).

Other factors besides zone. Your zone is not the only factor that determines whether or not a plant will thrive in your garden. Heat and daytime temperatures, rain- and snowfall, wind, humidity, and cloud cover are important, too. And within a zone, there are many pockets with their own microclimates due to elevation, a nearby body of water or mountain, or other factors. Even within your own garden, the shelter of a wall may encourage a less-hardy plant to flourish. Also, many plants that grow in one zone may do well in the southern part of the neighboring colder zone—although it's always safer to choose a plant that is hardy in a zone that's colder than yours.

Consider your plants. Some trees and bulbs, for example, need a period of cold to stimulate growth. Deciduous plants can usually tolerate more sun and heat than evergreens. And most plants withstand cold better in a dry area. If you want to be sure that a certain plant is hardy in your area, consult a local nursery or a knowledgeable gardener.

For more information. Here we have grouped closely related zones into four broad categories— cold, temperate, warm, and hot. For a closer look at your region, check your local library or go to www.usna.usda.gov/Hardzone and click on your state. For the nine similar climate zones developed by Natural Resources Canada, try sis.agr.gc.ca/cansis/nsdb/climate/hardiness.

Hawaii and Alaska are not shown on the maps here. Except for higher inland elevations, all of Hawaii is hot zone 11. Alaska's lower coastline and panhandle, where most gardeners live, are surprisingly in temperate zones 5 and 6, but most of the state is in the lower numbered cold zones.

The Cold Zones—1 to 4

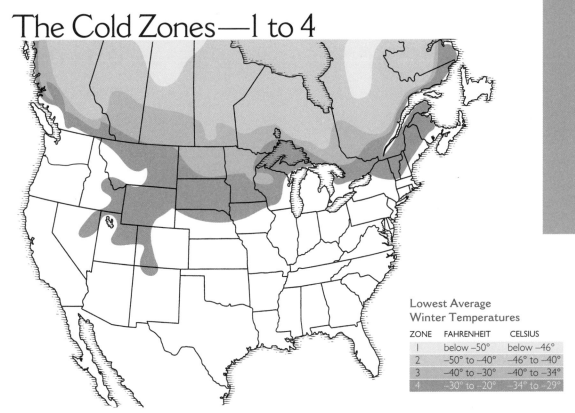

Lowest Average Winter Temperatures

ZONE	FAHRENHEIT	CELSIUS
1	below −50°	below −46°
2	−50° to −40°	−46° to −40°
3	−40° to −30°	−40° to −34°
4	−30° to −20°	−34° to −29°

ORNAMENTALS

The soil is slow to warm in spring, so perennials and shrubs that are already in the ground, ready to produce buds and blossoms, are especially valuable. Peonies, delphiniums, and lilacs make great anchor plants, and evergreen trees are invaluable for providing color and form through the long winter. Ornamental grasses planted in protected spots and left uncut until spring do a wonderful job of dramatizing winter wind.

Windbreaks help to tame winter gales. Low walls or hedges can serve the same purpose in smaller yards, provided they don't create excessive shade.

EDIBLES

Raised beds are a boon for vegetable and herb gardens because they warm up in spring faster than the ground. Cool-natured vegetables, such as cabbage and beets, thrive, and chives may grow so well that they become invasive. To warm the soil for tomatoes, peppers, and other warm-natured crops, use black plastic mulch. Starting seeds indoors and using cold frames and cloches can add weeks to the short growing season.

WISE ADVICE

Make space indoors for houseplants, which can help lift your spirits in winter while purifying stuffy indoor air. Outdoors, in your short growing season, use plenty of containers filled with annuals for summer color. In fall, empty the containers and store them in a dry place to keep them from cracking due to cold temperatures.

The Temperate Zones—5 to 6

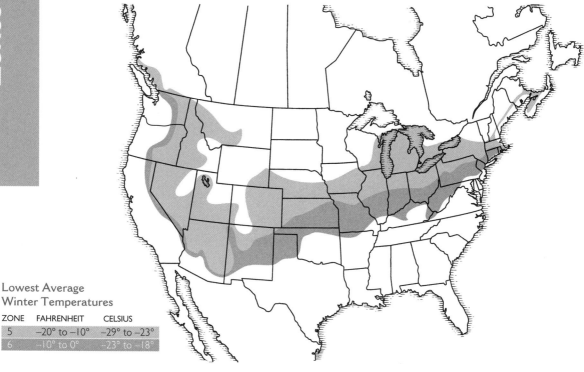

Lowest Average
Winter Temperatures

ZONE	FAHRENHEIT	CELSIUS
5	−20° to −10°	−29° to −23°
6	−10° to 0°	−23° to −18°

ORNAMENTALS

With four distinct seasons, gardeners are wise to invest heavily in spring-flowering bulbs, summer-blooming perennials and shrubs, and trees with vivid fall color. In winter, use evergreens and stone features to keep the garden attractive. Plants with ornamental bark, such as red-twig dogwoods and birches, can also help.

Summer calls for plenty of colorful annuals, as well as trellised clematis or annual vines. In naturally rich soil, fine-textured bluegrass thrives when given good care. In areas with low rainfall, buffalograss is an excellent choice. Stop feeding and watering shrubs and trees in late summer because new growth in late season is easily damaged by winter's cold.

EDIBLES

Perennial vegetables, including asparagus and rhubarb, will produce for many years, along with raspberries, strawberries, and many tree fruits. Perennial herbs may fall victim to cold, so it's a good idea to pot small specimens and grow them indoors in winter. Maximize production by planting cool-season veggies in early spring, tomatoes and other warm-season veggies in late spring, and plenty of fast-growing leafy greens in late summer.

WISE ADVICE

In many areas, limited wild habitat has created serious overpopulation problems with deer and other wild animals. Be prepared to fence in your garden if necessary and whenever possible, choose plants that animals don't like to eat.

The Warm Zones—7 to 8

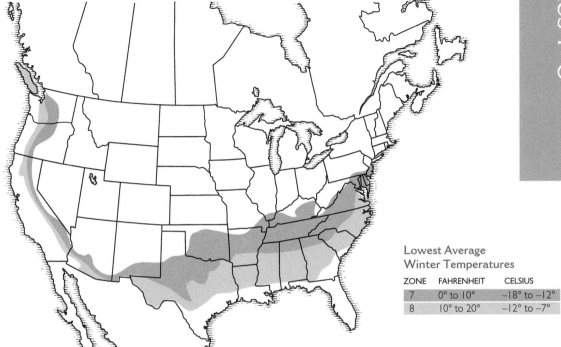

Lowest Average Winter Temperatures

ZONE	FAHRENHEIT	CELSIUS
7	0° to 10°	−18° to −12°
8	10° to 20°	−12° to −7°

ORNAMENTALS

Several popular flowers can be grown as perennials, including dahlias, gladiolus, and cannas. Spring-flowering bulbs, however, may suffer from short winter dormancy but can be enjoyed for one or two seasons. Versatile evergreen azaleas and camellias make excellent shrubs for partially shaded sites, and all types of hydrangeas can be grown with ease for summer color.

Water features are especially refreshing, where summers are hot and humid. Arbors and pergolas that create shade make great additions to sun-drenched yards. In yards dominated by large trees, woodland gardens provide fine places to grow spring-blooming wildflowers and many types of hardy fern.

EDIBLES

Long, hot summers make tomatoes and peppers phenomenally productive, along with semi-tropical vegetables including okra, sweet potatoes, and field peas. The long, mild fall favors growing leafy greens and cabbage-family crops. In eastern regions, rabbit-eye blueberries thrive in acid soil, as do figs and muscadine grapes. In western areas, warm days and cool nights combine to provide perfect growing conditions for many tree fruits, grapes, and raspberries.

WISE ADVICE

Insect populations are often huge in mild-winter areas, which is a great reason to grow plants that host beneficial insects such as ladybugs, lacewings, and numerous small wasps.

Garden Planning and Design **29**

The Hot Zones—9 to 11

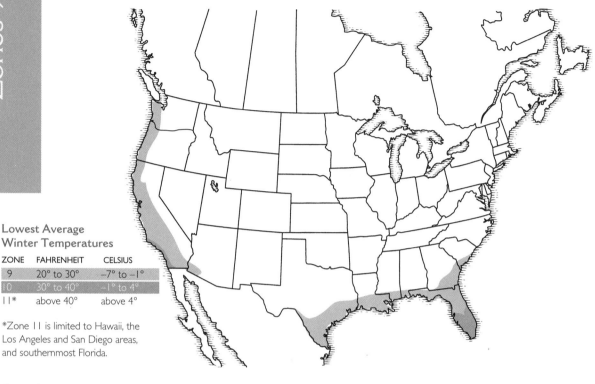

**Lowest Average
Winter Temperatures**

ZONE	FAHRENHEIT	CELSIUS
9	20° to 30°	−7° to −1°
10	30° to 40°	−1° to 4°
11*	above 40°	above 4°

*Zone 11 is limited to Hawaii, the
Los Angeles and San Diego areas,
and southernmost Florida.

ORNAMENTALS

In humid southeastern areas, big oaks dripping with Spanish moss set the scene for a rather sparse lower layer of vegetation. In sunnier sites, tropical trees and groundcovers help hold the garden through summer. Winter and spring are the big color seasons, with bougainvillea blooming in the company of brightly colored annuals.

In southwestern regions, mild year-round weather creates a paradise for marginally hardy plants, such as Rosemary, fuchsia, and gardenias. Roses with good resistance to mildew bloom over a long period. Limited rainfall often makes it necessary to provide supplemental water to all garden plants, which should be done in the most efficient way possible to avoid waste.

EDIBLES

In eastern regions, use fall to grow cool-season vegetables, and start warm-season crops in late winter. Explore semitropical fruits, including guava, papaya, and all types of citrus, which provide blossoms and fruit. Strawberries can be grown as annuals, planted in the fall. In western areas, manage your space well to keep your vegetable garden in production year round. Rain is usually more abundant in winter, so cool-season crops grown in fall and spring demand less supplemental water.

WISE ADVICE

Don't struggle to garden in hot summer weather. Working in the garden is more enjoyable in the milder temperatures of the fall-to-spring season.

SPECIAL GARDENS

What do you think makes a garden special? Maybe the feel of a miniature mountain conjured up by a rock garden? Or perhaps your idea of a special garden includes the presence of small shovels and watering cans—evidence that a young gardener is learning about the wonders of plants. Gardeners use their landscapes to explore a wide range of interests, from hosting pretty songbirds and luring butterflies to growing plants that actually eat insects. This chapter includes practical and creative ways to give your garden a distinctive difference, regardless of its size or location. A simple Japanese style, for example, can be carried out in a courtyard-size setting, or you may want to try a geometric, clipped knot garden if you often view your garden from second-story windows or a high deck.

How do you decide which special touches are right for your unique garden? Watch for ideas or projects that trigger a little thrill, whether it's making a homemade bird feeder or creating beauty by combining stones and water. The most special gardens of all do one simple thing: They provide their keepers with moments of deep satisfaction that can be found only in the garden.

31

❧ Natural Gardens

THERE IS A SPECIAL JOY that comes with devoting part of your landscape to a garden that re-creates how the area might appear if nature were allowed to work its wonders with the site. Depending on where you live, at least one of the following options is probably worthy of consideration.

WILDFLOWER MEADOWS

A meadow is a sunny area that supports a profusion of wildflowers along with a few grasses, which hold the soil in place and deter unwanted weeds. Transforming a pasture or area of lawn into a meadow takes time, but if you start small and implement your plans over a period of several years, you can create a beautiful meadow that's easy to maintain with yearly mowing.

Prepare the area in the fall by cultivating the soil, raking out debris, and sowing seeds of wildflowers native to your area, along with colorful annual wildflowers. Set aside one-third of your seeds and oversow the area first thing in spring. Include pathways throughout the meadow.

Throughout the first year, patrol the area often and nip out weeds. Instead of pulling them, which will disturb tiny wildflower seedlings, cut them off at ground level and toss the foliage into the paths. Fill open spaces with additional wildflower seeds, purchased seedlings, or rooted cuttings of native perennial wildflowers.

In the fall, mow the area high, rake up the debris, and compost it. Sow additional seeds in thin areas.

Weed often through the second year and expect to see plenty of color from year-old perennial plants. Continue filling gaps with seeds and delay mowing until spring so that seeds shed by mature wildflowers will have a chance to grow.

From the third season on, fine-tune your meadow by adding plants you like and taking out those you don't like. Expect to see plenty of wildlife, including birds, butterflies, and huge populations of native pollinating insects.

WOODLAND GARDENS

Nothing announces spring's arrival more beautifully than the pastel petals of woodland plants found on the forest floor. Your own woodland garden should match the conditions found in a natural wooded site: shaded protection from the summer sun; rich, moist soil with a high proportion of humus; leaf litter for mulch; and dappled sunlight in spring, which is the biggest bloom time for woodland flowers.

Most woodland flowers prefer acid soil. To provide it, work compost or leaf mold into planting pockets before setting out plants.

Increase sunlight by removing low branches from trees. Although woodland flowers need shade, they grow best in high, dappled shade rather than deep shade.

Make use of improved varieties. The popularity of shade gardening has led to huge improvements in woodland wildflowers, such as heuchera, foamflower, wild geranium, and many other species.

Include shrubs, such as native azaleas and serviceberry, as well as small trees like redbud, dogwood, and witch hazel.

Trim the edges with spring-flowering bulbs, which often thrive in sites that get winter sun followed by summer shade.

RESTORED PRAIRIES

North American prairies once stretched from the Rockies eastward almost even with the Great Lakes. Today, only small pockets of native prairie remain—yet replicas are turning up in more and more home landscapes. Creating a restored prairie is similar to growing a wildflower meadow, but with more emphasis on native grasses, which are foundation plants in a prairie ecosystem.

Visit local wild areas to learn about plants that are native to sites similar to yours. Keep in mind that dry prairies support different plants than prairies in low, damp areas.

Participate in plant rescues, which are often sponsored by local native plant or wildflower societies. As long as you have the owner's permission, you can dig and adopt native prairie plants that would otherwise be lost when land is developed for roads and houses.

Hold the water. Except for providing water to new transplants, don't water a restored prairie. Supplemental water often favors weeds over native prairie plants.

Burn wisely. Periodic burning is a natural part of a prairie's life cycle. Obtain any needed permits and plan a carefully controlled burn every three to four years.

Preserve a habitat. Restored prairies serve as home to quail and other ground-nesting birds as well as beneficial insects and grasshopper mice—little rodents that eat mostly grasshoppers. Mowing or burning in spring preserves their habitat through winter, when it's most needed.

BLOOMING DESERTS

A desert is one of the most inhospitable places on Earth because of extreme temperatures and long periods of drought. The fact that beautiful, exotic flora can thrive in desert climates is a never-ending miracle. Gardeners who learn to work with desert conditions can participate in this miracle by bringing the desert into bloom.

Stick with native plants that have made the necessary adaptations to survive under desert conditions. Cactus, agave, and deep-rooted perennials often perform best.

Plan for night viewing. Hot sun makes the desert inhospitable during the day, so many desert flowers open at night. Wildlife is more active then, too.

Leach out salts. Alkaline desert soils often contain high concentrations of salt. Many desert plants tolerate these conditions, but they will grow better if you add organic matter and water heavily several times a year.

Start with plants rather than seeds. Well-rooted plants will become established much more quickly than seeds. When working with seeds, plant them in the fall rather than in spring.

Include tall stones, fences, posts, or other elements that cast shadows. The tiny microclimates where shade is present can support a richer diversity of plants.

XERISCAPE GARDENS

Closely related to a desert garden is a Xeriscape garden, which is particularly well suited to terrain that is at least seasonally semiarid or arid but not full-blown desert. It may be an odd word, but Xeriscaping, or landscaping in ways that require little if any supplemental water, is an idea whose time has come. Based on the Greek word *xeros,* meaning "dry," a Xeriscape garden is built with plants that naturally thrive on the normal rainfall of the region. Xeriscaping saves water and time because when plants become established—usually after two years—you won't have to spend time watering when the weather is dry.

Don't limit your garden to cacti and rocks. A well-designed Xeriscape can be eye-catching and lush all year. If you limit the size of the garden, you can set aside a small portion for a vegetable or flower-cutting garden, both of which demand more water. It's best to avoid outright desert-like Xeriscapes with large areas of gravel and only a few succulents for interest. Such a sparce layout offers no respite from the sun and raises temperature by radiating heat back into the environment.

Add a trickle of water. A small fountain is a refreshing addition to a Xeriscape garden in hot, dry climates. Even the sound of splashing water is restful. A recirculating pump keeps water use to a minimum.

Include a little lawn. Lawns require more water than most groundcovers, but you can save water by confining your turf to a single focal point off the patio or between flowerbeds. Choose dry land grass species that need less water, such as tall fescue, blue grama, and buffalograss. Elsewhere in the garden, replace your lawn with drought-tolerant groundcovers, such as common yarrow, Portuguese broom, and sea thrift.

Annuals that adapt to Xeriscaping in both warm and cold climates include marigolds, cockscombs, African daisies, dusty miller, gazanias, moss roses, sunflowers, and zinnias.

Plant in water-use zones. Zone your Xeriscape garden according to the water needs of the plants. Group those that need more moisture, for example, where they can benefit from the runoff water from downspouts, driveways, and patios. Put plants that don't need full sun under the dappled shade of tall trees; this will keep down the soil temperature and minimize the need for water.

Put plants in the ground just before the rainy season to take advantage of whatever natural precipitation you get. Space them far enough apart so that roots will have plenty of room to spread and won't have to compete for moisture.

Establish your plants. Shape soil into basins around the base of new trees and shrubs to help catch water. Water infrequently and deeply to encourage deep roots. After two years, you can knock down the basins, install a low-volume irrigation system, and add mulch. By keeping soil temperatures cool, a 2- or 3-inch (5- or 8-cm) layer of organic mulch significantly reduces water loss.

Low-volume irrigation systems operate at low pressure and deliver a low but steady amount of water. They include soaker hoses, controlled drip emitters, miniature sprayers and sprinklers, and root irrigators that soak the soil beneath the surface.

❧ Theme Gardens

MOST GARDENERS HAVE A DREAM garden—a particularly harmonious setting designed around a specific theme or classic prototype. The romantic English cottage-style garden has been by far the most emulated model for decades, but the rustic alpine rock gardens, tranquil Japanese gardens, and formal knot gardens described here have much to recommend them. For any such theme garden to thrive, it's important that it be suited to the distinctive climate and soil characteristics of your yard.

ROCK GARDENS

Rock gardens are modeled on high-mountain terrain, where colonies of alpine wildflowers and shrubs thrive on the cool, sunny, arid stone slopes. You can create a rock garden of any size by working with an existing stone outcrop or by arranging rocks and filling the crevices between them with compost and gravel. Use these tried-and-true guidelines for creating your garden of stone.

A steep, hard-to-mow slope is an ideal setting for a rock garden, and it can easily be transformed from an eyesore into a showpiece. Structure the base of the slope with a low stone wall, then work your way up the slope by adding more stones and plants.

Use local rock. To help your garden of stone fit into the landscape, choose a type of rock found in your region and use it throughout the garden.

Arrange the stones. Place stones in odd-numbered groupings, which are usually more eye-catching than even numbers. On a steep slope, use the largest stones for the base.

Set up your stones. As you set stones in place, plant them by burying them by one-third their depth in the soil with the broadest side down. This will keep them from toppling. Slant stones so that they point backward, which channels water to plant roots and prevents erosion. And be sure to include a few flat stones to stand on when you're working in your garden.

Plants used in rock gardens are traditionally tough alpine wildflowers, along with ground-covers and dwarf shrubs, but you can use any low-growing plants to complement mountain natives. To ensure visual interest, choose a variety of plants that have different growth habits. Mix creeping perennials with upright bulbs and add in other tiny bloomers.

Dwarf perennials are mainstays of the rock garden. Choose among dwarf ferns, sempervivums, saxifrages, campanulas, tiny bulbs, and creeping phlox.

Put spreading plants in their own pocket to keep them contained; rock crevices form natural barriers against spreading roots.

Use soil that drains quickly. Adapted to harsh conditions, rock plants are accustomed to quick-draining soil. Heavy soil will suffocate the roots, while rich soil promotes lush growth that may overtake the stones. Fill crevices with a mix of coarse sand, compost, and fine gravel.

JAPANESE GARDENS

Ideal for small spaces, a Japanese garden involves the harmonious use of water, plants, and stone. A pleasure to look at year round, it needs only some attentive pruning and weeding. By combining native and Asian

plants, you can adapt this soothing garden style to your climate and location.

Don't overdo it. *Shibusa* is a word that the Japanese often use to describe their gardens. It has many meanings, but it mainly implies restraint, good taste, and elegant simplicity. Limit your choice of materials.

Water is a mandatory element. Whether running or still, water is essential to a Japanese garden. Install a birdbath, a small fountain, or a tiny shallow pond with a few goldfish. Always make sure the water is perfectly clean.

Look for contrasts when choosing plants and stones. Use lighter shades against darker shades. Mix fine and bold textures. And remember that in Japanese gardening, the emphasis is on foliage rather than flowers, although you can add a few flowering plants to punctuate the seasons.

Let a path meander. In a strolling or teahouse garden, the path becomes the garden. Stepping stones control the rate at which you proceed and the spacing of views. The long axis of the stones is generally perpendicular to the direction of movement. Interject larger stepping stones where you want to pause and view a special feature.

Select the right stones. Stones for the background should be fairly large and carefully chosen—either blocks of rock with a distinctive outline or large, table-like slabs laid on the ground. You can also add pebbles or river gravel, which are easy to maintain.

Gravel guidelines. Use off-white instead of pure white, which can produce a blinding glare. Smaller gravel holds patterns best. Before spreading, place a woven geotextile underneath. The material prevents weeds, but unlike black plastic, it lets air and water pass through. Rake carefully to make sure that no patches of the material show through the gravel.

When choosing plants for a Japanese-style garden, combine Asian natives with indigenous specimens. Plants appropriate for this style include bamboo, cherry, Japanese maple (*acer palmatum*), pine, azalea, camellia, ginkgo, wisteria, Japanese iris, and various ferns.

Compact, mound-forming plants are useful in creating rolling contours that suggest hills or clouds. Good choices include Japanese holly (*Ilex crenata*), inkberry holly (*I. glabra*), Swiss mountain pine (*Pinus mugo*), Korean boxwood (*Buxus microphylla* var. *koreana*), and dwarf red barberry (*Berberis thunbergii* 'Crimson Pygmy').

TYPES OF JAPANESE GARDENS

Strolling gardens are based on the idea of a journey. The path itself is the garden, and the stones on the path articulate the journey, showing where to walk and where to stop.

Hill-and-pond gardens are generally made for viewing. As the name suggests, a body of water dominates. Plants and shrubs are usually used to suggest rolling hills and clouds.

Teahouse gardens are designed around a path leading to a simple teahouse.

Courtyard gardens are usually in the entryways of homes. Often there is a basin of water for cleaning away the dirt of outdoors before entering the garden and then the home. *Shu-i-wa* is Japanese for this garden type. It means "point of energy," a term taken from acupuncture.

Dry-landscape gardens are classic rock-and-gravel types.

KNOT GARDENS

Known since Elizabethan times, knot gardens were common features at monasteries and aristocratic estates. Today, they are most often seen in public gardens, although they're enjoying a revival among home gardeners who want to create distinctive gardens in a formal style.

Try a knot garden. Because the pattern of a knot garden is best viewed from above, it's usually best to locate the garden where it can seen from a raised deck, porch, or balcony. You can also put one in a sunken garden.

Start with a plan. Sketch your design to scale on graph paper to determine the shapes and the number of plants you need. You can use a number of geometric designs, including interlocking circles, squares, triangles, and other shapes formed by low, narrow hedges.

Knot-garden plants must be both hardy and tolerant of regular shearing. Popular choices are dwarf boxwood, Japanese holly, gray or green santolina, lavender, germander, and Rosemary. Use several kinds of plants with different colors and textures to accent the interlocking design.

Before planting, make sure the ground is absolutely level, or the pattern will be distorted. As you set plants in place, exaggerate the design slightly so it will keep its definition once the plants mature.

Use mulch. Spread crushed marble, red shale chips, or pea gravel for permanent mulch, or use fine-textured organic mulch, such as shredded bark, and renew it annually.

When pruning plants, neatness counts. Clip plants lightly with sharp, thin-bladed shears every three to four weeks during the growing season. Clip conservatively at first so that you can judge the results as you proceed. Stop trimming four to six weeks before the first frost so the plants can harden off before winter.

Single-season knots. Historically, knot gardens are permanent garden features, but you can also use annuals to create a one-season garden. Take a painterly approach by planting a knot using different colors of coleus, or use herbs, such as parsley, red basil, and soft gray sage.

❧ Water Gardening

THE LIFE IN A GARDEN POND provides not only visual pleasure but also an ongoing education. The interaction between aquatic animals and plants is a lesson in the natural balance necessary for a healthy ecosystem. Aquatic plants add oxygen to the water and take up impurities, while fish eat mosquitoes and other insects, and their waste fertilizes the plants. In a small pond, the natural balance between plants and fish will keep the water clear. In a larger pond, install a submersible pump and add a filter to help circulate clear water.

PLANNING A POND

Select a location where the pond looks like it fits with the rest of the landscape. In a formal garden, for example, consider using a symmetrical pond as a centerpiece. For a naturalistic look, site a free-form pond where it can be easily seen and enjoyed from outdoor living areas. Also consider the view from indoors.

Nearby trees may block the sun needed by aquatic plants and litter the water with leaves in autumn. If you like the look of a pond set in a leafy glade, choose evergreen trees and shrubs, which don't shed, and site them far enough away so that they won't cast shade and their roots won't eventually weaken pond walls.

Hold in the water. Flexible, fish-safe liners can be fitted into any size or shape of pond. They are inexpensive and last for 10 years or more. Preformed fiberglass ponds are a bit more durable but are trickier to install because they must be perfectly fitted into the excavated hole.

Include a liner. For the best fit, line the hole with ½ to 1 inch (1 to 3 cm) of damp sand before installing a flexible liner for your pond. If the pond is small, a piece of scrap carpeting may save you some money. It's easier to work with a flexible liner on a warm, sunny day, when the liner is more pliable.

Level it off. If you're installing your own pond, make sure that the top edges are absolutely level. Use a long carpenter's level to check all sides.

No room? If your yard is too small to accommodate a full-size pond, you can create a mini-pond with a half barrel or other watertight container. Use only small aquatic plants that are suited to tub culture.

Landscape the edges with a combination of plants and edging stones. Brick edging gives a neat look to formal ponds. For a naturalistic pond, use stones. Instead of arranging them in a ring around the pond's edge, allow some to appear to tumble into the water.

Wait two weeks after filling your pond to add plants and another week to add fish. That way, neither plants nor fish will be harmed by possible chemical contaminants in the water.

Limit algae by growing plants, such as water lilies; they block the sun that algae need for growth. Also include rooted floating plants, which provide food for fish and help oxygenate the water.

Start with goldfish. Beautiful koi are great for large ponds, but they're too active to adapt to very small ones. Plain comet goldfish withstand cold weather well and are good at hiding from predators.

Make a proper introduction. Don't just plunk your fish into the pond. Let them adjust to their new surroundings by floating the unopened plastic bag containing the fish on the pond for 1 hour; then open it gently and set the fish free.

Don't overstock. Each fish needs a certain quantity of water to live. Calculate the required minimum by multiplying the length of the fish by five: A 4-inch (10-cm) goldfish, for example, needs at least 20 gallons (76 liters) of water. Another way to gauge is to allow 1 square foot (929 square cm) of pond surface area per 1 inch (25 mm) of fish. And remember that too much water is better than too many fish!

Watch their diet. Encourage fish to eat insects—especially mosquito eggs and larvae—

BOG GARDEN BASICS

If part of your yard drains poorly and stays constantly wet, why not create a bog garden? Or simply make a low edge of a garden pond into one. You can even make a tiny bog garden using a small plastic container with one or two drainage holes added. Hide the container's edges carefully. In a larger bog garden, install a sheet of thick plastic and pierce it with drainage holes 1 foot (30 cm) apart. Fill it with peat-rich soil, and include stepping stones or a wooden bridge so that you can enjoy your garden and tend the plants without getting your feet wet.

Good bog plants include many native species that grow naturally around ponds or lakes. Choices include marsh marigolds, water irises, and flowering rush in sun, or ferns and colorful primroses in shade. Carnivorous plants are ideal for a bog garden, too. In cool climates, use hardy pitcher plants (*Sarracenia* spp.), as well as butterworts (*Pinguicula* spp.) and sundews (*Drosera* spp.). In warmer climates, you can also grow the legendary Venus flytrap (*Dionaea muscipula*) and the California pitcher plant (*Darlingtonia californica*).

by letting them fend for themselves in summer. In spring and fall, feed them as long as the temperature is about 50°F (10°C). In winter, don't feed them at all. Never overfeed; excess food in the water upsets the pond's balance and can encourage algae.

Prevent ice damage. Frozen water expands and puts pressure on the pond sides. In late fall, weight the necks of sealed, empty plastic bottles

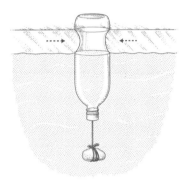

with stones tied to strings and place the bottles in the water. The ice will press on these flexible air pockets instead of the liner. You can also use rubber balls or floating logs.

Noisy neighbors. Despite their nighttime croaking, frogs and toads are welcome additions to the pond; they eat insects and are entertaining to watch. But don't let the population get out of control: tadpoles feed on aquatic plants. Keep their numbers in check by scooping the frogs' clear, jellylike eggs out of the water each spring.

MAKE A MUSICAL WATERFALL

If your yard is too narrow for a pond, you can still have a dramatic water feature with the help of a submersible pump. To create a small stream and waterfall, excavate a reservoir at the base of the stream and use the soil to form a berm above it. Install a liner and top it with a pump that will push the water to the top of the fall through a hidden pipe. The waterfall area must be lined, too, to prevent water loss. Try different ways of arranging rocks in the waterfall to alter the sound of the falling water.

Pond frozen? Fish become semidormant in winter, but they still must breathe. If the pond surface freezes for weeks, toxic gases in the water can build to harmful levels. Make a vent in the ice by heating a saucepan of water and setting it on top, repeating as needed. You can also buy an electric deicer, which ensures an opening in the ice at all times.

If aphids attack your plants, place plastic mesh over the leaves to sink them into the water; fish will find the pests an unexpected treat. After the leaves have been nibbled clean, remove the mesh.

Gardening with Children

If you have a child in your life who's interested in growing plants, make a space in the garden for him or her to explore the wonder of helping things grow. Instill a sense of ownership by providing a child-size watering can and tools, and place a sign with the child's name in the plot. And don't be too exacting—to a child, the thrill is in the process, not in producing something perfect.

Keep them interested by sowing quick-sprouting plants, such as lettuce, radishes, nasturtiums, and marigolds. Take them to a garden center and let them choose a few easy bedding plants, such as petunias, to add instant color to their garden.

❦ Watch Out!

Many plants are poisonous if ingested. Keep toddlers away from caladiums, philodendrons, English ivy, and many flowering bulbs.

Blue potatoes? Plant varieties that bear unusually colored or shaped fruits—blue potatoes, purple broccoli, speckled bush beans, or rounded yellow cucumbers.

A tunnel of flowering climbers becomes a playhouse for children. Anchor wire hoops in the ground and plant an easy-to-grow climber, such as morning glory or scarlet runner bean.

Watch it grow. Scratch the child's name or a silly face lightly into a young pumpkin growing on a vine. Over time, the drawing will grow and take shape. Or plant your child's initials in the soil with garden greens; red or green leaf lettuce or radishes work nicely.

Make mint tea. Plant easy-to-grow mint. When it's ready, whip up a batch of solar mint tea with your child by filling a 2-quart (2-liter) glass jar with water and a handful of mint leaves. Cover the jar with foil and let it sit in a sunny spot for 2 or 3 hours. Then pour into glasses, add ice and a dollop of honey, and have a tea party.

Make a sneaker planter. Stimulate a budding gardener's imagination by using an old sneaker as a planter. Help your child poke a couple of holes in the shoe and fill it partly with soil. Plant little rosettes of hens-and-chicks in the holes, firming the soil with your fingers. Add soil to the shoe's top opening and plant more rosettes there. Then nestle the sneaker into the soil amid some flowers or herbs.

Create a secret room. Mark a square in the soil and plant sunflowers on the outline to make a private garden "room" for children. Be sure to leave a little space for the door.

PART TWO

Caring for Your Plants

Every flower of the field,
every fiber of a plant,
every particle of an insect
carries with it the impress
of its Maker, and can—
if duly considered—read us
lectures of ethics or divinity.

—Sir Thomas Pope Blount, 1649-1697

SMALL FLOWERING PLANTS

Nothing in life pays back more for a gardener's efforts than flowers. Whether you enjoy them in patio pots, flowing flowerbeds, or garden-fresh arrangements, flowers bring joy to life. This chapter includes hundreds of tips on growing a range of beautiful bloomers, including single-season annuals, cold-hardy biennials, and dramatic bulbs for every season. And once your flowers burst into bloom, there are ideas for handling them as cut flowers, drying them for use in crafts, and even eating those worthy of your plate and palate.

Don't worry if you don't know a petunia from a pansy. Many of today's flowers are such eager bloomers that little skill is required to make them happy, and few things are easier than working with well-grown bedding plants. But do explore the wonderful returns you can get by growing flowers from inexpensive packets of seeds or by planting bulbs that reappear like magic at the perfect time each spring, summer, or fall. The world of flowers is a huge one, so you will never run out of new plants to try or new ways to use old favorites.

Annual Flowers

IF YOU WANT PLENTY of dazzling color for very little money and effort, annuals are the plants for you! Rollicking beds filled with marigolds, nasturtiums, and zinnias can be yours for the price of a packet of seeds, or you can buy transplants in six-packs and pop them into a bed—or perhaps create a beautiful container bouquet for your deck or patio. Like most vegetables, annual flowers grow for only one season, so they give you plenty of versatility from one year to the next. You can even choose between annuals that prefer cool weather, such as calendulas and pansies, and others that never complain when summer rolls into town. Annuals come in a huge range of shapes and sizes, too, from vigorous vines for covering a chain-link fence to compact dwarfs perfect for edging a walkway. Wherever you want a spot of color, there is an annual flower perfect for the job. In the next few pages, we'll take an in-depth look at 11 endearing annuals, but first a few tips on getting the most from these rewarding plants.

WHERE TO GROW ANNUALS

The right place for most annuals is a sunny location with good drainage and average garden soil. Repeating the same annual in different parts of your yard, such as in a flowerbed, along a walkway, and tucked into pots on your porch, will give your yard a magical feeling of unity.

A few are made for shade. Impatiens, coleus, begonias, and wishbone flower (torenia) tolerate more shade than other annuals, so they're great for bringing color to areas near trees or buildings. Remember that light colors tend to show better in shade than darker ones.

Use annuals as fillers. While you're waiting for small shrubs to grow, fill in the spaces between them with annuals. You can also use annuals to cover places where early-blooming bulbs and perennials have come and gone or to add color—and attract beneficial insects—to your vegetable garden.

Create container bouquets by growing bushy or trailing annuals in pots or window boxes. Petunias, verbenas, and lobelias are old window box standbys, but there are many new annuals you can add to the mix. Scaevola (fan flower) and silvery gray helichrysum or dusty miller are ideal annuals for bringing special shimmer to pots and window boxes.

Pot them up and bring them in. As summer winds down, you can pot up some of your favorite summer annuals and enjoy them for a few more weeks as blooming houseplants. Some of the best bets include begonias, coleus, impatiens, and geraniums. For best results, pot them up a few weeks before your first fall frost is expected. That way, they will recover from the trauma of being dug up and transplanted by the time you bring them indoors.

Have flowers all season. While you wait for perennials to take hold, dress up the garden with annuals. Since they germinate, bloom, and die within a single season, there's no need to dig them up once the later flowers are established. You can also plant them at the base of a trellis while you're waiting for a perennial vine to flower.

Try whimsical enclosures. If there's an old bed in your attic, why not move it outdoors and turn it into a bed of pansies? Fill an old wheelbarrow with nasturtiums or let petunias spill out of a pair of old boots filled with potting soil.

Don't start too early. Young nursery plants are often grown in sultry greenhouses and may not be hardened off properly. After you buy plants, keep them in a protected spot outdoors for a few days to give them a chance to get used to the sun and wind. Water daily to make sure they don't dry out. Unless the flowers are hardy types, wait until after the last frost to set them out in your garden.

Sow half-hardy annuals indoors to give them a head start. You can start seeds in individual containers or plant a whole tray if you want numerous plants in one color. To make sure

⅔SORTING THROUGH annuals

HARDY TYPES	
Dianthus, larkspur, pansy, sweet alyssum, sweet pea	Sow directly in the ground whenever the soil can be worked or set out seedlings in early spring or in fall in mild climates and early spring in cooler regions. These annuals tolerate cold weather and hard freezes.
HALF-HARDY TYPES	
Bachelor button, calendula, cosmos, lobelia, nasturtium, petunia, phlox, annual poppy, snapdragon, verbena	Sow indoors and plant outside at about the time of your last spring frost. These annuals prefer cool growing conditions and can tolerate light frosts.
TENDER TYPES	
Ageratum, begonia, celosia, cleome, coleus, geranium, impatiens, marigold, morning glory, salvia, sunflower, vinca, zinnia	Sow or transplant two weeks or more after the last spring frost, when the soil is warm. These annuals will blacken if touched by frost.

they're evenly spaced, place chicken wire over your seeding tray and put a seed in each opening. This makes it easier to separate the seedlings for transplanting.

Grandpa's wisdom

As cruel as it sounds, the best thing you can do for blooming bedding flowers is to snip off every bloom as you set the plants in beds or containers. This thoughtful pinching reminds the plants that they should get back to the business of growing roots and stems, which will result in many more blossoms over a much longer time.

Bag it up. Before setting out small plants in a windy or exposed area, put them in paper bags containing good soil, then set the bags in the ground, leaving 2 inches (5 cm) of the rims above soil level. The seedlings will be sheltered, and as they grow, the paper will decay and let the roots reach into the surrounding soil.

SEEDS OR PLANTS?

Why not plant both? Set out a few bedding plants of an annual you like and, at the same time, sow some seeds nearby. The bedders will bloom first, and the seed-sown flowers will fill in later and provide a season-long parade of color.

Tiny seeds take time to grow, which is the best reason to buy ageratum, begonias, impatiens, pansies, and many other popular annuals as bedding plants. Annuals with larger seeds, including nasturtiums and sunflowers, are fast, easy, and inexpensive to grow from seeds.

If you crave a certain color, you will have more colors to choose from if you start with seeds. If you go with bedding plants, shop early if you want a special shade or your planting plan calls for a large number of one color of a certain flower.

Keep your eye open for bargains. Young plants in six- or eight-packs of the same variety are often available at such good prices that they're a very wise choice. The best values are seedlings that are well rooted but not yet in bloom. Late in the season, beware of starved, dried-up leftovers, even if they are free.

Be wary of "grab bags." Many seed stores sell small packets of seed mixes described as "fragrant," "mixed colors," "for shady areas," or "drought tolerant." Too often, the packages lack the specific information you need. Unless you want a garden of surprises, buy individual seed packets labeled with advice on plant size, spacing, and care.

GET CREATIVE WITH ANNUALS

Plot out your planting. Make allowance for the height and proper spacing of each type of annual and put your plan on paper. Color it in with crayons or colored pencils to get an idea of the overall effect.

Avoid planting in straight lines or singles. Use staggered rows, trace curves in different directions, or simply plant in clumps or groups. Single annuals often get lost, but groups of three to five plants will grow into a colorful mound.

Play with sizes and forms. Provide height by placing tall flowers behind shorter ones and get great contrast by choosing some annuals that have daisy-like blossoms (zinnias) and others with upright spikes (salvias).

Get double use from color bowls. Many garden centers sell pots and planters already planted with painterly combinations of annuals. Enjoy a preplanted combo as a living work of art for a few weeks, then pinch the plants back, cut the roots apart with a sharp knife, and transplant them in your garden. Within three weeks, they should be growing vigorously again, and they will bloom stronger and longer than they would if you left them in their original pot. Clean it up and replant it with a new group of flowers.

Simplify to reduce maintenance. Massing a single color or a simple combination of two colors will create an elegant, unified effect suitable for entryways and window boxes. Sticking with only two or three types of annuals simplifies maintenance, too, because you can plant, groom, and feed many plants at the same time.

Play it soft, play it loud. Pastel pinks, lavenders, and yellows show up best in early morning light, evening light, or partial shade, but they tend to wash out in strong sun. Vivid reds and oranges hold up in bright light and are easily seen from a distance.

Try some colorful foliage. More and more annuals are available with vibrantly colored foliage that's perfect to mix and match with beautiful bloomers. Look for ornamental sweet potato vine, Persian shield, helichrysum, and other annuals with eye-catching leaves.

KEEPING ANNUALS IN BLOOM

Remove all spent flowers and any leaves that turn yellow. Occasionally pinching back your plants will encourage them to be bushier and flower more profusely. Use pruning shears or scissors to remove dead flowers from annuals about once a week from early summer to fall. When the plants begin to appear exhausted, or winter is around the corner, allow a few flowers to develop seeds to sow and grow next season.

Annuals don't like manure or heavy fertilizer. Too much nitrogen results in plants with too many leaves, too many stems, and too few flowers. The only manure suitable for use on annuals is composted manure that is thoroughly worked into the soil prior to planting, or you can use a slow-release fertilizer. If annuals show little new growth and seem to need feeding, drench them with a balanced, water-soluble plant food.

Let them nap. Some annuals need a rest from flowering, and if allowed to take a blooming break, they often come back bigger and better in late summer and early fall. Don't worry if your marigolds or nasturtiums look healthy but have few flowers in the heat of summer. As nights become longer and cooler, they will come back into bloom again.

BEGONIAS

Wax begonias are among the most versatile annuals. They grow well in sun or shade, are resistant to most pests and diseases, and don't take a lot of maintenance once they're established. The types sold as bedding plants bloom freely from early summer to frost, providing a mass of white, red, or pink color offset with light or dark green, bronze, or red foliage. See page 101 for tips on growing tuberous begonias in containers on your deck or patio.

Wait until after the last frost to plant begonias in your flowerbeds and window boxes. They can't stand the cold. If a late frost threatens after you have set out your plants, cover them with an old blanket until milder weather returns.

Seeds are tiny yet strong. Sow begonia seeds indoors by pressing them lightly into damp seed-starting mix, but don't cover them. They are very fine and need plenty of light to germinate. Water the seed-starting mix from below to avoid disturbing the seeds, soaking the base of

MULTITALENTED ANNUALS

Annuals for drying. Traditional favorites include everlasting (Helischrysum bracteatum) and its close relatives winged everlasting (Ammobium) and immortelle (Helipterum). Other candidates are statice, love-in-a-mist, globe amaranth, and bells of Ireland. Plan to start plants from seed if you want to grow unusual dried flowers, because bedding plants are hard to find. Harvest when the blooms are just opening and air-dry upside down in a warm, dry place away from strong sun. Use some of the blossoms to make colorful potpourri (see page 59).

Climbing annuals such as sweet peas and morning glories will quickly disguise a chain-link fence, or you can grow them over a trellis to hide an unsightly view, such as garbage cans. Other vigorous climbing annuals include scarlet runner beans, black-eyed Susan vines, and hyacinth beans. Most climbing annuals are easy to grow from seed.

Fragrant annuals can fill the garden with their perfume, and several are easy to grow. Try flowering tobacco (Nicotiana), vanilla-scented heliotropes, and old-fashioned sweet peas. Some types of petunias are surprisingly fragrant, too.

Cut-and-come-again annuals produce more flowers the more you gather them for bouquets. Instead of compact dwarf varieties, look for tall types of calendulas, snapdragons, and zinnias or sunflowers described as branching types. See page 74 for tips on conditioning and arranging annuals in beautiful bouquets.

the flat in a larger container of water. When the surface is moist, remove the flat and let it drip before putting it back into a semishaded spot.

Go for the bronze. Darker foliage helps wax begonias with bronze leaves tolerate more sun than varieties with green leaves, and bronze-leafed varieties look great, too. When planting any wax begonia in full sun, don't worry if some leaves scorch a little at first. They will fall off, and the new leaves will be acclimatized to the greater light intensity.

At the end of summer, transplant a few vigorous specimens from your flowerbeds into pots filled with potting soil. Potted-up bedding begonias often continue to bloom indoors for several months when kept next to a sunny window. Cut them back occasionally to encourage new shoots.

COSMOS

With their long, slender stems and lacy foliage, cosmos are an attractive, fast-growing way to add color to the garden, and they make great cut flowers, too. While hardy to Zones 9 and 10, most cosmos are grown as annuals. The most popular of several species is *Cosmos bipinnatus,* a native of Mexico, which sports red, white, pink, or purple flowers up to 4 inches (10 cm) in diameter on top of 4- to 5-foot (1.25- to 1.5-meters) stems. Another species, *C. sulphureus,* boasts 3-inch flowers in shades of yellow and orange, and it's a great choice if you live where summers are hot and humid.

Lean, well-drained, sandy soil is actually the preference for cosmos. Don't give them large doses of fertilizer, or the plants will become giants that won't bloom until late summer. Instead of fertilizer, make sure your cosmos get plenty of bright sunlight and adequate moisture.

Cosmos are easy to grow from seed. Sow seeds right in the garden from spring to early summer. If you buy seedlings or start seeds indoors, set out the little plants at about the time of your last spring frost.

Plant seedlings deep, so that all but the top 4 inches (10 cm) of stem is buried. Like tomatoes, cosmos often develop roots at the base of their stems. As the plants grow, hill up a little soil around the base of each plant, which encourages them to bush out and stand steady in gusty summer storms.

For a distinctive aroma of cocoa, try chocolate cosmos (*C. atrosanguineus*), which has dark burgundy blooms and velvety petals.

GERANIUMS

The plants Americans call geraniums are known as pelargoniums in the rest of the English-speaking world—from the plant's botanical name, *Pelargonium.* Even more confusing is the fact that true geraniums—of the genus *Geranium*—are commonly called cranesbills or hardy geraniums. The distinction between them is that garden geraniums are grown as tender perennials or annuals, whereas true geraniums are hardy perennials.

Garden geraniums are great for beds, pots, or window boxes. Many will bloom indoors when potted up and handled as winter houseplants.

Avoid shopping confusion. The geraniums sold in garden centers vary in price because some are grown from seed and others from rooted cuttings. Inexpensive, seed-grown geraniums are fine for planting in beds. More costly vegetatively propagated strains have bigger flowers, so they are showier plants suitable for growing in containers.

Rainy climate? Single-flowered geraniums and those with darker leaves will grow better than double-flowered varieties in areas that have few sunny days.

Keep a geranium forever. Potted up and kept indoors through winter, garden geraniums will start growing again in spring. But instead of regrowing an old plant, take stem cuttings and root them to create several healthy new plants. Dip the ends of the cuttings in rooting powder and plant in moist seed-starting mix. Cover them with a plastic bag to maintain humidity and transplant them into potting soil as soon as you see new growth—usually in about a month.

Don't overwater. It causes root rot, and geraniums would rather be dry than too wet. When growing geraniums in containers, add fertilizer to the water, diluting it to half the strength recommended on the label.

Going on vacation? Keep your geraniums from looking spent on your return by trimming

 SORTING THROUGH
garden geraniums

- **Garden geraniums** are also called zonal geraniums because many varieties develop dark or light bands, or zones, on their leaves. Most of the geraniums sold at garden centers in spring are zonals, and there are dozens of varieties to choose from.

- **Ivy-leafed geraniums** are trailing plants ideal for hanging baskets. They need cool nights and can be difficult to grow in very warm, humid climates. In addition to regular ivy-leafed geraniums, a newer type called exotic geraniums features flower clusters with spiky blossoms and are grown like other garden geraniums.

- **Regal geraniums,** also called Martha Washington geraniums, have serrated leaves and flowers similar to azaleas. They grow best in cool maritime climates and have a hard time with hot, humid nights.

- **Scented geraniums** are grown for their scented leaves, which, when rubbed, release fragrances, from apple to nutmeg. Try 'Mabel Gray' for lemon or 'Lady Plymouth' for rose.

off all flowers and buds. Water and mulch just before you leave. If you're going away for three weeks—the time it takes for new buds and blooms to form—a colorful plant will await your return.

IMPATIENS

Impatiens have earned enormous popularity for both their long-lasting display of showy blooms and their ability to thrive with little sun. Plant them beneath a shade tree or in borders or containers that receive partial to moderate shade. Given regular water and fertilizer, impatiens often bloom nonstop from late spring until well into fall. A few new varieties will tolerate more sun, but if you try them, be prepared to provide water twice a day in the heat of summer.

If you start with seeds, expect hybrid impatiens to grow fast. You can sow seeds as late as March, and they'll still be ready to set out in June in the warm 65°F (18°C), shady conditions they require. Don't cover the seed tray; the seeds need plenty of light to sprout.

For compact, well-branched plants covered with flowers, pinch out the growing tips of your impatiens before you plant them and keep pinching back stem tips every few weeks. So you'll always have a few flowers, nip out only half of the stem tips at a time on individual plants.

Try New Guinea impatiens in large pots or as feature plants in a small flowerbed. Many have beautifully variegated leaves, and the flowers can be more than 2 inches (5 cm) across.

Keep a broom handy when growing impatiens in patio pots, because the plants constantly shed old petals. If the pots are small, pick them up every few days, carry them to another part of your yard, and give them a good shake to get rid of the old flowers.

Delight your children by letting them grow touch-me-nots (*Impatiens balsamina*) in their own corner of the garden. These upright, old-timey flowers produce an abundance of plump capsules that explode at the slightest touch, sending seeds on their merry way. They produce so many seeds that they often come up on their own year after year.

MARIGOLDS

Tremendously popular and easy to grow, marigolds are the best source of sunny yellow color in the summer garden—or let orange or bronze marigolds carry your garden into fall. French and African marigolds are actually misnamed. Marigolds are native to the American Southwest and to Central and South America. In the 1500s, marigold seeds were taken by Spanish explorers from the Americas to Spain. From

❧ SORTING THROUGH marigolds

- **French marigolds** grow into bushy mounds less than 16 inches (45 cm) tall and are the best marigolds for edging a bed. Many varieties help to control the soilborne pests known as rootknot nematodes. French marigolds are available in yellow, orange, mahogany, and some bicolors.

- **African marigolds** grow to 3 feet (1 meter) tall and have tight pom-pom blooms up to 4 inches (10 cm) across in shades of yellow or orange. There are many hybrid marigolds with a little African ancestry that grow into big, robust plants.

- **Signet marigolds,** often called gem marigolds, have lacy foliage and small, dainty flowers. The blooms are edible, but signets often do not bloom for as long as other types of marigolds.

there, seeds were transported to France and parts of northern Africa, where the taller types eventually became naturalized. Today, most beautiful summer gardens include some type of marigold.

Choose this carefree annual. Adaptable and easy to please, marigolds perform well from seed sown directly in the garden in spring, or you can set out bedding plants. As long as the site is sunny and the soil is well drained, marigolds will thrive. Sow more in midsummer for a big burst of color in the fall.

Pinch off the first blooms, even if you have to grit your teeth to do it. It's the best way to encourage marigolds to develop more branches, which means more flowers. Once the plants begin to bloom heavily, regular deadheading accomplishes the same thing as pinching.

Strip down the stems. Marigold foliage rots quickly in water. When preparing to use marigolds in a cut flower arrangement, strip off the leaves that will be below the water line.

NASTURTIUMS

Informal and perky, nasturtiums are a wonderful choice for beginning gardeners, with their big, pea-size seeds, fast growth, and peppery edible leaves and flowers. Plants form a low, 12-inch-tall (30-cm-tall) mound and then begin to trail a bit, often forming a carpet of leaves and flowers. Nasturtium leaves are bright green and rounded, and the brightly colored flowers come in shades of red, yellow, orange, cream, or crimson.

Be direct. While seedlings are readily available in spring, nasturtiums are easy to grow from a packet of seeds. Sow in early spring by poking the seeds into sun-drenched soil about ½ inch (13 mm) deep. Thin seedlings to 6 inches (15 cm) apart, and the plants will soon be off and running.

Plant a pretty pyramid. Drive a stake into the center of a wooden barrel. Stretch about a dozen pieces of string from the top of the stake to the edges of the container and fasten with tacks. Plant climbing nasturtiums around the barrel perimeter and train the vines up the

strings, then use the barrel as a centerpiece in an herb garden or on a patio. You can also use trailing nasturtiums as a low screen by training the vines up a short trellis.

Pair with potted citrus. Plant bush-type nasturtiums around the base of a potted lemon, lime, or orange tree. Their bright yellow, orange, and red blooms will complement the colors of the citrus fruits.

Mix with your vegetables. Plant nasturtiums between rows of vegetables, 12 to 18 inches (30 to 45 cm) apart. They'll form a pretty groundcover and are said to repel some insects—and their blooms are edible!

PANSIES

Delightfully old-fashioned, pansies have never gone out of style. Pansies tolerate more cold than other annuals and are often grown from fall to spring in Zones 6 to 9. Available in a huge range of sizes and colors, pansies grow well in sun or part shade, reaching 6 to 10 inches (15 to 25 cm) tall and 10 to 12 inches (25 to 30 cm) across. Fanciful folks say the dark centers in some flowers look like little faces. The stems are cute in small bouquets, and you can use the edible blossoms to garnish dessert platters or punch bowls.

Snow survivors with natural antifreeze. Pansies do a great job of surviving cold because they can move water out of their leaves and replace it with natural antifreeze. When planting pansies in the fall, get them in before the cold

temperatures arrive. They need to be well rooted before soil temperatures drop below about 50°F (10°C). In cool climates such as New England, pansies can be set out in early spring provided the plants are hardened off for a few weeks first. They'll even survive an early-spring snow.

Get painterly with pansies. With so many colors available, it's easy to weave two colors into a beautiful spring tapestry. Yellow and blue pansies always look great together, or you can use white pansies to help showcase bright tulips and other spring-flowering bulbs.

For a big boom of blossoms, pinch off the first flush of buds and blossoms that appear in spring. Three to four weeks later, the sacrifice will pay off with a super-size show of blooms all at once. Deadhead pansies often to prolong their flowering period.

PETUNIAS

Petunias come in just about any color except orange, and they're a top choice among summer-flowering annuals. You can even choose between bushy and trailing types, and many hybrids do an amazing job of standing up to humid heat. Petunias prosper in beds, pots, or hanging baskets, and they're great for covering the bare bases of taller flowers. Some are fragrant, especially in the evening or early morning.

Tiny petunia seeds need extra attention. About 10 weeks before the last frost, sow them indoors in a tray prepared with fine soil on top.

Press the seeds well into the soil, but don't cover them, and water from below. Plant out after danger of frost has passed, in soil amended with compost or rotted manure.

Please pinch the petunias. When seedlings are 6 inches (15 cm) tall, pinch the stem tips to encourage side branching. In midsummer, petunias often stage a strong comeback if you use pruning shears or hedge clippers to cut back the plants by half their size.

Don't smoke. Petunias are particularly susceptible to tobacco mosaic virus. If you smoke, do so away from the plants, and always wash smoke or tobacco residue from your hands before touching them.

SORTING THROUGH
petunias

- These indispensable annuals come in most solid colors and numerous bicolors that have contrasting veins, edges, center stars, or stripes. Grow varieties with double, ruffled blossoms in pots that can be kept in a place that's protected from heavy rains.
- When buying petunias to fill flowerbeds, look for multiflora types, which produce a nonstop parade of medium-size flowers on compact, disease-resistant plants.
- Whenever you want a trailing plant to dress the edge of a container, consider a trailing petunia. White trailing petunias go with everything, or you can pair rich purples with plants that have chartreuse leaves or use soft pinks in a color scheme built around muted pastels.

Does it look like rain? Do you want your petunias to look perfect? Even the sturdiest petunias can be flattened by a heavy downpour. To preserve their good looks, cover them with a cardboard box or a plastic sheet draped over stakes to keep it off the plants. And always mulch petunias so mud won't splash up and mar the flowers when it rains.

POPPIES

Poppy family members are papery beauties, with over 50 species of annuals and perennials with crinkled, cuplike blooms reminiscent of crepe paper. They come in a range of solid and bicolor shades, with single or double blooms. The easiest poppies to grow are often called corn, Flanders, or Shirley poppies (*P. rhoes*)—the same dainty but hardy annual that turns the fields of Europe into seas of scarlet in spring. Now naturalized in North America, corn poppies self-sow readily, so plant them where they can spread.

Grow poppies in full sun in rich, very well drained soil. Sow them in the fall in Zones 7 to 9 or first thing in spring farther north. Sow seed directly, because the poppys' long taproot makes them difficult to transplant. In spring, be prepared to protect your plants from hungry rabbits.

Keep friends close. For all the beauty of their blossoms, poppies have coarse, hairy foliage that some find unappealing. Plant poppies behind other ornamentals that will shield their leaves and

Use Dried Flowers to Make Potpourri

Make use of faded flowers in potpourri, a spice- and oil-scented blend of dried petals, leaves, and other plant materials. If you grow flowers and herbs, you already have most of what you need to make potpourri.

Collect blossoms and herbs from your garden and dry them whole on a screen or sheet of newspaper. When they're crisp to the touch, store them in airtight jars until you're ready to make a batch of potpourri.

Go for color and texture rather than fragrance when collecting plant material to dry. You can add interesting textures to potpourri by foraging in the woods for seedpods, evergreen cones, and the berries of shrubs, such as holly and pyracantha.

Store different dried materials separately so you can layer them into glass jars or make special batches of rose, herb, or spicy holiday potpourri.

Fixing the fragrance. Much of potpourri's fragrance comes from essential oils, which are sold in small bottles at craft and health-food stores. From woodsy balsam to soothing lavender to sweet wisteria, essential oils are available in a wide variety of rich scents. Along with an essential oil, you will need a fixative, such as orrisroot, which is sold at most craft stores as small crystals or powder.

The first step in making potpourri is to mix the fixative with the essential oil in a glass jar. Stir with a chopstick, screw on the lid, and set the jar aside to let the mixture blend for several days. Then mix the scented fixative with your collection of dried flowers, seeds, and spices by shaking them together in a large, zip-close bag. In two to three weeks, your potpourri will be ready to use. If the scent fades, return the mixture to the bag and sprinkle in a few drops of essential oil. It will regain its fragrance within a few days.

fill in the gaps as they slowly fade away. Pull foliage when it begins to turn brown. Many people gather the dried seed capsules on long stems and use them in dried flower arrangements.

Grow poppy seeds for baking. Almost as easy to grow as corn poppies, bread seed poppies (*P. somniferum*) produce big flowers followed by egg-shaped seedpods that are full of black, edible seeds. Be sure to wait until the seedpods turn brown to harvest seeds for eating, and set aside some to replant next year.

Demanding, but worth it. The Iceland poppy (*P. nudicale*), a biennial grown as an annual, is the hardest to grow, but its silky petals are the most intensely colored and seem to glow with an inner light. This heavy bloomer, with up to 50 flowers per plant, is ideal for cutting. Sow in late summer for blooms the following year.

SUNFLOWERS

If you think all sunflowers are 8-foot (2.4-meter) giants, think again! There are dozens of varieties to choose from, including branching bushes and dwarfs small enough to grow in containers. Most sunflowers are yellow, but there are also deep reds, creamy whites, and lovely mahoganies. In any size or color, sunflowers attract bees and other beneficial insects and produce nutritious seeds enjoyed by people and their feathered friends.

Start with seeds. Sunflowers are among the easiest annuals to sow from seed. Plant seeds in late spring after the soil has warmed. In midsummer, sow another packet for a beautiful fall show.

Don't skimp on sun. If they run short of light, sunflowers will twist so their flowers face the sun. Use this trait to your advantage by choosing a site easily viewed from its south or west side, because sunflowers usually face those directions.

Plant a sunflower hedge. Branching sunflowers such as 'Italian White' produce dozens of blossoms on big, bushy plants. When grown 2 feet (60 cm) apart, they make a tall, dense hedge for the rear of a sunny flowerbed, and the blooms make great cut flowers, too.

Grow sunflowers as living trellises for pole beans. Use a tall, single-stemmed variety and let it grow at least 12 inches (30 cm) tall before planting pole bean seeds at its base.

Keep summer birds from eating seeds you want to save for winter. After the petals shrivel, slip a cut piece of old pantyhose over the ripening seed head. Allow at least 3 weeks of ripening time before gathering and storing your homegrown birdseed.

Save the stalks for next year. After sunflowers finish blooming, lop off the stalks near the soil line, trim off any branches, and store your "sunflower poles" in a dry place until spring. Use them to make a natural-looking teepee trellis for scarlet runner beans or morning glories.

ZINNIAS

Zinnias hail from Mexico, so they have what it takes to survive the hottest summer weather. Available in a huge range of colors and types, some zinnia blossoms are flat daisies, while others are more formal pom-poms. Tall varieties are great for cutting, while compact dwarf hybrids make wonderful, sun-tolerant edging plants. A great annual for color lovers, zinnias are hard to beat for their rich reds, sunny yellows, or pure pinks.

Grateful deadheads. Zinnias will respond enthusiastically to cutting. Deadheading the fading flowers—and cutting some fresh ones for arrangements—will keep the plants amazingly prolific. When gathering zinnias to show off indoors, choose blossoms that have just opened and cut them early in the day. Before putting them in a vase, strip off the lower leaves, which can quickly deteriorate.

Experiment with seeds. Bedding plants are widely available, but as long as the soil is warm, zinnias are easy to grow from seed sown directly in the garden. And, because the seedlings transplant so easily, you can also sow seeds in your vegetable garden and move them to flowerbeds when they're about 4 inches (10 cm) tall.

Try a zinnia hedge. Many compact hybrids bloom so heavily that they make a fantastic summer hedge. If you've wondered what a

SORTING THROUGH zinnias

- **Compact hybrid zinnias** (*Zinnia elegans*) for edging or hedging include several popular series, such as the award-winning 'Profusion' and tried-and-true 'Dreamland' series. For cutting, look for tall-timbered 'Benary's Giant', 'Oklahoma', or the heirloom strain simply called 'Cut and Come Again'.

- **Narrow-leafed zinnias** (*Z. angustifolia*) have smaller flowers, and these heat-resistant, fine-textured plants are ideal for edging beds that bake in hot sun. Colors include white, orange, and yellow.

- **Mexican zinnias** (*Z. haageana*) feature petals that are orange to mahogany and tipped with yellow. The color patterns often vary from one blossom to the next, so these are great flowers if you like surprises.

bright ribbon of red or hot pink might look like alongside your front walkway or driveway, try your plan with zinnias.

Outmaneuver mildew by growing disease-resistant varieties and replacing old plants with younger, more vigorous ones. Powdery mildew on zinnias is most common on plants that are nearly exhausted from a long season of bloom.

The Beauty of Biennials

Annual flowers grow for only one year, while perennials keep coming back season after season. In between, there are biennials, plants that sprout from seeds and produce leaves their first year, then bloom, set seed, and die in their second year.

True biennials are rare in nature, but many garden flowers behave like biennials, depending on the climate. Whether you're working with hardy annuals, short-lived perennials, or true biennials, starting flowers in late summer to bloom the following spring often seems like a form of green magic.

The rhythm of the biennial season. Plant biennial seeds in pots or prepared beds in late summer. Plant them outdoors in the fall at least six weeks before the first frost or over-winter them in a cold frame if you live in a cold climate. Don't keep them indoors all winter; they need a good winter chilling to trigger heavy spring blooming.

Marry biennials with bulbs. In early fall, plant low-growing biennials among spring-flowering bulbs. Plant the bulbs, then interplant them with biennials. The bulbs will pop up and bloom first, and the biennials will help hide their ripening foliage from view. Biennials also fill the color gap between spring-flowering bulbs and early annuals and perennials.

Let them naturalize. Many biennials are big seed producers and will shed so many seeds that volunteer seedlings pop up year after year. To help, let some flowers mature until they turn brown. In late summer, weed and water the area to give seedlings ideal conditions to sprout.

Grow long-lasting garden money. Money plant, also known as silver dollar plant, is a true biennial prized for its flat seedpods, which make great additions to dried flower arrangements. After the seedpods have dried out completely, rub the flat disks lightly between your fingers to remove the brown outer membranes. With luck and a bit of practice, the bright, silvery central membrane will be left intact for you to use in winter floral displays.

FLOWERS TO HANDLE AS BIENNIALS

Canterbury bells (*Campanula*), English daisy (*Bellis perennis*), Foxglove (*Digitalis purpurea*), Hollyhock (*Alcea rosea*), Money plant (*Lunaria*), Pansy (*Viola x wittrockiana*), Siberian wallflower (*Cherianthus allonii*), Stock (*Matthiola maritima*), Sweet William (*Dianthus barbatus*)

❧ Perennial Flowers

EXCITING AND ROMANTIC, perennials die back in winter and emerge anew in spring. They vary in winter hardiness and tolerance of humid heat. Peonies, for example, thrive where winters are cold and summers are mild. In warmer climates, some daylilies and daisies hold onto a little green growth through the coldest part of winter. Wherever you live, there are dozens of perennials that you can use to bring color and fragrance to your garden year after year.

A list of garden-worthy perennials would number in the hundreds, but many of the tips below can be used to help all perennials grow better. And eight long-lived lovelies are featured here. From shade-tolerant hostas to hibiscus that love to bake in summer sun, discovering perennials that like your yard as much as you like them turns every season of flower gardening into a fascinating adventure.

GETTING STARTED

Get your money's worth by looking for perennials that bear variety names, which often bloom longer and stronger than perennials that can be grown from seed. Named varieties often cost a little more because they're propagated from cuttings or divisions rather than from seed, but they're worth it.

Be patient with seeds. If you do start perennials from seed, be prepared to wait a year, or maybe more, for the plants to bloom well. Most perennials need to sit through a period of cold weather before they will develop lots of buds and flowers.

Find free flowers. If you need to cover an area quickly and economically, purchase perennials that reseed readily. Strong self-sowers include yarrow, columbine, lamb's ears, bellflower, and pulmonaria. Also collect plant seeds in fall and keep your eyes open for any volunteers for transplanting.

Learn to love leaves. Because perennials bloom for a brief period, select plants with attractive foliage. Bergenia, plumbago, and many sedums have waxy leaves. Bleeding heart, coral bells, and cranesbills exhibit "cut" leaves. Hostas offer interesting variegation patterns, and perennials with gray foliage, such as Russian sage, go with everything.

Plot out a plan. Before installing perennials, plot your basic plan on a piece of paper. If you like, use tracing paper to make overlays for each month of the growing season. Note the bloom time for your perennials, then add annuals and bulbs to fill color gaps.

Perennials look best planted in groups of at least three plants, or you can set more plants together in drifts. Locate perennials that bloom early and then fade away behind those that are at their best in late summer.

PERENNIAL BORDERS

Historically, collections of perennials have been grown in a border—a special bed that usually backs up to the yard's boundary. Tall plants in the rear form a backdrop, with smaller plants arranged in the foreground. Because perennials come and go throughout the season, a perennial border is a constantly changing tapestry of color and texture.

Use string and a board to trace a straight border. Stretch the string between two stakes to mark the line, then cut the ground with a sharp spade or edging tool, aligning the board with the string as you work.

To trace a curved border, use a hose or rope to mark out the shape of the border, securing it in several places. Cut the ground with a sharp spade or edging tool, following the lines of the hose.

Carefully consider texture, which is almost as important as color in a perennial border. Much of the beauty of a perennial border comes from the interplay between the foliage and flowers of different plants.

Avoid rampant spreaders in borders, where they can easily get out of hand. If a perennial in your garden shows signs that it likes to travel, put it to work as a groundcover instead.

Pay attention to the back. A good border has a distinct backdrop, which can be comprised of trees, shrubs, a wood fence, or vines trained up a trellis. In addition to showcasing other perennials, the backdrop adds vertical interest to a border.

Trim the sides. For a charming edge along the sides of a perennial border, use this simple and inexpensive technique. Insert sturdy 12- to 16-inch (30- to 40-cm) wood stakes every 6 inches (15 cm) along the edge of your border. Then interlace the uprights with pliable vines or willow stems to create a lattice.

WHEN WILL THEY BLOOM?

There are perennials for every site, style, and level of gardening skill. The following 50 easy-to-grow perennials are arranged by their bloom time.

Spring: Ajuga, baptisia, basket-of-gold, bergenia, bleeding heart, columbine, coral bells, foamflower, hellebore, lady's mantle, peony, poppy, primrose, pulmonaria, thrift, viola

Summer: Astilbe, baby's breath, bee balm, bellflower, blanket flower, catmint, coneflower, coreopsis, cranesbill, daylily, delphinium, dianthus, feverfew, goat's beard, helenium, helianthus, hosta, lupine, obedient plant, penstemon, phlox, rudbeckia, Russian sage, scabiosa, sedum, verbena, veronica, yarrow

Fall: Aster, boltonia, chrysanthemum, Japanese anemone, goldenrod, lobelia

Include edging. Borders that share their edges with lawn benefit from well-maintained edging, which can be created from mulch, bricks, or edging materials that are installed in the ground. Where borders adjoin walkways or other hard surfaces, use dwarf annuals to define and bring color to the edges.

GROWING PERENNIALS

Prepare the soil well, because perennials often remain in one spot for several years. Turn the soil over to at least 1 foot (30 cm), so the plants' long-lived roots will have a good home, and incorporate plenty of organic matter to ensure adequate water and air circulation.

Water often the first season. Prevent drought stress the first season after planting a new perennial, so it will develop plenty of strong roots that will help it get through winter.

Fertilize in spring. Perennials make much of their new growth in spring, so that's when they most need nutrients. Your best choice is a balanced, timed-release fertilizer or an organic fertilizer, such as aged compost or thoroughly rotted manure.

Mulch perennials year-round with an attractive organic mulch to suppress weeds, retain moisture, and prevent frost heaving in winter. In gardens where slugs or snails chew holes in plant leaves, rake up the mulch in spring and spread a fresh layer a few weeks later, after the soil has warmed.

To prolong bloom time, deadhead perennials religiously, snipping or snapping the spent flowers off the stems.

 Grandpa's wisdom

Dormant perennials may look dead, but late winter or early spring is still the best time to buy new perennials. If you buy plants when they're in bloom, you'll have to wait another year to enjoy the flowers.

Winterize your perennial garden by removing any dead flowers or foliage in autumn. After a hard freeze, cut back all stems to ground level and add extra mulch. Don't pull on withered foliage, or you may damage shallow roots.

DIVIDING PERENNIALS

With most perennials, you can increase your supply of plants by digging, dividing, and replanting the best specimens. Plus, most perennials need to be divided every few years to remain vigorous. When you dig and divide perennials depends mostly on when they bloom.

- Divide perennials that flower in mid- or late summer, including asters, chrysanthemums, sunflowers, and Japanese anemones, in spring.

- Divide spring and summer bloomers in late summer or fall so that they will have time to develop new roots before winter comes.

- Some perennials prefer to be divided very seldom, if at all. Peonies, for example, would just as soon be left alone for 10 years or more.

Don't dig more than you need to. When dividing perennials, you don't have to lift the entire clump. To separate one or two growing crowns for replanting, gently loosen stems and roots on one side and cut the small plants off cleanly with a butcher knife, another sharp knife, or a small spade. Be sure to retain growing points or buds as well as roots on each piece. Then replace the soil around the remaining roots and plant the little division right away.

Tackling a big job. To divide an entire clump, use a digging fork to loosen the soil around the clump, then lift it from beneath. Fine-rooted plants, such as dianthus and bee balm, can then be divided by simply pulling them apart with your hands. Use a knife or spade to separate those with tougher roots by cutting them into smaller clumps.

Divide older plants that have become woody by digging the clump and saving only the young plants growing near the outside edge. Dispose of the parent plant once you've saved the healthier offspring.

Pot up the extras. If you have no place to put all of your divided perennials, set some in pots. They will make themselves at home until you find a place for them, which may be in a friend's or neighbor's garden.

CHRYSANTHEMUMS

People in Asia have cultivated chrysanthemums for more than 2,000 years. Today, anyone with fertile, well-drained soil and full sun can grow these beautiful perennials, which usually wait until fall to cover themselves with long-lasting flowers. Colors range from whites and yellows to pinks and maroons. Most gardeners like to see bushy plants with hundreds of blossoms, but if you want only a few huge flowers, you can grow special large-flowered varieties and clip off most of the buds.

Mums for every climate. When shopping for chrysanthemums, choose varieties that bloom when you want them to. In northern areas, choose early-blooming cultivars. Midseason mums are best for Zones 5 to 7. In warmer climates where autumn comes later, choose late-blooming varieties to carry plenty of color well into fall.

Pinch out the growing tips of garden mums every three weeks from Easter to the Fourth of July. Pinching is essential if you want bushy, heavy-blooming plants.

Ready rooters. Chrysanthemums are a cinch to propagate from stem-tip cuttings. When you pinch back new shoots in late spring, remove the lowest leaves and set them to root in damp potting soil. They will be ready to transplant to new areas of your garden in only three weeks.

Cascades of chrysanthemums. Train button mums or other small-flowered chrysanthemums to cascade over the sides of their pots by tying them to bamboo canes that are slanted progressively downward as the plants grow. In September, when the plants are ready to flower, remove the canes and let the plants hang down on their own.

Shallow-rooted mums need extra winter protection to prevent heaving. After the first freeze, cut the stems back to ground level and mulch with about 3 or 4 inches (8 or 10 cm) of hay, straw, or shredded bark. This helps plants overwinter in temperatures as low as −10°F (−23°C) and escape the frost heaving caused by alternate freezing and thawing of the soil. In mild winter areas, do the opposite. Let mums retain their dead foliage through winter, which will protect the shallow roots from ice and cold winter winds.

What about florists' mums? The large-flowered chrysanthemum you received as a gift may not be hardy enough to grow as a perennial, but you can try cutting it back in winter and storing it in a cool garage where temperatures stay above freezing. In spring, set it in the sun, add water, and repot any green shoots that appear.

DAYLILIES

The colorful blooms of the popular daylily lasts only one day—hence its name. Native to Asia, daylilies have narrow leaves about 2 feet (60 cm) long, with funnel-shaped flowers atop leafless stalks that may grow to 5 feet (1.5 meters). Six to 12 flowers make up a cluster, and two or three open each day. Daylilies are a passion for some gardener-collectors, and hundreds of varieties are available. It's easy to expand your daylily collection, since they grow rapidly into large clumps that you can divide in late summer or early fall.

As long as the soil's not too wet, and they receive at least a half day of sun, daylilies will grow in a range of conditions. You can even use them to hold a slope that's prone to erosion. However, very showy varieties and all of the new reblooming daylilies (which bloom for months rather than weeks) need regular water and fertilizer and good-quality soil in order to produce plenty of flowers.

Look for at least two fans, or crowns, when buying a new daylily. It means that the plant is more mature, so it will be more likely to bloom well in its first season in your garden.

Give daylilies room to grow. Place plants at least 2 feet (60 cm) apart because every year, a daylily will grow one to three new crowns. Fill space between plants in a new daylily bed with small summer annuals.

Protect the reds. Plant red daylilies in a spot that gets relief from the hot afternoon sun, because many red daylilies bleach out in intense sun. Yellow daylilies tend to be easy to please in less-than-ideal growing conditions.

Use daylilies to mask the base of a fence. Instead of battling the grass and weeds that grow at the base of a fence with a weed trimmer, let

(Continued on page 70)

Enjoy Edible Flowers

The same colors that flowers bring to your garden can be enjoyed at the table if you open your kitchen to edible flowers. Not all flowers are edible, but those listed in "Please Do Eat These Flowers" can be used as garnishes or palate-pleasing ingredients. It's best to grow your own edible flowers because flowers raised for the florist trade often contain toxic pesticide residues.

Savor squash blossoms. In addition to their fruits, zucchini and other types of squash provide edible blossoms. Fry the flowers in batter, tempura-style, or lightly sauté them. You can also use squash blossoms as wrappers for cold salads or cut them into thin strips and toss them with hot pasta. Some people find the longer-stemmed male flowers more flavorful, and they are certainly more abundant. In the first weeks that a squash plant is in bloom, most of the blossoms are male.

Pick edible flowers just before you're ready to use them. They will not have wilted, and their flavor will be at its most intense. Harvested blooms can be loosely wrapped in dampened paper towels and kept in the refrigerator for about a day. Here are some ways to enjoy them.

- Garnish fruit salad, sorbet, or finger sandwiches with sage, rose, violet, or pansy blossoms.

- Mix rose petals, mint flowers, or violets into cake batter or cookie dough.

- Toss some blossoms from nasturtium, basil, or mustard plants with your favorite salad greens.

- Freeze flower petals or small blossoms in ice cubes and

enjoy them in cold drinks or float them in a bowl of party punch.

Try spicy tuberous begonia petals with yogurt or ice cream. Include several different colors for an especially festive presentation.

Let calendulas stand in for saffron. Yellow calendulas,

sometimes called pot marigolds, don't have the savory flavor of saffron, but a few chopped petals sprinkled into rice as it cooks will impart the same rich yellow color. Use a light hand because too much calendula can taste bitter.

Some edible flowers look better than they taste. Chrysanthemum petals, for example, are a beautiful garnish and quite safe to eat, but they won't win any contests in the flavor department.

With sunflowers and dianthus, the petal tips can be used to add color to a huge range of foods, but the bases of the petals, where they attach to the blossom's center, often taste bitter.

Try thin shreds of yellow or orange tulip petals in a dark green spinach salad. Or use them to line a plate of stuffed mushrooms.

Daylily blossoms are surprisingly tasty, with a slightly sweet, floral flavor. Be sure to snip out the stamens before preparing daylily blossoms for the table. You can also eat daylily buds that are almost ready to open. The blossoms are good when tossed with buttered pasta and Parmesan cheese, or you can cut them into strips and add them to any salad.

Use nasturtium blossoms to garnish cold summer soups. Nasturtium flowers have a peppery flavor, which is a welcome touch with chilled potato, cucumber, or carrot soup. You can also use large nasturtium blossoms as plate-size cups for special relishes or condiments, such as capers or tartar sauce.

DECORATE A CAKE

Even the best edible flowers wilt within a few hours after they're picked, but it's easy to make them last longer if you want to use them to decorate a cake.

To make candied flowers, pick violets, pansies, or nasturtiums with short stems attached; quickly rinse and pat dry. In a small bowl, beat an egg white until frothy, then mix in 2 tablespoons (30 grams) of superfine (not confectioners') sugar. Hold the blossom by the stem as you paint the mixture onto both sides of the petals. Let them dry on a baking rack in the refrigerator. When you're ready to use them, snip off the stem as you set each blossom in place.

vigorous daylilies take over the space. They will dominate lawn grass with ease and often win out over weeds.

Grandpa's wisdom

Local folks know the best daylilies, and many avid daylily gardeners sell plants from their collections in mid- to late summer. When you see a sign that says "Daylilies for Sale," put on your brakes.

DELPHINIUMS

Delphiniums, the royal cousins of larkspurs, preside over the garden with lacy, toothed foliage framing towering spikes of white, blue, or violet flowers. Beloved in cool-climate gardens, where they will thrive with reasonable care, delphiniums are not suitable for regions with very hot, humid, or arid summers. But where they can be grown, they should be grown. A delphinium in full bloom is a breathtaking sight.

Grow new plants from seeds sown in summer so that young seedlings won't have to endure summer heat. Delphiniums are naturally short-lived, so it's best to start new plants every other year. And, unlike many perennials, which must be propagated vegetatively, excellent hybrid delphiniums can be grown from seed.

Spoil their feet by providing them with rich, fertile soil that is deep, friable, and well drained. Plenty of organic matter dug into the

planting hole will help keep the soil moist during dry spells.

Fresh air and dry leaves help prevent botrytis, a fungal disease to which delphiniums are particularly susceptible. In damp weather, don't add to the plants' problems by wetting the foliage.

For blooms all season on established plants, pinch out the growing points of some of the green spikes early in the season. This will set back the flowering clock for the pinched spikes, but the unpinched ones will go ahead and bloom. Many gardeners pinch only outer spikes so the central ones will bloom first. That way, the later blossom spikes hide the early ones as they begin to fade.

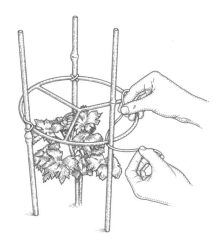

Tall giants fall hard. Begin staking delphiniums early, when they are only 1 foot (30 cm) tall. Use a grow-through type of plant support that will hold up the stems when they are holding heavy blooms and a thunderstorm moves through the garden.

☙ Watch Out!

Some people develop skin rashes from contact with delphinium sap, and delphinium foliage is moderately poisonous. That's why deer seldom nibble the plants.

Want a second crop? To enjoy a second flowering in September, cut back the stems of delphiniums as soon as the flowers have faded in June or July. Cut just above the basal leaves at a height of 4 to 9 inches (10 to 23 cm). Water the plants copiously and apply liquid fertilizer several times throughout the course of the summer. When nights cool in early fall, watch for a fast flush of flower spikes.

As perfect for highlighting a shady spot as they are for growing in the cool, green woods, the abundant varieties of hardy fern are handy on the north side of the house or as edging for shady borders. The small ones look natural in a rock garden or alongside a pond, and you can cut fronds from any fern to include in floral arrangements. Ferns may require supplemental water in dry weather, but once established, they often prosper for years with little care.

Shades of preference. Most hardy ferns prefer dappled rather than deep shade. The amount of sun a fern tolerates depends on the moisture

TEN FABULOUS FERNS

Hardy ferns for the garden

1. **Christmas fern**—Evergreen, hardy, and great for north-facing slopes

2. **Cinnamon fern**—Tall, reddish-brown "cinnamon stick" fronds followed by tall green ones

3. **Japanese painted fern**—Silvery fronds tinged with red and blue; a great foliage plant for the shade garden

4. **Japanese red shield fern**—Coppery young fronds

mature to green, with red spores

5. **Maidenhair fern**—Dark stems and feathery fronds; needs constant moisture

6. **Ostrich fern**—Tall plumes; likes marshy soil beside garden ponds

Tender ferns for containers

7. **Bear's-foot and hare's-foot ferns**—Long, "furry" rhizomes at base of fronds; great for hanging baskets

8. **Bird's-nest fern**—Rosette with lobed, flat fronds; easiest fern to grow as a houseplant

9. **Boston fern**—Easy to grow in outdoor hanging baskets; sheds badly when brought indoors

10. **Japanese holly fern**—Shiny, leathery foliage; easy to grow as an indoor-outdoor patio plant

content of the soil—the wetter the soil, the more sun the plant can handle.

Multiply ferns. Ferns develop dustlike spores rather than seeds. Unlike seeds, spores have no food reserves, and they need a wet environment in which to grow. Instead of trying to grow new plants from spores, divide ferns to increase your supply of plants. The best time to dig them is early spring, when the new fronds unfurl. You can dig and move wild ferns pretty easily, provided you have written permission from the property owner.

Feed ferns last year's leaves. Before you create a new leaf pile in the fall, turn and mix what's left from last year and spread the crumpled, half-rotted leaves over your fern bed. This mimics the natural habitat of most hardy ferns, which grow in the cushy leaf mulch that covers the forest floor.

Wait until spring to clean up old fronds. The dry fronds of deciduous ferns protect the base of the plant. Once the cute, curled fiddleheads show in spring, clip off old fronds at the soil line.

HIBISCUS

The hibiscus is a member of the mallow family and is prized for its oversize tropical blooms, which often exceed dinner-plate size. The lovely Chinese hibiscus, *Hibiscus rosa-sinensis,* is perhaps the best-known species, although it is hardy only in the warmest areas: Florida, the Gulf Coast, California, and Hawaii. However, recent

Grandpa's wisdom

In Jamaica and other West Indian islands, hibiscus is known as "shoe flower" or "shoe black." The juice from the flower petals can be used as a polish for black leather shoes.

advances in breeding work with rose mallow (*H. moscheutos*), a Louisiana native, have resulted in beautiful varieties that can be grown outdoors as far north as Zone 5. In colder regions, the plants can be kept in containers and stored through winter in a protected garage.

Which is which? Some nurseries lump all hibiscus together, so look for a plant with dull, medium-green, heart-shaped leaves and dinner plate-size white, pink, purple, or red flowers with buds 2 to 4 inches (5 to 10 cm) long. Many of the showiest varieties have two or even three colors in their blooms—the primary petal color, a contrasting throat, and a brightly colored stamen.

To plant hibiscus in containers, put each plant into a 5-gallon (19-liter) pot. Place outdoors in a warm, sunny spot after the danger of frost has passed. Plan to move the plant to a bigger pot in midsummer.

Watch for Japanese beetles. They love to munch hibiscus leaves and flowers. In most areas, you can cover plants loosely with a floating row cover during the six weeks in early summer when the beetles are active. Hibiscus usually bloom best late in the summer anyway, after the Japanese beetles have gone.

HOSTA

These hardy, drought-tolerant perennials, prized more for their large, beautiful leaves than for their trumpetlike flowers, are mainstays for shady borders and pondside beds. They are also effective as a groundcover, and there is no finer plant for growing around the base of a tree. Because hostas need a period of winter dormancy, they grow well anywhere where the temperature drops below freezing for two to three months of the year.

A rich diet helps. While hostas are adaptable, easy-care plants, they will thrive for years if given rich soil and plenty of moisture. Good nutrition also helps bring out the variegation patterns in varieties with gold- or white-striped leaves.

Watch for too much sun. Hostas are sun-shy: The large leaves they produce to collect light will scorch if exposed to too much sunshine. In cool climates, hostas can tolerate about 4 hours of sun daily; in warm climates, 2 hours of direct sun is the limit for most types. There are a few sun-tolerant varieties that can accept more light.

Don't get slimed. Hostas are notorious for attracting slugs and snails, which love to hide beneath their lush leaves by day and come out to eat at night. To thwart them, try trapping them with beer (see page 246). Or grow hostas in wooden containers encircled with copper tape, which slugs are reluctant to cross. The tape is available from garden supply companies; simply attach several strips all the way around the container.

Lessen slug damage by keeping the hosta bed free of weeds and decomposing leaves. The improved growing conditions will strengthen the plants, deprive the pests of nesting sites, and make it easier to detect and destroy eggs and adults. Where slugs aren't a problem, hostas love a year-round mulch.

Share the bounty. Hostas multiply fast, so a planting only a few years old will have plenty of crowns. When the first leaves poke through the surface in early spring, use a sharp spade to dig a crown from the outside of the clump. You can take divisions from hostas in late summer, too. The leaves of hostas divided late in the season often die, but in spring the plants will emerge magically.

PEONIES

Tremendously cold hardy and phenomenally long-lived, peonies are the queens of many perennial borders. Their glossy dark foliage frames flowers that can be huge, and many are fragrant, too. Whether white, pink, deep rose, or a combination of colors, peonies bloom dependably year after year. The biggest problem is that you must often wait two or three seasons for a new plant to begin blooming well. Peonies grow best where summers are cool, and they're not well adapted in Zones 9 and 10.

Terrible travelers. Peonies like to stay put, so select their location carefully and prepare their beds to last for years. Pick a sunny to partially

(Continued on page 76)

Enjoy Cut Flowers

You won't have to wait for a special occasion for a bouquet when you learn how to use your garden flowers as cut flowers. When you gather and arrange them with care, you can enjoy cut flowers throughout the house—and throughout the season.

Three simple steps will help your newly cut blossoms last longer in a vase.

- Most blossoms respond well to a rejuvenating conditioning period just after they are cut. Place them in a deep container of water and put it in a dark spot in the house for a few hours.

- After the stems have been conditioned, prepare the flowers for your arrangement. Remove any thorns and leaves that would be below the water line, where they would become slimy and rotten.

- Cut the bottoms of the stems diagonally so they have a larger surface to absorb water (this is best done under water so the vessels of the stems won't be obstructed by air bubbles). Asters, roses, and snapdragons in particular benefit from this treatment.

Now comes the fun part— arranging the flowers. Use these tips to make all of your creations turn out beautifully.

Keep cut flowers upright. To keep cut flowers from sagging in their vase, crisscross several pieces of transparent tape across the mouth of the vase before putting the flowers in. The flowers will look perky and fresh for a few extra days.

Cauterize stem ends. Daffodils, hollyhocks, hydrangeas, and poppies have difficulty drawing water into their stems because a milky, slimy substance inside seals the cut ends of the stems. The substance can have an adverse effect on other flowers in the same vase. To remedy the problem, briefly singe the stem ends with a flame after trimming the stems.

Give cut flowers extra height. Your flower arrangement would be perfect, except a few of the flowers aren't tall enough. You can improve on nature by sticking the too-short stems into plastic straws before putting them into the vase.

Hold flowers in place. Pros use a "frog" to keep cut flowers in place. To make your own, put an inverted berry basket into a vase (cut the basket to fit if necessary). It will keep your stalks standing tall. You can also fashion a homemade "frog" by bending a piece of chicken wire into a ball and placing it in the bottom of the vase.

Extend the life of your arrangement with hairspray. Just as it preserves your hairstyle, a spritz of hairspray can preserve your cut flowers. Stand a foot away from the bouquet and give it a quick spray, just on the undersides of the leaves and petals.

Hitting the road? Put your cut flowers in six-packs and arrange them when you arrive at your destination. Save a cardboard six-pack holder of

bottles. Place your cut flowers in the water-filled bottles, slip them into their holder, and you're ready to roll.

Bouquets to go. Don't bother with awkward, water-filled containers when traveling with a small bouquet. Simply fill a balloon with about ½ cup

(120 ml) of water and slip it over the cut ends of your flowers. Wrap a rubber band several times around the mouth of the balloon to keep it from slipping off.

AN OASIS FOR CUT FLOWERS

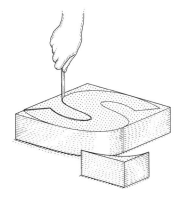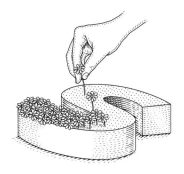

Florists' oasis, the synthetic "moss" used for flower arrangements, retains moisture long after the water in a vase has dried up. Before inserting stems into the moss, give it a good soaking by holding it underwater for several seconds. You can also use it to create original flower arrangements. Cut it with a knife according to your whim, changing the shape into a number, an initial, or even a heart, then attach it to a plate or dish with floral tape. Finally, soak the oasis for several hours before inserting the flowers, then blanket it with sphagnum moss or small pieces of greenery as camouflage.

MAKING YOUR CUT FLOWERS LAST

Sparkling-clean receptacles ensure longer life for cut flowers. Wash vases thoroughly after each use and add a few drops of bleach to the rinse water. For narrow-necked containers that are difficult to clean inside, add ½ cup (240 cc) of dried beans or peas to the wash water and swish them around to remove any vegetation that may be adhering to the surface. Here are some tried-and-true ways to "feed" cut flowers to make them last longer.

- Dissolve 3 tablespoons (45 grams) of sugar and 2 tablespoons (30 ml) of white vinegar in 1 quart (1 liter) of warm water and pour it into the vase. The sugar nourishes the plants, while the vinegar inhibits bacterial growth.

- Add a few drops of vodka to the vase water to kill bacteria, along with 1 teaspoon (5 grams) of sugar for energy.

- Another popular recipe calls for three drops of bleach and 1 teaspoon (5 grams) of sugar in 1 quart (1 liter) of water. Or just add ¼ teaspoon (1 ml) of bleach per quart of water.

- Put a crushed aspirin in the water before adding your flowers.

- Don't throw out that left-over soda. Instead, pour about ¼ cup (60 ml) into the water in a vase full of cut flowers (use clear soda in a clear vase). The sugar in the soda will make the blossoms last longer.

- Your posies and other cut flowers will stay fresh longer if you add a copper penny and a cube of sugar to the vase water.

- Other household items that you can put into the water to extend the life of your flower arrangements include a multivitamin or a pinch of salt or baking soda.

shaded spot that is protected from wind. Dig to a depth of 1 foot (30 cm) and amend the soil generously with compost or well-rotted manure; the soil should be slightly acidic and quick draining.

Cover their eyes. Plant peonies in autumn or early spring, when their "eyes"—little red buds on the crown—are visible. Set the eyes 1 to 2 inches (3 to 5 cm) below the soil line if you live in Zones 3 to 5. In less severe winter climates, set the roots so the eyes are right at the surface. You can add mulch in winter, but remove it first thing in spring.

Paint your garden with peonies. Interplant peonies with bearded irises for a stunning show in late spring. Pair crimson peonies with bright yellow or purple irises for a hot mix. For a subtle look, use white or pink peonies with pastel irises.

❦ Watch Out!

German primrose (*Primula obconica*), which is sometimes sold as a blooming houseplant, can cause skin irritations when handled. Some of the newer hybrids don't have this unfortunate characteristic, but be careful anyway if you have sensitive skin.

Use a green screen. Help prevent peonies' heavy blooms from snapping in the wind by shielding the plants with an evergreen hedge. A bonus: The flowers will sparkle all the more near the dark green backdrop.

Support peonies. To keep the blossoms from falling over, let peonies grow through the metal peony-support rings available at garden centers. Or make your own by cutting a circle from a piece of large-mesh fencing and attaching it securely to a trio of bamboo stakes.

Add peonies for drama. When you cut peonies for floral arrangements, select stems with buds that are just opening (the striking blooms will unfold in a few days) and cut the stems with only a few sets of leaves. The plants need the foliage to produce food for the following year. If you hear thunder, quickly cut any blossoms you've been planning to gather, because peonies with heavily ruffled flowers often crash to the ground when they become heavy with rain.

PRIMROSES

Most *Primula* species are called primrose, but this genus also includes other flowers and a few weeds. Yet there is nothing weedy about garden primroses, which prefer partial shade and cool, moist soil. Early-flowering polyanthus primroses make fine companions for delicate spring flowers, such as forget-me-nots and narcissus. They often grow beautifully in the moist nooks near water features.

Mixed blessings. Primroses cross easily, so if you plant different colors and see volunteer seedlings coming up the next year, they may show unique colors. Most of the primroses sold as bedding plants are hybrids, so they seldom produce offspring in the same color.

A rock garden favorite, the drumstick primrose (*P. denticulata*), has round clusters of lavender, purple, or white blossoms and is the first primrose to bloom in the spring. Sometimes called the Himalayan primrose, it performs best when planted in the moist spaces between rocks, where the roots will remain cool.

Two wildflowers for meadows. If you live in a temperate region and want to create a beautiful wildflower meadow, include cowslips (*P. veris*) and English primrose (*P. vulgaris*) around the shady edges. Both are charmers in this setting and bloom in early spring.

Indoor advice. Potted primroses sold as indoor bloomers in late winter and spring will grow outdoors, but wait until freezing weather has passed to plant them in a moist, shady spot. Or keep them in a window box or on the patio. Every two weeks, give them a little flowering-plant fertilizer that has been diluted to half the recommended strength.

❧ Bulbs, Corms, and Tubers

BULBS ARE A GREAT WAY to expand your flower garden's blooming repertoire. Pop them into the ground, and at precise times in the gardening year, your garden will benefit from their hardy nature, varied heights, and rich colors and forms. Hardy spring-flowering bulbs end their growing season in late spring or early summer, remain dormant through the hot, dry days of summer, and start growing roots again in the fall. The leaves and stems of lilies and other summer-flowering bulbs are frozen back by cold temperatures, and the bulbs then wait until spring to resume active growth. A few summer bulbs, such as caladiums, cannot tolerate freezing temperatures, so one of the fall rituals for bulb lovers is to dig up their tender tubers, pack them into boxes, and keep them cozy until planting time rolls around the following spring. To avoid confusion, you'll find tips for growing spring-flowering bulbs including the perennially popular daffodils, hyacinths, and tulips below, and then you can spend some time getting to know beautiful summer bulbs, such as dahlias, lilies, and irises.

ARE ALL BULBS BULBS?

Tulips and lilies are bulbs, but many of the other plants we call bulbs have important botanical differences in their roots, so they are more properly called corms, tubers, or rhizomes.

- **Bulbs** are modified stems that act as nutrient storage organs. They're made of fleshy scales wrapped around each other, similar to an onion.
- **Corms** don't have scales, and they are woodier than bulbs. Gladiolus grow from corms.
- **Tubers** are thickened, fleshy roots, like potatoes. Dahlias grow from tubers.
- **Rhizomes** are thickened underground stems. Most irises grow from rhizomes.

such as grape hyacinth and small daffodils, in groups, not singly or in rows. For the most natural look of all, just toss the bulbs on the ground and plant them wherever they fall. Some will be close together; others far apart. You'll avoid an artificial or contrived look.

Big bulbs make big flowers. When buying bulbs, look for the largest ones available. They have the greatest food reserves and will produce

SPRING-FLOWERING BULBS

Get a dazzling display. For the most natural appearance, plant small spring-flowering bulbs,

more and larger flowers. Also buy bulbs that show no sign of root or shoot growth, and feel the package to make sure the bulbs are firm rather than mushy. If a newly purchased bulb has begun to grow, plant it in a pot if you can't set it out in your garden immediately.

Mark a missing spot. What do you do when a hyacinth that was supposed to appear in spring doesn't show up? Push a colored golf tee into the soil at the spot where it didn't grow. In the fall, you'll know exactly where to plant a new bulb to avoid gaps in your planting plan.

Invite some company. Interplant bulbs with bushy biennials, perennials, or leafy creeping plants, which will use their foliage to conceal the bulbs' yellowing leaves. Use daylilies to camouflage the fading foliage of daffodils or let fall-blooming chrysanthemums hide the yellow legs of tired tulips.

What do they do in winter? Spring-flowering bulbs begin developing a root system in the fall, and this process may continue all winter. Roots develop best when the bulbs are cold, which also keeps them from sprouting too soon. When it's said that tulips need 12 weeks of chilling, it means that they need 12 weeks of growing roots in cold soil below 40°F (4°C) before warm temperatures trigger them to grow leaves and flowers.

DOS AND DON'TS FOR BETTER BULBS

Don't buy bulbs and leave them in poor storage conditions (too much light, moisture, cold, or heat) and then plant them after they have begun to rot.

Do plant in well-drained soil. If your garden soil is clay and drains poorly, add a good helping of sand, compost, and even a few handsful of gravel at the bottom of the planting holes.

Do add a bulb fertilizer or balanced, timed-release or organic fertilizer to the soil beneath the bulb at planting time. Fertilize established bulbs yearly, when they are in their most active season of growth.

Don't plant mixed bulbs that won't flower on the same date. The dramatic effect of massed blooms will be lost, and maintenance will be a headache.

Do form tight clusters of a single variety in a flower bed, in a patch of groundcover, or in a corner of your lawn.

Don't pull off or cut the foliage back after the petals fall. Bulbs need to rebuild their food reserves for the following season, and their leaves are the means by which sunlight is transformed into plant food. Don't remove or trim back leaves until after they have naturally turned yellow.

Force Spring-Flowering Bulbs

You can ask tulips, narcissus, and other spring-flowering bulbs to bloom ahead of schedule by using a technique known as "forcing." Basically, you mimic the chilly temperatures of winter. Then you provide warmth so the bulbs sense that spring has arrived.

To force bulbs in soil:

1. Place spring-flowering bulbs in a pot of fast-draining potting mix. Crowd several into a pot for a more colorful display. In a 6-inch (15-cm) pot, for example, use six tulips, three hyacinths, or up to a dozen crocuses.

2. Store the planted container at about 40°F (4°C) and keep it lightly moist, letting the bulbs root for 10 to 12 weeks. Dig a trench, place the pots in it, and cover them with a board (to keep out rodents) topped with soil and mulch. Or keep them in a box or old cooler in an unheated garage.

3. To stimulate sprouting, move the containers to a cool room after their chilling time is up.

Keep them lightly watered until new growth appears.

4. When sprouts are 1 inch (25 mm) tall, move the pots to a brightly lit place. Flowers will appear in three to six weeks, depending on the species.

5. Once the buds show color, move the pots to indirect light to prolong blooming. Keeping blooming bulbs in a cool room will help them hold their blossoms longer.

To force paperwhite narcissus:

1. The bulbs require no cold treatment or soil. Set them in a shallow, watertight container filled with pebbles, leaving ½ inch (13 mm) of the tops exposed and making sure they

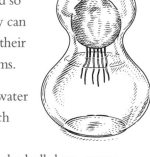

are well anchored so that they can support their long stems.

2. Add water to ⅛ inch (3 mm) beneath the bulb base, never letting it touch, or it will rot.

3. Place the container in a dark place until sprouts show (8 to 10 days), then move it to a sunny spot. The bulbs should flower in three to five weeks.

To force crocuses and hyacinths in water:

1. Use a narrow-necked bulb jar or vase that holds the bulb just above the water line and put it in a cool, dark place until roots form.

2. Move the vase to a sunny room after sprouts are 2 to 4 inches (5 to 10 cm) tall. Fragrant flowers will appear within a month.

Bulbs like a tight fit. When you plant a bulb, make sure it doesn't remain suspended between the sides of the planting hole with an air pocket underneath. The bottom of the bulb needs to be in firm contact with the soil to root properly.

How deep to plant? A bulb should usually be buried at a depth at least twice its height, so little crocuses should be planted only 2 inches (5 cm) deep, while big tulips may need 8-inch-deep (20-cm-deep) planting holes.

Plant in crates to end the bulb season fast. After the flowers are gone, bulbs need to spend some time storing up energy for next year, and they can't do it without their leaves. If you are in a rush to replant the space occupied by spring-flowering bulbs, plan ahead by planting the bulbs in wooden or plastic fruit crates buried at the proper depth. As soon as the leaves begin to yellow, you can lift them from the ground, crate and all. Then move the crated bulbs, complete with their soil, to another area of the garden until they die back completely.

Weed bulbs by hand. A cultivator or other sharp-pointed tool can easily damage shallowly planted bulbs and their roots.

All bulbs aren't for spring and summer. Fall-blooming bulbs include hardy cyclamens, autumn crocuses (*Colchicum*), and *Amaryllis belladonna,* with massive trumpet-shaped flowers of pink or white. Like spring-flowering bulbs, these hardy fall bloomers usually rest during the summer.

DAFFODILS

Daffodil is the most popular name for members of the genus *Narcissus*, a diverse bulb family that includes about 25 species and thousands of varieties that bloom between February and May. All have a central trumpet, or corona, but the size, color, and shape of the blossoms varies from plant to plant. Many classic daffodils have long, fringed, tube-shaped coronas, but others have flat, ruffled ones. Colors of the petals and coronas range from soft white, lemon, and salmon pink to vibrant gold and orange. Squirrels and rodents usually leave daffodils alone, and most types bloom for many years with very little care. Daffodils and narcissus can also tolerate more shade than other bulbs.

Don't worry about the name. Technically, all daffodils are narcissus, but not all narcissus are daffodils. Most of the bright yellow and white daffodils seen in gardens in spring really are daffodils, but smaller-flowered varieties that bloom later, often with several flowers per stem, are properly called narcissus. Jonquils are a specific class of narcissus.

Pinch off faded flowers with your fingernails or pruning shears, leaving the green stem in place. Removing the blooms speeds storage of food reserves that the bulb needs in order to bloom next year. Feed your daffodils and other narcissus with a balanced fertilizer sprinkled around the plants in spring. If you have a lot of bulbs, invest in a high-phosphorus bulb fertilizer.

Daylilies make fine daffodil companions because fading daffodil foliage will be neatly masked by the daylilies' similar leaves. Other good green screens include peonies (in the North) and Shasta daisies (in the North and South).

Go natural with dainty narcissus. The best way to plant small-flowered narcissus is in naturalistic drifts, with dozens of bulbs creating meadows or rivers of color. Try them along the base of a fence or another place where their fading foliage won't interfere with your late spring lawn mowing.

Confuse tulip-hungry rodents. Narcissus are slightly toxic and unpalatable, so pests will generally leave them—and their neighboring plants—alone. Use them as decoys. Interplant daffodils with tulips, hyacinths, and other bulbs beloved by chipmunks, mice, and moles. Some types are even bypassed by browsing deer.

Prevent leaf burn. If a spring cold snap threatens to injure plants, protect them with an overturned flowerpot, a cardboard box, or even an old blanket. The new growth of most daffodils will not be injured unless temperatures drop into the low 20s (-7°C), and early daffodils often push up blooms through wet spring snow.

Divide narcissus every four years in early summer, just as the foliage has died back. Lift the clump with a fork, shake off soil, and let the bulbs dry in the shade for a few days. Pull the bulbs apart and either replant them immediately

 SORTING THROUGH
daffodils

Among gardeners' favorite daffodils are bright yellow 'King Alfred', creamy white 'Ice Follies', and many others that bloom in mid-spring. Smaller miniatures often bloom earlier, and the little guys look great in tight spaces. Use a variety of types to stretch the narcissus season from late winter to late spring.

- **Cyclamen narcissus** (*Narcissus cyclamineus*) has reflexed petals that resemble a cyclamen's and long trumpets with crinkled ends. It is one of the first narcissus to bloom.

- **Poet's narcissus** (*N. poeticus*) features scented blooms, which open in mid- to late-spring with white petals surrounding a contrasting "eye" that is usually rimmed in red.

- **Sweetly scented jonquil** (*N. jonquilla*) has slender leaves and clusters of blooms with small cups that appear in late spring. The scented flowers, in white and yellow, are ideal for cutting.

or store them in a box until you're ready to replant them in the fall.

HYACINTHS

The sweet scent of hyacinth has made it a favorite flower of spring. Spikes clad with bell-shaped blue, pink, white, yellow, or purple flowers grow 10 inches (25 cm) high, and bulbs typically bloom well for three or more years before weakening. Under good conditions, hyacinths will keep coming back for decades, although the flowers will not be as close together as they are with first season Dutch-grown bulbs.

THE FIRST HYACINTH

According to Greek mythology, Hyacinth was a handsome young athlete and an inseparable friend of Apollo, god of the sun. Zephyr, the West Wind, became fond of the young man, but Hyacinth spurned his affection. One day, as Hyacinth was throwing the discus with Apollo, Zephyr created a violent wind that blew the discus off course and into the young man's forehead at full speed. Hyacinth fell, mortally wounded, his blood staining the grass. Overcome with grief, Apollo transformed the blood drops into the delicately fragrant flower that still bears his friend's name.

Remedy short-stemmed blooming. If your hyacinths are flowering on short stems, force them to grow longer ones. Before the hyacinths bloom, place the cardboard rolls from paper towels or toilet paper over the green spikes to force them to elongate toward the light. When they reach the height you want, remove the rolls. They will then bloom on long spikes.

Indoors or out? While hyacinths herald spring's arrival in the garden, you can enjoy them indoors in winter by forcing bloom. Plant bulbs with their "shoulders" exposed in moist, well-drained potting mix and store at 40°F (4°C) for 12 to 15 weeks before the desired bloom time. To break their dormancy, move them to a cool 55° to 65°F (13°C to 18°C), bright but not sunny spot until sprouts appear. Then place them in direct sun and keep the soil

moist. Once the buds show color, put the plants in indirect light, which will help prolong flowering. The fragrant blooms will last about two weeks in a cool room.

Save used bulbs. Don't throw away forced hyacinths after they've flowered indoors. Keep them well lit and well watered and feed with liquid fertilizer. After the foliage has yellowed and died back, plant the bulbs outdoors to bloom the following season. You may have only a few flowers the first year, but the spikes will become more robust in the next two seasons.

Planting delays? Place hyacinth bulbs in the vegetable compartment of your refrigerator, where they will keep for two weeks. Wrap them in paper towels so their pungent skins won't impart their odor to the food. Or plant them in pots of damp peat moss and enclose the planted pots in plastic bags before storing them in your refrigerator.

TULIPS

The stately tulips that herald spring are mostly hybrids that have resulted from 300 years of passionate plant breeding. Available in a huge range of colors and forms, tulips always bloom beautifully their first year and may bloom well for several seasons thereafter. In addition to the dazzling hybrids, species (or botanical) tulips are smaller, hardy bulbs that will naturalize in informal spots for years of bloom. They usually have open, starry blooms that close in wet weather, with a "wild" look that recalls their native mountain habitats.

Good tulip bulbs are pretty, with firm, smooth flesh covered by chestnut-colored papery skin. Don't worry if the papery outer layer is tattered, but avoid bulbs with soft spots, bruises, or nicks. Plant tulip bulbs with the skins intact because they help protect the bulbs from pests and disease.

To purchase species tulips and lesser-known hybrids, seek out catalogs from specialty bulb growers, who are more likely than garden centers to carry them. Be sure to order them in late summer or fall, the seasons when all spring-flowering bulbs are shipped.

THE TULIPOMANIA CRAZE

"Tulipomania" was the name given to the tulip-growing frenzy that swept Europe in the 17th century. The seed of this phenomenon was sown in the mid-1500's, when native tulip bulbs were imported from Turkey to the imperial gardens of Emperor Ferdinand I of Vienna. From there, a royal botanist who had zealously bred the unusual new plants carted his tulip bulbs to Holland, where, in 1593, they debuted in the botanical gardens. It has been said that the flowers were so coveted by the public that all 600 bulbs were stolen—all in one night. Thereafter, the passion for tulips increased, peaking in 1637, when three Rembrandt tulip bulbs commanded the equivalent of $25,000.

Climate too hot for tulips? Most tulips need a period of cold dormancy, but some will perform well in warm climates with minimal chilling, at least for one season. Try *Tulipa sylvestris*, *T. bakeri* 'Lilac Wonder', 'Blue Parrot', 'White Triumphator', or 'Sweet Harmony'. Some mail-order companies sell prechilled tulips to grow as annuals in mild winter climates.

Use the right soil. While tulips can usually adjust to many soil types, they grow best in rich, quick-draining loam.

Team tulips with mini-pansies. Small-flowered mini-pansies start blooming sooner in spring than larger-flowered types, and they are hardy enough to be planted with tulips in the fall in most areas. By the time the tulips bloom, the mini-pansies will form a sea of color at their feet.

The edge of a tree's shade canopy is a great place to plant tulips. They will get full sun during their early stage of growth and enjoy cool shade as the flowers appear. Light shade helps tulip blooms last longer, while hot weather makes them shatter quickly. Be careful with too much shade, because light-starved tulips will bend and twist toward brighter light.

A second-year slump is common for some tulips in some soils. You never know until you try! If you're not happy with some tulips, lift the bulbs at season's end and replant them in an inconspicuous spot, where their less-than-perfect blooms won't matter. They may surprise you by coming back better than ever.

🌿 SORTING THROUGH
tulips

To prolong the thrill of seeing tulips in bloom, plant cultivars that flower at different times. There is no dearth of choices: The tulip industry produces 1.5 billion bulbs in more than 3,000 varieties annually.

- **Species tulips** such as *Tulipa Kaufmanniana* grow less than 8 inches (20 cm) tall and bloom in early spring, along with early daffodils.

- **Fosteriana tulips** bloom in mid-spring on 10- to 18-inch-tall (25- to 45-cm-tall) plants, in pure colors ranging from yellow to deepest purple. If you crave a certain color, try these sturdy plants. Triumph types are slightly taller yet similar, and they often naturalize well.

- **Darwin hybrids** are big and beautiful, and they often grow more than 2 feet (60 cm) tall, producing large, richly colored blooms.

- **Parrot tulips** are but one type of novelty tulip. In addition to parrot types, which have frilled petal edges, there are fringed, streaked, and big double-flowered tulips, many with dramatically streaked petals.

For long-lasting bouquets, cut tulips in the morning. Select fairly tight buds with good color on the upper two-thirds of the petals. Give tulips plenty of room in a vase because the blooms can expand by as much as 50 percent.

SUMMER-FLOWERING BULBS

Make a colorful summer splash. Summer-flowering bulbs provide a great opportunity to create splashes of color in the sultry summer garden. From late spring irises to summer lilies, summer-flowering bulbs are naturals as feature flowers in mixed beds.

Plant new bulbs in warm soil. Even hardy summer-blooming bulbs, such as lilies, should be planted in spring after the soil has begun to warm. You can plant irises in summer as well.

Try them in containers. Dwarf varieties of many summer-blooming bulbs make beautiful container subjects. After the flowers fade, you can move the pots to an out-of-the-way place while the bulbs finish their life cycle.

Excellent drainage is crucial because bulbs will rot quickly in overly wet soil. If you have heavy clay and questionable drainage, create a special raised bed for summer bulbs and include a layer of gravel about 12 inches (30 cm) below the surface.

Hardy is as hardy does. Most irises and lilies are winter hardy, and dahlias and gladiolus can be left in the garden as far north as Zone 7. However, caladiums must always be dug and stored through winter.

Guard against rot. Store tender bulbs in dry peat, sand, or sawdust that is kept slightly damp. Arrange the bulbs in layers, being careful that they don't touch each other. Store in a dark place where the temperature is around 50°F (10°C).

Put on your pantyhose. Pantyhose legs make terrific sacks for storing flower bulbs over winter, because they let air circulate freely around the bulbs to prevent mold and rot. Cut a leg from a pair of pantyhose and place your bulbs inside, knot the end, and use strips of masking tape to make ID tags for the sacks. Hang them up in a cool, dry space, and they'll be ready for planting in the spring.

Don't let your bulbs dry out. Whether you store them in boxes or hanging bags, dahlias, cannas, and caladiums tend to dry out during winter storage. Check them every three to four weeks and lightly sprinkle water on any that appear to be starting to shrivel.

CALADIUMS

These foliage plants offer a splash of color to any shade-filled spot in your garden. In the South, you'll often see them around the trunks of spreading shade trees. They also do well in patio containers, with their veined leaves nodding in every breeze. 'Candidum', probably the most popular caladium, has large snow-white leaves laced with green veins, and it does a wonderful job of cooling down sultry shade. The dwarf variety 'Little Miss Muffet' has lime green leaves speckled with red, and it grows beautifully in containers.

Think tropical. In May, buy dormant, knobby tubers and pot them in humus-rich potting soil with the tops of the tubers buried 1 inch (25 mm) deep. Dampen well and keep the pots in a place where the temperature is 75° to 80°F (24° to 27°C), such as on top of your refrigerator or water heater. Wait until the weather is warm to set them out.

 SORTING THROUGH
caladiums

More and more nurseries sell unusual caladiums. Use them to set a tropical mood in your garden.

- **Most caladiums** have large heart-shaped leaves with contrasting veins or edges. Pink, white, green, and red combine differently in each variety.

- **More adaptable caladiums** with elongated, lance-shaped leaves tolerate more sun, as well as slightly cooler temperatures. Most caladiums with 'Florida' in their name fall into this group.

- **Smaller species caladiums,** such as *Caladium humboldtii*, grow only 5 inches (13 cm) tall, so they're great for patio-size summer dish gardens.

- **Gigantic elephant ears** (*Colocasia* and *Alocasia* species) are not the same species as caladiums, but they are grown the same way. Many have beautifully variegated green leaves.

Can't tell the top from the bottom? Caladium tubers can be confusing, but they will always grow if you bypass the mystery by planting them on their sides. Of course, the preferred planting position is top side up.

Although caladiums crave shade, too little light may make them leggy and weak-stemmed. This seldom happens outdoors, but watch indoor caladiums for signs of light starvation.

Satisfy their hunger. Caladiums need plenty of fertilizer to grow big, lush leaves. Instead of applying fertilizer all at once, give them regular rations of a balanced or high-nitrogen fertilizer all through the summer months.

Use leaves in arrangements. The painterly patterns and clean lines of caladium leaves make them ideal for simple flower arrangements, such as a single leaf paired with a rosebud in a glass vase.

Take them for a swim. Caladiums do well when they get plenty of water. If you have a garden pool, pot the tubers in porous terra-cotta pots. Once the plants have developed one or two leaves, place the pots on a ledge or cement blocks at the pool's edge, with the rims just above water level. They'll respond with lush growth.

Expect no flowers from caladiums unless you live in a hot, humid climate. If an odd-looking, leafless, elongated stem does appear, clip it off so that the plant will concentrate its energy on growing leaves rather than flowers, which are not at all showy.

Try storing them in pots. If you grow your caladiums in pots, you can store them that way, too. Gradually withhold water from the plants in early fall; they will slowly die back and become dormant. Clip off all top growth and store the almost-dry pots in an indoor closet. In late spring, repot the corms in clean containers filled with fresh potting soil.

Keep stored caladiums warm. Caladiums flourish in heat and can't abide temperatures below 65°F (18°C). Even dormant tubers will rot if the temperature drops much below 60°F (16°C), so give caladiums warmer storage temperatures than dahlias or gladiolus.

DAHLIAS

Dahlias deliver brilliant color for as long as warm weather lasts. As with daylilies and roses, growing dahlias tends to be habit forming because they are as beautiful in a vase as they are in a garden. Dwarf types can be used to fill window boxes or edge sunny beds, or you can grow tall, large-flowered varieties if you prefer. Some produce blooms as big as dinner plates!

Give dahlias a head start by planting the tubers in early spring in a warm (at least 60°F or 16°C), sunny place, such as a sunroom or in pots kept by your patio doors. Plant them in a shallow box filled with a light planting medium, such as seed-starting mix or light-textured potting soil.

The right depth. In the garden, larger dahlia varieties need a planting depth of 6 to 8 inches (15 to 20 cm). Dwarf types can be planted only 3 to 4 inches (8 to 10 cm) deep. Many gardeners plant dahlias in well-enriched planting holes and cover them with 1 inch (25 mm) of soil weekly as the stems grow. Always wait until the last spring frost has passed to plant dahlias.

Double your dahlias. When the shoots of tubers reach 6 to 7 inches (15 to 18 cm) in length, cut them 2 inches (5 cm) above the soil line and set the cuttings to root in pots filled with seed-starting mix. Enclose the potted cuttings in plastic bags and keep them warm. In three weeks, they will root, and you'll have twice as many dahlias!

Keep them well fed. Dahlias don't like to go hungry, so include a water-soluble plant food in the water you give them, or sidedress them monthly with a balanced granular fertilizer.

Stake inconspicuously. For tall dahlia varieties, stake when the stems reach 18 to 20 inches (45 to 50 cm) high. Select three or four bamboo canes of the same height as the mature plant and drive them into the soil beside the main stems. Tie the stems at two heights with soft twine and incorporate the new growth as it develops.

Easy does it. Don't tug on the stems when you lift dahlias. Delicately lift the entire clump with a spading fork to keep from damaging the tubers. Let the tubers dry in the open air for at least a

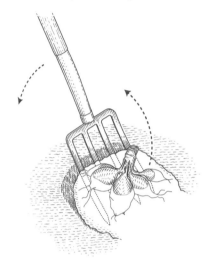

BAFFLE BULB-EATING CRITTERS

Chipmunks, squirrels, and mice are drawn to bulbs like hungry humans to a breakfast buffet. Daffodils are naturally squirrel resistant, but try these techniques to protect other bulbs.

- Bury a piece of wire mesh, such as landscape fencing, over the plantings.

- Sprinkle moth crystals over the freshly planted bulbs.

- Use medicated baby powder to dust flower bulbs before planting them. Place five or six bulbs and about 3 tablespoons of baby powder in a sealed plastic bag, then give it a few gentle shakes. The medicated-powder coating helps both reduce the chance of rot and keep away moles, voles, grubs, and other bulb-munching pests.

- To keep burrowing rodents out, line the bottom and sides of a prepared bed with chicken wire, plant the bulbs, and cover with soil.

- Plant bulbs in berry baskets. Be sure to place the basket at the correct depth, then insert the bulb and cover it with soil.

day, preferably in the sun, before knocking off the dry soil and storing them for the winter.

Prolong flowering by deadheading. When faded flowers are promptly removed, many small-flowered varieties will bloom nonstop for four months or longer.

To get dinner-dish-size flowers, choose cactus- or decorative-type dahlias. Remove the weakest stems, leaving only two or three of the strongest. When the plants are about 12 inches (30 cm) tall, tie them to stakes. As flower buds form, pinch them off or remove side shoots, leaving only the top bud. Pros get blooms up to 10 inches (25 cm) in diameter.

❧ SORTING THROUGH
dahlias

Dahlias come in a wide range of flower forms and some have vivid reddish-black foliage. The larger the flowers, the later a variety tends to bloom.

- **Single-flowered dahlias** produce flat, open, daisy-type blossoms. Blooms are often numerous, and these varieties tend to bloom for a long time.

- **Anemone and collerette dahlias** have clusters of short petals around their centers, which are framed by larger petals on the outsides of the blossoms. They make great cut flowers.

- **Classic dahlias** show the decorative flower form, in which new petals slowly emerge from the blossoms' centers over a period of more than a week. Many of the best garden dahlias are of this type.

- **Ball, cactus, and dinner plate dahlias** feature large, showy blooms. They are most often grown as exhibition plants.

Sometimes called sword lily, gladiolus produce spikes of large silky blossoms that are gorgeous in cut flower arrangements. They grow from round corms, and new corms develop above the old ones. The flowers come in all sizes— from miniatures to giants—with plenty of color choices. If you plan to use your glads primarily as cut flowers, choose colors that will work well with your home's interior décor. Many gardeners grow glads, for cutting, in their vegetable gardens.

For gladiolus all summer, plant a few corms every 2 weeks, starting at about the time of the last spring frost. The plants will bloom about two months later. Stop planting 10 weeks before your first fall frost is expected.

Don't plant in rows when using glads in flowerbeds. The plants look better in groups of five, and the shelter provided by surrounding plants will help hold them upright.

Stake the giants. Stake large-flowered gladiolus, which can grow 4 to 6 feet (1.2 to 1.8 meters) tall, with a soft cloth tied to a bamboo cane. Place the stake behind the flower spike as soon as you can tell which way the florets will face.

Hasten blooming. Gladiolus florets open from the lower part of the stem upward. Pinch out the top bud to speed the opening of flowers all along the spike or allow the florets to open naturally and pinch off the lowest ones as they begin to shrivel.

🌸 SORTING THROUGH
gladiolus

All gladiolus are not alike. In addition to a wide range of colors, gladiolus vary in height and hardiness.

- **Tall, large-flowered glads** often grow more than 3 feet (1 meter) tall, and they are available in almost any color and numerous bicolors. However, they are dependably hardy only in Zones 8 to 10.

- **Intermediate-size gladiolus** are easier to work with in a garden, because they don't require staking. The 'Flevo' series grows about 2 feet (60 cm) tall, and the corms are hardy to Zone 7.

- **Several species glads** make dependable perennials in Zones 7 to 9. Cultivars of *Gladiolus nanus* are most common. For something unusual, try the white-flowered *G. callianthus*, sometimes called Abyssinian gladiolus, which produces fragrant, nodding flowers in late summer.

Dig corms when the leaves begin to turn yellow—usually about six weeks after the plants bloom. Lift the plants carefully with a spade, shake off the soil, and set them aside to dry for a few days. Then cut the leaves to 2 inches (50 mm) before storing the corms in a cool, dry place.

IRISES

Some irises grow from bulbs, but the popular bearded iris—so called for the hairs on the down-turned petals—grows from thick, shallow rhizomes. Although the iris blooming season is short, the blossoms rival those of orchids in their exotic details. And, when the plants are not in bloom, they provide sleek texture with their stiff, pointed leaves. When designing iris plantings, remember that they're most striking when massed; their blooms will look like a swarm of butterflies hovering over the garden.

Bearded irises need sun and well-drained soil. Sidedress plants with a balanced, timed-release fertilizer in spring. If drainage is questionable, plant rhizomes in a mound of soil amended with coarse sand.

The best time to plant new irises is in early summer, soon after the plants have bloomed. Planting season continues into the summer, for as long as the soil stays warm.

Healthy plants seldom need dividing more often than every three years. Irises tend to skip a

ADOPT AN AMARYLLIS

The big bulbs known as amaryllis are popular holiday gifts, and with good care, they will continue to bloom for many seasons. If you grow one indoors in winter, keep it watered and fed until spring, then bury the pot in the garden almost up to the rim. In fall, dig up and clean up the pot and allow the bulb to dry indoors for six to eight weeks. Six weeks before you want it to bloom, replant the bulb in fresh soil, add water, and place it near a bright, warm window. A new shoot will appear within days, followed shortly by a beautiful new bud.

season of bloom after they have been divided, so it's usually best to postpone division as long as possible. When dividing irises, keep only the healthy outer parts of the clump, with a fan of new growth attached. Let the cut rhizomes dry in the sun for several hours, then replant them 12 to 15 inches (30 to 45 cm) apart.

The worst pest of bearded irises is the iris stem borer, which tunnels into new leaves and bores holes in the rhizomes. Dig up and destroy badly affected plantings. In areas where problems with this pest are severe, treat irises with a pesticide that contains imidacloprid, which doesn't kill earthworms or beneficial insects.

❧ SORTING THROUGH irises

Beyond bearded irises, there are many more types to try in your garden.

- **Dwarf irises** bloom in spring, and they mix easily with little daffodils. Hardy to Zone 3, many dwarf irises are slightly fragrant.

- **Dutch irises** grow to about 20 inches (50 cm) tall and bloom in late spring. Adapted in Zones 6 to 8, Dutch irises make better cut flowers than other types.

- **Siberian irises** offer a good change. Stiffly upright with purple, white, or bicolor blossoms, a clump of these hardy irises makes a great vertical accent in a mixed perennial border.

- **Louisiana irises** are hybrids that are great for the edge of a water garden. There are numerous other irises that grow in shallow water.

Keep plantings neat by cutting back leaves by about half their length in late summer so that they have an attractive fan shape.

LILIES

Lilies are reliable summer performers, bringing color and fragrance to the garden when other flowers have faded. Lily blooms are usually shaped like elegant trumpets, and colors range from pure white to deep burgundy, with pastels and eye-popping hot hues in between.

Give lilies your best site. Lilies like moist, loamy, slightly acidic soil. If your soil is too heavy or light, dig very well rotted manure, composted leaves, or other organic matter into the planting bed. Also work in some bonemeal or superphosphate. Lilies love a site with good air circulation, wind protection, and excellent drainage.

Plant in groups of three or more. Because of their tall, thin stems, lilies sometimes look awkward and bare when planted alone. You can surround them with small companion plants, such as dwarf dianthus or ageratum.

Plant and forget? Lilies seldom need to be dug and divided, and there are few things more beautiful than a happy lily that has grown into a robust clump. Do remember to fertilize in spring and again in late summer, but don't worry about digging and replanting established bulbs.

Hold the tigers. One of the few problems lilies face is lily virus, which causes distorted growth and weakens the plants. Although easy to grow, tiger lilies can secretly host this virus, which is spread to susceptible plants by aphids. Don't grow tiger lilies if this disease is known to be present in your area.

To stake or not? Some gardeners prefer the look of a full-flowered stem nodding in the sun. But if you want to stake lilies, do so in spring, inserting a green metal or bamboo stake by each stem, being careful not to injure the bulb. The stake should reach about 9 inches (22 cm) below the flowers. Tie loosely with a figure-8 loop.

Add some friends. Underplant lilies with noncompeting companions, like primroses, violets, or baby's breath—these will keep lily roots cool and may support thin lily stems.

Take seasonal precautions. In cold climates, prevent frost heaves with a deep layer of straw, conifer needles, or chopped leaves. If shoots emerge prematurely in early spring, cover them with a cloche, basket, or other device. Work around the shoots gently—if you snap them off, you'll have no blooms.

Cut lilies carefully. When cutting blooms for arrangements, leave a third of the stems on the plants so that the foliage can replenish nutrients for the bulbs. Lily blooms often last a week or more in a vase of cool water.

Try Asiatic lilies in containers. Although they're not fragrant like Oriental lilies, compact Asiatic hybrids grow well in beds or pots. You can pot them in fall and keep the containers in a cool place where they won't freeze, or wait to plant the bulbs first thing in spring.

❧ SORTING THROUGH lilies

For success with lilies, match your choice to the growing conditions in your garden. Regardless of type, yellow, pink, or white lilies are usually the strongest bloomers.

- **Asiatic hybrids** are the easiest lilies to grow, and they are hardy to Zone 4. Try several varieties and stick with those that prove worthy of your garden.

- **Oriental lilies** produce large fragrant blossoms and often persist in the garden for many years. Hardy to Zone 4, these lilies often have beautifully speckled throats.

- **Easter lilies** are usually hardy only to Zone 7, but if they are transplanted to the garden in spring, they will often bloom for many years in late spring or early summer.

- **Trumpet lilies** often grow 6 feet (2 meters) tall, so they always need staking. Hardy to Zone 4, a trio of towering trumpet lilies makes a great accent in the back of a mixed border.

CONTAINER
PLANTS

Container gardening allows you to quickly and easily brighten any area, indoors or out, with a vibrant green plant—or maybe several beautiful bloomers. In this chapter, you will find tips for potting up plants to use in very different ways—some to bring seasonal color to your deck or patio, others to grow in window boxes—and dozens of ways to handle versatile plants like aloe and palms, which like to spend the winter indoors and move outside in summer. There are plenty of ideas for keeping your houseplants healthy and happy, too, whether you grow them in pots, hanging baskets, or in a little terrarium.

There is a reason that more and more gardeners are enjoying the company of green companions in containers. Container gardening requires little space or muscle, and plants in pots can be enjoyed during every season of the year. You can be endlessly creative with container-grown plants, too, and rearrange them to take advantage of their colors, fragrances, and textures in a matter of minutes. Many houseplants will thrive for years when given good care and often will offer up cuttings or divisions which can be shared with family or friends.

❧ Container-Gardening Basics

WHEN PLANTS ARE IN CONTAINERS rather than being grown more naturally in the earth, they require special care—especially when they are being grown in a climate far removed from their normal habitat, as container plants often are. Whether you are working with house-plants or containers on your patio or deck, here are some hints to keep in mind.

Make big planters more portable. Don't strain your back moving a planter loaded with heavy soil. Reduce the amount of soil and lighten the load by first filling one-third to one-half of the pot with empty aluminum cans, crushed plastic milk containers, or Styrofoam packing peanuts. It will save on mess when repotting if you enclose these filler materials in mesh onion bags. Finish filling the planter with soil and add your plants. In addition to making the planter lighter, the bottom layer of lightweight filler will improve the drainage in large containers.

Drill for drainage. Every pot that holds a plant must have drainage holes so excess water can escape. You can drill holes into wood or fiberglass containers, but concrete or ceramic planters may break when drilled, even if you use a masonry bit. When you want to use a pretty planter that lacks drainage holes, line the bottom with an inch of pebbles and set a pot with proper drainage holes inside on the pebble bed.

Plant a cache of tea bags. For healthier potted plants, place a few used tea bags on top of the drainage layer at the bottom of the planter before adding a plant. The tea bags will retain water and leach nutrients to the soil.

Prevent potting soil leakage. When you're repotting a plant, line the bottom of the pot with a coffee filter, a used dryer sheet, a small piece of window screening, or a few dried leaves to keep the soil from leaking out through the drain hole.

Another way to erase erosion. Soil from potted plants won't slip-slide away if you place pieces of broken clay flowerpots in the bottom of the pot when replanting. When you water your plants, water will drain out through the bottom, but not the soil.

Put in a quick refresher. Before you spend time repotting a container-grown plant, try topdressing the surface with a fresh helping of potting soil instead. Remove an inch or two from the surface of the old potting mix and use a fresh mixture to refill to the original level. Dump the used soil in your flowerbeds.

Help plants with a pencil. Got a houseplant that needs some support? Don't know if it needs watering? A pencil can help with both problems. It's the perfect size stake for a small plant, tied with string or a strip of cloth. To gauge moisture in the soil, stick a pencil into the soil and leave it there for 30 minutes. If the tip is dry when you pull it out, the plant needs a good watering.

Blend by shaking. If you want to add peat moss, sand, or another soil amendment to packaged potting soil, there's an easier way than stirring the ingredients together in a bucket. Shake them together instead. Fill a heavy plastic trash bag halfway, blow in a few puffs of air, and hold the bag shut while you shake it up. Let the mixture settle before opening the bag.

Stop cats from digging. If your feline companions like to scratch in the soil of potted plants, cover the soil with pebbles, seashells, aluminum foil, or plastic wrap. Just as cats can't stand a dirty litter box, they will change their minds about scratching in a difficult material.

Clean pots with vinegar. When you have several pots that need cleaning before they can be

☘ Watch Out!

Moving heavy plants can be risky for them and you. To avoid injuries or accidents, try these safe strategies.

- If you know certain plants will eventually be moved, keep them in a child's wagon, which can easily be wheeled from place to place.

- Borrow a skateboard and use it to move a heavy plant.

- Build a plant caddy by attaching casters to the bottom of a scrap piece of lumber.

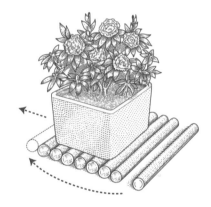

- Like the Egyptians who built the great pyramids, you can move a heavy planter on a "conveyor belt" of round logs or pipes. Keep the planter rolling by continually bringing the last log to the front.

- Tilt a heavy plant on its edge and rock and roll it to its new location.

- Use a "hand truck" or dolly.

reused, soak them in warm, soapy water, scrub them with a stiff brush, and transfer them to a bucket filled with 1 cup (250 ml) vinegar to

PICKING PRIME POTTING SOIL

Potting soil usually contains equal parts loamy, sterilized topsoil; sphagnum moss or peat moss; and either perlite, vermiculite, or sand. There are many brands, including some blended especially for containers. These container potting soils often include polymer crystals, which absorb and hold water better than other types of particles, as well as enough balanced fertilizer to get plants off to a good start.

Specialty potting soils for African violets, orchids, and cacti are good choices if you have several plants to repot. African violet soil often contains extra peat; orchid soil includes chunky bits of tree bark; and cactus soil has a fine, gritty texture so that it will drain fast. Since most people don't need very much of a specialty potting soil, these mixtures are often sold in small bags with zip closures.

Whatever you do, don't try to use ordinary garden soil for your container plants. It's much too heavy and may contain soilborne diseases. You may read about using "compost" for potting plants in gardening books and magazines of British origin, but they don't mean compost from your compost heap. It's just that one country's compost is another country's potting soil.

each gallon (4 liters) of water. The vinegar will help dissolve any mineral deposits that survived scrubbing. Rinse the pots well before refilling.

Plan for neat feet. Setting pots on a solid surface makes it impossible for excess water to drain away. Indoors, set pots in plant saucers filled with pebbles—an easy way to aid drainage and raise humidity at the same time. Outdoors, you can use decorative "feet" or make your own from small wood blocks, used thread spools, or plastic jar lids.

Use a chopstick. When plants are potted up, it's important to eliminate any air pockets around the roots. Rap the bottom of the pot on a solid surface to tamp soil into place or, when working with pots or plants that are difficult to

lift, use a chopstick to poke potting soil between the roots and the inside of the pot.

Need to feed? It isn't necessary to add fertilizer for the first few weeks after repotting, especially if the potting soil includes fertilizer. But each time a plant is watered, some of the nutrients leach out with the excess water. Plants kept outdoors in summer and watered frequently need regular fertilizer. Indoor plants that are pale and show little new growth are usually in need of feeding.

Save cleanup time after potting sessions by covering your work area with newspaper before you start. Tidying up will take only seconds, and little potting soil will be wasted because you can quickly put any that spilled back into the bag.

❧ Deck and Patio Gardening

NEARLY EVERY HOUSE or apartment has a place outdoors where you can grow a few special plants when the weather is warm. Whether that space is a deck, balcony, patio, or porch, it can serve as a delightful outdoor room when furnished with beautiful plants. Some may be indoor-outdoor plants—houseplants that you keep indoors in winter and move outdoors when the weather warms. Others may be herbs, patio-size tomatoes, or plants with special talents for bringing color and drama to outdoor living areas. Here are more than 20 tips for arranging, choosing, and using some of the finest deck and patio plants.

PLANNING YOUR PLANTINGS

Put plants to work by turning your deck or patio into a private oasis. Tall plants or vines trained up trellises can work like green walls in summer, when you're most likely to spend time enjoying your outdoor room.

Make the most of limited space on your deck, patio, or balcony by arranging plants in layers. Put some of the plants in pots on the floor, others in hanging baskets, and some in boxes attached to railings.

Lift patio plants to new heights by placing some on top of upside-down flowerpots. Or get a piece of 6-inch (15-cm) PVC pipe and cut it

---

MAKE POTTED PRESENTS

Use a clean, new terra-cotta flowerpot as a container for gifts to fellow gardeners. Use a terra-cotta saucer as a top and tie the pot with a colorful ribbon. Once the gifts are removed, any avid gardener will be quick to find a use for this little clay essential. For friends who do propagating, you could wrap a nested set of new terra-cotta pots, from 2- to 8-inch (5- to 20-cm) sizes.

For a springtime surprise, fill a pot with packets of seeds for vegetables, herbs, or flowers. In fall, a pot filled with choice bulbs for fall planting will become a lasting reminder of your friendship. In winter, pair pots with paperwhite narcissus or amaryllis, which begin growing as soon as they are planted and bloom within a few weeks.

---

into pieces that can be used as stiltlike sleeves for plants growing in 6-inch pots. If you like, you can paint the pipe with enamel paint to make it look like wood or terra-cotta.

Try crazy containers. It's fun to grow flowers in old boots or baskets, but how about that bird feeder that got mangled by squirrels? Bird feeders are naturally leaky, so they make fine containers for little petunias or other trailing plants.

Raise color to eye level with hanging baskets. Place hanging baskets anywhere you need a spot of color—a lamppost, tree limb, roof overhang, fence, gazebo, or balcony. In all cases, make certain that the baskets are hung securely enough to withstand strong winds and the weight of wet soil.

Easy watering. Like most container plants, hanging baskets dry out readily. Water with a spraying wand attached to a garden hose or use a turkey baster to spritz water into a small basket. Either way, watering hanging baskets can be messy, so position them where a bit of dripping won't matter.

CHOOSING CONTAINERS

Choose colors with care. Colorful containers that coordinate with the colors in your house or the cushions on your outdoor furniture will relieve the sameness of terra-cotta pots. But keep in mind that the color of the container will affect the temperature inside the pot. Dark colors absorb solar heat, while light ones reflect it.

Quick-change containers. Make it easy to replant large containers by using 4-inch (10-cm) removable plastic pots buried just to their rims. Use mulch or Spanish moss to hide the plastic pots from view. When you want a seasonal change—from pansies to begonias, for example—simply switch the pots for a whole new look.

Strawberry pots need special handling to help water flow down through the middle of the

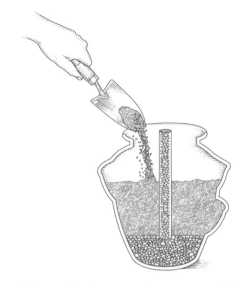

pot. When planting a strawberry pot with herbs, flowers, or strawberries, first fill the bottom with 1 inch (25 mm) of gravel topped by 2 inches (5 cm) of potting soil. Then insert a cardboard tube from a roll of paper towels and fill it with gravel. Fill the rest of the container with potting mix, then gently withdraw the tube, leaving the column of gravel in place. Each time you water the container from the top, the gravel column will help distribute water where it needs to go.

Garden with discarded buckets. Need some inexpensive containers for plantings on your patio or apartment balcony? Five-gallon (19-liter) plastic buckets are just the right size for big plants or mini-gardens. And you can find them almost everywhere; try the deli department at your supermarket, which receives bulk salads and pickles in them. Don't forget to put drainage holes in the bottom with a hammer and a large nail. Paint your plant buckets with enamel paint to make them more attractive.

Filling a large patio container? When planting shallow-rooted plants in a deep patio container, don't go to the bother—and expense—of completely filling that huge container with potting soil. Find a smaller flowerpot that will fit upside down in the base of the deeper pot and occupy a lot of that space.

CREATING VARIETY

Grow for flavor and color. If you're a food gardener at heart, try using your sunniest spots to grow dwarf tomatoes, small-fruited cucumbers, or a hanging basket of frilly lettuce. Then move on to colorful flowers. Light pastels are great for areas that are used at night because they reflect the glow of the moon. Brighter reds and oranges will attract hummingbirds and dazzle you with their rich hues.

Buy extra bedding plants. After you have filled flowerbeds with bright bloomers, plant extras in containers placed near entryways or outdoor living areas. They will help bring together splashes of color from other parts of your yard, and you'll be able to appreciate the intricacies of otherwise simple flowers because you can view them up close.

Don't forget fragrance. Add to your enjoyment of your outdoor living areas by including pots of fragrant flowers, such as heliotrope, as well as fragrant herbs, such as basil, scented geraniums, or Rosemary, in your potted garden. Swish your hand through the foliage of fragrant herbs to help them release their spicy perfumes.

Include some evergreens. For winter interest, try growing a dwarf juniper or arborvitae in a pot, or even a shapely evergreen holly. You will love having their evergreen foliage close at hand, and you can use them in your holiday decorating plan, too. Hardy bonsai plants kept on a deck or patio work like living sculptures (see page 102).

Try topiary in a pot. Ivy, jasmine, and other small-leafed climbers can be trained over wire frames into a variety of shapes, such as hearts, arches, or cones. Make a wire frame or buy one from a garden shop. It should be twice as tall as

the plant's pot. Insert its base firmly in the soil around the plant. Wind one plant stem around one wire and repeat with remaining stems. If a stem is stiff, tie it in place with soft green twine until it conforms to the shape. Pinch or snip any stems that grow out of place.

Watch out for wind. If you live in a windy area, you can keep potted plants from toppling by driving a 3-inch (8-cm) nail into that spot on the deck where you always keep a plant. Then slip the drain hole in the bottom of the pot over the nail.

If you often forget to water, try growing sedums and other succulents as patio plants. They store water in their juicy leaves, so they require less care than many plants. A few are cold hardy enough to be left outdoors in mild winters.

Bring potted geraniums indoors before the first fall freeze and keep them near a sunny window. With luck, regular watering, and occasional fertilizing, they may bloom off and on all winter long.

Anticipate winter's chill. Use plastic, wood, or fiberglass planters if you intend to leave them out year-round in a cold climate. Protect both plant and container by wrapping wire mesh loosely around the planter, then fill the space with plastic packing peanuts, bubble wrap, or dead leaves.

Protect patio plants with bubble wrap. Keep your outdoor container plants warm and protected from winter frost damage. Wrap each container with bubble wrap and use duct tape or string to hold it in place. Make sure the wrap extends a couple of inches above the lip of the container. The added insulation will keep the soil warmer all winter long.

FUCHSIAS

The dramatic beauty of fuchsias has made them top choices for growing in pots kept near

> ## BEST SUMMER FLOWERS FOR DECKS AND PATIOS
>
> Most annuals are happy to grow in containers, but a few grow better in pots than in flowerbeds. These special summer flowers show their appreciation for the excellent drainage and reduced humidity that container culture has to offer.
>
> - Fuchsia
> - Geraniums, especially large-flowered zonal types
> - Helichrysum
> - Lobelia
> - New Guinea impatiens
> - Petunias, especially trailing or double-flowered types
> - Scaevola (fan flower)
> - Tuberous begonia

outdoor living areas. Healthy plants on the brink of bloom are widely available at garden centers in spring. With good care, they will stay in bloom all summer long, but unless you live in a mild coastal climate, it's best to regard them as summer annuals and not try to keep them from year to year. Fuchsias readily accept morning sun, but they prefer partial shade.

For best blooms, spoil your fuchsias with rich, premium-quality potting soil. Keep the soil evenly moist, but don't overwater. Feed container-grown fuchsias with a balanced fertilizer once a week all summer.

Pinching is essential. For lush fuchsias, pinch back stems after they have produced flowers during the first few weeks of summer. Pinched plants produce more side shoots, which in turn produce more flowers. You can stop pinching as often after midsummer, when your plants will have developed a strong, symmetrical shape.

Use fuchsias for baskets. Fuchsias' pendant flowers make these plants very popular for outdoor hanging baskets. To increase your supply of plants, take 3-inch (8-cm) stem-tip cuttings, dip the stems in a rooting hormone powder, and place them in a container filled with damp seed-starting mix or sand. Cover with glass or plastic, keep the cuttings in a warm place, and in three to five weeks, they will be rooted and ready for their permanent pot.

BEGONIAS

Unlike the wax begonias you can use to edge sunny flowerbeds, tuberous begonias grow from flattened tubers. Happiest when grown in containers in filtered shade, tuberous begonias produce big, richly colored blossoms packed with velvety (and edible) petals. If you give them good care, it's easy to keep them for many years.

Start with the best. In spring, buy high quality tubers, because big tubers produce more flowers. Invest in a premium-quality potting soil for your tuberous begonias, too. An extra handful of peat moss mixed into each pot will help to keep the roots moist and free of disease.

Plant the right way. To plant tubers, find the small point on the top, which is the concave side of the tuber, and plant it so it's barely covered with potting soil. If you can't identify the concave top, plant the tubers on their sides. The new shoots will grow their way up to the light at the surface. Plant three tubers per 6-inch (15-cm) pot. Keep the soil lightly moist, and place the planted containers in a spot where the temperatures stay around 70°F (20°C).

Fertilize plants weekly throughout the summer, using a balanced, water soluble plant food mixed at half the rate recommended on the package. Clip off old blooms to encourage the formation of new buds.

Bring pots indoors before the first fall frost, and let them dry out. Clip off the old stems, and place the almost-dry pots in a cool room. In spring, empty the pots and replant the tubers in clean pots filled with fresh potting soil.

Grow a Bit of Bonsai

Interested in transforming a dwarf potted plant into a living green sculpture? That's the idea behind the ancient art of bonsai (pronounced *bone'-sy*). As an absorbing hobby, bonsai requires a patient approach, and there are many books available to help you learn what you need to know, but if you have a deck, patio, or balcony, you have the perfect spot to grow beautiful bonsai.

Start with something easy.
Dozens of plants can be used for outdoor bonsai, but it's best to begin with plants that adapt to many climates and have a strong natural structural growth habit. A dwarf Japanese maple is an excellent choice for beginners, as are Chinese junipers and dwarf cotoneaster. These plants can be kept outdoors year round in many areas. Where winters are very cold, they can be kept in an unheated garage.

Choose a healthy specimen.
Check the roots by examining the clump; the roots should spread evenly from the trunk and not overlap. The structure of the tree should look natural and untrained, and the leaves should be bushy. Deciduous trees, which lose their leaves in winter, should have pleasingly shaped trunks and branches. Also check that the pot has unobstructed drainage holes.

The best way to display bonsai
is on a shelf, tabletop, or pedestal that raises the most dramatic part of the plant to eye level. For care and grooming, it's good to have a revolving stool that you can set the plant upon, making it accessible from all sides. Most bonsai grow best in filtered light in a place where they are shielded from the scorching

midday sun. Also be sure to provide protection from strong wind.

Grow moss beneath your bonsai. Aside from being decorative, moss is a good indicator of the plant's water needs. When the moss appears parched, spray it with water. If you can't water for several days, wrap the moss-covered base of your bonsai in a clear plastic bag, which acts like a greenhouse and maintains high humidity.

Limit movement, because moving bonsai around can cause the leaves to drop. Find the right place for your plant and let it stay put.

Too much water can drown the roots of bonsai. If an outdoor bonsai gets flooded by a heavy rain, prop the pot on its side to help drain off the excess water. Also watch for very dry conditions. In hot summer weather, you may need to water your bonsai twice a day.

Freeze-wrap containers.
When cold weather comes, wrap the pots in bubble wrap or several thicknesses of newspaper, burlap, wool, straw, strips of tarp, or old rags. Or place the tray inside a larger pot filled with peat moss to provide insulation. If your outdoor bonsai is completely covered with snow, don't brush it off; it makes excellent natural insulation.

Buy fertilizer that is released slowly, and never use fertilizer on young or newly transplanted bonsai. For healthy older specimens, fertilize fairly often in small increments in both spring and fall.

ESSENTIAL ELEMENTS OF BONSAI

- **Train the plant's trunks and branches** so that it appears to have been shaped by natural forces, especially time and wind. Copper or aluminum wire is used to bend branches to desired shapes, which may be slanted, twisted, or outstretched. Branches may be wired to the trunk or to other branches, or they can be pulled downward by small fishing weights. You can wire the plant at any time of year, but conifers are best done in winter. Once a branch has achieved the shape you want, gently remove the wire.

- **Landscape the base of the plant** so that it looks like a miniaturized version of a time-hewn outdoor scene. Exposed roots, stones, moss, and other natural elements combine to create this illusion.

- **Use broad, shallow containers,** called bonsai dishes to have a strong dwarfing effect on long-lived plants. Plants are further dwarfed by regular root pruning. Prune the roots of evergreens every three to five years, deciduous plants every two to three years, and flowering or fruit trees every year. When root pruning, cut off a third of the roots and provide a fresh supply of soil.

Window Box Gardening

EVERY HOUSE HAS WINDOWS, so every house can have window boxes—unique planters that look beautiful from the outside and can also be enjoyed from the inside. Make sure you can reach window boxes easily, because they need frequent watering in hot weather. Replanting window boxes is a breeze if you use removable plastic liners that are slipped inside more decorative boxes. Change plants in keeping with the seasons. Start in spring with pretty primroses, switch to petunias or impatiens in summer, and shift gears in fall by plugging in dwarf chrysanthemums or ornamental kale. In addition, small vegetables, herbs, and all of the annuals that thrive on decks or patios will work in window boxes.

WHAT KIND OF BOX?

Measure before you buy or build. You can find window boxes in a range of sizes or build them to fit, but you can't change the size of your windows. Install any needed hanging hardware before you fill the boxes with potting soil—the best time to make adjustments if the fit is not right.

Make a mini-greenhouse. To convert a window box into a mini-greenhouse, bend three or four lengths of coat-hanger wire into ∪-shaped hoops and push the ends into the soil.

Punch small holes in a dry cleaning bag and wrap it around the box before putting it back at the window. Or cover the hoop with a piece of bubble wrap and hold it in place with clothespins.

Give fruit crates a second life by using them as window boxes. You may need to install support posts to hold up their outer edges or prop them up with sturdy sticks gathered from the woods. Ask your grocer for wood crates used to pack oranges, grapes, or peaches. If you attach screw eyes to the corners and tie on pieces of string, you can use the crates as containers for hanging plants, too.

Wood's the word. Window boxes made of cedar, redwood, or other rot-resistant lumber insulate plant roots from heat and cold better than metal or plastic. Paint them a light color on the outside to reflect heat, or use a waterseal product. Use a plastic or metal liner to keep the wood from rotting and warping from prolonged contact with wet soil.

Insulate the sunny side. If a window box will cook in hot afternoon sun, insert a sheet of Styrofoam or thick corrugated cardboard before filling it with soil. You can also set a smaller box inside the larger one and pack the space between the two with peat moss. Keeping the soil cool will promote more vigorous growth.

PLANTING A WINDOW BOX

Let them spill. The most beautiful window boxes include plants that trail over the edges. Cascading or trailing plants, such as lobelia, ivy, periwinkle, petunia, and nasturtium, are very attractive additions, which do a great job of softening the edges.

Crowd them in. Window boxes look best when they're bursting with plants, so keep plants close together. Crowded plants need extra water and fertilizer, which you can provide together if you use water-soluble plant food.

Grow window box veggies. Dwarf tomatoes or peppers can grow in a sunny spot on your balcony or your windowsill. You can combine them with your favorite herbs, such as compact basil or curly parsley.

Grow savory snippings. If you have a sunny kitchen window, grow herbs, such as thyme, chives, parsley, sage, or sorrel, in your window box, along with leafy lettuce and other salad greens.

Start fresh each season. A window box's soil quickly becomes exhausted, so replace it annually with a fresh supply. Dump the old soil in an outdoor flowerbed or scatter it over your lawn.

Keep color year round. In winter, when your window box flowers are finished, fill the boxes with dried flowers from your garden or artificial greenery in muted colors.

Growing Indoor-Outdoor Plants

MANY OF THE PLANTS you keep indoors in winter grow best when they spend the summer outdoors, where light is more abundant and there is usually a difference of at least 10 degrees F (6 degrees C) between day and nighttime temperatures. Changes in day length enhance the growth of indoor-outdoor plants, too. When kept outdoors well into fall, plants, such as kalanchoe, holiday cactus, and most other cacti, respond to the shorter, cooler days by producing lots of buds that open several weeks later, when winter is well under way. Besides cacti, other terrific indoor-outdoor plant choices include aloes, bromeliads, orchids, and palms.

Prevent sunburn by letting plants gradually become accustomed to brighter light when you move them outdoors in spring. Start them out on a table placed in a shady spot, then move them to slightly brighter light after a week or so. Do the reverse in fall so that plants accustomed to bright outdoor light won't sulk when suddenly shifted to a dim indoor environment.

Plan ahead for growth spurts. While it's in the great outdoors, you may not notice how much a philodendron or tree ivy has grown. Don't be surprised if you need to change the indoor location of plants that respond to summer outdoors by gaining size.

Watch for hitchhikers. Plants kept outdoors in summer often host secret visitors, including earthworms, earwigs, and aphids. Two weeks before bringing them back indoors in winter, begin checking for evidence of hitchhikers. A thorough cleaning or quick repotting may be in order.

ALOE

Warmth and sunlight are keys to growing aloe plants, so give them bright light indoors and partial shade when they're moved outdoors in summer. Water the plants before they begin to shrivel or appear limp, but don't keep them too wet, or they will rot. Bring them indoors in fall before temperatures drop below 40°F (4°C).

Grow your own burn medicine. The gelatinous sap of *Aloe vera barbadensis* can soothe minor burns, skin rashes, and sunburn. Cut off a leaf of the plant at its fleshy base and split it open with a knife or razor blade. Apply the sap to the irritation as quickly as possible and repeat often for the first few hours. If you love to cook, keep an aloe plant on your kitchen windowsill to treat any minor mishaps.

Pot up the babies. Aloe plants seldom bloom when they are grown indoors through winter, but they often produce little offsets, called pups.

When the pups are 2 inches (5 cm) tall, cut them from the mother plant and pot them up in small containers. They make great gifts.

BROMELIADS

Water their hearts. Most bromeliads have a central cup, or reservoir, that holds water until they need it. Every week or so, dump out any

water left in the cup and refill it with a fresh supply. Bromeliads also take up water through little scales on their leaves. Water air plants (*Tillandsias* spp.) by misting them with a fine spray of room-temperature water.

Grow a bromeliad branch. Arrange several small bromeliads together on a shapely branch or piece of driftwood. Secure them with florists' wire atop a small pad of humus-rich potting soil, such as orchid potting mix. Indoors, keep your bromeliad branch in a room with high humidity. Outdoors, place it where drips won't be a zproblem; spray it often with your hose.

Nurture the next generation. After a bromeliad blooms, the parent plant slowly dies. Before it expires, it will produce one or more offsets, or pups. Wait until the pups are one-third to one-half the parent's size, then cut them away and pot them up. Enclose the planted pups in a plastic bag for a couple of weeks to maintain high humidity while they grow little roots.

CACTUS

Coax a cactus into bloom by keeping it outdoors in summer, in a place that gets a few hours of direct sun. Water often in summer, but let the soil get drier as the days become shorter in fall. Move it to your coolest room in early winter, then give it more light and warmth during winter's second half. Most cacti need a cool, dry rest period to develop buds and blossoms.

Handle with care. When repotting a cactus, don't depend on gloves to protect your hands. Instead, make a large band from newspaper folded over several times. Wrap it around the plant whenever you're repotting it or picking it up.

Remove cactus prickles from your fingers with adhesive tape or a thin layer of all-purpose white glue. Let the glue dry and then peel it off, prickles and all.

ORCHIDS

Hard to grow? Orchids are commonly perceived as delicate and demanding, but they really need only two things—some time outdoors in summer to soak up plenty of filtered light, warmth, and humidity, and a 10- to 15-degree F

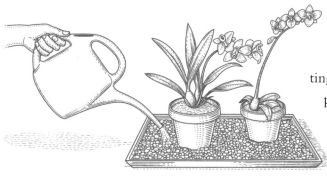

(6- to 8-degree C) difference between day and nighttime temperatures when they're indoors in winter. Provide them with high humidity by keeping them on a tray of damp pebbles.

Expensive orchids are not necessarily better than strains that have been around for years and proven their ability to thrive when grown in pots. Moth orchids (*Phalaenopsis* spp.) are easy for beginners and are usually quite affordable. Start small, with one or two orchids, because orchid growing is addictive.

Orchids rest between bloom cycles, so it's best to buy plants that are just beginning to show buds. Blooms often last four to six weeks, but after that, it may be months or years before the plant blooms again.

PALMS

Pots for palms should be deep, because strong palm roots push down through the soil and can lift the tree out of a shallow pot once they hit the bottom. Repot palms only every two years, because the brittle roots are often damaged during repotting. Between repottings, freshen the soil of potted palms by digging out the top 2 inches (5 cm) of soil and replacing it with fresh potting mix.

Brown tips on palm leaves are often caused by fluoride or other chemicals in water. Collect rainwater to use on affected palms or use bottled distilled water. Use sharp scissors to snip off the brown tips.

Before bringing palms back indoors in fall, check the leaves carefully for signs of scale—small brown bumps on stems or leaf undersides. Remove them by hand with a soft cloth dipped into soapy water. Go back the next day and use a toothpick to pick off any survivors.

Houseplants

YOU CAN USE A HUGE RANGE of beautiful plants to create a bit of garden magic inside your home. Use bright windows to provide the perfect settings for a wonderful variety of foliage plants, grown for their beautiful leaves, as well as houseplants that produce colorful flowers.

BASIC CARE

Keep out strange invaders. Before you buy a new houseplant, lift the leaves gently to check for scale, mealybugs, whiteflies, or other pests. Then look under the pot. If the plant passes inspection, isolate it in a room away from your other houseplants for two weeks to allow time for hidden pests to appear.

Read the newspaper to your plants. This can benefit them in two ways. The carbon dioxide in your breath may energize their gas exchange cycles, and if there's enough natural light in their location for you to read by, you'll be assured that the plants are getting the minimum amount of light needed for good growth.

Be gentle with budders. Don't move plants around for short periods of time. Sudden changes can cause droopy leaves, increase susceptibility to pests and diseases, and cause flowering plants to drop healthy-looking buds.

As soon as a blooming plant shows signs of flowering, put it in a spot where it can stay.

Know your light. When you're deciding where to put a plant, keep in mind that south-facing windows receive much more light than north-facing ones. With east- or west-facing windows, observe the amounts of morning or afternoon sun they get before putting plants next to them. Also remember that plants with brightly colored foliage need more light than others.

Site in the right light. Because the light is more intense in summer than in winter, you may need to move sun-sensitive plants from a west- to an east-facing window in the hot months. Also keep in mind that plants can tolerate more sun in the house than out; an indoor sun lover may scorch if placed outside in bright summer light.

Keep it even. A half-turn of the pot every day or two will keep the growth of your houseplant even, since its foliage automatically bends toward the light.

Don't overheat your house. Your plants won't like it! The ideal temperature to set the thermostat at is between 55° and 70°F (13° and 21°C), with cooler temperatures always being better than hotter.

Give them a good soaking. In spring or summer when the weather is warm and dry, give plants a good watering at least once a season; it's the easiest way to leach out excess salts and thoroughly moisten the inside of the root mass. Place the plant in the sink or a pail of water and leave it for 15 minutes, or until no more bubbles come to the surface. Let it drain well before putting it on a saucer. This is also a great way to rehydrate plants that have dried out badly while you've been away.

Insulate before you vacate. You also can limit moisture loss from your potted plants another

way. Cut rings from several layers of newspaper and moisten them well. Water your plants thoroughly, then place a ring on the soil in each pot.

Wash away dust, smoke, and other residues by giving your plants a shower with lukewarm water. You can also dislodge dirt, especially on

KEEPING HOUSEPLANTS BEAUTIFUL

- Regularly remove all faded flowers, dried leaves, and bare stems.

- When you cut brown tips, leave a small brown border. Cutting into live tissue will cause more drying and dieback.

- Fertilize your houseplants regularly during active growing and flowering periods—typically March through September. Reduce the fertilizer dose to half of the recommended amount in fall. Don't fertilize at all in winter.

- Don't use wax or leaf shine products. They may give the foliage luster, but they can clog the pores. Another reason not to wax: It makes houseplants look artificial. For a natural glow, wipe down the leaves with a wet sponge.

fuzzy or prickly leaves, with a hair dryer set on cool or low.

Going on vacation? Water your houseplants thoroughly and arrange them, without saucers, on a dampened plush towel in your sink or tub; make sure the drain holes are in contact with the towel. Turn on the cold tap until water drips slowly onto the towel and leave the water on; the moisture in the fabric will be drawn up by the roots.

Must you mist? Contrary to lore, squirting foliage with water is not an efficient way to increase humidity for houseplants. A humidifier works better, for both plants and for people. Misting does, however, help keep leaves clean and fresh, and it's a good way to provide moisture to cuttings that are slowly developing new roots. Use soft water (water low in minerals) when misting, and make sure it's no cooler than room temperature. Mist in the morning whenever possible, and never mist plants that are exposed to full sun.

Feed your ferns. Schedule an occasional teatime for your ferns, gardenias, and other acid-loving houseplants. Substitute brewed tea when watering or work wet tea leaves into the soil to give the plants a lush, luxurious look.

To increase humidity for indoor ferns and other plants that can't tolerate dry air, set the

plant on a dish of pebbles and add just enough water to touch the bottom of the pot.

Give plants a group shower. Group together plants that need high humidity and enjoy being spritzed with water. Keep them separate from cacti and such fuzzy-leaved specimens as African violets, gloxinias, and gynuras, whose foliage will discolor if subjected to slow-drying water droplets.

Block plant overspray with an umbrella. Houseplants love to be misted, but your walls don't love being soaked with overspray. Stick an open umbrella between the plants and the wall when you want to give your plants a shower.

Make flower pots hold water longer. If your potted houseplants dry out too quickly after watering, try this simple trick for keeping the soil moist longer. When repotting, tuck a damp sponge into the bottom of the pot before filling it with soil. It will act as a water reservoir and may help prevent a gusher if you accidentally overwater.

Shampoo your houseplants by hand. Houseplants get dusty, but unlike furniture, they need to breathe. Make a soapy solution with a few drops of dishwashing liquid added to a pot of water, dunk in a cloth and wring it out, and wipe those dusty leaves clean.

Give your plants a mineral bath. Don't throw out that leftover club soda—use it to water your indoor plants. The minerals in the soda water help green plants grow. For maximum benefit, give your plants a drink of soda once a week.

Hydrate your plants with egg water. After boiling eggs, don't toss the cooking water down the drain. Instead, let it cool and water your houseplants with the nutrient-filled fluid.

(Continued on page 114)

Try a Terrarium

The air in many homes is so dry that houseplants that need high humidity levels suffer or refuse to grow at all. An enclosed glass container filled with plants solves this problem because it works like a miniature greenhouse.

Plants will grow indefinitely in sealed glass containers because of the greenhouse effect. Water evaporates from the soil and provides humidity; droplets then condense on the sides of the glass and roll down the sides into the potting mix, bringing moisture to the roots.

Terrariums never spill, and they grow beautifully beneath fluorescent light, so they're a great way to grow plants in an office. You can make one from anything from a large wine jug to an old aquarium tank.

True terrariums are available as plastic or alloy-framed models or as more expensive brass-framed or leaded glass models, often with automatic ventilation controls. But you can grow a bottle garden in any glass or plastic vessel.

Naturally, the best plants for terrariums are small ones that that like low light and high humidity. Start with a clean container, and layer in ½ inch (1 cm) of sphagnum moss, ½ inch of fine gravel (such as aquarium gravel), a thin topping of aquarium charcoal, and 2 to 3 inches (5 to 8 cm) of sterile, peat-based potting mix that is moist to the touch.

- A paper funnel makes it easy to fill a jug or bottle without getting the sides dirty. Simply roll butcher paper or sheets of newspaper into a funnel and pour the potting mix and drainage materials through it.

- Use a fork taped to a chopstick or an artist's paintbrush to make planting holes for terrarium plants.

- Set plants in place with another chopstick fitted with a small wire hook or loop. In containers with wide openings, you can use tweezers or tongs.

- Tamp down the soil around plant roots with a cork or spool attached to a stick. When you're done, lightly spray the plants and soil surface with water.

Don't rush to replant. When given proper water and light, terrarium plants often grow happily for more than a year between feedings, and they may need replanting only

TRY THESE TERRARIUM CONTAINERS

As long as a container is made of clear glass, very lightly tinted glass, or clear plastic, it deserves to be considered for a new life as a terrarium. Remember that containers with wide openings will require more frequent watering, or you can cover the opening with a piece of glass or other type of translucent cover. Try any of these:

Aquarium tank, large tea jar, brandy snifter, liquor bottle, food canister, pitcher, goldfish bowl, or wine jug.

It's normal to see a little condensation inside a terrarium, but if the glass is so foggy that you can hardly see the plants, it's too wet. Leave the top open to help excess moisture evaporate, and wait until no new droplets appear to add more water, a teaspoon (5 ml) at a time.

Cover your container with its lid, a cork, plastic wrap, or a piece of glass to trap moisture and create condensation.

Hold the food. Don't fertilize bottle garden plants the first year. Thereafter, feed very lightly, diluting an all-purpose houseplant fertilizer to about ⅛ strength. If plants grow too large, prune them, transfer them to a larger vessel, or replace them.

Terrariums kept at normal room temperatures are great places to grow tiny ferns, palms, fittonias, and other plants that need high humidity. Or you can take a different approach and use a terrarium to grow tiny plants that prefer dry conditions, such as little cacti or succulents.

Place it properly. Put the container in indirect sunlight or place it under a fluorescent light for 12 hours daily. Turn it regularly to keep plants growing evenly.

every three to four years. When a plant's leaves begin to stick to the sides of a terrarium, remove it and give it its own little pot.

Never run short. Keep a filled plastic water bottle tucked away among groups of houseplants so it will always be handy. If plants are hard to reach, try using a bulb-type turkey baster to dribble water into their pots.

Use ice cubes to water. Place them around the soil, but not touching the stem. The ice will melt slowly, releasing water gradually and evenly into the soil.

HELPFUL HINTS

Construct a rustic indoor trellis. Tired of draping trailing plants over doorframes and windows? Give them something to climb on instead. Using wall anchors, if necessary, attach vinyl-covered hooks (available at hardware stores) to a wall and hang any reasonably attractive ladder from them, positioning the ladder's legs on the floor a couple of inches from the wall. It's easy to train potted plants to grow up and around this rustic support. It looks nice on a porch, too.

Mouse pad your plants. To keep plant containers from scratching or damaging your furniture or floors, just set the pots atop old computer mouse pads. Your floor will remain scratch-free. You may need to use multiple mouse pads for large pots.

Use plastic jar lids as coasters. Plastic lids placed top side down beneath drainage holes do a good job of capturing water beneath plants that aren't kept on saucers or trays. Turn the lids over to raise pots from wood furniture, where saucers might leave watermarks.

Create a sun box. A sunny window is a great place to keep plants that love a lot of light, as do many blooming houseplants. However, since the light always comes from the same direction, usually the south or west, plants tend to bend toward it. Instead of turning them every few days, you can help high-light plants bathe in the light they crave in a homemade sun box. Remove the top and one side from a cardboard box and line the other three sides with aluminum foil, shiny side out, then tape or glue the foil in place. Put plants in the box and set it near a bright window.

Turn a coat hanger into a pot hanger. Need a fast way to hang a pot on a wall or post? Bend the long edge of a wire hanger into a circle and fit it just below the lip of a 6- to 8-inch (15- to 20-cm) flowerpot. Then use pliers to twist the hanger until the wire ring fits snugly. Attach the curved top of the hanger to a hook or nail.

Lure fungus gnat larvae with potatoes. When you water your houseplants, do tiny gnats fly into the air? They are fungus gnats, which will be less of a problem if you let the soil dry between waterings. Meanwhile, you can use a potato to trap their larvae, which are tiny worms that often injure plant roots. Push slices of raw potato around the base of the plant, leave them for two days, and then start over with fresh bait.

Brighten up houseplants. Are the leaves of your plants looking dull? Wipe down each leaf with a soft cloth dipped in a half-and-half mixture of warm water and milk. You'll get a nice shine, but there won't be enough residue left behind to clog the leaf pores.

Try another way to make leaves shiny. Professional florists use this trick to keep houseplant leaves shiny and clean. You can do the same thing at home. Just rub a tiny amount of mayonnaise on the leaves with a paper towel and they will stay bright and shiny for weeks and even months at a time.

Use pulleys on hanging baskets. Suspending your hanging baskets from a pulley makes it easier to lower them for watering and other care. Special plant pulleys are sold in garden centers, but you can save some pocket change if you shop at the hardware store.

Start buds early in a dark bag. Want that Christmas poinsettia to look gorgeous by the time the holidays arrive? Speed up mother nature by placing the poinsettia in a large, dark garbage bag for several weeks to wake up the plant's buds.

Kill bugs on a potted plant. To exterminate bugs on a houseplant, put the plant in a clear plastic bag, such as a cleaning bag, add a few mothballs, and seal for a week. When you take the plant out of the bag, your plant will be bug-free. It will also keep moths away for a while.

Tired of ugly dirt? Use small ground covers, such as creeping fig or Swedish ivy, at the base of large houseplants to dress up the bare soil. Choose a plant with the same cultural requirements as the houseplant and pot them at the same time.

REPOTTING

When to repot? Repotting can be done at any time, but the best time is just before growth begins, which is in spring for most houseplants. Here are four signs that a plant is ready for repotting:

- New leaves appear slowly and are very small compared to older leaves.
- Soil dries out very quickly, or water runs down the inside of the pot without soaking in.
- Roots are growing out through the drainage holes or are appearing above the soil's surface in the pots.
- Roots are so tightly coiled that when you pull the plant from the pot, you see all roots and no soil.

Try an ice cream scoop. Does dirt scatter everywhere when you are replanting your houseplants? An ice cream scoop is the perfect way to add soil to the new pot without making a mess.

Never pull on a houseplant's head. To help loosen a plant from a pot, water it well, then run a table knife around the inside of the pot. Sometimes you'll need to break a pot to get the plant out. When this is necessary, tap the pot gently with a hammer or mallet to avoid damaging plant roots.

You don't have to repot big plants as often as smaller ones. Instead, give the soil new life by removing an inch or two (3-5 cm) of the old potting mix from the surface. Then replace it with fresh potting soil to the original level. When topdressing long-lived rubber plants, palms, or Norfolk pines, you can incorporate timed-release fertilizer at the same time.

Have a spring propagation party. Most houseplants make most of their new growth in spring, so that's the best time to divide and propagate them. If you think you'll end up with more plants than you want, invite some friends over and have a propagation party.

Be considerate of shedders. Some houseplants, such as the weeping fig (*Ficus benjamina*) or Boston fern, can be traumatized by repotting, moving to a new location, or sometimes even a change of seasons. They show their displeasure by shedding leaves. Let them sulk, clean up the mess, and be patient. If the plants otherwise receive good care, they will recover from their bad mood.

Just a reminder—always keep the plant label even after repotting, so that you won't forget the plant's name or the care it needs.

LANDSCAPING
PLANTS

It is a gardener's nature to love plants, especially plants that love us back. When chosen and planted with care, shrubs, vines, and trees will do exactly that, growing bigger and better with time. This section includes hundreds of tips for using these hardworking, permanent plants, from simple boxwoods to lacy weeping cherries—and for groundcovers and ornamental grasses as well.

Far from being boring, the plants in this section dramatize the changing seasons, and many provide habitat and food for wildlife. But be forewarned: Growing roses—especially disease-resistant shrub roses or historic heirlooms—can be addictive! The syndrome known as azalea fever can strike unexpectedly, too, or you may fall in love with the alluring textures of stately ornamental grasses. And each time you indulge your passion for these special plants, your landscape will benefit for years to come.

Go ahead. Try a spirited vine or flatter the corner of your house with a shapely flowering tree. Plant a shade tree that will outlive you. As long as you stick with species that match the site and soil you have to offer, you can't go wrong.

❧ Shrubs

SHRUBS ARE THE BACKBONE of a garden's structure, and they often require little care once they are established. Season after season, shrubs can help anchor your house in the landscape, define boundaries, direct foot traffic, and provide a constantly changing tapestry of color. Dwarf shrubs are the perfect choices for small gardens, where there may not be room enough for trees. In larger yards, shrub hedges—or even individual specimen plants—are the easiest way to divide and define open spaces. Before any landscape can appear completely dressed, it must include carefully chosen shrubs.

SHRUB SELECTION AND CARE

Designing with shrubs can begin at the nursery, where you can place shrubs together to see how they work when growing side by side. In addition to color and texture, take a plant's natural profile into account when designing with shrubs. Upright and pyramidal shapes are rigid and more formal, while mounding or spreading growth habits appear more relaxed. Weeping shrubs make dramatic focal points.

Look for many talents. Some shrubs bloom in spring and early summer and then offer little else. Choose shrubs that have many talents: interesting fruits, fall color, attractive bark, and a pleasing silhouette, even when bare. Good choices for a long-term display include barberry, euonymus, leucothoe, pieris, privet, mahonia, nandina, snowberry, and viburnum.

Get wise on size. Matching a shrub's mature size to the proposed planting site will save you years of struggle to keep it in bounds. Good-quality shrubs sold by reputable nurseries include plant tags that tell you their mature height and width.

Reduce weeding chores around shrubs by covering the ground with a fabric weed barrier. Then cover the barrier with attractive organic mulch, such as bark nuggets or pine needles.

Special-effects shrubs. Leaves may be a shrub's dominant feature, but not all shrubs are green. Foliage color can range from burgundy to gold to blue-gray to all shades of green. Red-twig dogwoods are most valued for the striking color of their bare branches, which are particularly vivid against a background of winter snow.

Fertilize each spring with a complete timed-release fertilizer, which will slowly provide nutrients for several months. Use an acid-based fertilizer for acid-loving shrubs, such as azaleas, camellias, garden pieris, and rhododendrons. For more information on fertilizer, see page 293.

Most shrubs require little pruning in the first few years. At first, confine pruning to removing crossing branches that spoil the plant's shape, along with damaged or unhealthy branches.

Try going natural. A natural hedge comprised of several different shrubs is not pruned like a neatly clipped one, yet it can provide privacy and food and habitat for wildlife. Viburnums and other shrubs that produce flowers and berries make great additions to a natural hedge.

Prune with purpose. Pruning methods vary from shrub to shrub, depending in part on their flowering habits. A basic rule of thumb is always to follow the natural shape of the plant; don't just shear away unless you're trimming a hedge or topiary. Cut back to an outward-facing bud or remove the whole stem at the base.

The best time to prune flowering shrubs. Time the pruning of your flowering shrubs to enhance the quality of their blooms. Prune forsythias, rhododendrons, and other early bloomers immediately after they flower. Late bloomers, such as hybrid tea roses, which flower on new growth, are best pruned in early spring to encourage more new growth.

Keep hedge bottoms leafy. Leave a hedge full to the very bottom by pruning at a slight angle, with the base wider than the top. This will let sunlight penetrate to the lower branches and prevent dieback.

WHAT'S WRONG WITH MY SHRUB?

Overall decline or death

- The site doesn't suit the shrub's needs for light, water, soil type, or pH.
- The site doesn't suit the shrub's tolerance of temperature extremes, wind, or pollution.
- The planting depth is improper.
- The roots have been burned by herbicide, fertilizer, or road salt.
- Pests or diseases have attacked leaves or roots.

No blooms or fruits

- The shrub is still too young to bloom.
- Pruning was done at the wrong time.
- Excessive high-nitrogen fertilizer was used.
- Frost nipped the shrub at bud formation.
- The buds or flowers were eaten by birds, animals, or insects or affected by disease.

Keep variegation vivid. Is a variegated shrub growing a branch with all green leaves? Prune it out as soon as you spot it. Left unattended, the shrub may revert to solid green.

MOVING SHRUBS

Need to move an established shrub? Move a woody plant when it's dormant, but prepare for the move a few weeks ahead of time. Use a sharp spade to cut a circle 18 inches (45 cm) from the base of the shrub. This severs the lateral roots and encourages growth of shallow feeder roots, which will help the plant readjust quickly.

Trim it back. Shrubs will recover more quickly from transplanting if you prune back one-quarter to one-third of the topgrowth. The reduced foliage mass loses less moisture and places fewer demands on the roots—plus, it makes a big shrub easier to handle.

When moving day comes, dig from outside the dripline, digging all the way around the plant. Don't try to lift the plant right away—keep prying the spade under the roots and rocking the plant away from you until it comes free.

Wrap the roots. To help keep the root ball intact and make it easier to move, wrap it in a tarp or old blanket while it's still in the hole. Rock the plant to one side and tuck the fabric in under the roots, then tip it in the opposite direction and pull up the burlap around the root ball. Tie it around the trunk or stem with heavy twine.

Pour on the water. Water is essential—both to keep the disturbed roots moist until they can take up water from the soil and to eliminate air pockets. Soak the base of the relocated plant once a week through the growing season if rainfall is insufficient. Let the soil dry slightly between waterings so the roots don't rot. Mulch well to retain moisture.

BOXWOOD

Evergreen shrubs never go out of season. Dwarf evergreens make great accents for entryways, or

SPECIAL SHRUBS FOR WARM CLIMATES

- **Evergreen camellias,** with dark green foliage and delicate blossoms, prefer a humid climate like that of the Southeast and parts of the West Coast as far north as Seattle. Plant camellias in soil that is slightly acidic, in a site that provides shelter from strong sun and cold wind.

- **Gardenias** love the South, thriving in hot, humid summers and mild winters. They are usually used as border shrubs and hedges. Plant them close to your house, where the fragrance of the white flowers can be easily enjoyed.

- **Aucubas** have the valuable talent of being able to grow in shade, and the variegated leaves remain fresh and glossy in the hottest weather. Although not grown for their flowers, aucubas that do bloom then produce bright red berries.

you can use larger varieties to balance a view that's dominated by large trees. Evergreen shrubs also do a great job of defining boundaries or structuring outdoor activity areas. Boxwoods can be pruned to create a formal hedge, or you can use other evergreens, such as the low-maintenance junipers or dwarf hollies described in the following sections, in simple foundation plantings.

Ideal shrubs for low hedges, boxwoods are incredibly uniform. To plant a low hedge of dwarf boxwoods, stretch a string between two posts and dig a trench 16 inches (40 cm) deep. Put rotted manure or compost at the bottom of the hole and plant a boxwood every 6 inches (15 cm); don't remove the leaves at the base.

Firm the soil, then water. Mulch to cover the roots, but leave an open space around the trunk to keep stems from rotting.

Boxwood is famous for being drought resistant once it is established. If you maintain even soil moisture the first year after planting, you may never need to water your boxwoods again.

Pruned or natural? Boxwood takes well to pruning, from the simplest form to the most complex topiary. But be conservative; develop the shape slowly, permitting some extra growth each year. Unpruned boxwoods are beautiful, too—in an informal setting.

HOLLY

If you're bothered by the sharp spines of holly leaves, select a type that has few or no spines, such as Chinese holly, Japanese holly, or longstalk holly. In warm climates, yaupon hollies make fantastic, low-maintenance shrubs.

Check plant tags for the plant's mature height, since pruning spiny hollies is no fun. Varieties are available in a huge range of sizes.

For profuse red berries, you will need both male and female plants of most species. Only female holly specimens will produce berries—and only when pollinated by a male. One male holly will provide ample pollen for several female plants.

Not all hollies are evergreen. Cold-hardy winterberry holly sheds its leaves in the fall but compensates with a profusion of bright red, orange, or yellow berries all winter. In addition to providing spectacular color in a drab season, it is tolerant of wet soil and partial shade, and adapts to almost all parts of North America.

JUNIPER

Shape shifters. There are dozens of junipers, which may be tall and thin, compact 2-foot (60 cm) bushes, or sprawling plants that hug the ground. Colors vary as well, from dark pine green to bright blue-green, and there are even junipers with gold or icy gray foliage. All junipers need full sun, and require little if any pruning.

Perfect for slopes, dwarf junipers do a great job of turning a slippery slope into a lush wave of greenery. Use a weed barrier mat to hold the soil while the plants become established; hide it with a mulch of pine needles or bark.

Birds love juniper berries, which are small and dark and often escape notice by people. Birds typically wait until late winter to gather them up. Try trimming a few berry-bearing branches and using them in cut flower arrangements.

AZALEAS AND RHODODENDRONS

A large shrub covered with blossoms is always a dazzling show, and some flowering shrubs bloom so heavily that the leaves are temporarily hidden from view. For generations, forsythias have been the flagship shrubs of spring, followed by azaleas, lilacs, and the roses and hydrangeas of summer. Of these, azaleas and rhododendrons are ideal shrubs for partial shade. They're native to woodlands where the soil is naturally acidic, so they grow best in soil with a pH below 6. Grow azaleas and rhododendrons near large shade trees or mix them with other shrubs in foundation plantings.

Botanically speaking, azaleas and rhododendrons are first cousins. In the past, the plants called azaleas were deciduous, while rhododendrons were those that held their leaves through the winter. Today, there are both evergreen and deciduous hybrid azaleas, as well as evergreen rhododendrons in a range of sizes and colors.

Moderation in all things. Remember that azaleas and rhododendrons respond best to moderation in all aspects of cultivation: moderate light, moderate water, and moderate pruning.

Don't fertilize when planting. The common practice of putting fertilizer directly in the bottom of a planting hole can be fatal to azaleas and rhododendrons. Wait until the plant is established before you start feeding it. However, do enrich the planting hole with several spadefuls of good compost.

Be generous with mulch. Azaleas and rhododendrons need a 3-inch (8-cm) mulch of wood chips, pine needles, bark chips, salt hay, or oak leaves to keep the shallow roots cool and moist.

Adequate moisture is critical until new azaleas or rhododendrons become established—at least two years. Once mature, they can survive moderate drought, although drought-stressed plants are more susceptible to disease, insects, and cold. Help out wilted plants with a deep soaking.

Rejuvenate old plants gradually over a three-year period, cutting back a third of the branches each year. Prune in early summer after the flowers have faded. Complete pruning then to avoid injuring next year's flower buds.

Prevent yellowing of azaleas. Sudden yellowing of acid-loving plants, such as dwarf azaleas, hydrangeas, and gardenias, could signal a drop in the plant's iron intake or a shift in the soil's pH level. To resolve either problem, mix 2 tablespoons (30 ml) of apple cider vinegar in 1 quart (1 liter) of water and pour a cup around the plants once a week for three weeks.

To encourage blooms in acid-loving azaleas, water them every week during their nonflowering period with 3 tablespoons (45 ml) of vinegar in 1 gallon (4 liters) of water.

Fight insects with soap. Yellowish speckling of upper leaf surfaces and black spots on the undersides of azalea leaves indicate the presence of lace bugs or thrips. Get rid of them with insecticidal soap spray applied on a cloudy day.

HYDRANGEAS

Hydrangeas have in common a need for moist soil in spring, when they make most of their new growth. Most adapt well to partial shade, so they make fine plants to work into boundary plantings. The best flowers are produced from buds that grew the previous season, so it's wise to locate hydrangeas where they will receive shelter from cold winter winds. In cold climates, the south side of the house is often the best place to grow colorful bigleaf hydrangeas, which have been favorites in gardens for over a century.

Watch out for tree roots. Although hydrangeas like partial shade, they suffer when forced to compete with tree roots that rob the

---

⅋ SORTING THROUGH hydrangeas

• **Smooth hydrangea** (*Hydrangea arborescens*), Zones 3 to 8, is native to eastern North America. The wide, mounding plants adapt to full sun or partial shade and grow 3 to 5 feet (1 to 1.5 meters) high and wide. Improved cultivars, including 'Annabelle', produce huge, creamy white flower clusters in early summer.

• **Bigleaf hydrangea** (*H. macrophylla*), Zones 6 to 9, is sometimes called French hydrangea, although it's native to Japan. This popular shrub grows about 4 feet (1 meter) high and wide and produces large blue or pink flower clusters in early summer. Lacecap varieties bloom for a longer period and produce smaller flower clusters in which a ring of blossoms encircles a flattened center. The 'Endless Summer' variety blooms on both old and new wood.

• **Peegee hydrangea** (*H. paniculata*), Zones 3 to 8, is native to China and Japan, and is the biggest of the free-standing types, growing 15 to 20 feet (5 to 6 meters) high and 10 to 15 feet (3 to 5 meters) wide. Elongated white flower panicles appear in late summer and persist until winter. Older plants often thin out at the bottom and resemble small trees.

• **Oakleaf hydrangea** (*H. quercifolia*), Zones 5 to 9, is native to the southeastern United States. It grows 4 to 6 feet (1 to 2 meters) high and wide, and its large, lobed leaves often turn rich burgundy red in the fall. Elongated cream flower panicles appear in early summer and persist through winter. This hydrangea thrives in rich, acid soil and partial shade. There are many improved cultivars.

• **Climbing hydrangea** (*H. anomala petiolaris*), Zones 4 to 8, originated in China and Japan. Climbing hydrangea can climb to 60 feet (18 meters), and the stems cling to walls or other supports with sticky roots. Airy white flower clusters appear in early summer. This beauty requires extremely sturdy support; it's a great plant to grow up a failing tree.

soil of moisture. Plant them where their roots can enjoy moist soil, and provide a mulch to help keep the soil from drying out too quickly.

Try them in threes. If you have the space, plant three hydrangeas together; they look spectacular when massed. In smaller yards, a single plant makes a great specimen. Try growing daylilies on the sunny sides of your hydrangeas.

Don't deadhead. The dried flower heads are not only beautiful, adding interest to the winter garden, but also useful: They help protect the tender emerging buds from frost damage. Leave them on until early spring, then prune them back to just above a bud. Use spent heads for mulch or in the compost pile.

When to prune. Prune hydrangeas in late winter or early spring, cutting out damaged limbs and very old branches. Don't remove live wood that grew the previous season unless the plant needs serious shaping, because this is the wood that will produce the best blooms. After plants leaf out, trim off any bare branches, which were probably damaged by cold winter weather.

Changing a bigleaf hydrangea's color. The color of a bigleaf hydrangea's blossoms reveals the chemistry of your soil. Blue flowers indicate acid soil (below pH 7), while pink indicates alkalinity (above pH 7). To make a blue hydrangea bluer, acidify your soil with aluminum sulfate, iron sulfate, or soil sulfur. To make it change to pink, add lime to the soil to raise alkalinity. Be patient, nudging the pH in the direction you want

gradually, over a period of one to two years, because adding too much sulfur or lime at once can damage the plant's roots.

LILACS

Lilacs have been garden favorites for 300 years, and they grow especially well in midwestern regions, where every landscape includes a lilac. The most common species, *Syringa vulgaris*, is the fragrant common lilac from southern Europe and is hardy in the coldest winter climates. In addition, numerous other species, including many from Asia, make excellent garden shrubs, especially in the South, although few have the sweet fragrance of common lilac.

Lilacs demand neutral, well-drained soil. If your site is wet, plant them in a mound so that surface water will drain off. They also need 5 hours of sun daily and an occasional dose of lime to keep the soil neutral to slightly alkaline. Be patient; young lilacs need a few years to establish and produce maximum blooms.

Painless deadheading. Clip plenty of bouquets for indoor arrangements—it will lessen deadheading chores, and you'll have fragrant flower clusters to scent the house. Smash the woody stem ends with a hammer, which helps cut lilacs take up more water. Lilacs bloom on the previous year's wood, so also cut back the plants after blossoming ends to stimulate new growth.

To rejuvinate an overgrown lilac, either cut the whole plant back to the ground or remove a third of the oldest stems each year over three years to promote new sprouts from the base. Conscientious annual pruning makes drastic measures unnecessary.

Watch out for mildew. Lilacs are prone to powdery mildew, which covers foliage with white fuzz in late summer. Prevent the problem by pruning to promote air circulation. Also keep shrubs away from walls and reduce stress by watering and fertilizing regularly. Dust affected areas with sulfur.

ROSES

If you want to plant a new rose, you have two choices. Early in the spring, while roses are fully dormant, they are often available bare rooted. If you buy a bare-rooted rose but can't plant it right away, open the container and moisten the roots. Reclose and store it for up to two weeks in a dark place where the temperature stays 35° to 40°F (2° to 4°C). Just before planting, rehydrate the roots by soaking them overnight.

As spring gets under way, nurseries stock roses actively growing in pots. Some may already be in bloom. Try not to disturb the roots when planting a blooming rose. Cut out the bottom of the container and set the still-packaged root ball into the planting hole. Then slit one side of the container and gently remove it before backfilling the hole with soil that has been amended with compost.

Check the drainage. Roses must have good drainage, so check the site if you're not sure. Dig a hole 18 inches (45 cm) deep at the desired planting spot and fill it with water. If the water is gone within 2 hours, the site is suitable for roses. If water is still standing after 2 hours, build a raised bed for your bushes.

Be considerate of grafted roses, which often show a bulge on the main stem just above the roots. In cold climates, plant grafted roses 1 to 2 inches (3 to 5 cm) deep to protect the graft union from winter cold. Where winters are mild, plant the roses higher, so the graft union sits an inch or more above the soil's surface. Prune off any canes that emerge from below the graft union.

 Grandpa's wisdom

Planted near rosebushes, lavender drives away aphids; sage, hyssop, and thyme deter caterpillars; and French marigolds may discourage nematodes.

For early spring color, plant little bulbs such as miniature narcissus, grape hyacinth, or crocus 1 foot (30 cm) or so from the base of a big rose. The bulbs will bloom before the rose leafs out. Be sure to let the bulb foliage die back naturally in early summer.

Rotate buds to the north. Carefully check the canes on new roses. If most of the buds appear to face in one direction, place the plant in the planting hole so that the heavily budded

ROSE-PRUNING BASICS

Use the right tools. For the cleanest, least traumatic cuts on rose canes, use a sharp pair of bypass, or scissors-type, pruning shears; anvil-type shears can do damage by smashing the stems. To prune the largest canes on your bushes, use long-handled lopping shears.

Deadhead wisely. To keep modern hybrid tea and floribunda roses blooming throughout the growing season, remove fading flowers before the seeds, or rosehips, can form. As the petals start to drop, cut off the flower just above the fourth leaf cluster, or the highest node that has five leaflets just below it. A new flowering stem will sprout from the node.

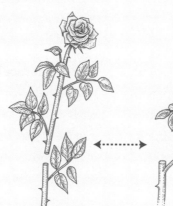

Prune reblooming roses in early spring just as the leaf buds swell. Begin by removing any dead or damaged canes, then take out any canes that grow in toward the center of the bush and any that cross and rub each other. Cut off the suckers that sprout from below the graft

union. Choose three to six of the strongest canes to keep and cut all the others off at ground level. Then trim the remaining canes to the desired height.

Roses that flower once a year should be pruned just after blooming. Trim as needed to create an open, balanced framework of sturdy branches. To keep the growth compact, cut back each cane by a quarter.

Rake up pruned clippings and dispose of them, since they may harbor disease spores or insect eggs and larvae. For the same reason, rake up and dispose of fallen rose leaves in autumn.

---

side faces north. This trick helps produce a well-shaped, mature rose bush, because strong southern sun will stimulate new growth on the other side of the plant.

Shape a basin of soil or mulch to help retain water around the rose's roots. In hot, dry weather, roses need an inch (30 cm) of water a week from either rain or a hose. Use a bubbler (available at garden centers) on the hose so the water seeps into the soil around the rose's roots without wetting foliage; damp leaves invite fungal diseases.

Give roses a lift with tea leaves. To give your rosebushes a midsummer boost, tuck old tea bags under the mulch. When you water the plants, the nutrients from the tea will be released into the soil, spurring growth. Roses love the tannic acid in tea.

Don't scrimp on sun. Most roses grow best where they get at least 6 hours a day of direct sun.

Growing climbers? Climbing roses will flower more profusely if you train them to follow a horizontal line along a trellis or frame while the canes are still young and supple. Forming an arch by fastening the end of a cane to a peg in the ground will encourage even more blooms.

The second blooming. To stimulate continued flowering of everblooming roses throughout the summer, drench the roots of each bush immediately after the first blooming with 2 to 4 tablespoons (30 to 60 cc) of brewer's yeast dissolved in 2 gallons (8 liters) of water.

Remedy low iron levels. Yellowed leaves with dark green veins are signs of chlorosis, a condition caused by an iron deficiency. Apply fertilizer containing chelated iron, but first test your soil: To keep iron from "locking up," the soil's pH must be between 5.5 and 6.5. If the pH is higher, apply sulfur; if it's lower, apply lime.

Dress standards for winter. Standard roses, often called tree roses, are actually rosebushes grafted onto long rootstock trunks. To protect the graft union over the winter, simply cut off the sleeve of an old sweater or sweatshirt. Prune back the rose's top growth in late fall so that you can slip the sleeve over the branches and around the graft union on the trunk below. Then stuff the sleeve with peat moss, dry leaves, or straw for insulation; tie a plastic bag over it to keep out ice and snow. Remove the sleeve in early spring.

A baking soda cure. At the first sign of blackspot—a common leaf disease for roses in humid weather—pinch off affected leaves and protect those that remain with a baking soda spray. Mix 2 teaspoons (10 cc) of baking soda and a few drops of liquid soap with 1 gallon (4 liters) of water. Spray the whole bush with the mixture. Reapply every four or five days until the spots disappear and the weather becomes drier.

Want to make more roses? Take cuttings from roses that grow on their own roots (that is, ones that are not grafted onto rootstock) and set them to root. In June, look for a vigorous pencil-thick cane; one bearing a bloom is at the right stage of maturity. Cut it into 6- to 8-inch (15- to 20-cm) lengths, making sure that each one has at least three leaves. Without damaging the buds at their bases, trim off all but the top leaf on each. Cut a cross into the base of each cutting with a sharp knife and slip a grain of rice into the center of each cut. To keep the grains in place, bind the cuttings' bases (not too tightly) with twine. Stand the cuttings in water overnight, then pot them in a mix of equal parts sand and soil. Water the pots thoroughly, set them in a cool and bright but shaded spot, and keep them well watered. The cuttings should root in two to three weeks.

❧Vines

WHETHER YOU WANT to transform a dull wall or fence into a magnificent living barrier or simply call attention to your mailbox, vines are the plants for the job. You can start with a short-lived annual vine, decide how you like it, and then switch to a long-lived woody vine. Chain-link fences in particular benefit from the presence of vines. To further obscure a fence, paint it green before the vine begins to grow and flower.

VINE SELECTION AND CARE

Buy vines in containers. Never buy a climbing plant with exposed roots. The odds are that the plant has suffered, and the roots have dried out. Replanting may be difficult. Look for several stems growing close to the base of the plant rather than a single tall one.

Plant perennial vines in spring just as the buds are beginning to swell. Give the soil in the pot a good soaking before planting a vine in a hole enriched with compost or organic fertilizer.

Beware of invasive species. Vines are often able to grow by throwing new stems over other plants, so they can become invasive if not kept in check. Some, such as Oriental bittersweet and Japanese honeysuckle, grow so exuberantly that they shouldn't be planted at all. Choose native species, such as Virginia creeper (now available in a variegated form) or coral honeysuckle instead.

Keep the roots cool. Most vines like to have their feet in the shade and their heads in the sun. Plant a low, shallow-rooted shrub, evergreen if possible, on the sunny side of the climber's base. Its cool shade will help the vine establish itself and reach its full potential. Keep the soil around both plants cool by spreading a thick layer of organic mulch over the surface.

❦ Watch Out!

Beware of poisonous climbers—and not just poison ivy! Wisteria, sweet pea, and some other climbers have poisonous parts that can be dangerous when eaten. Teach children not to eat berries or seedpods from ornamental plants.

Keep your house cool. A climbing vine that covers a south- or west-facing wall provides insulation in summer, keeping the house cooler and air-conditioning costs down. This is a great use for annual vines, which grow only during the summer.

Don't plant ivy or other vines where they can climb on wood siding; they can quickly cause the wood to rot. In some states, English ivy is so invasive that it's considered a noxious weed.

SORTING THROUGH vines

Not sure if you can handle the sprawling habit of a vine? Try an annual type first. If you're pleased with the results, you can install a permanent perennial vine in its place.

Six easy annual vines: Black-eyed Susan vine, cup-and-saucer vine, hyacinth bean, morning glory, scarlet runner bean, sweet pea

Six long-lived perennial vines: Clematis (Zones 4 to 8), climbing hydrangea (Zones 4 to 8), golden hops (Zones 4 to 9), honeysuckle (Zones 4 to 9), trumpet creeper (Zones 5 to 9), wisteria (Zones 5 to 9)

Use an old tree as a trellis. Some vines will climb a tree, adding color and texture to the trunk. Select vigorous species that can tolerate shade and tree-root competition and can climb unassisted. Ivy, winter creeper, and cross vine are good choices. Install plants carefully around tree roots in humus-rich soil and give extra food and water as needed. Train the stems by tying them loosely to the trunk.

Let them wind on wire. Heavy vines, such as those of honeysuckle and passionflower, can be supported on strong copper wires. The wires will eventually oxidize to an attractive green that blends into the foliage.

A handy removable trellis. If you regularly repaint the wall on which you install a climbing plant, mount a trellis on hooks so that it's easy to remove when the time comes to paint. Or put the base on hinges so the trellis and plant can be folded down in one piece when you need to work on the wall.

CLEMATIS

Queen of the climbers, clematis is prized for its long flowering period, the variety of flower shapes and colors, and its ability to thrive in a range of climates. Equipped with curling leaf stems, the vine will attach itself and rapidly grow through a lath or lattice trellis. In some neighborhoods, clematis is known as mailbox vine because it's such a popular choice for growing up a light trellis attached to a mailbox post. Most people like to showcase clematis by growing it on its own trellis, but you can also let it gently twine its way through the branches of a shrub or small tree. Colors range from pure white to deep purple to rich burgundy red. Blossoms of the spring-blooming types can be as large as saucers, while the blooms of fragrant autumn clematis are less than 1 inch (25 mm) across.

Plant a dynamic duo. Plant two different varieties side by side for a spectacular bicolor show of flowers. Or, to prolong the floral display, plant adjoining spring- and summer-blooming varieties so that you'll have flowers for months instead of weeks.

Withering away? If the foliage of your clematis withers and dies from a girdling stem canker at the soil line, it's a victim of a common disease:

clematis wilt. Remove and burn diseased stems, cutting well below the infected area. Plant new plants in a new location in moist, neutral, well-drained soil.

Spring training. Let your clematis cover—and beautify—a blank wall or fence by training it on a plastic-covered wire grid secured to the surface

with nails. *Note:* Plastic-covered wire is preferable to bare wire, which can often heat up and burn the plant. Position the wire at least ½ inch (13 mm) from the surface so the tendrils have room to twine. For smaller wall spaces, a narrow-lath trellis makes a good support.

Prune at the right time. Clematis that flower in spring do so on the previous year's ripened wood and require only light grooming. Late-blooming types flower on young wood produced the same year, and require a hard annual pruning in late winter or early spring.

Easy cuttings. In summer, select a half-ripe branch from the middle part of a shoot. Cut below the bud and pull off the leaves and lower bark. Dip the cut end in rooting hormone and insert the cutting into damp rooting medium. Keep shaded until roots form.

For winter decoration, leave the feathery fruits on your clematis. With the first frost or snow, the fruits will be transformed into dazzling little jewels. If you want to use them in a dried arrangement, cut them before they mature and fall from the plant.

New life for an old umbrella. Slide the framework of an old umbrella into a metal pipe driven into the ground. Plant two clematis at the foot of the frame. The flowering vines will quickly blanket it.

Spoil the soil your clematis calls home by blanketing it with a 3-inch (8-cm) layer of good compost every spring. If your soil is naturally acidic, add a little lime to the mixture before spreading it on.

Feed with baking soda. Give your clematis—and other flowering, alkaline-loving plants, such as delphiniums and dianthus—an occasional shower with a mild solution of 1 tablespoon (15 cc) of baking soda in 2 quarts (2 liters) of water. They'll show their appreciation with fuller, healthier blooms.

Clematis in containers. Many small-flowered varieties make excellent container plants, although you need to provide them with a twig or wire trellis. If you have a deck, try positioning the pot so the vine can find its way to the railing and spill over into a cascade of flowers.

WISTERIA

Pretty but pushy, wisteria can be an awesome vine provided you are willing to train it properly. It's a fast-growing climber that produces heavily scented cascades of white or lavender blooms in late spring. But it's also a willful beauty that can quickly outgrow its boundaries and latch onto gutters, shingles, and shutters. It can also literally pull apart all but the strongest trellis. The safest approach is to train a wisteria to grow as an umbrella-shaped specimen in which branches emerge from a short, muscular trunk.

Prune summer and winter. Regular, careful pruning not only keeps wisteria contained but also promotes next year's blooms. Clip it after flowering in summer by cutting off the long, stringy shoots to 6 inches (15 cm), leaving six leaves (the buds form on short spurs); prune again in winter, shortening the shoots to 3 inches (8 cm) with three buds. Also snip off any side shoots emerging from the base of the trunk.

A good spot. Don't plant wisteria near your house, trees, or utility lines, where it could become a nuisance. Instead, train it to twine along a strong fence or tie a young vine to an upright stake and begin topping it back after it grows 4 feet (1.2 meter) tall.

Only feed the young. Feed a young wisteria vine each spring with timed-release shrub fertilizer. Mature plants bloom better without supplements.

Shock treatment for stubborn plants. Root-prune mature wisteria vines that fail to flower; forcing roots to branch out encourages bud formation. Use a spade to cut a circle about 4 feet (1.2 meter) in diameter around the trunk, slicing through any roots you encounter.

✿ Trees

TREES GIVE ANY LANDSCAPE a sense of permanence, and even small trees can be a great investment—not only in your landscape but also in the future. Most trees live for decades, and some feature ornamental bark, flowers, and dazzling fall color. Take your time when choosing the perfect tree to plant, and meanwhile, do everything you can to make sure the trees you already have enjoy long, healthy lives.

CHOOSING TREES

Nature's air conditioners. Shade trees are invaluable for shielding houses from heat. Locate open-branched deciduous trees on the southern or western exposure so their limbs block high-angled summer sun. Don't use densely branched deciduous or evergreen trees, which won't allow low-angled winter sun to penetrate.

Know your needs. What do you want from a tree? Shade in summer or color in autumn? A hardworking windbreak or an easy-care foundation planting? Choose a species that meets your needs instead of forcing one into a role that doesn't suit it.

Trees are big underground, too. Consider a tree's ultimate height and spread, but don't forget its root mass, which can reach three times the size of the canopy. Before bringing that sweet little sapling home from the nursery, select a spot where it can develop without encroaching on power lines, buildings, driveways or walkways, underground pipes, or neighboring plants.

Small but sturdy. Don't select the tallest, biggest tree you can find unless you need to fill in a spot immediately. Look for a small, young one with a sturdy trunk, well-formed branches, and no signs of pests or diseases. It will cost less, be easier to move and plant, and adjust more readily to its new home than an older tree would.

Naughty ladies. The female trees of some species have unattractive habits and are best avoided. Flowers of the female poplar, for example, can cause allergies. The female ginkgo produces foul-smelling fruits.

Small garden? If so, buy one of many excellent trees that stay small, such as redbud, crabapple, dogwood, or Japanese maple. It's impossible to prune a large tree into a smaller one.

Shade lovers. While most trees need full sun, some tolerate or even prefer shade. If your best site for a new tree provides a half day of shade, look for dogwood, serviceberry, stewartia, redbud, sourwood, Carolina silverbell, Japanese snowbell, or threadleaf maple.

PERFECT PLACES FOR LANDSCAPE TREES

- **Use trees to soften** the hard angles made by building corners and to mark the ends of foundation beds. Imagine a diagonal line coming out from the front corners of your house toward the front edge of your lawn. Somewhere along that line should be a great place for a tree.

- **Keep scale in mind.** A towering spruce will dwarf a small house, while a large house will overshadow a dainty dogwood.

- **If you want to showcase a tree** as a single specimen, select one that offers more than one season of beauty A tree with flaking bark, pretty leaves, colorful fruits or fall foliage, and a pleasing silhouette works harder in the landscape than a dazzling spring bloomer that soon fades.

- **Look out the window.** Consider not only how your tree will look outdoors but also how it will be viewed from inside. If you use the tree to block an unattractive vista, however, don't place it where it will completely obstruct your sightline.

- **Neatness counts.** Plant only tidy trees near decks, driveways, entryways, and patios. You'll be spared the mess of fruits, seedpods, bark, petals, or twigs.

Follow the old adage: Never plant a $5 tree in a 5¢ hole! Dig the hole large enough to allow you to spread out the roots of a bare-rooted tree or to fill in around the soil ball of others—usually three times wider than the root spread but no deeper. If you disturb the base of the hole, the soil may settle and cause the tree to sink. To help tree roots penetrate the soil beyond the planting hole, score the sides of the hole with a spading fork or spade before setting the tree in place.

Check the depth. To position your tree, place a stick or tool handle across the hole to mark the ground level. Never plant the trunk-root juncture deeper than it was at the nursery. Turn the tree in the hole until the trunk is straight and the most attractive side is on view.

CARING FOR TREES

Water attentively. Young trees need plenty of water until the roots are established. When they mature, water them deeply so that moisture soaks the roots. When rainfall is low, use a soaker hose around the base of the tree or let water run very slowly out of the hose end for several hours. If the soil or mulch is disturbed by the water flow, turn the pressure down to a trickle.

Multipurpose mulch. Mulch not only retains moisture and suppresses weeds but also keeps potentially damaging lawn-care equipment at a safe distance. Use year-round organic material like shredded bark or wood chips—not fresh grass clippings or sawdust. Spread it around the base of the tree, starting 6 inches (15 cm) from the trunk and keeping it only 2 to 4 inches (5 to 10 cm) deep; any deeper, and it could suffocate the roots.

Prevent sunscald. This condition can injure young, thin-barked trees—especially ashes, lindens, maples, oaks, willows, and fruit trees. It occurs on warm winter days when the sun's rays activate dormant cells underneath the bark. When the temperature drops at night, it kills the cells and damages the tree. To prevent sunscald, wrap young tree trunks with a couple of layers of aluminum foil during the winter or use protective tape sold for this purpose.

Protect the trunks. Mice, rabbits, and other animals often feed on the bark of young trees during winter. A cheap and effective deterrent is to wrap the trunks with a double layer of heavy-duty aluminum foil in late fall. Be sure to remove it in the spring.

Watch out when whacking weeds. Weed trimmers can quickly do permanent damage to an otherwise healthy tree. To avoid accidentally scarring the trunk of a young tree when you're whacking weeds, cut a cardboard mailing tube in half lengthwise and tie the two halves around the trunk while you work around the tree. Then slip it off and use it on another tree. If you entrust weed trimming to others, use pieces of perforated plastic drainage pipe slit down the side and slipped over the base of the trunks to protect young trees.

Stake for stability. A newly transplanted tree usually needs support to help it stay straight until its roots can take hold. Drive three stakes into the ground around the tree and attach the trunk to the stakes with guy wires. Split a piece of old garden hose or use discarded inner tubes to cushion the bark from contact with the wires.

Young tree in trouble? Prune the foliage by 15 percent to reduce stress on the roots. Keep the tree thoroughly watered and mulch with compost. Wind paper tree wrap around the trunk to limit moisture loss. Check for and eliminate any air pockets in the soil. Wait until the following spring to decide whether the tree is a lost cause, because some trees that shed their leaves after transplanting make a comeback the following year.

Good neighbors. A tree growing on your property is yours, but it's often legal for a neighbor to trim branches that hang over the

property line. Talk to your neighbors about intrusive branches that may need to be trimmed, whether the tree is your property or theirs.

Remove sap from skin. Tree sap is sticky stuff and often won't come off easily. Don't worry:

Just rub butter on your hand, and the gunky sap will wash right off with soap and water.

Feeding trees. Putting fertilizer in the planting hole can harm the roots of young trees, so give them a season to get established before you begin feeding them. Fertilize adolescent trees with balanced timed-release tree and shrub fertilizer in spring. Drilling holes in the soil and filling them with fertilizer is a good way to make sure the fertilizer goes to the tree and not to surrounding grass.

Let it be. Unless you're creating topiary, let a tree be itself: Its natural shape is part of its beauty. Prune only to stimulate natural growth patterns.

Never top a mature tree. Bluntly cutting off a tree's branches reduces its size but often leads to a rebound of awkward crowded stems—and may even kill the tree. Thin out branches instead, following the natural shape of the tree. If the tree is quite large, hire a trained arborist to do the job right.

Avoid accidents. Promptly prune off any dead, diseased, or damaged limbs, which can easily fall and cause injury. But take note: Because of their huge size, some older specimens can be difficult—and dangerous—to handle. If you need to prune large limbs, transplant an established tree, or remove a dead tree, don't attempt it yourself. Hire an arborist to do it for you.

Start a rap sheet. If one of your trees has recurring problems with pests or diseases, keep a file on it. Record when the incident occurred, the symptoms, and the measures that were taken to correct them—whether successful or not.

FLOWERING TREES

All trees flower, even if their "blooms" are barely visible. While shade trees are grown for their dense foliage, those categorized as flowering trees are grown specifically for their showy displays of blossoms. No matter where you live, you can plant a flowering tree that will grow and thrive, requiring no more maintenance than any other tree.

Good for small spaces. Because many flowering trees are of low to moderate height, they are ideal for gardens with little space. Plant one as an individual specimen to provide a colorful focal point.

In large gardens, plant several flowering trees in a group to create a dramatic cloud of blooms in the season of your choice.

Accent your flower garden with a flowering tree. Place it at the back of a border or slightly off-center in the middle of a bed, where it will add a welcome vertical dimension to a horizontal look. Or use a flowing bed of groundcover plants to tie together three similar flowering trees.

City specimens. Several hardy, resistant flowering trees stand up well to air pollution. Try a hawthorn tree (*Crataegus* spp.), saucer magnolia, or pagoda tree (*Sophora japonica*) if you want a flowering tree to plant on a busy street.

Flowers plus! For visual interest all year, select trees that have not only beautiful flowers but also decorative foliage, intense fall color, ornamental fruit, or attractive bark and branching. Dogwoods, crab apples, and ornamental cherries are excellent choices.

In winter, when most trees are bare, evergreens serve as much-needed columns of green, which dramatize wind and appear even darker when cloaked with snow. Birds need evergreen trees for shelter, and people need them for the same

🥀 SORTING THROUGH flowering trees

- **Crab apples** develop white, pink, or rose blossoms in spring followed by red or yellow fruits in late summer or fall. Growth habit may be upright or weeping, and some varieties have purple foliage.

- **Dogwoods,** such as the native *Cornus florida*, a garden favorite since the 1700s, have gotten better and better in recent years. New hybrids resist disease and extend the bloom time well into early summer.

- **Golden rain tree** celebrates spring by showing foot-long clusters of tiny yellow blooms, which persist as reddish brown seedpods until fall.

- **Ornamental cherries** have beautiful pink or white blossoms and many have an elegant weeping growth habit. The shiny, sometimes banded bark keeps the trees attractive through the winter.

- **Persian parrotia** (*Parrotia persica*) has a graceful branching habit and striking amber, crimson, and gold autumn foliage. The bark on older trees flakes away in patches, creating a patterned effect.

- **Redbuds** cover themselves with tiny rose-pink blossoms in spring, and a few varieties bloom white. Large, heart-shaped leaves help young trees to grow quickly.

- **Serviceberry,** prized for its billowy white flowers in spring and bright foliage in fall, is also known as shadbush or shadblow—so called because it blooms when the shad start spawning in eastern rivers. Among the best species are the 50-foot (15-meter) downy serviceberry (*Amelanchier canadensis*), the widely available Allegheny serviceberry (*A. laevis*), and the big-blossomed apple ser-

viceberry (*A. × grandiflora*). All are hardy to −20°F (−29°C).

- **Stewartia** has eye-catching white flowers, pretty flaking bark, and leaves that turn bright red or orange in the fall.

- **Witch hazel trees** are small enough for tiny yards, and their fringe-like flowers are valued mostly for their sweet scents and for their timing. Depending on the variety and climate, witch hazel can bloom in fall, winter, or first thing in spring.

- **Yellowwood** (*Cladrastis lutea*), native to the South, can take 10 years to produce its first blooms. But be patient: you'll be rewarded with an abundance of long, drooping chains of fragrant, white, pealike flowers. Try the 'Rosea' variety for light pink blooms. Both trees boast beautiful yellow-orange foliage in fall.

reason. Planted on the north side of your house, an evergreen tree can shelter it from biting winter winds, and its shade pattern won't block the warming rays of the Southern sun. From large American hollies to cypress, pines, magnolias, or yews, every landscape should have a space for a carefully selected evergreen tree.

When to plant? In most climates, set out new evergreen trees either before growth starts in early spring or after the tree has finished growing in early fall. If planting in the fall, make sure the roots will have time to establish themselves before the ground freezes.

In mild-winter areas where the ground doesn't freeze, fall is preferred for planting evergreen trees. Fall-planted trees can take advantage of winter rains and should be well rooted by the time stressful summer weather arrives.

Sun or shade? Most evergreen trees need full sun for at least three-quarters of the day. Those planted in the shade—including shade-tolerant hemlocks, arborvitaes, and yews—sprout fewer branches and have less attractive shapes.

A backdrop for flowering vines. Brighten evergreen foliage in summer by training colorful climbing vines, such as clematis, nasturtium, morning glory, and cup-and-saucer vine to twine prettily on the tree's south-facing side.

Not all evergreens have needles. The southern magnolia (*Magnolia grandiflora*), or bull bay, is a fixture in the Deep South. Newer dwarf forms, such as the award-winning 'Little Gem' variety make magnolias much easier to fit into the landscape.

An all-round favorite. Yews (*Taxus* spp.) are among the world's most popular needle-leaf evergreens. Hundreds of species and cultivars are available, and they range in size from 40-foot (12-meter) columnar trees to sturdy, dense shrubs good for hedges and 2-foot (60-cm) spreading shrubs, which are wider than they are tall.

Reduce a conifer's spread by pinching back or pruning the new green shoots that appear each spring. Be careful not to prune past the

point where leaves are growing, since only a few conifers can produce new growth from branches without live foliage present.

A winter mulch. Branches pruned from evergreen trees—especially conifers—make ideal winter mulch for perennials, small border shrubs, and strawberries. Either shred the branches with a wood chipper or lay pieces of whole boughs atop the soil.

❧ Groundcovers

WHAT EXACTLY *IS* a groundcover? Basically, it's any low-growing plant that spreads out to cover the soil. The workhorses of the plant world, groundcovers look great, take less work than lawn to maintain, and can grow where turf grasses simply won't thrive.

GETTING STARTED

Right plant, right place. The secret to success with groundcovers is choosing those that are suited to the growing conditions in your yard. If your site gets at least 6 hours of sun a day, select groundcovers that can take full sun. Partial-shade plants can get by with 3 to 6 hours of sun; fewer than 3 hours usually qualifies as full shade. Also consider the soil. Most groundcovers grow best in average conditions, but some can tolerate very wet or very dry soil.

Choices, choices. Once you've come up with a list of groundcovers suited to your site, narrow it down by deciding what you want from your planting. If you need a lawn-like effect without regular mowing, a low-growing ornamental grass can do the trick; for a carpet of green all year long, consider growing an evergreen plant such as pachysandra. Flowering groundcovers do double duty: They suppress weeds and dress up your landscape with seasonal color as well. Ground-hugging plants are best between stepping stones and along paths; taller plants—to about 3 feet (1 meter)—are fine for planting on slopes or under trees.

Frame it up. A ribbon of groundcover plants 1 to 2 feet (30 to 60 cm) wide around a small lawn area creates a finished look and reduces the time you'll spend on edging. Evergreen groundcovers work best, but you can also use deciduous plants, which die back during the winter. (While the groundcover is dormant, cover it with attractive mulch, such as shredded bark.)

Weeding is fundamental. The single most important step in getting groundcovers off to a good start is getting rid of all the weeds *before* you plant. Hand-dig weeds with taproots, such as dock and dandelions, to make sure you remove them completely. Then remove the remaining grass and weeds with a sod cutter or (in small areas) with a spade or shovel. After you dig or till the soil, water the site and let it sit for a week or two, then weed again before planting.

Fall into planting. Autumn is the ideal time to get new groundcover patches started. Come spring, they'll be settled in and be ready to sprout quickly, so they'll get a jump-start on crowding out weeds. Plus, they'll need less watering since their roots will be well established before hot, dry summer weather arrives.

The strongest link. To make mowing easier and minimize tedious trimming, use beds of groundcovers to link individual shrubs and trees into larger beds. Flowering groundcovers are fabulous for adding color around non-blooming trees and shrubs; evergreen groundcovers make an elegant backdrop for bright-flowered bushes.

Create planting pockets. Need to get ground-covers growing under trees and shrubs? The abundant roots can make it tough to dig or till the whole site, so dig individual planting holes as best you can and add a shovelful of compost to each. After planting, mulch with leaf mold or more compost and keep the groundcover well watered for the first year or two.

Slope savvy. Groundcovers are super solutions for slopes, eliminating the need for regular mowing in awkward spaces. To prevent erosion while the plants are getting established, lay a per-meable, biodegradable mat, such as jute netting, over the prepared soil. Cut planting holes, set in the plants, and cover the mat with mulch.

Stepping up. Another option that works well for a steep slope is laying boards, logs, or stones across it to create low walls. Add some topsoil to fill in behind each wall, and you'll create level "steps" that are easy to plant with groundcovers, and are much less prone to erosion.

MAINTAINING GROUNDCOVERS

Annual aid. It's natural for new groundcover patches to look a little sparse, but avoid the urge to set the plants close together; otherwise, they'll become crowded and prone to disease problems. Instead, tuck annuals into the bare spaces to fill in for the first year or two. They'll add extra color and stop weeds from getting started.

Pin 'em down. Groundcovers with trailing stems, such as vinca and wintercreeper, tend to root where they touch the soil. Help them along by pinning them down with short pieces of wire bent into a "∪" shape.

Make the most of mulch to suppress weeds and keep the soil evenly moist while your groundcovers are filling in. To make the job of mulching go quickly, cover each plant with an overturned pot, then spread 1 to 2 inches (3 to 5 cm) of compost, shredded bark, or other organic mulch over the whole bed. Remove

(Continued on page 142)

❦ SORTING THROUGH groundcovers

Steep slopes tend to be very dry because rainfall runs off instead of soaking in, so they call for sturdy groundcovers that can survive without much moisture. Similarly, shady areas require groundcovers that can thrive without much sunlight. And under shrubs and trees, groundcovers should not compete for nourishment. Groundcovers for edging should be particularily dense and hardy. Here's a sample of some top-notch choices for these tough sites.

For slopes

NAME	SPECIES	DESCRIPTION	PLANTING	ZONES
Creeping juniper	*Juniperus horizontalis*	Dense, shrubby, evergreen mounds of woody stems with short green or bluish needles; about 2 feet (60 cm) tall.	Full sun	3 to 9
Daylilies	*Hemerocallis* spp. and hybrids	Deciduous clumps of narrow, strap-like leaves plus trumpet-shaped summer flowers in a wide range of colors; 1 to 4 feet (30 cm to 1.2 meters) tall.	Sun to partial shade	3 to 9
English ivy	*Hedera helix*	Long, vining stems with shiny evergreen leaves that are deep green, green and white, or green and yellow; 6 to 12 inches (15 to 30 cm) tall.	Partial to full shade	5 to 9
Ice plant	*Delosperma cooperi*	Evergreen or semi-evergreen mats of narrow, succulent, green leaves and daisy-like purple flowers all summer long; 3 to 6 inches (8 to 15 cm) tall.	Full sun	6 to 9
Rock rose	*Helianthemum nummularium*	Low, mounding shrubs with gray-green leaves plus pink, orange, yellow, or white flowers in late spring; 1 to 2 feet (30 to 60 cm) tall.	Full sun	5 to 8
Rockspray cotoneaster	*Cotoneaster horizontalis*	Spreading mounds with deciduous, glossy green leaves that turn red in fall; 2 to 3 feet (60 cm to 1 meter) tall.	Full sun	4 to 8
St. John's wort	*Hypericum calycinum*	Evergreen carpets of blue-green leaves with yellow flowers in spring and summer; 12 to 18 inches (30 to 45 cm) tall.	Sun to partial shade	6 to 9
Wintercreeper	*Euonymus fortunei*	Fast-growing creeping or mounding plants with deep green or variegated evergreen leaves; 1 to 4 feet (30 cm to 1 meter) tall.	Full sun to full shade	5 to 9

As lawn alternatives in shade

NAME	SPECIES	DESCRIPTION	PLANTING	ZONES
Pachysandra	*Pachysandra terminalis*	Upright, 6- to 8-inch (15- to 20-cm) stems bear whorls of glossy, rich green foliage all year long, plus short spikes of fragrant white flowers in late spring.	Space plants 6 to 12 inches (15 to 30 cm) apart	4 to 8
Periwinkle	*Vinca minor*	Slender, trailing stems clad in small, glossy, deep green leaves create dense evergreen carpets that are 6 to 8 inches (15 to 20 cm) high. The pretty sky-blue spring blooms are a bonus!	Space plants about 1 foot (30 cm) apart	4 to 9

For under shrubs and trees

NAME	SPECIES	DESCRIPTION	PLANTING	ZONES
Dwarf Chinese astilbe	*Astilbe chinensis* var. pumila	Low, dense masses of lacy green leaves are accented with brushy, 1-foot (30-cm) plumes of pink flowers in summer.	Space plants 8 to 12 inches (20 to 30 cm) apart	4 to 8
Spotted lamium	*Lamium maculatum*	Dense, mounding plants form 6- to 8-inch mats of silver-and-green leaves 6 to 8 inches (15 to 20 cm) high and accented with pink or white flowers from midspring to midsummer.	Set plants about 1 foot (30 cm) apart	3 to 8

As broad edgings for lawns and hard surfaces

NAME	SPECIES	DESCRIPTION	PLANTING	ZONES
Bugleweed	*Ajuga reptans*	Low rosettes of deep green, bronze, or variegated leaves are 3 to 4 inches (8 to 10 cm) tall; they are evergreen in mild climates. Four- to 6-inch (10- to 15-cm) spikes of blue or pink flowers bloom in late spring.	Space plants 8 to 12 inches (20 to 30 cm) apart	3 to 8
Liriope	*Liriope* spp.	Also known as lilyturf, this groundcover produces an evergreen, lawn-like effect, with narrow, deep green or variegated leaves that are 10 to 18 inches (25 to 45 cm) tall. Short spikes of purple-blue or white flowers appear in mid- to late summer.	Set plants 1 foot (30 cm) apart	6 to 9

the pots, and *voilà!*—a perfectly mulched groundcover patch!

Keep groundcovers well fed and watered while they mature. An easy way to fertilize large drifts is to use soluble food that you can apply with a hose-end sprayer.

Fall cleanup. It's fine if some leaves fall on your groundcover beds (they'll serve as a natural mulch). But if the plants are buried by an abundance of leaves, clear them off with a rake or leaf blower before winter.

Spring into action. In early spring, spruce up your groundcovers by cutting back any evergreen stems that are too long or winter damaged. To rejuvenate old groundcover patches, give them a hard trim with hedge clippers or a lawnmower (adjust the blade to its highest setting). A string trimmer can work great on slopes, but test it on a small area first to see if it's powerful enough for the job; if not, you may need a blade attachment.

Watch out for woody weeds in groundcover plantings beneath trees. Oaks, maples, and many other tree seedlings may appear in spring. Use pliers to pull them while they're young. Woody weeds are easiest to pull when the soil is wet.

AGGRESSIVE GROUNDCOVERS

Vigorous growth is an important trait for a good groundcover, but it's smart to check out just how vigorous a particular plant is before you let it loose in your landscape. Some spread so quickly that they can creep right into your lawn or flowerbeds, making more work for you instead of less! Groundcovers that need careful watching include ajuga, goutweed (*Aegopodium podagraria*), houttuynia, ivies, Mexican primrose (*Oenothera speciosa*), moneywort (*Lysimachia nummularia*), sweet woodruff (*Galium odoratum*), and wintercreeper.

Regular pruning or pulling out unwanted plants can work to control a small patch, but in large areas, it's more practical to separate groundcovers from lawn or garden areas with metal or plastic edging strips. The strips should extend at least 4 inches (10 cm) into the soil—and ideally 6 inches (15 cm) or more—to discourage creeping roots from crawling underneath. Or give the plants a site where they can spread freely, such as a slope or an area surrounded by paving.

✢ Ornamental Grasses

WHEN IT COMES TO PLANNING your home landscape, what comes to mind first? The lawns and flowerbeds, probably, and then maybe a few trees and shrubs for good measure. But if you overlook the incredible array of great plants classified as ornamental grasses, you'll miss out on some super opportunities for adding year-round interest to your yard!

Grasses aren't just for lawns anymore! Ornamental grasses come in an amazing array of sizes, forms, and colors, and they can adapt to just about any growing conditions, from sun to shade, from wet soil to dry. Low growers are marvelous in masses as a no-mow lawn substitute or as edgings around beds or along paths. Enjoy single clumps of large grasses as eye-catching accents or plant them in a row for a stunning summer and fall screen around your pool or patio. They look great mixed with flowering plants in beds, too!

SELECTING AND MAINTAINING

Explore your options. The key to growing gorgeous grasses is choosing those that are naturally adapted to the site where you'll plant them. Otherwise, they'll take more work to maintain, be more prone to problems, and never look their best. Sun lovers, such as miscanthus and pampas grass (*Cortaderia*), tend to have weak stems and need staking if they get too much shade. Sedges

(*Carex* spp.) and other ornamental grasses that prefer shade can turn crispy brown in sun-baked sites, even if you give them lots of extra water.

For flower beds, stick with ornamental grasses that are described as clump forming. These well-behaved grasses form tidy mounds or tufts that expand gradually over time, but basically stay in one place. That means you can pair them with flowering annuals, bulbs, and perennials without fear that they'll crowd out their more delicate companions. Examples of clumpers include fescues, miscanthus, and feather reed grasses (*Calamagrostis* spp.).

The reason for the seasons. You'll often see ornamental grasses described as warm season or cool season. Warm-season grasses, such as miscanthus (*Miscanthus* spp.) and fountain grasses (*Pennisetum* spp.), are slow to sprout in spring, but they shoot up once the weather heats up, producing their flowers and showy seedheads in late summer. They're fantastic for adding autumn interest to your landscape!

Cool-season grasses, such as fescues and blue oat grass (*Helictotrichon sempervirens*), do most of their growing when temperatures are below 75°F (24°C). During the dog days, they slow down or stop growing altogether. Enjoy them with spring bulbs and early perennials, then combine them with later-blooming plants to take over the show in summer and fall.

Timing is everything. Early spring is the best time to plant warm-season grasses so they'll have time to get their roots down before their summer growth spurt begins. You can plant cool-season grasses just about any time the ground isn't frozen, but early-spring planting usually works best for them, too.

Before you plant, weed the area thoroughly. It's especially important to remove any turf or weed grasses. Otherwise, they can grow into your ornamental grasses, and you'll have a tough time getting the bad grasses out without pulling out the good grasses as well!

Keep 'em lean. Ornamental grasses typically grow best in average garden soil, so don't put a lot of work into preparing a perfect planting site. Rich soil leads to lush growth, which can lead to disease problems or cause weak stems that need staking. It's fine to add a few handsful of compost to the planting hole, but avoid using manure or high-nitrogen fertilizers.

The kindest cut. Warm-season grasses usually turn tan or coppery by late fall, but their foliage often stays good-looking well into winter. To tidy them up in spring, use hand shears to snip small grasses back to about 2 inches (5 cm) or a pruning saw. Electric hedge shears work better for cutting large grasses to about 6 inches (15 cm) above the soil. Wear gloves while working with grasses, because their leaves can have sharp edges.

> ## NOW, THAT'S CREEPY!
>
> Creeping grasses spread outward by horizontal stems or roots. They look like clumpers for the first year or two, but by the third year, you'll find their shoots popping up all over, often far from the original plant! Common creepers include blue Lyme grass (*Leymus arenarius*), ribbon grass (*Phalaris arundinacea* var. *picta*), and silver banner grass (*Miscanthus sacchariflorus*).
>
> If you really want to grow these invasive grasses in a bed or border, you could try dividing and replanting them every year to slow their spread or plant them in a bottomless bucket sunk almost to its rim into the soil to restrain the roots. The easiest route, though, is simply to give them room to run. Try them on a difficult-to-mow slope (they make great groundcovers) or in an area surrounded by paving, such as the strip between a sidewalk and the street. Or plant them in pots and set them on a hard surface so their roots can't escape from the drainage holes!

Lift and separate. Digging up and dividing your ornamental grasses every three or four years in early spring will help keep them healthy and vigorous. Separate small clumps by hand; divide large ones with a sharp spade or an ax.

Here comes the groom. Cool-season grasses benefit from a little cleanup in midsummer. Cut them back by about half their height, and they'll produce a flush of fresh leaves that look good for the rest of the growing season.

❧ SORTING THROUGH ornamental grasses

Here's a rundown of some super clump-forming grasses that are guaranteed to please!

NAME	SPECIES	DESCRIPTION	TYPE	LIGHT	ZONES
Blue fescue	*Festuca glauca*	Blue-green to gray-green foliage is 6 to 10 inches (15 to 25 cm) tall; flowers are 12 to 18 inches (30 to 45 cm) tall.	Cool season	Full sun	4 to 8
Feather reed grass	*Calamagrostis × acutiflora*	Deep green leaves are up to about 3 feet (1 meter) tall; pinkish to tan plumes are 4 to 6 feet (1 to 2 meters) tall.	Cool season	Full sun to light shade	4 to 9
Fountain grass	*Pennisetum alopecuroides*	Green foliage is up to about 2 feet (60 cm) tall; brushy flower spikes are up to about 3 feet (1 meter) tall.	Warm season	Full sun to light shade	5 to 9
Golden Hakone grass	*Hakonechloa macra* var. *aureola*	Arching blades striped with green and yellow; mounds are 1 to 2 feet (30 to 60 cm) tall.	Warm season	Partial shade	5 to 9
Miscanthus	*Miscanthus sinensis*	Also known as Japanese silver grass or eulalia. Green or variegated foliage is from 4 to 6 feet (1 to 2 meters) tall; showy fall plumes are 5 to 8 feet (1.5 to 2.5 meters) tall.	Warm season	Full sun to light shade	4 to 9
Dwarf pampas grass	*Cortaderia selloana* var. *pumila*	Green foliage is up to about 3 feet (1 meter) tall; creamy white flower plumes are 4 to 6 feet (1 to 2 meters) tall.	Warm season	Full sun to light shade	7 to 9
Switch grass	*Panicum virgatum*	Green to blue-gray foliage is 3 to 6 feet (1 to 2 meters) tall; 4 to 7 feet (1 to 2 meters) tall in bloom.	Warm season	Full sun to light shade	4 to 9
Tufted hair grass	*Deschampsia cespitosa*	Deep green foliage is 2 to 3 feet (60 cm to 1 meter) tall; 3 to 5 feet (1 to 1.5 meters) tall in bloom.	Cool season	Partial shade	4 to 9

BAMBOO

Bamboo plants can add grace and beauty to any landscape, but they can also cause a maintenance nightmare if you don't choose and use them carefully. Bamboos are actually a type of grass, and like grasses, they come in two different forms: clump formers and creepers. Do some research before you plant, and you'll save yourself time and money in the long run!

Think twice. The creeping kinds, such as black bamboo (*Phyllostachys nigra*) and golden bamboo (*Pleioblastus viridistriatus*), are the ones that can cause problems because their roots spread far and wide and are very hard to control. If you really want to grow them, try them in large pots or use them as groundcovers in very difficult sites, such as steep slopes. Otherwise, you'll need to surround their roots with barriers of sheet metal or very heavy plastic 3 to 4 feet (1 meter) deep, and even that might not stop them completely. Or site them in the middle of a grassy area so you can mow around them regularly.

Try these instead. Luckily for bamboo lovers, there *are* some clump-forming kinds, too! They tend to be slow growing, but once they're established, they'll provide many years of easy-care elegance without making pests of themselves. The best of the bunch are the umbrella or fountain bamboos (*Fargesia* spp.). These well-behaved evergreen bamboos typically thrive in Zones 5 to 8, and they usually grow best with morning sun and afternoon shade.

To get bamboo plants off to a good start, prepare a planting hole that's just as deep as the root ball but at least twice as wide. After planting, water daily for the first week or two if rainfall is lacking, then once or twice a week for another month. Taper off to once every few weeks by the end of the growing season. By the following year, your bamboo should be fine without extra water except during extended dry spells.

☙ Watch Out!

Many grasses produce attractive flowering plumes that turn into pretty seedheads, but some of them can also turn into weed problems if you let those seedheads ripen! Sometimes—as with fescues and fountain grasses—it's simply a matter of having lots of seedlings to pull out of your own garden. To prevent this, cut off the flower heads as they turn brown or mulch heavily each spring to smother the seedlings.

In other cases—as with miscanthus and purple pampas grass (*Cortaderia jubata*), for example, wind can carry the seeds to meadows, woods, and other natural areas, where they sprout and crowd out the native vegetation. Before planting, check with your local Cooperative Extension agent to find out which grasses could be a problem in your area.

Mulch, mulch, mulch! A 2- to 3-inch (5- to 8-cm) layer of organic mulch helps keep the soil cool and moist, encouraging good rooting and healthy top growth. In spring and summer, grass clippings are great for mulching bamboo. In the fall, spread a thick layer of leaves around the base of the plant to protect the shallow roots from freezing.

Bye-bye, bugs. Bamboos are seldom troubled by insects. If you do find scale or other sucking pests on your plants, cut and burn the infested stalks or spray with an insecticide.

VEGETABLES, FRUITS,
AND HERBS

Why grow your own food? If you've ever sunk your teeth into a sun-ripened tomato right off the vine, you know the answer—incomparable flavor. Corn tastes sweeter, radishes snappier, and beans crisper when they are harvested from your own garden. Homegrown vegetables and fruits also supply more vitamins and minerals because they're fresher, they save money on the family food bill, and you get the chance to try unusual varieties that you won't find at the local market.

That said, the best reason to grow your own food is because it's so much fun. Along the way, growing what you eat always brings a satisfying feeling of accomplishment. What's more, if you garden with your nose, you'll find live, green herbs to be a neverending source of delight. From the romantic aroma of lavender to the sharp spiciness of Rosemary, herbs offer fragrance, flavor, and sometimes health benefits—all for very little effort.

It's true that growing fruits can sometimes be challenging, but every yard has room for one or two easy ones, such as blueberries or raspberries. If you have more space—and a passion for fruits—you can expand your collection to include family favorites.

✣ Vegetables

WHERE TO BEGIN? The sunniest spot in your yard is the best place to stake out your plot, because most vegetables need a minimum of 6 hours of sun daily. And, because vegetables like plenty of moisture, grow yours near a water source. Finally, vegetables always have the unwanted company of weeds. Monitor your plot weekly to pull up invaders, which can be enjoyable work as you watch your favorites from the 30-plus vegetables described here grow from tiny seeds or plants to big, meal-enhancing vegetables.

PLANNING YOUR PATCH

Which way should your rows run? In temperate climates, make your vegetable rows from east to west so that all the plants receive maximum sunshine. In hot, arid climates, run the rows from north to south so that each plant will be shaded by a neighbor on the warm south side.

The neatest gardens have straight rows, which is important if you use a tiller to cultivate between plantings. But it's harder than it looks to make straight garden rows freehand. For planting heavy seeds, such as beans, put sticks in the ground at each end of a row and run a piece of string between them to guide you as you plant. To plant dozens of lightweight seeds in a snap, cut a piece of string the same length as the row, wet it thoroughly, and sprinkle the seeds directly on it. The moisture will make seeds stick long enough to lay the string in a prepared furrow. Just cover the string with soil, and you're done!

Keep everything within easy reach. To make tending beds easier, make them no wider than the spread of your arms—that's about 4 feet (1.2 meters). Design a main path wide enough for a wheelbarrow, at least 3 feet (1 meter) wide, and include footpaths 1 foot (30 cm) wide between beds. To suppress weeds and provide a clean place to walk, keep paths covered with straw, chopped leaves, boards, or strips of scrap carpeting.

Make the most of limited space. Plant vertical crops, such as peas and pole beans, which take up little ground space. Or try dwarf varieties, such as 'Tom Thumb Midget' lettuce and 'Tiny Dill' cucumbers. Many dwarf varieties can also be grown in roomy containers kept on a deck or patio.

Protect vegetables with old tires. If you're eager to get an early start in spring, plant your tomatoes, potatoes, eggplants, peppers, or other vegetables inside old tires laid on the ground. The tires will protect the plants from harsh winds, and the dark rubber will absorb heat from the sun and warm the surrounding soil.

Leave room for blooms. Flowers in the vegetable garden not only make it a more pleasant place to work, but also have practical uses. Many flowers attract beneficial insects, such as bees, ladybugs, and lacewings, while others may repel pests in search of your vegetables. Try French marigolds, cosmos, and zinnias as well as edible flowers like nasturtiums and violets.

Beans boost soil nitrogen. Beans, peas, and other legumes are among the few plants that enrich the soil with nitrogen—an element essential for plant growth. Legumes begin using up the nitrogen they've stored when they blossom and set fruit. If you pull them up early, they will leave nutrients behind in the soil that can be used by other plants.

Fill up the season. After harvesting a cool-weather crop (spring peas or spinach, for example), replant the space with a warm-weather vegetable (green beans or summer squash). Interplant quick growers (radishes) with slower ones (tomatoes). The short-term crop will be up and out before the slow grower can crowd or shade it.

Grow vegetables that look as good as they taste. Many common vegetables are attractive enough to be used as ornamentals. Use 'Tequila Sunrise' or 'Chocolate Bell' peppers and 'Violet Queen' cauliflower to add color to the vegetable garden. For textured or colorful leaves, plant red chard, savoy cabbage, or 'Red Sails' lettuce.

Scare off birds with reflective tape. An innovative way to keep birds away from your vegetables is to hang strips of reflective tape over the plants. When the tape flutters in the breeze, it casts light across the garden, which spooks wary birds.

Shield your vegetable garden. For centuries, maybe millennia, gardeners have used companion planting to repel insect pests. Aromatic plants, such as basil, tansy, marigolds, and sage are all reputed to send a signal to bugs to go elsewhere, so try some near your prized vegetables. Mint, thyme, dill, and sage are old-time favorites

THE VEGETABLE FAMILY TREE

Like all living things, vegetables belong to families. Knowing which plants are kindred will come in handy when rotating your crops.

Allium family (*Alliaceae* spp.): Garlic, leeks, onions, shallots, chives

Brassica or mustard family (*Brassicaceae* spp.): Broccoli, Brussels sprouts, cabbage, kale, cauliflower, radishes, turnips

Carrot family (*Umbelliferae* spp.): Carrots, celery, parsley

Cucurbit family (*Cucurbitaceae* spp.): Cucumbers, gourds, melons, pumpkins, squash

Goosefoot family (*Chenopodiaceae* spp.): Beets, spinach, Swiss chard

Legume family (*Fabaceae* spp.): Beans, lentils, peas

Nightshade family (*Solanaceae* spp.): Eggplant, peppers, potatoes, tomatoes

Sunflower family (*Asteraceae* spp.): Artichokes, Jerusalem artichokes, lettuce

near cabbage family plants (cabbage, broccoli, cauliflower, and Brussels sprouts) for their supposed ability to fend off cabbage moths. Best of all, you can eat most of these savory herbs!

Move things around. Crop rotation is essential for preventing a buildup of harmful soilborne microbes that prefer certain plants. For this reason, don't plant a vegetable or a member of its family in the same place year after year. Instead, divide the garden into sections and move the plants from one area to another. As a general rule, a plant should be replanted in its original spot only every three or four years.

BEANS

Choose short or tall snap beans. Bush-type snap beans yield their bounty for a shorter time than pole beans—usually for about 3 weeks in the summer. Because of their shorter maturation time—about 55 days, or almost 2 weeks earlier than pole beans—it's a good idea to plant them successively so you'll have a constant supply of beans throughout the summer. Pole beans usually start producing after 65 days and then continue to provide fresh beans for up to 12 weeks. You have to plant them only once.

Beans like it hot. Sow bean seeds only when the soil is very warm. Try this toe-tingling test: If you can walk barefoot in the soil without feeling the cold, it's ready. Don't bother to start beans ahead of schedule indoors. Plant seeds directly in the garden three weeks after the last

 SORTING THROUGH
beans

Loosely categorized by the stage at which you harvest them, there are enough bean varieties to keep you in fresh produce for much of the growing season and to enjoy dry or frozen beans during the rest of the year.

- **Snap or string beans** are eaten young and fresh in the pods and include bush, pole, and runner varieties. French filet beans are the slender, succulent beans that the French call *haricots verts*, while colorful snap beans include yellow (or wax) varieties like 'Roc d'Or' and 'Goldkist'. There are also purple-podded beauties such as 'Royal Burgundy'.

- **Shell beans,** including fava, lima, and cranberry beans, mature in the pods and are then shelled to cook fresh. They can also be frozen when fresh or allowed to mature into dry edible beans.

- **Dry edible beans,** or field beans, are dried in the pod, stored dry, and soaked before cooking. Types include kidney, navy, pinto, and black beans, which are all just different types of a single species, *Phaseolus vulgaris*. They're also the same type of plant as snap beans—just varieties that produce lots of seeds per pod.

frost, planting them 2 inches (5 cm) deep and 6 inches (15 cm) apart. Install a trellis as you plant pole beans.

Limas love hot weather, but a few varieties can accept a cooler climate. Cool-weather varieties like 'Geneva' and 'Thoroughgreen' have been bred for gardeners in the northern states.

What's the secret of long snap bean production? Keep 'em picked! If you take their pods away, beans feel obliged to make more flowers—and thus more beans. Pole beans should be harvested every two days, and bush beans should be picked twice a week. Leave shell types like 'Great Northern' and pinto beans on the plant until the foliage begins to wither. Then harvest whole plants and hang them upside down in a warm place.

Keep the leaves dry. Instead of wielding a hose or watering can when watering beans, place a soaker hose between the rows— or simply poke more holes in an already leaky hose. Never pick snap beans that are wet from dew or rain. Jostling a wet plant can spread the spores that cause one of the many fungal and bacterial diseases that attack most types of beans.

You'll know it's time to pick shell beans when the pods are plump and tightly closed, looking as if the beans inside are ready to burst out. Shelled, fresh limas should be bright green, favas light gray-green, and soybeans yellow-green; cranberry beans should have bright red markings.

Grow a bean tepee for the kids. Train your pole beans on a tripod constructed from 10-foot (3-meter) bamboo poles tied at the top with cord. Kids love bean tepees—and they can pick and eat fresh beans while they're playing inside.

Trellis pole beans the easy way by making a string trellis. Attach strings to wood spikes just outside the planted row and loop them over a

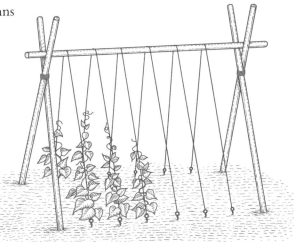

cross pole held up by posts at the ends of the row. When the season is done, you can simply snip the strings to take down the trellis.

BEETS

Develop your beet palate. When too many seedlings appear in a direct-seeded row, let them grow 3 inches (8 cm) tall before harvesting them as baby salad greens. Try a few fresh beets raw, grated like carrots. Roast beets whole and then slip off the skins before chilling them for a delicious cold beet salad.

Try a different color. Beyond red beets, 'Burpee Golden' looks like sunshine in a salad, and 'Chiogga' is candy-striped in pink and white.

For an early harvest, start beets in a cold frame in pots filled with a half-and-half mixture of potting soil and garden soil. Transplant to the garden as soon as all danger of frost is past, and keep the soil constantly moist. Direct-seed more beets when you set out the seedlings. Whether planted early or late, beets are tastiest when they're the size of golf balls.

Have beets in winter. Late varieties will keep for several months if you harvest before the first frost. Let the roots dry for a day outside, sheltered from the rain. Twist the leaves off and shake the soil from the roots, then store the roots in a root cellar or basement at a temperature of 30° to 41°F (−1° to 5°C). To keep them from drying out, pack them into a box filled with sand or barely moist peat moss.

BROCCOLI

Broccoli is best in the fall. Cool weather is essential for broccoli, so it often can be grown in both spring and fall. Although the plants often become bitter and bolt when days get long and hot in late spring, this never happens in the fall. Set out plants in late summer, and they will continue to grow through the first few frosts. Instead of ruining broccoli, frost actually improves its flavor.

Pack more into the same space by planting seedlings only 8 inches (20 cm) apart. Although the heads will be smaller, the total yield will be up to twice that of the recommended 18- to 24-inch (45- to 60-cm) spacing. Broccoli is a heavy feeder, so use plenty of compost, add lime if the soil is naturally acidic, and rake in 1 pound

(450 grams) of 5-10-10 fertilizer for every 25 feet (8 meters) of row.

Get it to cut and come again. If you give plants wider spacing, you can often harvest small secondary heads after the first head is cut.

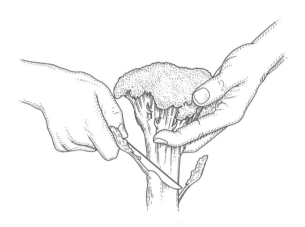

Varieties called sprouting types often produce so many sprouts that you can pick them for more than a month, but even nonsprouting types often produce good sideshoots. Always use angled cuts on the stalks so that rain or other moisture doesn't collect on the butt of the stem and set plant-killing rot into motion.

Try an offbeat broccoli. Two plants related to the familiar green-heading broccoli are gaining favor in American gardens. Broccoli raab, from Italy, has succulent leaves and button-size florets. Flowering gailon, also called Oriental broccoli, has leaves and buds with a sweet broccoli flavor. Both can be grown from seed sown directly in the garden first thing in spring. Better yet, sow them in late summer for a fall crop.

Try this season-stretching veggie. Brussels sprouts are tailor-made for the tail end of the season because cold temperatures bring out the best in the sprouts' sweet, nutty flavor. Start seeds indoors in midsummer and set the seedlings in the garden 8 to 10 weeks before your first fall frost. The plants will keep growing after that, and they can even withstand hard freezes. Where winters are mild, you can pick sprouts all winter long. In cold-winter areas, pull up the plants and stash them in an unheated garage, where they will keep for several weeks.

Give them plenty of legroom. Brussels sprouts need rich soil, full sun, and lots of space—2 feet (60 cm)—between plants. While the plants are young, fill spaces between them with quick crops of lettuce and radishes, which will happily grow to maturity in the gaps between the growing sprouts.

Push out your sprouts. A few days before harvesting sprouts, snap off a few of the lowest leaves to give the sprouts more room to grow. A month before harsh winter weather arrives, lop off the top 4 inches (10 cm) from each plant to help them hurry to produce big sprouts.

Not all sprouts are green. Fast-maturing 'Jade Cross' and 'Prince Marvel' varieties of Brussels sprouts are dependable and easy to grow, but why not grow what you can't buy? Look in seed catalogs for 'Rubine', a unique variety that produces rosy red sprouts.

Grow triple-season cabbage. If you love cabbage, set out a few seedlings in early spring for harvest in summer. Then make a larger planting in mid- to late summer to harvest in early winter. While you're waiting for heads to form, grow a small bed from direct-sown seeds and harvest them as leafy cooking greens as soon as they've been sweetened by a light frost.

Get a second cabbage crop from the same plants. If space is tight in your garden, get two cuttings from one planting. When you harvest the first batch, instead of cutting the stem at soil level, cut just below the head without removing the big "wrapper" leaves. With proper watering, smaller heads will develop on the stem near the base of the leaves.

You'll need to feed. Unless your soil is especially rich, fertilize your cabbage crop once a month by scattering a band of 10-10-10 fertilizer—or high-nitrogen organic fertilizer—in a band 6 inches (15 cm) wide around the base of each cabbage plant.

Watch for white butterflies. If you see white butterflies flitting among your cabbage, check the undersides of leaves for small yellow eggs. These will hatch into velvety green cabbageworms. They are easily controlled by applying *Bacillus thuringiensis* (Bt) insecticide, which is harmless to earthworms and beneficial insects. Reapply Bt every 7 to 10 days, especially after a good rain.

Go Asian for a change. Chinese cabbages combine the crunchy texture of lettuce with the flavor of cabbage. They come in two forms: tall, cylindrical Michihli cabbages, including 'China Express' and 'Orient Express', and barrel-shaped Napa types, such as 'Jade Pagoda'. Either type is a cinch to grow in the fall garden.

CARROTS

Plant carrots with coffee and radishes. To increase your carrot harvest, mix the seeds with unused ground coffee before sowing. Not only does the extra bulk make the tiny seeds easier to sow, but the coffee aroma may repel root maggots and other pests. As a bonus, the coffee will help add nutrients to the soil as it decomposes around the plants. You might also like to add a few radish seeds to the mix before sowing. The radishes will be up in a few days to mark the rows. When you pull them, you'll thin the carrot row and cultivate the soil at the same time.

Sow seeds in a row or a band as thinly as possible—no more than three seeds per inch (25 mm). Planting in rows is preferable, since it makes weeding easier. Tamp seeds in with the back of a rake to bury them ¼ to ½ inch (6 to 12 mm) deep. A few weeks later, thin the seedlings, leaving the strongest plant every 2 inches (5 cm) in the row for small varieties. Thin larger varieties to 3 inches (8 cm) apart.

Match varieties to soil type. Follow this rule when choosing varieties: The heavier the soil,

---

PLANT YOUR VEGGIES IN SEASON

Some like it hot, some like it cool, and vegetables also notice when days get longer in spring and shorter in the fall. Here's when to plant your favorites.

Early spring: Peas, potatoes, bread beans
Mid-spring: Beets, broccoli, cabbage, carrots, cauliflower, celery, fennel, lettuce, onions, radishes, Swiss chard
Late spring (after last frost): Beans, corn, cucumbers, eggplant, gourds, melons, peppers, squash, tomatoes
Early summer: Lima beans, okra, pumpkins, sweet potatoes
Late summer: Broccoli, cabbage, cauliflower, fennel, greens, lettuce
Fall: Garlic

---

the shorter the carrot should be. Varieties sold as either half-long or baby types are preferable to long, slim carrots for heavy clay soil. In extremely heavy soil, plant round varieties, which won't have to penetrate as deeply. Or you can plant carrots in raised beds. Locate the beds in full sun except in the hottest climates, where a little shade and extra watering are advisable.

There is a secret to growing sweet carrots. First, avoid high-nitrogen fertilizer, which can lead to coarse, hairy roots that are devoid of flavor. Second, time planting so the roots will mature in cool soil. Get a prompt start in spring, sowing seeds when apples are in bloom. Plant carrots again in late summer for harvest in the fall.

Store carrots in the ground. In most areas, you can cut off carrot tops in late fall, cover the bed with thick, organic mulch or bales of straw or hay, and dig carrots as you need them through most of the winter.

Try carrots of a different color. Most carrots are orange, and deep-orange carrots usually contain the most vitamin A. However, there are beautiful yellow, red, and purple carrots, too, such as 'Purple Haze', an All America Selections award winner with purple skin. All carrots with unusual skin colors have orange flesh.

CAULIFLOWER

Give cauliflower a stress-free life. The "queen of the brassicas" is a temperamental beauty that must grow quickly without any stress. Set out seedlings before they become root-bound, and time plantings to avoid both cold and heat. Set out your spring crop at about the time of your last frost, and plant fall cauliflower about 10 weeks before the first frost is expected.

Use leaves as a sunscreen. Sunlight will quickly turn the creamy-white heart of a ripening cauliflower yellow or even brown. As soon as the heads are 2 inches (5 cm) across, bend three or four of the innermost leaves over the center and secure them with a clothespin. Or simply break the leaves so they form a light-blocking blanket over the ripening head. Harvest the heads before they begin to look "ricey."

Try unusual varieties. You can buy white cauliflower in stores, so why not grow unique yellow, purple, or lime green varieties in your garden? Yellow-orange 'Cheddar' looks as if it's already been buttered, and purple 'Violet Queen' turns green when it's cooked.

CELERY

Expect something different. Celery from your garden will probably be much greener and leafier than the type you buy in the store, but it will be packed with flavor. Grow celery in cool weather and expect slender stalks. For tender,

WHAT'S WRONG WITH MY CARROTS?

SYMPTOM	EXPLANATION
Roots are forked	Soil is rocky or contains undecomposed organic matter
Roots are too short	Plants are too crowded, or weather has been too hot
Core is hard and woody	Lack of nutrients caused plants to grow too slowly, or roots were left in warm soil too long
Carrots have cracks	Uneven watering (carrots crack when subjected to dry, then wet conditions)
Shoulders are green and bitter	Tops of roots were exposed to strong sun; hill up a little soil over root tops or use mulch

light green stalks, you will need to blanch the plants. Two weeks before harvest time, wrap the stalk cluster in a cardboard sleeve tied with string, with the leafy top exposed to the sun.

Try celery's big-rooted cousin. Celeriac produces big, knobby roots just above the soil line, and you can use the leaves to flavor stocks and soups. Peeled and cooked, the roots are a uniquely crisp and flavorful vegetable.

The salad lover's celery is sometimes called par-cel, or cutting celery. It's much leafier than stalk-type celery but doesn't develop knobby roots like celeriac. Cutting celery is easy to grow in any fertile soil, and the young leaves can be chopped into salads or used as pot herbs. One or two plants is all you need for a full season of big celery flavor.

CORN

The perfect anchor crop for large gardens. Because it is pollinated by wind (with a little help from insects), sweet corn produces the best and biggest ears when it's planted in blocks of three or more adjoining rows. In small plantings, you can improve pollination by gathering pollen from the tassels at the tops of the plants and sprinkling it onto the silks as they emerge from the tips of the ears.

Fertilize twice. Corn is a heavy feeder, and the best way to keep it from going hungry is to fertilize it twice. Work balanced fertilizer into the soil before you plant seeds in mid- to late spring, then feed it again just as the tassels emerge from the tops of the plants. Use a fast-release fertilizer, such as inexpensive 10-10-10, for the second feeding, or use ammonium nitrate, a potent source of fast-acting nitrogen.

Practice artful hoeing. Use a sharp hoe to get rid of weeds that threaten to crowd out your corn. When it's knee high, use your hoe to hill up

SORTING THROUGH sweet corn

Hybrid sweet corn comes in several different packages, which are listed in catalogs by their genotype, each with its own code.

- **Sugary hybrids** (Su) have kernels with a sugar content of 5 to 10 percent and include traditional favorites like white 'Silver Queen' and yellow 'Early Sunglow'. Harvest ears when they are young and tender, because they will quickly become starchy if allowed to get overripe.

- **Sugary enhanced hybrids** (Se) combine the tenderness and the complex flavor of traditional sweet corn with a higher sugar content—15 to 18 percent—that holds for several days or even a week after the corn is ripe. Most home gardeners prefer Se types, which are available in dozens of different varieties.

- **Supersweet hybrids** (Sh2) have the highest sugar content of all (20 to 30 percent) but often at the expense of tenderness and flavor. The seeds are not strong sprouters, and the plants cannot be grown near other types of corn. Supersweets are fine for freezing and are available in white, yellow, or bicolor versions.ø

soil around the bases of the plants, which helps keep them from falling over when blasted by strong gusts of wind from summer thunderstorms.

Defeat corn earworms. This common corn pest wiggles into the tips of ears and helps itself to tender young kernels. A few days after the silk emerges from the developing ears, fill a medicine syringe with vegetable or mineral oil and apply several drops to the base of the silk. Then pop a clothespin over the tips of the ears.

Double-crop with beans. When your corn is about 1 foot (30 cm) tall, plant pole beans along the outermost row. The beans will twine up the stalks and be ready to start picking soon after the corn is ripe.

CUCUMBERS

Trellis cucumbers to save space and fight foliage diseases. Getting the leaves up high improves air circulation and allows them to dry more quickly. It also keeps the fruits off the soil, where they are susceptible to rust and rot. Gravity may help trellised fruits grow straighter, too, but the plants may need more water than usual because of increased exposure to wind and sun.

Sow cucumbers in peat pots instead of flats since the delicate seedlings won't tolerate any disturbance of their roots. Plant them out when they've grown two or three true leaves.

Encourage branching by pruning young plants as soon as they are carrying four leaves. Pinch off the tip of the stem, leaving two leaves at the bottom. Two stems will quickly grow where there once was only one.

Grow better, stronger fruits by leaving only four fruits on a plant at a time. When the tiny fruits begin to appear, thin them down to four by picking them by hand—they'll pop off easily. Baby cucumbers are a treat to eat after being marinated overnight in a vinaigrette dressing.

SORTING THROUGH cucumbers

- **Dark green slicing types** like 'Marketmore' and 'Straight 8' are the most popular cucumbers. All should be peeled before using, because the chemicals that cause digestive gas are found just below a cucumber's skin.

- **Chinese or hybrid "burpless" types** lack the chemicals that cause gas, so they are more easily digested. Varieties include the original 'Burpless', 'Orient Express', 'Green Knight', and 'Sweet Success'.

- **Pickling cucumbers** are shorter, thicker, and lighter in color than the slicing types. They typically produce more and smaller fruits—all at one time, making them ideal for harvesting in large batches. Good choices include 'National Pickle', 'Calypso', and compact 'Picklebush', a good choice for containers.

- **Unusual varieties** are fun to grow. 'Lemon' is a sweet-tasting heirloom variety with round yellow fruits that grow to the size of baseballs. An heirloom from Maine, 'Boothby's Blond' is a pale yellow pickler with black spines. Scan catalogs for the rare 'White Wonder', an ivory pickling cucumber that's popular in Europe.

Space savers. If your garden is small, sow compact hybrid varieties such as 'Salad Bush' or 'Spacemaster'. As long as you keep them watered, you can even grow them in a large pot or half barrel on a balcony or patio.

EGGPLANT

Help eggplant run on solar power. Eggplant loves sun and heat, so wait until the soil is warm before setting out seedlings, and plant the seedlings in the sunniest part of your garden. If your climate is cool, stick with small-fruited, fast-maturing varieties or grow eggplant in roomy black containers, which absorb solar heat. Eggplant's starry purple flowers make it a fine edible ornamental to grow in pots on your deck or patio. In cooler climates, space the plants 18 inches (45 cm) apart; in southern climates, space them 24 inches (60 cm) apart.

Foil flea beetles. Little black flea beetles love to chew hundreds of little holes in eggplant leaves. They may not manage to find eggplant grown in containers set on a high bench or table, but they will definitely find it in the garden. The best defense is to cover plants with lightweight floating row cover.

Cut the fruits before they become seedy. You will need pruning shears or a sharp knife to harvest eggplant fruits, complete with their little green or purple caps. Perfectly ripe fruits have glossy skins, and the seeds inside should be newly formed and far from mature.

FENNEL

Essential in the gourmet garden. The culinary herb known as fennel (*Foeniculum vulgare*) produces licorice-flavored seeds, but vegetable fennel (*F. vulgare* var. azoricum), also called finocchio or Florence fennel, is a true garden delicacy. The bulbous base is delicious raw or cooked, and you can use the ferny leaves as a flavorful garnish.

Spoil fennel with rich soil and cool temperatures. Vegetable fennel grows best in soil that has been generously enriched with compost and holds moisture well. Plant seeds in well-prepared soil at about the time of your last spring frost or you can set out seedlings in late summer for a luscious fall crop.

Get bigger bulbs. Make sure your fennel never runs short of water. When the bases begin to swell, mulch them with a light blanket of straw—a trick that helps the outer stalks stay as tender as those in the middle of the bulb.

GARLIC

Buy bulbs from catalogs or garden centers, which often offer varieties that you will never taste if you don't grow them yourself. Some are mild and some are hot, but when fresh from the garden, all are delicious.

Plant in fall about 4 inches (10 cm) deep. The best time is around mid-October (in the North) or November (in the South), so that cloves can establish a good root system that will withstand heaving. In cold climates, mulch over your garlic bed unless you anticipate a good cover of snow, which is a wonderful insulator.

For maximum production, plant only the biggest cloves from the outside of the largest bulbs and eat the culls and runts.

Garlic hates weeds. Weed by hand as often as needed to eliminate wild competitors, or use mulch, which also helps keep the soil moist the way garlic likes it.

As a companion plant, garlic is said to enhance the growth of fruit trees, strawberries, tomatoes, cabbage, and roses. Garlic planted near peas, beans, and asparagus supposedly hinders their growth.

Pull garlic once three-quarters of the stems become dry and brown. Leave the crop in the sun for a day or two and then move it to a dark, dry place for a week. Trim off the tops and store the heads in mesh bags at 40° to 50°F (4° to 10°C) in relatively low humidity. Never keep garlic in a moist root cellar, where it will rot.

Eat the leaves, too. Plant a few small cloves in a pot and snip the green sprouts as needed in the kitchen, just as you would use chives.

GOURDS

Only for show. Gourds are unusual-shaped vegetables in the cucurbit family, which also includes pumpkins, squashes, melons, and cucumbers. While they are edible when young, gourds are grown chiefly for the ornamental value of their shells when mature and dried. Some have brightly colored patterns of yellow, orange, and green, which can be preserved with varnish or wax. Others, called lagenarias or hard-shell gourds, dry to tan and can be crafted into dippers, bottles, rattles, or birdhouses.

Treat hardshells like tropicals. Sow these frost-tender plants where they'll get plenty of warmth and sunshine, and use black plastic mulch if your summers are on the cool side. They need at least 115 days to reach maturity, and the big ones take even longer. Colorful ornamental gourds are better for cool climates because they mature in only 80 to 90 days.

A dry climate? Create a basin in the soil around your gourds to hold moisture. Mulch with straw or shredded dead leaves to keep from wasting a drop of water.

In wet areas, plant gourds in mounds spaced 5 feet (1.5 meters) apart. Mulch to prevent soil erosion and inhibit weeds, as the fleshy roots grow very close to the soil surface.

Prevent rotting by keeping gourds off the ground. Once the fruits form, put them on a board supported by four overturned flowerpots or bricks or place them on several sheets of folded newspaper.

Time to harvest? Leave gourds on the vine until they are completely ripe, with hard rinds and dry stems. A light frost or two won't hurt gourds, but move them into a dry place before a hard freeze. Cut, don't pull, fruits from the vine, leaving 2 to 3 inches (5 to 8 cm) of stem attached. Handle carefully to avoid bruises, where rot can develop.

Cure gourds by letting them dry and harden in a warm, well-ventilated place for two to six months. Don't worry about any mold spots that develop on the surface—they won't damage fruits. Just scrub off the patches after the gourds have dried until you can hear seeds rattling around inside them.

GREENS

Mix and match. Greens comprise a range of vegetables grown for their leafy, dark green tops, and each type has a distinctive flavor and texture. Plant a mixture of collards, kale, broccoli raab, and turnip and mustard greens. To ensure a ready supply, plant a small bed or short row of the greens of your choice every 10 days in spring, then again in late summer or early fall. That way, you can always harvest the leaves in their prime.

Make a rich bed by turning compost or rotted manure into the ground before planting kale or collards, which are heavy feeders. Add 1 to 2 pounds (0.5 to 1 kg) of 10-10-10 fertilizer for every 50 square feet (5 square meters). Kale and collards prefer soil with a pH of 6.5 or above, so amend acidic soil with lime if needed.

Fertilize again for maximum production of nutritious leaves and stems. Feed greens when they are about 6 inches (15 cm) tall by spreading a band of 10-10-10 fertilizer at the rate of 1 cup per 10-foot (3-meter) row. Or douse them with a balanced, water-soluble fertilizer.

Grow kale as a winter crop. The hardiest of the greens, kale planted in late summer can often be enjoyed through most of the winter. In

TRY TECHNICOLOR GREENS

Not all greens are green, and some of the colored ones are pretty enough to grow in your vegetable garden. Try 'Red Giant' or 'Osaka Purple' mustard. Among kale, many gardeners love the color and flavor of 'Russian Red', also known as 'Rugged Jack'. 'Scarlet Queen Red Stem' turnips have bright red leaf veins, and beautiful red-skinned roots. Colorful greens lose most of their color when cooked.

Zones 7 to 9, collards are usually winter hardy, too. Don't worry if your kale and collards taste strong at first, because a few frosts trigger the production of sugar in the leaves. So, these greens taste best after cold weather arrives.

Not just for boiling. When grown in cool spring weather, baby mustard greens add a pleasant bite to salads. Clip leaves when they are less than 6 inches long. If you leave the crowns behind, the plants will quickly produce more tender leaves. Be sure to keep plants well watered. Dry soil or hot weather makes mustard greens taste hot and sometimes bitter. In early summer, pull up plants and compost them.

Use greens to smother weeds. The broad leaves of mustard greens make them a good edible cover crop to sow beneath taller plants. The leaves of the greens shade the surrounding soil, making it more difficult for weeds to germinate and grow there.

Go Asian in the fall. Numerous Asian greens such as mizuna and tatsoi grow beautifully in fall, when days are getting shorter and cooler rather than longer and hotter. These are often beautiful plants, as good for the flower garden as for your vegetable beds.

The best way to wash greens is to fill a large washtub or the kitchen sink with cold water. Put the greens into the water and swish them vigorously to remove dirt. Repeat with fresh water if the greens still hold dirt, then drain them in a colander or salad spinner.

Stir-fried or steamed? Tender young greens can be stir-fried or steamed briefly before being served. If you want to freeze them, you can steam them quickly in a covered container. Mature greens are tougher, so cook them longer to tenderize them and improve flavor.

LETTUCE

A cool customer. Lettuce prefers temperatures around 60° to 65°F (16° to 18°C) and turns bitter and bolts when days become long and hot. It needs full sun in cool weather but appreciates a little afternoon shade when days become warm.

Water well. Lettuce needs constant moisture for good growth. If too much water washes away nutrients, turning the leaves yellow, feed them with balanced water-soluble fertilizer.

To grow lettuce from seed, sow seeds barely covered in well-drained, moderately rich soil. Do several small sowings two weeks apart rather than one large planting.

Rabbits and other creatures love lettuce. To keep them away, fence with chicken wire or use a scent repellent. Some gardeners swear by interplanting with marigolds.

Harvest heading lettuces by cutting plants at the base. With leaf lettuces you can pick the outer leaves when they are still young, which encourages inner ones to grow. You can also cut a young plant 1 inch (13 mm) above the ground—it will grow back in a few weeks.

SORTING THROUGH
lettuce

Keep your lettuce patch lively by including different types, which vary in size, color, and, most of all, texture. Your garden will look more interesting, and so will your salads.

- **Butterhead or Boston lettuces** form loose heads with soft, buttery leaves. Try 'Buttercrunch', 'Nancy', 'Bibb', or 'Gem'. Butterheads mature in 60 to 75 days and often survive light frosts. Grown beneath a plastic tunnel, some will even survive winter.

- **Crisphead varieties** develop round or oblong heads with crisp, crunchy leaves. 'Iceberg' (60 days) is the best known, but French crisp varieties such as 'Nevada' or red-tinged 'Magenta' (50 days) grow faster and easier.

- **Looseleaf lettuces** quickly form spreading bunches of leaves, and new leaves keep coming as you pick the older ones. Very fast, easy, and tolerant of heat, looseleaf lettuces are available in a huge range of leaf colors and textures. Baby leaf lettuce is ready in 30 days; plants are mature in 50 days.

- **Romaine lettuce** produces long, narrow leaves with crisp stems that form an upright head. It tolerates both heat and cold well. Miniature varieties mature in only 45 to 50 days. Full-size romaines need 60 days to form crisp heads.

MELONS

Set seeds tip down. Melon seeds sprout best when planted with their pointy tips facing down. For a head start, sow seed indoors three weeks before your last spring frost and set the plants out when they are a month old.

Keep melons off the soil. To prevent rot, slip a board or flat tile underneath the fruits once they reach the size of an orange. Heat-absorbing tiles will also provide extra warmth in cool climates.

Support small melons. Keep small melons such as cantaloupes and muskmelons off the ground and free of pests and disease by using legs cut from old pantyhose as protective sleeves for them. As young melons start to develop, slide each one into the foot section of a leg and tie it to a stake to suspend the melon above the ground. The nylon "hammocks" will stretch as the melons mature and keep them from touching the soil.

Mulch, don't weed. Because working around vines may disturb the transmission of nutrients to the fruits, avoid pulling weeds in your melon patch. The easiest way is to prepare the planting site and then cover it with a weed barrier mat, sold at garden centers. Anchor the edges with rocks, cut slits where you want to plant, and put in your seeds or transplants. If you take up the barrier at the end of the season and store it in a dry place, it will last for several years.

For the best fruits, allow only four or five melons to ripen on each plant. Pinch off all the other young fruits while they are small and green.

Sweeten the crop. Give melons 1 inch (3 cm) of water weekly until three weeks before harvest. When the melons are almost ripe, withhold moisture, to concentrate their sugars.

SORTING THROUGH
melons

- **Cantaloupe** is a type of muskmelon. For short-season regions, try 'Delicious' or 'Earli-Sweet'. In warmer areas, grow 'Ambrosia' or a cousin of the cantaloupe, such as the Persian or crenshaw.
- **Honeydew** varieties include 'Rocky Sweet Hybrid', 'Limelight', and 'Snow Charm'.
- **Watermelon** choices include 'Sugar Baby', a small, round melon with crimson fruit, and the yellow-fleshed 'Yellow Baby' or 'Sunshine'.

Is it ripe? Good question! With cantaloupes, you can press against the blossom end (not the end with the stem). It will give slightly and smell sweet when the fruit is ripe. Honeydews usually change rind color as they reach full ripeness. With watermelons, look at the curled tendril nearest the stem. If it's dry and brown, tap the melon with your knuckles. A ripe melon gives off a deeper sound than one that isn't quite ready.

OKRA

A tropical shrub that can reach a full 6 feet (2 meters) tall, okra is grown as a warm-weather annual. Not too fussy about soil, okra thrives in heat and full sun and will grow wherever corn succeeds. You can tell it's a member of the hibiscus family by its showy yellow blooms.

Many okra varieties no longer have tiny, prickly spines that will make you itch, but it's still wise to wear long sleeves when cutting the pods. You'll need a sharp knife or pruning shears to harvest okra, which must be cut from the stem just above the pods' green caps.

The best pods are small and tender, so try to get them when they're less than 5 inches (13 cm) long. Pods grow fast in hot weather and more slowly when temperatures are below 70°F (21°C).

Try going red. Red-tinted varieties, such as 'Burgundy', look great as edible ornamentals, and you can even use them as living trellises for flowering vines. You can grow red or green okra in containers, too, where it makes a fine upright focal point.

Rejuvenate tired plants in late summer by pruning them back by about one-third their size. Side shoots will then grow into new bearing branches, providing you with a late-season bumper crop of tender pods.

Try it grilled. It's true that boiled okra is slimy, but grilled okra will convert the most finicky eaters. Thread pods crosswise onto a skewer, douse them with Italian salad dressing, and grill them for 3 minutes on each side, or until nicely browned.

ONIONS

Familiar bulb onions may be white, yellow, or red and range from the size of tiny pearls to that of softballs. When growing onions for big bulbs, be sure to choose a variety that matures in keeping with your climate. In the North, choose long-day varieties, because onions form bulbs in response to day length. Short-day varieties are better for southern areas.

Bunching onions, often called scallions or green onions, are easy and productive, and you can even transplant grocery store scallions to your garden and pull them when you need them in the kitchen. They make great row markers, too. Simply stick a scallion in the ground to mark where you left off seeding lettuce or another direct-seeded crop.

❧ Grandpa's wisdom

Folklore has it that you can tell how brutal the coming winter will be by counting an onion's outer skins at harvest. If the layers are thin and few, winter will be mild; if they are thick and numerous, get out your long johns.

Sets or seeds? Onion sets (young bulbs grown the previous year) are convenient, fast growing, and quick to mature. But only a limited number of cultivars—many with a pungent taste—are available as sets. Good sweet onions are grown from seed, but because onion seedlings grow slowly, it's best to buy them in bundles instead of growing them yourself.

Don't plant too early. Although onion seedlings tolerate cold weather well, exposure to spring freezes sometimes encourages them to develop flowering stalks at the expense of big bulbs. Set out sets or seedlings no more than a month before your last spring frost date.

Feed them early. Fertilize onions with high-nitrogen fertilizer such as fish emulsion early in the season, because big plants grow big bulbs. Bulbs ripen better under dry, less fertile conditions, so cut back on food and water in midsummer.

Give bulbs a push that speeds ripening by loosening the soil around them with a hoe as soon as they begin to swell. Or keep them mulched with a fine-textured material, such as grass clippings, spread around the plants in thin layers.

When are they ready? When the tops begin to turn yellow, bend the leaves over with the back of a rake; this will divert the plant's energy to the bulbs instead of the stems. A few days later, after the tops have turned brown, lift the bulbs with a fork. Lay them out to dry in a warm, shady spot protected from rain.

To cure onions, drape the tops over the edges of a large pail or hang them on a clothesline and fasten them in place with clothespins. When the skins feel dry and papery, cut the onions from the stems and store them in a cool, dry place.

PEAS

Pick your perfect pea. Peas come in three forms: garden peas (also called shell peas), snap peas, and snow peas—the latter two with crisp, edible pods. Select from dwarf, midsize, or tall types and early, mid-season, or late varieties. Go with snap peas if you want the most food per foot of row.

Spring standouts. Peas need cool weather, so plant them in early spring. Young seedlings are quite hardy and will sometimes come up through late spring snows. To make sure the site is ready for timely planting, prepare the bed or row in the fall. That way, you won't have to cultivate before poking the seeds into the ground.

A pea tepee. A decorative and practical way to plant peas is in a ring around a tepee. Use

slender tree branches with plenty of twigs. Push 5-foot (1.5-meter) stakes about 1 foot (30 cm) into the soil and plant peas at their base.

Get 'em when they're sweet. If you give peas a raw taste test, you'll quickly learn when they

are at their best. The pods of perfect shell peas are bumpy and slightly waxy, while perfect snap peas are plump, with small, slightly immature seeds inside. Pick snow peas when the pods are still flat or when the seeds in the pods have just begun to swell. Eat or chill peas right away because their sugars quickly convert to starch.

PEPPERS

These tropical natives, whether sweet or hot, need warmth to thrive. Big, sweet bell peppers need plenty of moisture, too, although hot peppers like slightly drier conditions. Start seeds indoors six weeks before you want to set out plants and keep them at about 70°F (21°C). Transplant outdoors a month after the last frost, once the soil temperature is above 65°F (18°C).

Don't plant peppers where you previously grew potatoes, eggplant, or tomatoes. All of these members of the nightshade family are prone to the same soilborne diseases.

Dig deep and plant deep. Peppers like a well-aerated bed. Turn the soil to 1 foot (30 cm) deep and amend with a generous shovelful of compost for each plant. Set seedlings a little deeper than they grew in their containers, so that the low seedling leaves are barely covered. Peppers don't develop roots along their stems; deep planting insulates roots from heat and dryness.

Mulch with plastic for great peppers. For healthy, productive peppers, mulch around the plants with black plastic: split-open garbage bags

SORTING THROUGH peppers

Peppers come in so many different packages that it's easy to get confused.

- **Bell peppers** are considered sweet peppers, although they don't actually taste sweet until they change colors and become red, orange, or yellow. Pimiento peppers are similar, with very thick flesh.

- **Unusual sweet peppers** include 'Gypsy', which has a conical shape. There are also sweet bananas and wonderfully flavorful frying and roasting peppers with long, tapered fruits. These unusual sweet peppers often produce better in short-season areas than large-fruited bell peppers.

- **Mildy hot peppers** include jalapeño, Anaheim, and poblano peppers, as well as many slightly hot varieties seldom seen in stores, such as 'Garden Salsa'. If you like only a little heat, check catalogs for these low-burn varieties.

- **Hot peppers** include Serranos and cayennes, which are plenty hot, but some people really go for the burn by growing habaneros.

are fine. It warms the soil for these heat-loving plants and protects against soil-borne fungal diseases transmitted by splashing water.

The way to water. Sweet peppers need even, moderate moisture around their roots. Water with a drip irrigation or soaker hose hidden beneath a mulch of grass clippings or hay.

To grow the hottest chiles, plant them in your sunniest spot and harvest on the warmest days. Hot weather brings out their heat.

Help sweet peppers set more fruit in hot weather by using some kind of shade cover. You can angle one over the south side of your plantings or tie a piece of lightweight cloth to stakes.

Taste of honey. When your peppers blossom, put several drops of honey on each plant. This attracts bees, which pollinate the plants. Repeat regularly and you'll get more and larger peppers.

POTATOES

Don't go for big bakers—unless you live in Idaho. Large baking potatoes require a long, cool season, but smaller varieties mature much faster. Grow what you can't buy, such as little potatoes with buttery yellow flesh or oblong "fingerling" types. Blue potatoes are fun to grow, too, such as the 'All Blue' variety, or try 'Caribe', which has snowy white flesh beneath purple skins.

Help potatoes keep their cool. Plant early, two to three weeks before your last expected frost, while the soil is still chilly. When leaves and stems appear, start mulching to keep the soil cool and moist. Potatoes stop growing new tubers when the soil gets warm, so it's best to help them get a fast start in spring.

Keep them in the dark. Light turns potatoes green and causes solanine, a mildly toxic substance that tastes bitter, to develop. As plants grow, keep mounding soil or mulch up around them to prevent sun from reaching the tubers, some of which are just below the soil surface. Wait for a cloudy day to harvest so your potatoes won't be exposed to bright light.

Sneak new potatoes. True new potatoes are small potatoes gathered while the plants are still green. Carefully pull back the mulch, feel around for a few treasures, and put the mulch back in place after you've gathered your dinner potatoes. The plants won't even notice they're gone. Harvest the rest of your crop when the plants begin to die back naturally.

Watch for Colorado potato beetle larvae. Fat, reddish bugs chewing potato leaves and flowers are the larvae of Colorado potato beetles. Pick them off, spray them with a neem-based insecticide, or better yet, nab them before they hatch. Check leaf undersides for clusters of yellow eggs and pinch off the egg-bearing leaves.

PUMPKINS

Pumpkins love summer, and some large-fruited varieties require about 110 frost-free days to mature. In northern areas, some pumpkin-loving gardeners start seeds indoors under lights three weeks before their last frost date. Farther south, the Fourth of July is considered prime time for planting pumpkins.

Records to beat. If you want to win a blue ribbon for the biggest pumpkin at the county fair, choose one of the *Cucurbita maxima* varieties.

'Mammoth Gold' will tip the scales at 100 pounds (45 kg), 'Big Moon' may hit 200 pounds (90 kg), and 'Atlantic Giant' will grow to a whopping 400 pounds (180 kg). The latter holds the world record. Let the plant form three fruits, then cut off two, leaving only the largest one to grow.

Say cheese. Pumpkins with *cheese* in their names—including 'Long Island Cheese,' which has a round, flattened shape like a wheel of cheese—are resistant to squash vine borers. Cheese pumpkins are also better than jack o'lantern types for making pies.

Cure harvested pumpkins for a week in a dry place at a temperature of about 75°F (24°C). To kill bacteria and fungi on the skin, dip the pumpkin in a weak chlorine solution (1 part bleach to 10 parts water). Store in an unheated attic away from dampness.

Miniature pumpkins are easy to grow, and they're great for a child's garden. Simply plant the seeds in an old compost heap, and in 10 weeks or so, you will have dozens of palm-size pumpkins.

RADISHES

Often the first vegetables harvested in spring, radishes are great for salads or relishes, and the best-quality ones are grown quickly in cool soil. Because they grow so fast, radishes make good row markers to separate small plantings of lettuce or other salad crops.

(Continued on page 170)

Perpetual Perennial Vegetables

If you have enough space, consider setting aside part of your garden for vegetables that will come back year after year. Incorporate them into parts of your yard where you grow shrubs or fruits, and you can harvest good things to eat without replanting each year. Here are three easy-to-grow perennial vegetables for your garden.

ASPARAGUS

Grow an all-male asparagus plot. Older open-pollinated strains, such as 'Martha Washington', include both male and female plants, but all-male hybrids grow faster and bear much bigger spears. To make sure your plants are male, use ' Jersey Giant', 'Jersey General', 'Jersey Knight', or other all-male Jersey hybrids. Another reliable hybrid is the productive 'UC 157'.

Be sure to plant plenty. Put in about 25 asparagus roots for each member of your family—more if you want to freeze some for later. To set out 50 plants, use a 30-foot (9-meter) double row, 3 feet (1 meter) wide. Beyond attentive weeding for 2 years, an asparagus plot needs little attention to produce well for 10 to 20 years.

Give the plants a soft blanket. Mulch your asparagus bed every fall and spring to maintain a continuous 4- to 6-inch (10- to 15-cm) cover of compost and rotted manure. Not only will you keep weeds away and conserve moisture, but you'll build a compost pile right on top of the dormant crowns, assuring your crop a long, productive life. Don't use sawdust or bark; both are too acidic for asparagus. Asparagus likes near-neutral soil, with a pH of 6.5.

No need to wait. Despite what you've heard, you don't have to wait until the third year to pick asparagus. Begin harvesting a few spears the second year during the month before your last spring frost. Each season, harvest all of the spears that emerge early, because they will probably be frozen back anyway. Once your patch is three or more years old, harvest for six weeks every spring, or until the average size of the spears declines to the diameter of a pencil.

Use asparagus fronds in cut flower arrangements. Fern-like asparagus foliage is so lovely in cut flower arrangements that some florists depend on it for green filler. Combine it with pretty summer flowers, such as cosmos or zinnias.

JERUSALEM ARTICHOKES

Pair them with asparagus. Jerusalem artichokes—also called sunchokes—aren't artichokes at all, but rather native perennial sunflowers. Even though you will dig up most of the roots every fall, a few will slip by you and grow into new plants the next spring, so plant them behind asparagus, which often stays put for decades.

Use them as flowering screens. In rich soil and partial shade, Jerusalem artichokes can grow 6 to 12 feet (2 to 4 meters) tall. Pick a spot where they shade other plants. With their head-high yellow flowers, they make a good screen for compost heaps or other unsightly areas.

Watch out for problems. Dig all the roots you can find in fall until the ground freezes and then again in spring as soon as the soil has thawed. In a heavily mulched bed, the tubers can even be dug from underneath a blanket of winter snow. Plots left undug can grow so well that the plants become invasive.

Problems to watch for. The tubers are often attacked by cutworms. And root-rot fungi may occur when the soil is too wet.

RHUBARB

Staying power. A rare vegetable perennial well suited to cool climates, rhubarb plants live for a long time. A well-tended rhubarb plant, started from seed or a root crown, can be harvested from for decades. 'MacDonald' has bright red stalks and excellent flavor, while 'Starkrimson' is less acidic and prized for its sweetness and deep red color.

For a heartier harvest, prune rhubarb flowers as soon as they form. The ornamental spikes—prized for their beauty by some gardeners—draw nutrients from the edible stalks.

☙ Watch Out!

Never eat rhubarb greens, which contain very high levels of oxalic acid. The stems are the only plant part that should be consumed.

Red alert. Rhubarb stalks are ready to pull when they are 1 to 1½ feet (30 to 45 cm) long. The newly developing stalks of the deepest red usually have the best flavor. Pulling season is over when emerging stalks stay small.

Spare the knife. When harvesting, never cut a rhubarb stalk off the plant, or the remaining stub will bleed and invite rot. Instead, hold the stalk near the base and give it a slight twist as you pull it away.

For something different, look for the popular 'Easter Egg' mix: radishes with skins of purple, lavender, pink, or rose. 'French Breakfast' is a red oblong type with a white tip, while 'White Icicle', with pure white skin, grows into a graceful tapered form up to 5 inches (13 cm) long.

Grandpa's wisdom

If your radishes have begun to plump up and you hear thunder, go ahead and pull them. Sudden deluges of rain often cause radishes to crack. You can eat cracked radishes, but they're not as pretty as perfect ones.

Encourage fast growth by giving radishes plenty of water; they can't tolerate drought conditions or heat waves. Sow them where they'll have partial shade at the hottest times of the day—planting near climbing beans or corn is ideal. If no shade is available, mulch the crop so it stays cool or use a summer-weight floating row cover. The right conditions will result in crunchy radishes that aren't too peppery hot.

SPINACH

Long, hot days cause spinach to bolt—that is, to flower and stop growing before maturing into the size you want for the table. Because of this, spinach grown in spring is naturally short-lived, but fall crops last much longer because days are getting shorter and cooler instead of longer and warmer. In many areas, fall spinach will survive winter and grow new leaves in spring, so don't miss that fall planting. Frost makes spinach sweeter, which is another reason to plant your biggest crop in late summer or early fall.

Grow spinach from fish. Spinach goes into high gear when it gets plenty of nitrogen. Plant in rich, fertile soil and feed plants weekly with 1 tablespoon (15 ml) fish emulsion mixed with 1 gallon (4 liters) of water, up until the week before you begin harvesting big, crisp leaves.

Try different textures. Smooth-leafed varieties like 'Space' grow fast and make great baby salad greens, but varieties with crinkled, savoyed leaves, such as 'Tyee' and 'Bloomsdale Longstanding', become super-crisp in cold weather.

Harvest in the morning. Spinach picked in the morning, rinsed clean, and promptly refrigerated is crispier than leaves harvested later in the day—and more nutritious. During the night, spinach leaves replenish their supply of moisture and nutrients.

SQUASH

Squash all season. Summer squash, including yellow crookneck and straightneck, zucchini, and scallop (also called pattypan) squash, grow fast and produce heavily when planted in late spring. A few weeks later, plant winter squash in hills, sowing five seeds in each and thinning to the best three seedlings. Be sure to allow at least 6 to 8 feet (2 to 2.5 meters) around the hill for the vines to spread. Most summer squash grow into big, bushy plants, but winter squash run a little or a lot, depending on the variety.

Try two-season butternuts. Butternuts are the most nutritious winter squash you can grow, and they are naturally resistant to squash vine borers. Plant plenty, and harvest some of the fruits when they're immature, like summer squash. They're as tasty as zucchini, and picking some young ones will increase the size of the fruits you allow to mature.

All squash like rich soil and plenty of sunshine. Prepare for planting by digging a hole large enough to hold a bushel of cow manure or compost; dump it in and top off with 3 inches (8 cm) of good garden loam.

Where to plant. Don't place where squash and its relatives have been grown in the past year or so. To confuse squash vine borers and cucumber beetles, interplant squash with radishes or basil.

Squash's best friend. Black plastic mulch may not be pretty, but squash love it anyway. Use it to raise the soil temperature, conserve moisture, reduce weeds, and deter pests.

To save space, pinch off the vine ends after enough fruit has set and turn the tips of the vines back toward the hill. Or train the plants on a trellis or tripod, supporting the fruits in a sling of pantyhose or soft cloth—perhaps an old bedsheet. Keeping them off the ground also exposes the fruits to more sun, prevents rotting, and makes harvesting easier.

Harvest winter squash once the rinds are firm and the vines begin to shrivel. Cut the stem about 2 inches (5 cm) above the fruit. While no

SORTING THROUGH squash

With so many types of squash to choose from, you will never be bored in the squash patch.

Summer Squash

- **Yellow squash** can have straight or curved necks, and all have a mild flavor.
- **Zucchini** is not always green. Gardeners can also grow gold or striped zucchini.
- **Scallop or pattypan squash** is much loved by trendy chefs, probably because the young, immature squash are so pretty on a plate.
- **Middle Eastern varieties** have smooth green skins and are often even more productive than zucchini.

Winter Squash

- **Buttercup types** are the favorites of Midwestern pie makers, and the vigorous vines produce supplemental roots along their stems.
- **Acorn squash** mature faster than other winter types, are available in space-saving bush varieties, and they're great for stuffing.
- **Delicata or sweet potato squash** are just the right size for single servings, and these pretty squash are good for stuffing, too.
- **Hubbards** can be huge, and they store well when kept in a cool, dry place.
- **Butternuts** are tops in nutrition, and many people think they are the most versatile winter squash for cooking. They resist pests and store for a long time.

FRIED FLOWERS, ANYONE?

Male summer squash blossoms—identifiable by their lack of a swelling at the base of the petals—can be picked for hors d'oeuvres without slowing down production in your squash patch. Here's a good way to prepare them. Wash the flowers and pat them dry. Make a thin batter by beating an egg with 1 cup (240 ml) of ice-cold water. Put 1 cup (240 cc) of flour into a bowl, add the egg mixture, and stir; the batter should be thin, with a few small lumps. Heat 1 to 2 inches (2 to 5 cm) of oil to 360°F (182°C) in a skillet. Dip the blossoms in the batter and fry four at a time for 1 minute on each side. Drain on paper towels, sprinkle with salt and pepper, and serve warm.

squash is frost hardy, don't worry about cool fall nights—they intensify the sugars in the flesh and produce the sweet flavor.

SWEET POTATOES

Savor a sweet-tasting tuber. Related to the morning glory, the sweet potato is a tropical vine that performs best in regions with long, hot summers and makes a fine summer groundcover. Grown from slips, or rooted sprouts, sweet potatoes develop best in sandy loam and need full sun and about 120 days of warm temperatures.

Make a mound by pushing soil to about 1 foot (30 cm) high and 1 foot wide—sweet potatoes will appreciate the good drainage. Plant the slips

4 inches (10 cm) deep at 15-inch (38-cm) intervals and keep them moist for several days. Sweet potato slips are usually planted in hot weather, so it helps to cover them with a box or flowerpot to shield them from strong sun for a few days after planting.

Watch them run. Lush sweet potato vines make a beautiful groundcover, and some are grown strictly as ornamentals. With either edible or ornamental sweet potatoes, you can increase your supply by snipping off 6-inch (15-cm) stem tips and rooting them in moist potting soil.

Give them the cure. After digging sweet potatoes, cure them in a warm—85°F (29°C)—place for 7 to 10 days. This curing period helps to toughen the skins and makes the tubers taste sweeter. After curing, switch your tubers to a cooler spot where temperatures are between 55° and 65°F (13° and 18°C). They will keep for four to five months.

SWISS CHARD

A beautiful green related to beets, Swiss chard is grown for both its crunchy leaf ribs and its deep green leaves. More tolerant of hot weather than other cooking greens, chard retains its mild flavor through the summer. You can eat Swiss chard raw, but it's better when lightly cooked.

Turn on the lights. 'Bright Lights' is a colorful variety that includes plants with stems of electric colors, from yellows to deep violet red, and outside leaves that can be harvested to cut and come again all season long. Other varieties have red or white ribs.

The more fertilizer and compost you give chard, the more it will grow. Dig in plenty of well-aged manure before planting this big eater. Once plants are 6 inches (15 cm) tall, feed with 5-10-5 fertilizer every month or so, using 3 ounces (85 grams) per 10-foot (3-meter) row.

Prolong the harvest by picking the outer leaves a few at a time after the plants grow to 10 inches (25 cm) tall. The best tool for harvesting chard is your hands; simply twist off the stem at its base. Don't use a knife, which might injure the inner stems and prevent further growth.

TOMATOES

A nightshade cousin, the tomato was long believed poisonous—or at the very least unpalatable. Legend holds that it was shunned in America until Robert Johnson of Salem, New Jersey, took it upon himself to popularize it. In 1820, standing before an assembled crowd of dubious townsfolk at the courthouse, he consumed a basketful of the vile fruit. After he suffered no ill effects, tomatoes were accepted at last, and these days, every vegetable gardener grows them. With tomatoes available in many shapes, colors, and sizes, a garden delivers few rewards more cherished than the flavor of a ripe, homegrown beauty.

How many to plant? Estimate two plants per household tomato lover. Tomatoes aren't difficult

STRANGE APPETITES

Good tomato fertilizers are low in nitrogen because too much nitrogen promotes foliage growth and makes fruits taste watery and bland. Creative gardeners have discovered other tricks to satisfy tomatoes' appetites.

Epsom salts. Every week, for every foot (30 ml) of height of your tomato plant, add 1 tablespoon (15 cc) to a gallon (4 liters) of water and pour it on. The magnesium in Epsom salts is a good nutritional supplement.

Banana peels. When buried in the bottom of a tomato planting hole, fresh banana peels act as a slow-release fertilizer, providing potassium and trace elements.

Eggshells. Every week or two, crush eggshells in a blender and add them to the water for your tomatoes—about six shells per quart (liter). The extra calcium aids growth of the leaf tips and blossom ends and prevents blossom-end rot.

to grow if you have a sunny spot for them. Garden centers offer a good selection of seedlings in spring, or you can grow seedlings indoors starting a month before the last spring frost.

Plant leggy seedlings in trenches because tomatoes grow roots from buried sections of stem. Lay the root ball on its side in a rectangular hole dug to a depth of at least 6 inches (15 cm). Hold the stem erect while covering the root ball and the lower part of the stem with soil.

Saving the Harvest

If you're lucky, you will grow more than your family can eat, which means you'll need to handle your largess.

Some vegetables, such as winter squash, onions, potatoes, and cabbage, only need cool storage to last a longtime. With most vegetables, you have three main options—freezing, canning, or drying. Drying is the most practical in arid climates. Canning is more complicated because most vegetables are low-acid foods, so they must be canned in a pressure canner. Freezing is the most practiced and easiest option. Here are some tips on freezing.

Blanch vegetables in boiling water before freezing them, which helps fix nutrients and keeps them in better condition after they're frozen. It can also improve their color. Blanching means plunging them in boiling water for about 30 seconds, then quickly cooling them in ice water before preparing them for the freezer.

Allow expansion space. When freezing vegetables in broth or water, leave a bit of extra space in the container. Freezing increases volume, and without extra room, the bags or containers will burst.

Freeze by the piece. After veggies have been blanched and have cooled slightly, place them on baking sheets and pop them into the freezer. When they're frozen hard, switch them to freezer-safe plastic containers.

Help your freezer door shut tightly by raising the front edge of the appliance slightly with a thin piece of wood. If you forget to close the door firmly, it will shut itself.

Keep it full. In case of a breakdown or blackout, a full freezer will stay cold longer than a half-empty one. Fill plastic milk jugs or drink bottles nearly full and use them to fill in empty freezer space. If a prolonged blackout does occur, cover your freezer with a thick blanket and avoid opening it.

WHAT'S YOUR TOMATO TYPE?

Determinate, or bush, tomatoes are bred to be compact, and the tallest determinate varieties grow to only 4 feet (1 meter). Smaller ones are happy to grow in pots, and determinate varieties often mature early and require very little staking. The tradeoff? All the tomatoes ripen at about the same time, and then the plants go downhill. However, vigorous deteminates, such as 'Celebrity' will often make a comeback if you prune the plants back by half their size.

Indeterminate, or vining, tomatoes continue to blossom and set fruits for as long as the plants are healthy. They tend to have very long branches that require serious staking, but their flavor is often excellent. Popular indeterminate tomato varieties include the red hybrid 'Better Boy' and cherry tomatoes such as 'Sweet 100'.

Tomatoes in the round? Try planting tomatoes in a circle around a central compost bin. As nutrients from the compost are washed down into the surrounding soil, the tomatoes can help themselves to a buffet of nutrients.

Protect tomatoes from aphids by surrounding plants with aluminum foil, shiny side up. In cool climates, radiant heat reflected from the foil will speed ripening of the fruits by about two weeks.

Compensate for blossom drop, which often occurs in cool, wet weather or on hot, windy days, by helping the remaining blossoms set fruit. On a day that's warm, calm, and dry, aid pollination by gently shaking the plant or tapping its stake. Welcome big bumblebees: they are excellent pollinators.

Water with sugar. When the fruits begin showing color, add a spoonful of sugar to their water—the tomatoes will be sweeter and juicier. But go easy: minimizing water while fruits ripen enhances their flavor.

What about heirlooms? Historical old varieties that have been treasured for many years have earned their way into the tomato flavor hall of fame. However, few heirlooms resist common diseases, and they are rarely as productive as hybrids. When selecting heirloom varieties, stick with names that are known to grow well in your area. Local greenhouse growers are often a good source of locally adapted heirloom tomato plants.

❧ Herbs

GROWING HERBS CREATES A FEAST for the senses. In summer, you might see a striking red bee balm blossom against a backdrop of green, or lacy dill fronds exploding with a crown of delicate yellow blooms. Meanwhile, you might sample the sunny Mediterranean flavor of basil or inhale the tart citrus aroma of lemon balm. Or, months after winter has begun, you might open a drawer and catch a sweet, clean whiff of a lavender sachet. Whether you're in it for the sensory pleasures, to provide material for crafts, or to have garden-fresh herbs for gourmet meals, herbs are among a gardener's most beloved friends. In this section, you'll find tips for growing and using more than a dozen garden herbs that are guaranteed to tantalize your senses and draw you out to the garden.

BASIL

A warm-natured annual, basil (*Ocimum basilicum*) cannot stand cold soil. Wait until your last frost is long gone to plant purchased seedlings in your garden or in pots kept in a sunny spot. If you can't get enough of this delicious herb, sow some seeds at the same time you set out purchased seedlings.

Bargain basil. When you buy basil plants, don't be surprised if you find several seedlings in a container. Gently separate them without pulling on the stems and transplant them to individual pots or directly to your garden. After transplanting, water the plants well and cover them with an upside-down flowerpot for a couple of days to protect them from strong sun.

The secret of long production. Pinching back basil shoots keeps the plants from flowering, which reduces flavor, and promotes the growth of bushy branches. Pinch plants every one to two weeks, just above the point where two little leaf buds cling to the stem.

Try different varieties. 'Sweet Genovese' is popular and versatile, and there are wonderful basils with purple leaves, too. Small-leafed globe basil is ideal for small pots or for planting in a large container with other culinary herbs.

Basil blackens when cut, so chop it at the last minute, just before adding it to a dish. Heat or vinegar-based salad dressing helps to fix its color. Basil also blackens when you freeze it, but once thawed, frozen basil holds its flavor better than the dried version.

CHIVES

A hardy perennial, chives (*Allium schoenoprasum*) are members of the onion family and are quite handy as a culinary herb. The entire plant is tasty, with the white shanks acting as a delicate substitute for scallions; the leaves making a versatile flavoring for dips, salads, spreads, and, of course, baked potatoes; and the flower heads lending a splash of color to salads. Don't overlook Chinese chives, also known as garlic chives. They bear flat leaves that are edible when young and produce a beautiful show of white flowers in late summer.

Chives will grow in almost all soils, but the ideal site is comprised of well-dug soil that has been amended with compost or organic material and a handful or two of bonemeal. Chives are equally happy in full sun or partial shade and are fairly drought tolerant—just don't plant them in very dry places.

Grow chives in pots in cold-weather regions. At the end of summer, cut back a few of the tufts to the base and transplant the clumps to a pot with other hardy herbs—perhaps parsley or thyme. Bring them inside to a sunny spot. With enough light, they will last for weeks and even for months.

Garden décor. Employ chives' blue-green foliage and pastel flowers to best effect along low borders in vegetable gardens or flowerbeds. Alternate with bellflowers or carnations for a pleasing look.

Divide crowded clumps in early spring in temperate climates. In hot climates, wait until fall. Your chives will remain tender and fragrant.

Harvest often for maximum growth, cutting tufts about 2 inches (5 cm) from ground level. If the tufts are large, harvest only half the plant at any one time. To prevent yellowing, don't harvest the leaves in small bits. Use scissors or a knife to snip off whole stems or portions of tufts instead; this spurs the growth of new leaves.

Mini-bouquets. The flowers that look so dainty in borders or beds ultimately hinder production and harvest of the leaves. Cut the flowers off at the base when they're buds and make little bouquets out of them, or pinch them apart and add the florets to spring salads.

The best way to store. Chives don't dry well, so freeze what you want to use later. Harvest the tufts, being careful to keep leaves pointing in the same direction. Pick them over and remove yellow foliage, rinse, and dry with paper towels. Lift a small handful, fold it in half, and place it in a small freezer bag. Never chop chives before freezing because the pieces will stick to your fingers and the plastic bag, and many will be lost.

Winter forcing. Lift the prettiest tufts in November and cut back the tops to 1 inch (3 cm) above the crown. Plant them in a small pot and store it in a dry root cellar for a few weeks. This period of rest is necessary before growth restarts. Bring the pot inside after a month, cut off any yellowed leaves, and place the pot in a warm, sunny spot. Young leaves will quickly develop.

DILL

A fast-growing annual herb that likes cool weather, dill (*Anethum graveolens*) originated in eastern Europe and can be grown in a container or garden patch. Fresh, frozen, or dried, the wispy, fern-like foliage and flat seeds lend a tasty flavor to fish, potatoes, peas, and, of course, pickles. Dill tolerates most growing conditions and germinates readily, so it's ideal for novice gardeners or youngsters.

Let some dill flowers go to seed. Doing so will give you plenty of seedlings every year, and they're easy to move.

Succession plantings can be made, but don't plant dill until after the danger of hard frost in spring is past—about a month before the frost-free date in your area. In warm regions, continue to sow dill into early fall.

Add to a border. Dill's fine texture and yellow blooms are pretty enough for a flower garden. Plus, you can use the stems and blossoms in cut flower arrangements.

HERBS FOR BETTER COOKING

Make an Italian scramble by adding 1 teaspoon (5 ml) each of minced fresh oregano, basil, and thyme to about eight large eggs before scrambling them. Round out the flavors with a bit of minced onion, either raw or sautéed.

Herbed pancakes turn breakfast into a light supper. Add 1 teaspoon (5 ml) of fresh sage and 1 tablespoon (15 ml) each of chopped chives and Parmesan cheese to pancake or crepe batter. If you like, roll up thin slices of ham or cheese in the finished flapjacks.

Marry tarragon with healthy root vegetables by adding 1 tablespoon (15 ml) of minced tarragon to 2 cups (475 ml) each of grated parsnips and grated carrots. Quickly stir-fry the mixture in 2 tablespoons (30 ml) of clarified butter or canola oil.

Spice up burgers by mixing 1 tablespoon (15 ml) each of minced fresh chives and parsley to 1 pound (450 grams) of ground beef, along with an egg and ½ teaspoon (2 ml) of seasoned salt, before forming into patties and grilling.

To brew tea from home-grown herbs, warm a china or glass teapot (don't use metal) and put in 2 tablespoons (30 ml) of chopped fresh herbs or 2 teaspoons (10 ml) of dried herbs. Pour in 2 cups (0.5 liter) of boiling water and steep for 6 or 7 minutes if using fresh herbs; for dried herbs, steep a minute longer. Strain, then sweeten with honey or sugar to taste.

Lots of room. If you decide to grow dill for the mature seed heads—which make wonderful fresh or dried material for flower arrangements—allow the plants 1 foot (30 cm) of space all around. By the time they develop mature seeds, some dill plants stand 4 feet (1.2 meters) tall.

To use dill in dried arrangements, cut the flower head before the seeds turn brown and hang the seed-bearing stems upside down to dry. To harvest seeds for cooking, allow them to turn light brown, hang them up in small bunches, and enclose them in a paper bag. After a week or so, you can knock the seeds from the stems and gather them in the bottom of the bag.

HORSERADISH

Each spring, horseradish (*Amoracia rusticana*) grows back from a thick, woody taproot, which is also the plant part used to flavor condiments. Peel and grate the roots and then add vinegar. Horseradish becomes spicier when exposed to air, so the faster you add vinegar, the milder the horseradish will taste.

To prevent forked roots, plant horseradish in drainage-pipe sections placed vertically in the ground and filled with a rich soil mixture. Roots will grow straight and thick until fall harvest.

Use the leaves. Horseradish leaves are known to have fungus-fighting properties, especially against brown rot, which attacks fruit trees. Mash the leaves in warm water to extract their juice, strain, and spray on plants.

COMPANION PLANTING WITH HERBS

• **Mix dill with carrots or cabbage.** Dill confuses carrot rust flies, which lay their eggs on carrot roots, and may deter cabbage pests as well.

• **Plant basil close to tomatoes.** Folklore says these plants encourage each other, and they also taste great together.

• **Grow chives with roses** to discourage insects and diseases.

• **Most any kind of mint** is a good idea planted next to cabbage or tomatoes to ward off white cabbage moths, aphids, and flea beetles.

• **Oregano enhances the flavor** of beans in the garden and repels insects that bother broccoli.

• **Sage should stay away from cucumbers,** but it enhances Rosemary, cabbage, and carrots, deterring cabbage moths, carrot flies, flea beetles, and slugs.

• **Plant thyme next to tomatoes,** where its flowers will attract bees for pollination.

Mark where it sleeps. When growing horseradish near a cultivated garden, be sure to mark its location before the leaves die back for the winter. If you accidentally till over the roots, small chopped pieces may turn up all over your garden.

LAVENDER

A Mediterranean herb that's usually winter hardy to Zone 5, lavender (*Lavendula* spp.) sports thin, fragrant, gray-green leaves and purple flowers in summer. It grows well in a sunny border with other herbs and flowers. Dried lavender flowers and leaves are a delight in sachets, wreaths, and potpourri. The flowers also attract bees and other beneficial insects.

Give lavender full sun and light, well-drained, slightly alkaline soil. Aid drainage in heavy soil by adding a layer of coarse sand or gravel to the base of the planting hole. Feed and water sparingly. Clean sand makes fine mulch for lavender.

Soften hard edges. With its airy texture and upright, slightly sprawling habit, lavender is an excellent choice for softening hard structural lines in the landscape. Plant it at the corners of buildings or steps, at the front or edges of raised beds, or along paths and terraces.

Pruning pointers. Lavender needs regular clipping to keep it from becoming leggy. In fall or early spring, remove the dead flower spikes and withered branches and shape new growth to form a bushy silhouette. If a plant appears dead in spring, wait a while in case new stems emerge from the base when the weather becomes warmer.

Harvest lavender for drying when the buds just open, or you can wait until they're in full bloom. Dry stems in bundles in a cool, airy spot.

In the laundry, put dried lavender flowers on a handkerchief, tie it tightly, and toss it into the dryer. Your clothes will emerge perfumed with a light herbal scent.

 SORTING THROUGH
lavender

Lavenders vary in their appearance, fragrance, and, most important, how well they grow in different climates.

- **True lavender** (*Lavandula angustifolia*) is the most common and is beloved for its gray-green foliage and spiky flower heads with their characteristic blue-purple—that is, lavender—flowers. It grows best where winters are cold and summers mild.

- **Hybrid lavenders,** such as *L. × intermedia* 'Provence', have been developed to be super-fragrant. They grow best where neither summer nor winter is too extreme.

- **Spanish lavender** (*L. stoechus*) looks different from other lavenders, and it isn't as fragrant. However, it stands up beautifully to hot, humid weather, which can be a problem with the other types.

Sweet slumber. Lavender is a prime ingredient in potpourri and is especially nice combined with rose petals. Folklore holds that a little bag of dried blooms slipped inside your pillowcase will help you sleep. To make sachets, fill handkerchiefs or tea napkins with petals and tie them with pretty ribbons.

Make a wand. Clip a bunch of blossoming sprigs about 6 inches (15 cm) long and use thin ribbon to bind the stems together into a cigar-shaped bundle. Use this "wand" to freshen closets and drawers or slip it onto a shelf in a bathroom cabinet.

Winter air freshener. For a festive occasion, sprinkle dried lavender stems into the fireplace. As they burn, they'll delicately scent the air.

In the bath. Sprinkle lavender blooms into the tub or add them to a footbath to soothe, scent, and refresh your skin.

MINTS

The various mints (*Mentha* spp.) are sprawling perennial herbs that prosper in rich, moist, cool soil in partial shade. In addition to the common peppermint and spearmint, lesser-known mints can add variety and extra fragrance to the home garden or containers. Apple mint has downy foliage, orange mint emits a citrus aroma, and the white-rimmed leaves of pineapple mint smell fruity-sweet.

A rambunctious grower, mint can quickly become invasive. To contain the roots, plant mint in a large pot and bury it, setting the rim slightly above the soil line. Or sink plastic edging strips 1 foot (30 cm) deep around the roots.

Harvest mint until a few weeks before the first frost of fall. It has countless culinary uses—for teas, jellies, garnishes, marinades, salads, and, of course, juleps.

Fragrant repellent. Plant mint near entrances to prevent ants from coming into your house. In the pantry, keep insects from invading jars of seeds, beans, and rice by placing a few stems of dried mint inside.

Bug-chasing cocktail. Drive away aphids and caterpillars with a homemade mint cocktail. In a blender, mix 8 ounces (225 grams) of mint leaves with 1 quart (1 liter) of water. Strain and spray on plants every 10 days.

Corsican mint (*Mentha requienii*) is a miniature species that makes a great crevice plant for walls or walkways, or you can use it as a peppermint-scented groundcover.

Snip away. Clip off young shoots regularly to promote bushiness. Most mints are such strong growers that it's impossible to gather stems too often. If plants become tattered, prune them back almost to the ground. Don't worry: you can be sure they will quickly regrow.

HERBS YOUR PETS WILL LOVE

Why shouldn't your pets enjoy herbs, too? Dogs are fond of fennel, which can be used to scent their favorite sleeping places, and a majority of cats are crazy for catnip. This hardy perennial should not be eaten by humans, but most cats love it. To keep them from rolling on plants or chewing them to death, grow catnip under a wire cage or in a hanging basket. Then you can determine when your cats get it as a treat. Even better, put an 8-inch (20-cm) square box made of chicken wire over your plant, tied to sturdy stakes. As the catnip grows through the wire and is eaten by the cats, the roots will remain intact and keep growing new stems.

OREGANO AND MARJORAM

This herb comes in two packages. True oregano (*Origanum vulgare*) is a vigorous perennial that gives off scents and flavors ranging from sweet to peppery, depending on the variety. Sweet marjoram (*O. majorana*) is a close cousin with better flavor and a more restrained growth habit. Sweet marjoram is grown as an annual in all but the warmest climates. In cold climates, you can bring potted plants indoors and grow them through winter on a sunny windowsill.

Harvest oregano or marjoram leaves just before the plants begin to flower. If you harvest when the flowers have set seed, the leaves will taste bitter. Marjoram's unusual flowers are borne on round structures that look like little balls.

🌱 Watch Out!

Grow herbs far from plants that might be sprayed with pesticides, and never grow them in soil where systemic pesticides are used. Always read pesticide labels, because many products that are fine for roses and other ornamental plants should never be used on herbs and other edible plants.

Use oregano as a groundcover in the vegetable patch to cool the soil and suppress weeds between rows or at the foot of tomatoes, corn, and other large plants. If the plants grow too big, cut them back as much as you like.

Marjoram is easy to propagate from stem tip cuttings set to root in moist seed-starting mix. You can take cuttings any time that the plants are not in bloom, and you can even root cuttings from marjoram stems purchased at the supermarket.

PARSLEY

Whether it has tightly curled leaves (*Petroselinum crispum*) or thicker, flat ones (*P. neapolitanum*), parsley is a hardy biennial often grown as an annual. It prefers well-drained soil and partial shade and will reward your efforts with lavish amounts of vitamin-packed leaves you can chop to season butter, sauces, salads, or any type of vegetable, grilled meat, or fish. Parsley is also rich in iron.

Flat-leaf parsley has a stronger flavor, so it's preferred for cooked dishes. Seeds or plants that are labeled as Italian parsley are of this type.

Curled-leaf parsley has a milder flavor, makes an attractive garnish, and adds a fresh "green" taste to cold dishes. You can even use dwarf types as edible edging for your flower garden.

Speed up a slow starter. Parsley seeds can take several weeks to sprout and need moisture to break dormancy. Speed germination by soaking the seeds in lukewarm water for two days before sowing. Or purchase seedlings and set them out gently, disturbing the roots as little as possible.

Sow a parsley sidekick. Sow some fast-sprouting radish seeds in the furrow with parsley. Radishes sprout first, marking the row so you won't disturb the parsley seeds while weeding.

For fresh parsley all winter, sow in October. In the North, sow seeds in pots and keep them in a sunny window. In the South, sow them in the garden. In warm climates, parsley grows best from fall to late spring.

A true biennial, parsley produces flowers and seeds after it has been through a spell of cold winter weather. The flowers make good filler for cut flower arrangements.

Keep leaves clean. Mulch parsley plants with straw to keep soil from splashing on the leaves during rainstorms or watering. To dislodge any grit before using parsley, swish your harvested stems in cool water.

Going on vacation? Before you leave, cut parsley tops and freeze them for later use. Water the remaining stems well with dilute liquid fertilizer to encourage new leaves.

Save the scent. To preserve parsley's delicate flavor, freeze it in plastic bags. Gather some sprigs, trim off long stems, wash the parsley and pat it dry, and then pack it into freezer bags. When you need some, simply rub the bag from the outside to crumble the leaves and scoop them out.

DRYING, FREEZING, AND USING YOUR HERBS

Dry your herbs the easy way. The day before you plan to gather long-stemmed herbs for drying, clean them with a fine spray of water from your hose. The next day, after the dew has dried, cut the stems, remove the lower leaves, and gather them in bunches secured with a rubber band. Pin the bunches to a clothes hanger and let them dry for two weeks in a warm, airy place away from strong light. When nearly crisp, strip the leaves from the stems and store them in airtight containers. Wait to crumble until you use them, because whole leaves retain their flavors longer.

Dry seed-bearing herbs like dill or coriander by hanging bunches inside roomy paper bags with a few ventilation holes punched into them. After two weeks, the dried seeds will drop into the bottom of the bag, where they'll be easy to gather and store.

Freeze parsley and basil, which quickly lose their flavors when dried. The easiest way to freeze them is to simply chop clean leaves, place them in ice cube trays, and cover them with water or stock. When the cubes are frozen hard, shift them to labeled freezer bags.

Make herb butters or cheese spreads when you have a few sprigs you need to use up. Mix the finely chopped herbs into softened butter, cream cheese, or any finely grated cheese. Herb butters and spreads will keep in airtight freezer containers for up to two months.

Make herb pesto by pureeing herbs with oil. Classic pesto is made from basil, garlic. and olive oil, but you can also make pesto from parsley, cilantro, or even mint. Pesto will keep in the refrigerator for several days, or you can freeze it for later use.

Coriander and cilantro, sometimes called Chinese or Mexican parsley, are from the same plant (*Coriandrum sativum*). The leaves of this fast-growing annual are known as cilantro, and the nutty seeds become the spice called coriander, both mainstays of Mexican, Thai, and other types of ethnic cuisine. Grow a quick crop in the fall in warm climates. In cooler regions, grow cilantro in both spring and fall. It needs rich, well-drained soil and full sun to partial shade. Pick fresh leaves as needed, but harvest seeds only when they are plump and changing color.

A parsley cure for puffy eyes. Don't discard parsley seeds that you didn't sow—use them in a refreshing compress. Mix 1 tablespoon (15 cc) of seeds with 1 cup (240 ml) of boiling water, then let it cool. Soak a washcloth in the infusion, wring it out until damp, and fold it in thirds lengthwise. Lie down, place the cloth over your eyes, and relax.

ROSEMARY

A Mediterranean native, Rosemary (*Rosmarinus officinalis*) grows as a shrub in southern California, Texas, and other areas with dry summers and mild winters. Its hardiness in other regions is iffy without protection, because cold, dry winds will quickly dehydrate the leaves. To be safe, grow some of your Rosemary in pots and bring it into a cool room during frigid weather. In any climate, Rosemary's strong, resinous scent and delicious flavor are perfect with grilled fish, meats, and Mediterranean-style vegetables.

Light, well-drained soil is essential for Rosemary, especially for container-grown plants. Water only as often as needed to keep the soil slightly moist.

Plants need full sun in summer, and it's best to keep them indoors in winter near a sunny south- or west-facing window.

Shapely plants. Fast-growing and tough, Rosemary is ideal for simple topiary shapes. To make a tree-shaped standard, choose a plant with a straight central stalk. Prune off the lowest branches a few at a time and shorten branches near the top to keep them from becoming too heavy. When the plant reaches the height you want, trim the head into a bushy ball.

To store Rosemary for cooking, strip leaves from branches and freeze in a freezer bag. Or dry and store in airtight jars.

Barbecuing? If you toss Rosemary sprigs on the coals or grate of the barbecue during the last 10 minutes of cooking it will impart a wonderful flavor and aroma to lamb, veal, or chicken. Rosemary branches can be used as skewers for kebabs or tied together to make an aromatic brush for applying sauce to the meat as it cooks.

SAGE

Sage (*Salvia officinalis*) is a hardy yet often short-lived perennial. Garden sage is woody, with soft gray-green foliage. The most familiar of the culinary sages, it's used primarily as a sausage and

SORTING THROUGH sages

These plants lack the rich flavor of garden sage, but they make fine additions to the flower garden.

- **Pineapple sage** (*Salvia elegans*) earns its name with its distinctive fragrance. It bears brilliant red flowers and grows to 3 feet (90 cm). Add leaves and flowers to fruit salads, jams, and tea.

- **Scarlet salvia** (*S. splendens*) is a long-blooming mainstay of the annual bed. Hybrids come in pink, purple, or ivory. It grows up to 3 feet (90 cm).

- **Silver sage** (*S. argentea*) is grown for its foliage—broad, scallop-edged leaves covered with silvery down. Its blooms are white to lavender, and it grows to 2 feet (60 cm).

stuffing ingredient, but it also adds great flavor to breads, cheese, poultry, and vegetable dishes.

Some varieties are variegated, which makes them ideal for large containers planted with an assortment of herbs. 'Aurea' has gold and green leaves, 'Purpurea' has purple foliage, and 'Icterina' has yellowish foliage blotched with green. All grow to 2½ feet (75 cm) tall.

Sage advice. Catalogs often describe sages as short-lived perennials or half-hardy annuals. In fact, some annual sages may survive mild winters, while extreme cold or hot, humid conditions may kill some perennials. When you try a new sage, mulch over its roots in late fall, then wait and see if it survives until spring.

Sun lovers. Garden sage loves sun and well-drained soil. Water young plants regularly until they become established. After a few weeks, they can tolerate drier conditions.

Pinch individual leaves as you need them in the kitchen. In addition to chopping them into dishes, lay whole sage leaves over roasted meats or breads. To use sage in salads, lightly fry whole leaves in a little olive oil, drain on paper towels, and crumble the crisp leaves over the finished salad.

Sage tea is good medicine and has an honorable history as an antiseptic mouthwash and digestive aid. Indeed, an old adage holds that "no man need be ill if sage grows in his garden."

To dry sage for wreaths or potpourri, cut flowering stems about 8 inches (20 cm) long, secure a bunch with a rubber band, and hang it upside down in a cool place to dry.

TARRAGON

Native to prairies and rocky, barren environments, tarragon (*Artemisia dracunculus*) will happily make its home in poor, dry soil. Tarragon grows to 2 feet (60 cm) or more, depending on the climate. Its aromatic leaves, used in a variety of recipes, are thin blades with pointed tips. Because tarragon needs winter dormancy, it's treated as an annual in very hot climates, but in most areas is grown as a perennial. Tarragon's basic needs prevail in all regions: loose, well-drained soil and plenty of light sunshine.

Buy plants, not seeds. Tarragon seed in packets is Russian tarragon—a less aromatic variety than French tarragon, which has sterile seeds. For the true anise-scented herb with a savory "bite," buy plants of *A. dracunculus* var. sativa. Not all garden centers distinguish between the two, so ask questions and pinch a sample leaf. French tarragon has a strong, sweet smell and a rich, distinctive flavor.

Time for a haircut. Tarragon likes to be snipped, so don't be afraid to cut back the tips whenever you think a dish can use a little of the herb.

"The little dragon." The herb's name (*dracunculus*) is related to the Latin word for "dragon"—a reference to the plant's serpent-like root system. Divide plants in spring every two years to untangle the roots and keep the plants vigorous.

For extra flavor, steep tarragon sprigs in white-wine vinegar. You can leave them in or strain them out after a month or so and use the vinegar in vinaigrettes, potato salad, poultry dishes, and the like.

THYME

Thyme (*Thymus* spp.) includes the classic culinary herb called common thyme (*T. vulgaris*), but you can also grow varieties that smell of lemon, caraway, or nutmeg—some culinary, some not. Silver thyme has leaves banded in white, and woolly thyme has fuzzy foliage. Mother-of-thyme is a name often used for several species that self-sow readily after they bloom: *T. praecox* spp. *articus, T. pulegiodes,* and *T. serpyllum.*

A creeping carpet? Some thyme varieties, including caraway, lemon, and coconut, are ground-hugging evergreens and like to sprawl. Use them as soft edging for borders, plant them between roses, or grow them as a fragrant crevice filler between stepping stones.

Time with thyme. For a clever garden show-piece, create a living sundial with thyme. Mark out a circle and divide it into 12 equal wedges like a pie. Alternate three or four thyme varieties, planting each wedge separately. For a working sundial, make sure that the 12 o'clock position is oriented due north. Install a gnomon, or pointer, to cast a shadow—perhaps a pretty birdhouse or a pole. Set stones around the perimeter to mark the hours.

Warmth-loving thyme thrives in well-drained soil and full sun. Plant it around a stone or brick path so it can take advantage of the reflected heat and light. You also can tuck it into a stone wall, which provides extra warmth and quick drainage.

Keep it neat. For bushy plants, prune back the stems in spring if you live in a cool climate; in warm areas, prune in fall. Replace plants when they start to die back in the center—usually after three to five years.

In the kitchen, drop whole sprigs into soups, stews, or sauces; the tiny leaves will cook in a few minutes. Use thyme generously when roasting vegetables and when you feel like being creative with a rice or pasta dish.

Be bee friendly. Thyme flowers, which bloom in white, lavender, pink, and magenta, lure bees. Place thyme wherever you need plants pollinated or want to watch bees at work. To prevent bees attracted by thyme from becoming a garden nuisance, plant it in a quiet corner where the bees are unlikely to be disturbed, or clip off flowers before they open.

Make a sachet. Wrap dried thyme in handkerchiefs or tea napkins and place them in drawers, closets, and bookshelves. The sachets add a fresh aroma and repel silverfish and other household pests.

Keep it coming. Even with the best care, thyme lives for only a few years. Replace one or two plants annually so the patch doesn't die out all at once.

✿ Fruits and Nuts

ONE OF A GARDENER'S greatest accomplishments is growing sun-sweetened fruits, which might be glossy red apples or juicy raspberries. Indeed, though most of us think of fruits as growing on trees, many of the easiest fruits to fit into a home landscape are so-called small fruits, or berries. Ground-hugging strawberries will knit themselves into a leafy green groundcover in a sunny spot, and blueberries are at home nestled among ornamental shrubs. Every yard has room for at least a few fruits, and perhaps a long-lived nut tree, too. If you dream of growing your favorite fruits in your backyard, the following pages include lots of tips for growing yard-worthy fruits, which you can use to turn your dream into a reality. And, because fruits often bear bumper crops in good years, there also are tips for preserving the harvest to enjoy months after summer is long gone.

WHAT FRUITS NEED

Fruits run on sun, and plenty of sun is the key to growing healthy plants that produce big harvests. Place all fruits where they will receive at least a half day of full sun. Gentle south-facing slopes are ideal for most fruits.

Abundant fresh air discourages fungal diseases and loss of spring blossoms to late spring frosts. If good space for growing fruits is limited, select dwarf trees. Apple, pear, cherry, peach, nectarine, and plum trees are all available grafted onto dwarfing rootstocks that restricts their size, yet they still bear full-size fruit.

Get beauty *and* bounty. While fruit trees are functional, they can also be decorative. Apples, pears, and cherries make particularly attractive landscape specimens when in full flower. Bramble-type fruits, such as blackberries or raspberries, can be used to define a boundary—and discourage trespassers. Or you can grow fruits upward by training grapes or kiwi vines to cover an overhead arbor.

Some fruits can't pollinate themselves, so they need a compatible partner. Study varieties closely and make sure you have good combinations of varieties when growing tree fruits and blueberries that are not self-fertile.

Practice good housekeeping. Always clean up leaves, fruits, and other debris around fruit plantings to discourage pests. Prune and destroy any diseased fruits or foliage. Monitor fruits often for signs of insect or disease problems so you can treat them promptly.

Fruits need bees and other pollinating insects, which are easy to attract to your garden with a diverse assortment of flowers. In addition to pollinators, you can encourage predator insects, such as parasitic wasps and ladybugs, to visit your fruits by planting mint, Queen Anne's lace, catmint, yarrow, and other favorite food sources in a nearby bed.

PLANTING FRUITS

Get started in spring, when fruits are just emerging from winter dormancy. In some areas, you can plant strawberries in the fall, but most fruits are best planted in late winter or early spring.

Dig planting holes in advance so they'll be ready when planting time comes. Dig planting holes for trees 2 feet (60 cm) wide and 2 feet deep and mix in plenty of compost or other organic matter. You can grow small fruits in broad rows or even raised beds. If you plan ahead, you can prepare planting sites in fall and winter, then refill the holes and cover them with a board or mulch until spring.

Mulch after planting to keep the soil moist and discourage weeds. Spread a deep layer of straw or wood chips around the base of newly planted fruits. The mulch will also protect the plants' shallow feeder roots. When mulching trees, keep the mulch 1 foot (30 cm) away from the trunks to deny rodents a hiding place and to promote good air circulation.

PREVENTING PEST PROBLEMS

Protect fruit on the tree with plastic bags. Are there some apples you want to protect or some grapes that need a little more time on the vine? Slip the fruit into clear perforated plastic bags as it approaches perfection. You'll keep out critters while the fruit continues to ripen.

Scare away crows and other birds. Are the birds eating the fruit before you do? To foil them, dangle strips of aluminum foil or used CD's from the branches using monofilament fishing line. Even better, hang some foil-wrapped seashells, which will make a bit of noise, to further startle fine-feathered thieves.

Protect strawberries from birds with ¾-inch (2-cm) mesh rigged over hoops. Tie

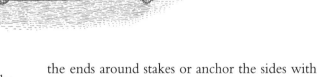

the ends around stakes or anchor the sides with bricks or stones.

Wrap tree trunks with plastic guards to protect them against sunscald, nicks from lawn equipment, and rodents that like to nibble on bark. Choose the type that expands as your tree grows and has ventilation holes.

Grandpa's wisdom

Many insect pests that bother fruits rest in tree crevices during the winter, and one of their worst enemies is the little bird called the tufted titmouse. Lure them to your winter bird feeders with sunflower seeds, but don't worry that the titmice will come around in summer to eat your fruits. They eat mostly insects and seeds.

Horticultural oil is an effective all-purpose pest preventive on fruit trees. To suffocate overwintering insects, use the heavier kind, called dormant oil, before trees leaf out. Use the lighter oil—known as summer oil—during the growing season.

APPLES

Apple trees are somewhat slow to become established, but they often bear for many years when given good care. Fruit set is usually best when you plant more than one variety, and dwarf trees take up very little space. The spring blossoms are beautiful and often fragrant, and you can save the pruned wood for barbecue season.

Choose varieties right for your climate. Apples and many other fruits vary in how many hours of winter chilling they need before they bloom and produce fruits. Your local extension service can provide you with a list of apple varieties that are known to grow well in your area.

To rejuvenate an old apple tree, prune it back into shape gradually by removing only one-third of the old, overgrown branches each winter for three years. Meanwhile, plant new dwarf trees nearby that will be pollinated by the flowers borne by the older tree.

Young apples require pruning, so be prepared to do some cutting and sawing each winter, usually in February. Productive trees should have open forms so that their branches have space to develop and are bathed in sunshine. Most apples are trained to grow upright so a single main stem supports several long side branches.

Reduce codling moth infestation by installing a collar of corrugated cardboard around the trunk of the tree. The larvae will nest in the cardboard. Remove it periodically, dispose of it in the garbage, then replace it with a new collar. In the spring, rub loose scales of bark from the tree trunk to eliminate the crevices in which codling moth larvae can readily pupate.

Thin out excess fruits as they develop so that those that remain will grow big and sweet. Thin right after the tree thins itself by shedding green fruitlets in early summer. Leave the largest and healthiest fruits alone—but remove even smaller ones less than 4 inches (10 cm) from the biggest ones.

Apples that are dimpled and tunneled with brown trails show signs that apple maggots, or railroad worms, have been at work. Trap egg-laying female maggots by hanging red tennis balls coated with commercial insect adhesive in your trees. Use one ball per dwarf tree and four to eight per full-size tree. Hang them at eye level, just within the canopy but not obscured by leaves.

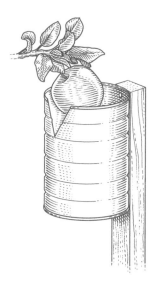

Make a homemade picker. Cut a **V** shape into the rim of an old 2-pound (1-kg) coffee can and bend the points slightly inward so they will grab the fruit. Lay a piece of carpet or foam in the bottom of the can as a cushion for the fruit, then nail or wire the can to a broomstick or pole.

Apples will stay fresh for months provided they have enough moisture and are kept a few degrees above freezing. Put the fruit into plastic bags in which you've poked a few holes and store in the refrigerator.

Dry some apples for healthy, tasty snacks. First, core the apples. Slice them into thin rounds, dip them in lemon juice to keep them from turning brown, and run a string through the center of each round. Tack the ends of the string to the ceiling of your pantry. After the slices are thoroughly dry, store them in plastic bags.

BLACKBERRIES

Easy to grow and always productive, blackberries seldom have problems with pests and diseases. Several varieties are thornless, although many of the best-tasting blackberries grow on canes that are well-defended with stickers. All blackberries bear fruit on one-year-old canes. In other words, the new canes that grow one summer bear fruit the next. Try blackberries in a place where they can grow into a robust hedge that deters unwanted visitors—including hungry deer.

Simplify pruning and maintenance. Prune annually after the final harvest. Cut to the ground any canes that bore fruit, which reduces possible disease problems and makes way for a new crop of canes. In late summer, pinch off the tips of the new canes to encourage short lateral branches to form.

Wear beekeeping gloves when pruning thorny blackberry plants. The gloves' protective gauntlets reach up to your elbows.

Want more plants? Bend the tip of a blackberry stem to the ground in summer and weigh it down with a stone. By the following spring, the tip will have roots, and it can be dug and moved to a new spot.

Plant a new patch every 5 to 10 years because cultivated blackberries pick up pests that lower productivity over time. Choose a new spot as far from the old site—and any wild brambles—as possible. Purchase only plants certified as virus- or disease-free.

In frigid climates, separate the blackberry stems from the support and spread them out on the ground. Cover them thickly with conifer branches or dried mulch to protect against severe cold. Uncover them in spring and prune back any canes that show no leaf buds by late spring.

Enhance an archway or fence with the lush foliage and pretty white flowers of thornless

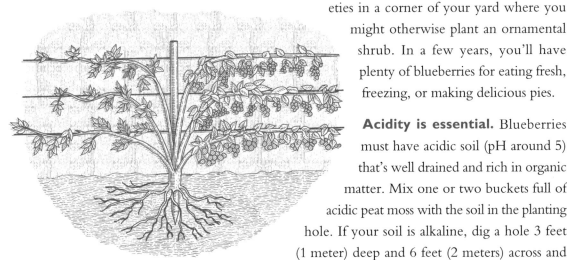

blackberries, such as 'Navaho' or 'Chester'. Or create a fan espalier to best see stems and fruit. In midsummer, when the current year's canes

are pruned back to the ground, begin training the new green stems into a fan shape by fastening them with plastic ties to a grid or trellis.

Pick them dead ripe. Blackberries taste best when they are fully ripe, which is often a day or two after they turn black. Harvest when they're still glossy but have just begun to soften. Blackberries are easy to freeze, or you can use them to make cobblers, pies, or wonderful jelly.

BLUEBERRIES

True Native American fruits, blueberries grow wild in open woodlands where the soil is quite acidic. Improved blueberries bear bigger, more flavorful fruits than their wild ancestors, and they are very easy to grow. Try a mound of three varieties in a corner of your yard where you might otherwise plant an ornamental shrub. In a few years, you'll have plenty of blueberries for eating fresh, freezing, or making delicious pies.

Acidity is essential. Blueberries must have acidic soil (pH around 5) that's well drained and rich in organic matter. Mix one or two buckets full of acidic peat moss with the soil in the planting hole. If your soil is alkaline, dig a hole 3 feet (1 meter) deep and 6 feet (2 meters) across and fill with a mixture of 1 part peat moss to 1 part sand. Fertilize blueberries with cottonseed meal or a timed-release fertilizer intended for use on azaleas, which also love acidic soil.

🍂 SORTING THROUGH
blueberries

Blueberries vary in their tolerance of cold, so there isn't a single blueberry that's right for all climates. Don't know which varieties you most like to eat? Visit a local blueberry farm and sample different varieties.

- **Northern highbush blueberries** are best for cold winter climates.

- **Rabbiteye blueberries** are the best bets in the South.

- **Lowbush blueberries** aren't as productive as taller types, but they make a nice knee-high groundcover for partial shade.

Oak leaves and other acidic mulches— including pine needles, wood chips, or sawdust—help blueberries thrive. Spread an inch or two (3 to 5 cm) over the ground beneath your bushes to protect the plant's shallow roots.

Birds love blueberries, and the only sure way to thwart them is with netting—from the top of the bush all the way down to ground level.

For superior flavor, don't pick the berries as soon as they turn blue. Let them hang on the branches a few more days to develop their mellow sweetness, then "tickle" the bunches; the ripe fruits will fall into your hands.

A long-term fruit bearer. As long as you harvest all the good berries and clean up any damaged fruits or cover them with deep mulch, your blueberry bushes should bear year after year with no disease problems.

Plant more than one variety. Even though cross-pollination isn't absolutely essential for blueberries, planting more than one variety will make both bushes bear more and larger fruits than either would alone. Another plus: Planting early-season, midseason, and later varieties enables you to have fresh berries for weeks on end.

CHERRIES

Cherry trees are so beautiful when they are in bloom that they are an ideal choice if you want a tree that doubles as an edible ornamental. Fruit-producing types don't have double flowers or weeping habits like ornamental cherries, but they make up for this shortcoming by producing buckets of juicy fruits. Cherry trees always bloom in spring, but in some years they fail to set fruit, even when conditions seem perfect. Perhaps they're saving their energy, because when a cherry tree does have a good year, the harvest is huge.

Sweet or tart? Choose from the two types of cherries: sweet and tart. Sweet cherries are for plucking right off the tree and eating fresh, but the trees often don't fruit well in climates with mild winters. Tart cherries, which are fine for cooking, are more widely adapted and often easier to grow. All cherries mature in early summer.

Use a pair of dwarf cherries to anchor a strawberry bed, or plant the ground beneath them with little spring-flowering bulbs. Dwarf cherries have a neat, upright growth habit that makes them easy to fit into any type of landscaping plan. If you want a more sculptural tree, a standard-size cherry may be an ideal choice.

Fine netting is the surest way to discourage birds from devouring your crop. Cover the whole tree with the netting and remove it as soon as your harvest is done. Alternatively, string black cotton thread among the branches just before ripening begins. Take a spool of thread, grab the free end, and toss the spool back and forth over the tree to a helper; continue until the spool is empty. Birds will hit the invisible thread and find it too much trouble to return to the tree.

Plant a dwarf cherry in a tub. Select a tub or other large container at least 20 inches (50 cm) in height and width. Fill it with a mixture of equal parts garden soil, compost, and perlite, plant your cherry, and grow it on your deck or patio.

GRAPES

A healthy grapevine will often grow for decades, and with their large, broad leaves, grapes make excellent shade-giving vines for an arbor. Many of the best garden varieties are descended from native strains and have fewer problems with disease than European wine grapes. Still, grapes do have plenty of enemies, so in most climates, you should expect big crops only in years when the weather is in your favor.

HOW ABOUT KIWIS?

Although not common in American gardens, kiwi vines are easy to grow, and they can be gigantic. Both the common (*Actinidia deliciosa*) and hardy kiwi (*A. arguta*) are fast-growing vines that need the support of a sturdy trellis or arbor, or you can let them take over a fence at the far end of your yard. The common kiwi produces the fuzzy fruits sold in supermarkets; hardy kiwis yield sweet, green, grape-like berries with smooth skins. When planning a kiwi planting project, be sure to include a male plant—one male is sufficient to fertilize several female plants. Kiwis need little extra attention besides pruning and regular feeding. Cut stems that fruited the previous year to 1½ feet (45 cm) in winter and control the shape of your vines by giving them a light trimming in summer.

What kinds? European grapes are most often grown in the parts of the west with long warm seasons, while American types, such as 'Concord', have fewer problems with cold and disease in the Northeast and Midwest. In the South, muscadine grapes—another native type—is often quite easy to grow.

Plant vines in early spring or fall in a weed-free, well-drained site in soil that has been amended with plenty of organic matter. Grapes prefer a slightly acidic pH of around 6. Space vines 8 feet (2.5 meters) apart and erect a trellis right away.

Sun makes grapes sweet. To ensure that fruits develop high sugar content, plant the vines where they'll receive maximum sun and heat. Site vines against a wall or on a slope with a southern exposure.

Use leaves in the kitchen. Clean grape leaves that are blanched in boiling water for 30 seconds make great wrappers for savory meat or rice stuffings, or you can use them to line the bottom of a serving plate in the same way you might use lettuce leaves.

Cultivate vines in pots for your balcony or porch. Fill large pots—at least 14 to 16 inches (35 to 40 cm) in diameter—with 2 parts garden loam to 1 part each leaf mold and coarse sand. Plant a vigorous variety and set up a support for the vines. At summer's end, you may even reap a few grapes. Repot every two years in fresh soil when the plant is dormant.

When to prune. Prune a grapevine in late winter, just before new growth begins. Waiting until late winter makes it easier to spot the swelling buds, and it's important to prune vines back so that each one retains fewer than 10 good buds.

Keep old vines well fed. Grapevines exhaust the soil after a few years, so it's important to fertilize old vines yearly with a 6-inch (15-cm) ring of balanced organic or timed-release fertilizer. Or blanket the ground with 1 pound (0.5 kg) of compost per 1 foot (30 cm) of row in late winter each year.

PEACHES

Juicy, succulent peaches are on many gardeners' most-wanted lists, but they aren't always easy to grow. Peaches are temperate-zone trees, growing well along both coasts, around the Great Lakes, and southwest of the Rockies. While most peaches require a period of cold dormancy before flowering, others that are adapted to the South are "low-chill" types that don't need and won't tolerate a harsh winter. Be sure to select peaches that suit your climate and are resistant to disease. Several common diseases and insects make growing peaches more challenging than growing apples, pears, and other tree fruits.

Pick your spot. Peaches need excellent drainage, full sun, and protection from wind. If late-spring cold snaps are common, plant your trees on a north-facing slope, where frost-bitten buds will have a chance to thaw gradually before being exposed to the sun.

For a reliable harvest, plant new trees every 5 years. Peach trees live only 10 to 15 years, and the new trees will begin producing just as the old trees are fading.

Pamper your peaches. Keep the trees well watered during the growing season; they need about 3 inches (8 cm) of water each month. Spread organic mulch or compost at the tree base, keeping it 1 foot (30 cm) from the trunk. After the petals drop, feed with 10-10-10 fertilizer as growth begins in spring and spread 2 cups (475 cc) of bonemeal outward to the dripline.

Prune peaches more severely than most other fruit trees to increase fruit quality and promote growth. Remove any limbs that form a narrow angle and train to create a spreading shape with an open center. Wait to prune until the flower buds are just starting to show pink. You'll easily be able to spot which branches will yield fruit and which have suffered winter damage.

Banish borers. A gummy substance oozing from holes in the trunk is a sign of peach-tree borers. Poke wire into their holes to kill them or place a ring of mothballs on the soil around the trunk in late summer, before the soil cools below 60°F (16°C). Mound a thin layer of soil over the mothballs and against the trunk; after one month, level the soil.

Harvest peaches when ripe, as green peaches won't mature off the tree. Select fruits that are slightly soft but still firm, have good color, and come free from the stem with a twist. Let them ripen further at room temperature for three days. Don't fret about a split pit or a little mold on the seed; it won't affect the flavor and quality.

Easy peeling. You can slip peaches right out of their skins if you plunge them into boiling water for 15 seconds. Peeled, sliced peaches are easy to freeze and keep their summer-fresh flavor for months.

PEARS

You might think of pears as the patient fruit. You will need patience as you wait for the slow-growing trees to reach maturity, but once they begin setting fruit, they will be patient as they wait for you to gather the pears. Pears are often less fussy than other tree fruits, so they're a good investment for gardeners who want a tree that's lovely in spring, when it's covered with blooms, and produces fruit for many years with little care.

European or Asian? European pear species boast buttery-smooth fruits but may become afflicted with fire blight, a bacterial disease that causes leaves to suddenly blacken in cool late-spring weather. Asian species have small, crisp, somewhat gritty fruits, but they are more resistant to disease.

A pair of pears. Pears require cross-pollination to produce fruit, so always plant two compatible varieties. 'Bartlett' and 'Comice' are good pollinators and yield delectable fruits.

No room? If you have room for only one pear tree, select one with several varieties grafted onto a single rootstock. Your tree will be self-pollinating and bear different kinds of pears at different times.

Hold the fertilizer. Feed pears sparingly with nitrogen; it stimulates succulent new shoots susceptible to fire blight. On trees three years and older, use only enough 5-10-5 fertilizer to produce 6 to 12 inches (15 to 30 cm) of new growth each season.

For perfect pears, pick when the fruit is slightly underripe and just turning a lighter green. Then let the pears slowly ripen at 65° to 70°F (18° to 21°C); cooler temperatures will slow the ripening process, which is good if you have a big crop of pears.

Faster to grow and less finicky than peaches, dwarf plums make wonderful little landscape trees. Many newer varieties of plums are resistant to common diseases, and all plums are lovely in spring, when they're covered with blossoms. Be sure to choose locally adapted varieties and plant more than one variety to ensure good pollination.

Early bloomers. Because plum trees, especially Japanese plums, bloom early in spring, the blossoms—and your crop—can be lost to a late frost. Plant the trees on a north-facing slope, which often delays blooming and thereby keeps the blossoms safe from cold.

Poor competitors. Shallow-rooted plum trees can't tolerate much competition, even from grass. If you plant a plum on the lawn, keep the soil beneath it free of grass or weeds out to the dripline; mulch with organic matter instead.

Plums like it rich. These heavy bearers need plenty of organic matter and fertilizer for maximum fruiting. Dress with 2 cups (475 cc) of bonemeal and 1 cup (240 cc) of alfalfa meal each spring, adding extra nitrogen if growth is not vigorous. In winter, spread 10 pounds (5 kg) of compost from trunk to dripline.

Pick plums for eating fresh when they are fully ripe; the fruit should have good color and be slightly soft. Pick fruits for cooking when they're slightly underripe.

Perhaps you've loved raspberries since you were a kid and always wanted to have them in your yard. Great! New varieties make raspberries easier to grow than ever, although even old standbys produce beautiful crops for very little effort. You can even extend the harvest season by growing spring-, summer-, and fall-bearing raspberries. All raspberries have thorns, so do grow them away from heavy traffic areas.

June-bearing raspberries produce a big crop all at once in early summer. These raspberries are like blackberries: they produce fruit on canes that grew the year before. If you want plenty of raspberries to freeze or make jam, choose traditional June-bearing varieties for most of your plot.

Everbearing, or primocane raspberries, produce berries on new growth. You can cut the canes down to the ground in the late fall or winter and start picking berries from the new canes the following fall. Cutting the canes back only halfway will coax an in-between summer crop. Include a few primocane plants to help stretch the raspberry harvest.

Too little space? Tie two raspberry bushes around a stake about 5 feet (1.5 meters) tall.

(Continued on page 200)

Preserving Your Fruits

Even if you've never canned a thing, you can make fruit preserves if you know how to boil and stir. Preserves are basically fruit that is cooked in a thick sugar syrup, and once the preserves are made, they can be stored in the refrigerator for a couple of weeks, frozen for a couple of months, or canned and stored for a couple of years. The choice is yours!

What about jam and jelly? Jams and jellies have a thicker consistency than preserves because of pectin—a substance present in most fruits, but often in modest amounts. You can add pectin by stirring in a box of a pectin product, which you can find with canning supplies in supermarkets. For jellies, the pectin is added after the juice has been extracted from the fruit, a process that frees the pectin in apples and some other fruits that often have plenty of pectin.

Because they have plenty of pectin and sugar, jams and jellies are easy to can in a waterbath canner, which can be any large pot in which the filled and capped hot canning jars can be covered with at least 1 inch (3 cm) of water and held at the simmering point for about 10 minutes. Here are the basic steps.

STEP 1. Prepare the fruit using a recipe from any basic cookbook. Citrus rinds, spices, and other flavorings can be added to create slightly different taste twists. While the fruit is cooking with sugar, sterilize canning jars and lids in another pot of boiling water. Keep the sterilized jars warm by placing them in a pan in a 250°F (120°C) oven.

STEP 2. Fill the jars to within ½ inch (12 mm) of the tops with the prepared preserves,

Raspberry Preserves

Plum Preserves

Peach Cinnamon Preserves

Crab apple Preserves

WHAT ABOUT FREEZING?

Most fruits can be frozen with ease, and unlike most vegetables, fruits freeze best if they aren't cooked first. Simply wash berries with plenty of cool water, pat them dry, and loosely pack into freezer-safe containers. If you like, though, you can cook apples, peaches, or pears before freezing so they're ready to eat as soon as they thaw. Better yet, go ahead and make pies or cobblers and freeze them ready to pop into the oven.

More flavorful fruit. To add zip to the flavor of thawed frozen fruit, add a few tablespoons of brandy, fruit-flavored liqueur, or honey.

Crisper pie crusts. When making a pie with frozen fruit, which releases a lot of water as it thaws, keep the bottom crust from getting soggy by sprinkling it with granulated sugar, ground almonds mixed with an egg yolk, or plain flour. All of these will absorb any excess moisture from the thawing fruit like a dry sponge.

When freezing pies, bake them until just done, then cool them, wrap them in freezer-safe plastic wrap, and freeze. Another method is to freeze the crust, fill it with cooled cooked fruit, and top it with a streusel-type topping before wrapping and freezing.

---

jam, or jelly. To make sure jam is ready to put into jars, pour ½ tablespoon (7 ml) of boiling jam onto a plate. Let it cool and slant the plate. If the jam doesn't slide, it's ready to be put up. If it slides easily, cook it a bit longer. Hot jelly is easier to put in jars if you pour it into a Pyrex or other heat-resistant glass pitcher first.

STEP 3. Keep lids and rubber seals in simmering water before putting them on the hot jars. Screw the tops on firmly and place the jars in gently boiling water for 10 minutes. Don't let hot-packed jars cool before processing in a waterbath canner. Once they lose their heat, they can crack when submerged in the hot water.

STEP 4. Remove the jars and let them cool. Listen for the telltale pop that lets you know that the jars are sealing. Recheck all jars the day after canning. If there's a slight depression in the lid and a jar gives off a light "ping" when tapped, it's firmly sealed. If any processed jars failed to seal, place them in the refrigerator and use the contents within two weeks.

Note: Because of their acidity, properly sterilized fruit preserves rarely become contaminated by bacteria. But to be safe, store them in a basement or other area where temperatures stay between 50° and 70° F (10° and 20° C). Before serving, check the jar. Discard it if the contents seem foamy or discolored, if the lid bulges or is misshapen, or if the rim is leaking. Odd odors, mold, or spurting liquid are also warnings to steer clear.

Gather the branches together gently with strips of soft cloth, being sure to leave space between the canes for air circulation.

Give them support. To keep long raspberry canes from touching the ground or blowing around in the wind, build a support. Drive sturdy posts 2 to 2½ feet (60 to 75 cm) into the ground, then stretch wire between them at knee and chest height. There's usually no need to attach the canes to the wires.

Japanese beetles love raspberries. In early summer, when Japanese beetles are out and about, jiggle them into a pan of soapy water. Aphids can be controlled by a heavy spray from a garden hose or an application of insecticidal soap. Raspberries are also vulnerable to viral diseases, which cause the berries to fall apart as you pick them. Remove affected plants and replace them with plants that are certified to be virus-free.

Save the old canes. Don't discard old raspberry canes after pruning. They make excellent kindling for your fireplace, or you can lay them over newly seeded beds to discourage dogs and cats from digging there.

STRAWBERRIES

The most landscape-friendly of fruits, strawberries grow wild in temperate regions across America and Europe. Today's cultivated varieties are descended from a mid-18th-century hybrid of two species that are native to the Americas and prized for their large, prolific fruits. In recent

SORTING THROUGH strawberries

Strawberries are sensitive to day length, but different varieties respond to the changing lengths in different ways.

- **June-bearing strawberries** bloom all at once in early spring, and their fruits are ready to harvest by early summer. 'Earliglow' and 'Surecrop' are June bearers.

- **Everbearing varieties** produce some berries in spring and many more in fall. 'Ogallala' and 'Ozark Beauty' are everbearers.

- **Day-neutral varieties** help fill the fruiting gap by blooming later in spring and producing in early summer. They often continue to bloom for a longer time than June bearers.

- **Alpine strawberries** are small, but they produce intensely scented fruits. 'Alexandria' boasts juicy fruits, and 'Alpine Yellow' has small golden fruits.

years, strawberries have gotten bigger and bigger as commercial growers have learned how to please them. Your homegrown berries won't be as large, but they'll be twice as flavorful.

How much is enough? For a family of four, plant about a dozen June-bearing strawberries, which fruit all at once in early summer, and a dozen plants of an everbearing type, which produce crops in spring and late summer. Each plant should yield about a cup per year.

The right soil. Strawberries like their soil to be rich, acidic, and well drained. In early spring (or fall in mild winter areas), prepare a thoroughly tilled, well-weeded bed amended with plenty of compost or aged manure. Plant strawberries on an overcast day so the plants won't be stressed by strong sunshine.

Neither deep nor shallow. Strawberries are fussy about their planting depth. Plant so that the crowns are just above the soil line. If planted too deep, the plants will rot; if too shallow, they'll dry out. Mulch between plants with pine needles, straw, or chopped leaves.

Berries on the balcony. Keep strawberries close at hand for munching by planting them in containers for the terrace. If you don't have an actual strawberry pot, use any tub or barrel with holes in its sides where you can tuck in plants. To water evenly, insert a perforated pipe down the center of the pot; it can be left in or filled with gravel, which stays in place when the pipe is pulled out.

Keep moving. Once an existing strawberry bed becomes less productive, start a new one in another part of the garden. But don't choose a spot where tomatoes, peppers, or potatoes have been grown in the previous three years; strawberries are prone to the same soilborne diseases that attack these vegetables.

A morning shower. Strawberries need to be kept moist, but take care: Water only in the morning so the plants can dry before sundown. This lessens the chances of seeing fruit-rot diseases and also discourages slugs.

Take a pinch. Get young plants off to a good start and ensure bountiful harvests in succeeding years by pinching off the flower buds the first season. With June-bearing strawberries, this means forfeiting fruit; on everbearing plants, removing the buds through July 1 stimulates the late-summer crop.

Speed the harvest. Strawberries will ripen and be ready to pick sooner if you protect the beds with plastic tunnels or row covers very early in spring. Be sure to leave the ends of the

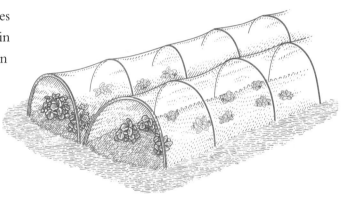

tunnels open on warm days so pollinating insects can get to the blossoms.

Store ripe berries unwashed in the refrigerator; wash them and remove the stems and caps just before using. Wet strawberries spoil quickly even if kept chilled.

Thwart thieving birds by stretching nets over the rows when the berries begin to redden. You can also set up wires that whir in the wind; twist the wires slightly so they vibrate and "sing" even louder.

The next generation. Help young runners put down roots by pinning them directly to the soil with 4-inch (10-cm) lengths of wire bent into a U shape. You can also bury 3-inch (8-cm) pots in the soil and peg the runners into them. Cut the runner from its parent six weeks later and wait another week to transplant it.

Feed them twice. Fertilize established strawberries in early spring just as new growth begins. Mow back the tops in midsummer, which helps prevent diseases, and watch for signs of new growth before feeding a second time in early fall. The fall feeding helps the plants develop buds that will grow into the next season's blossoms.

Cold comfort. In areas with hard freezes, mulch after the first frost with several inches of straw, hay, or other coarse material. Remove it the following spring after all danger of frost has passed.

GROWING NUTS

What is a nut? Botanically, it's a one-seeded dry fruit with a tough shell that won't split when ripe. True nuts include acorns and beechnuts, but the term can be applied to any hard fruit, such as the almond, chestnut, macadamia, or coconut. Almost all nuts grow on trees or shrubs, with the notable exception of annual peanuts, which produce their nuts underground on their roots.

Nut trees are valued for providing not only edible fruits but also natural beauty, shade, and habitats for wildlife. Because nut trees are usually

> ### SIX SUPER NUTS
>
> **Good cold-climate nuts:** Chinese chestnuts, filberts (hazelnuts), walnuts
>
> **Good warm-climate nuts:** Almonds, pecans, pistachios

slow-growing hardwoods, they take many years to reach their full size. Choose a planting site carefully and make sure that falling nuts won't create a problem overhead or underfoot.

Once they're planted, nut trees don't require much attention. Water young trees deeply once a week until they are established, which usually takes less than one season. Then mulch with 6 inches (15 cm) of compost to retain moisture and deter weeds. Snap off any suckers that appear around the base of grafted trees, because they will weaken the topgrowth and diminish production of the nut crop. Finally, steer clear of young nut trees when working with lawn mowers and weed trimmers—the number one enemy of nut trees grown in home landscapes.

Go for grafted trees. To get a good crop, choose a selected cultivar that has been grafted onto a seedling stock; trees raised from seed may not produce fruits of good quality. Plant more than one tree because many nut trees, including pecans and walnuts, require cross-pollination in order to bear fruit.

Whither the chestnut? Devastated by fungal blight, the majestic native American species has virtually disappeared, although plant breeders hope to soon have blight-resistant varieties available. As a substitute, you can plant the smaller, disease-resistant Chinese chestnut. To get fruit, be sure to plant at least two varieties.

Grow gourmet pine nuts. Piñon pines, natives of arid southwestern regions, bear resinous nuts in cones. Plant the small, slow-growing trees in a rock garden in areas where temperatures don't drop below 10°F (−12°C). Even more tender is the Italian stone pine, the source of the pignoli used in pesto. Northern gardeners can plant the nut-bearing Swiss stone pine, which is hardy to −10°F (−23°C).

Want almonds? Related to the cherry, almonds are pretty flowering trees whose blooms—and fruits—can be devastated by spring frost. Plant them in a protected site where temperatures don't dip below 10°F (−12°C).

To harvest black walnuts without getting stained by their sticky juice, spread plastic sheets under the tree before you beat the branches. You can gather up the crop in the tarps without having to touch the nuts.

To harvest pecans, mow beneath the trees before the nuts begin to fall. Gather nuts on a dry day, because pecans store best when dry.

Maintaining Your Garden

Any garden demands as much
of its maker as he has to give.
But I do not need to tell you,
if you are a gardener, that
no other undertaking will
give as great a return for the
amount of effort put into it.

—Elizabeth Lawrence, 1904-1985,
Gardening for Love.

LAWNS AND YARD
CARE

Although majestic lawns often were included in the grounds of fine French castles, beautiful home-size lawns are largely an American invention. Almost every yard includes some lawn, which provides space to play or relax and flatters nearby shrubs, trees, and flowers with its fine texture. And, although you may want to shrink the size of your lawn in the interest of reduced maintenance, why make compromises when it comes to the quality of your green carpet? In many ways, it is easier to meet the needs of a healthy, attractive lawn than to struggle with one that is underfed, weedy, or riddled with pests. As for those sites that simply refuse to support nice lawns, there are plenty of alternatives, including groundcovers, native wildflowers, and cushiony blankets of mulch.

Pursuing the dream of a lush lawn requires dedication as well as a good dose of positive thinking. Here to smooth the way are tips on selecting grass that suits your style and growing conditions, mowing like a pro, and all sorts of other bits of wisdom for avoiding pests, weeds, and back pain. Take care of your lawn's needs, and it will likely bring you more satisfaction than any other part of your landscape.

❧ Lawn Care Basics

FAR BEYOND MEETING your neighbors' expectations, a soft carpet of green grass is a fine place to play, an ecological boon, and bound to lift your spirits. Lawns are sometimes criticized by environmentalists, but if you use restraint with chemicals and leave room in your landscape for a diverse collection of other plants, a lawn can be a valuable feature in your home's outdoor ecosystem.

- A healthy lawn absorbs rainfall six times more effectively than a wheat field and prevents runoff and erosion of topsoil.

- Lawngrasses trap dust and dirt, and their roots (and the soil microbes they host) act as filters to capture and break down lots of different pollutants.

- An average front yard lawn has about twice the cooling capacity of the average home-size central air-conditioning unit.

- An attractive landscape with a well-maintained lawn can add 15 percent to a home's value.

KNOW YOUR TURF

Lawngrasses vary in their appearance and most active seasons of growth, but they all have several things in common. If you want to make a good lawn better, check these tips to make sure you're on the right track.

Fertilize when the grass is actively growing. Feeding a lawn that's resting or dormant often means you may be feeding weeds, wasting time and money, or causing unnecessary water pollution. Hold the food until your grass is ready to eat.

Check your soil's pH. Many naturally acidic soils need to have the pH raised with the addition of lime, which helps the grass take up nutrients better and enhances its resistance to disease. Inexpensive soil-test kits are available at garden centers, and pelleted or granular lime is as easy to apply as fertilizer.

Don't mow too low. "Scalping" a lawn invites weeds by weakening the grass and creating space for weeds to sprout and grow. Ideal mowing heights vary with the type of grass, but it's always better to mow a little high than to mow too low.

Make the most of your lawn's best season. All grasses have a time during the year when they naturally become lush and full. That's the best time to attend to small weed outbreaks or to give your grass a little extra fertilizer or water. The result will be tighter turf with deeper roots—exactly what will be needed if you're later faced with drought or other stressful conditions.

GRASS-RELATED ALLERGIES

With a bit of consideration on your part, your lawn need not add to your allergy suffering—and it may even help you breathe easier. The best lawngrasses won't produce pollen, either because they don't bloom at all (like hybrid Bermuda) or because regular mowing never gives them the chance. On the contrary, a thick lawn can trap billions of airborne pollen grains each season between its millions of long, slim leaves. When it rains or when you use the sprinkler, the airborne pollen is pushed down to the ground, where it remains.

Certain types of lawnmowers can help ease allergies, too. A rear-bagging mower traps and bags pollen along with the grass clippings. A well-maintained mulching mower dumps pollen below the mower along with the finely chopped clippings, and rain quickly pushes it into the soil.

Green it up. How green is your valley? Not green enough? Epsom salts, which add needed magnesium and iron to the soil, may be the answer. Add 2 tablespoons (30 ml) to 1 gallon (4 liters) of water, then spread it on your lawn. Afterward, water it with plain water to make sure the mixture soaks into the grass.

Use the right fertilizer. All lawn fertilizers contain abundant nitrogen, so the first number in the fertilizer analysis should be high. Whenever possible, buy fertilizer formulated for your type of grass. Timed-release or organic fertilizers cost a little more, but they don't need to be applied as often. With most grasses, a good feeding in spring, followed by the application of a "winterizer" fertilizer in late summer, provides ample nutrition.

There are exceptions. Turf-type tall fescue makes much of its strongest growth in fall, so the best time to feed is in September or October. A second feeding in early spring is often beneficial.

Don't overfeed. Excessive fertilizing stimulates blade instead of root growth, promotes thatch buildup, and "addicts" the grass to nitrogen so that it requires ever-increasing doses. Overfed lawns need to be mowed more often, too.

Help your lawn feed itself. Grass clippings contain nitrogen, and the first clippings of spring are the richest of all. Even if you bag your clippings to use as garden mulch at other times of year, allow them to "grasscycle" back into the lawn in spring and early summer.

A compost treat. Just as it does in your garden beds, compost works wonders on lawns. Spread ½ inch (12 mm) of screened, weed-free compost over the grass each spring or fall.

Another way to help grass thrive in heavy soil is to spread gypsum each spring. Made from powdered rock, gypsum helps grass roots penetrate more deeply and aids drainage. Depending on soil type, apply 4 to 5 pounds (2 kg) per 100 square feet (9 square meters) with a spreader or by hand.

(Continued on page 212)

Get to Know Your Grass

To bring out the best in your lawn, you need to know what kind of grass—or grasses—are growing beneath your feet. Many lawns are comprised of a single species, but just as many include several species grown together to form a happy community of intertwined plants. Climate is the major factor that influences the health and vigor of lawngrass, but sun, soil, and rainfall also play important roles.

Bluegrass is often the preferred lawngrass in cold northern climates. Its narrow, dark green blades create a fine, uniform texture, which makes it the grass of choice on sites where it's likely to grow well. Ideal sites are sunny and well drained, with deep, fertile soil. Bluegrass grows vigorously in spring and stays lush and green through summer and fall in regions where nights cool off. On the downside, bluegrass is susceptible to several diseases and needs extra water if dry spells last longer than a week. Bluegrass can be planted from seed or sod. Its ideal mowing height is 2½ to 3 inches (6 to 8 cm).

Perennial ryegrass and fine fescue are often combined with bluegrass in what are called cool-season blends for cold-climate lawns that receive partial shade. The resulting turf tolerates shade and foot traffic better than an all-bluegrass lawn, and the mixture cuts the risk of damage from pests and diseases. Cool-season blends can be planted from seed or sod. Mow at 2½ to 3 inches (6 to 8 cm).

Turf-type tall fescue adapts well to both winter cold and summer heat in the mid-Atlantic regions and upper South, and it grows well in light shade. Tall fescue does not creep like most other lawn-grasses, but close spacing forces the plants to become thin and upright. Also, this fescue has remarkably deep roots, so it grows well in a variety of soil types and needs less nitrogen than other cool-season grasses. In many sites, the limits of tall fescue can be overcome by combining it with small amounts of other grasses, such as fine fescue, which grows well in shade, and perennial ryegrass, which tolerates foot traffic. All are usually planted from seed. Mow high, at about 3 inches (8 cm).

Buffalograss is an American native that is now available in improved strains. And because it is a native, it often thrives in conditions too extreme for other lawngrasses, notably where summers are hot and dry. It also tolerates cold, and alkaline soil. Buffalograss has a fine texture, gray-green color, and rarely needs water once it is established. This same drought resistance makes buffalograss a misfit in climates with more than 30 inches (76 cm) of rainfall per year, since it can't compete well with weeds. Buffalograss spreads by runners, but is a strong, upright grower. A close cut can cause serious damage, so it must be mowed high, at 4 inches (10 cm).

Zoysia is the most attractive grass for sunny, well-drained lawns in warm climates. It has a luxurious look, and it forms dense, dark green turf. Long, hot Sunbelt summers are ideal for this warm-season grass, which is dormant in winter and greens up when temperatures rise in the spring. In the winter, it turns light buff and contrasts well with evergreens. Zoysia is slow to establish and requires regular feeding, yet tolerates cold winter weather and moderate shade. It must be planted from sod and it

must be mowed often at about 2 inches (5 cm).

Hybrid Bermuda loves hot weather, and it's a strong creeper that knits itself into tight turf. It also has a fine texture, and its dense growth makes it naturally weed resistant. Vigorous and disease-resistant, hybrid Bermuda greens up in spring and maintains its color up to the first frost. It grows best in full sun and requires regular fertilizing and frequent mowing. It is best planted from sod, although small repairs can be made with sprigs. Mow at 2 inches (4 cm).

Common Bermuda is quick to fill out, forms a deep green lawn, grows for decades with very little maintenance, and can bear up quite well under heavy traffic. On the downside, it's terrifically invasive and aggressively invades flowerbeds and vegetable gardens. It can be grown from seed. Mow at 2 inches (5 cm).

Centipede is a lawngrass that prefers not to be pampered and is the perfect choice for a combination of sandy acidic soil, high summer humidity, and mild winter temperatures. Centipede grows quite slowly and won't withstand heavy traffic, but it requires less frequent mowing than other warm-season grasses, and much less fertilizer. It can be grown from sod or densely planted sprigs. Mow at 1½ to 2 inches (4 to 5 cm).

St. Augustine is a favorite shade-tolerant grass in warm, high-rainfall climates. It forms coarse, yet attractive, low-growing turf with a rich, dark blue-green color. While it will not take much wear, it's great beneath tall pines, and its vigorous runners fill in fast. A few insects can cause problems for St. Augustine. This type of grass can be planted from sod or sprigs. Mow at 2 to 3 inches (5 to 8 cm).

Fertilize when rain is coming, because fertilizer works best when it's washed down to the grass's roots within 24 hours. Prompt watering will also wash down any granules that come to rest on the grass blades and keep them from burning the grass.

❦ Watch Out!

Never allow children to handle lawn fertilizer, and store all fertilizers and other lawn-care chemicals out of children's reach. These products can be harmful if swallowed.

If bagged fertilizer gets wet, you can still use it if you can crumble it into spreadable bits. This is easiest to do when it's still slightly damp. Write off the loss, though, if the fertilizer has hardened into large chunks, which can damage grass. To make the best of things, place a chunk the size of a table tennis ball in a watering can, stir well, and use the water to feed other plants.

Lime and fertilizer can be applied to the same area at the same time, but put them into the spreader separately. To avoid light and dark green stripes in the grass, apply half of the fertilizer by walking back and forth across the lawn in one direction, such as north to south. Then apply the second half by following an east-to-west pattern.

If you spill fertilizer or apply too much, remove as much as you can and flush the area with water to dilute the salt buildup that causes fertilizer damage. If you realize your mistake in time, go over the spot with a mower that has a

bag attached. In a small spot, try a wet/dry shop vac to pick up as much excess fertilizer as you can. If those strategies aren't an option, make a last-ditch effort by watering the affected space thoroughly for four days in a row. It just might work.

MOWING GRASS

Plan ahead. If you're designing a landscape from scratch—or planning changes that will affect large areas of space—take mowing into account. Decide how much lawn you're willing to mow, then plan features to make mowing

WHAT ABOUT WEED-AND-FEEDS?

In spring, when crabgrass and other weed seeds begin to germinate, many gardeners like to apply so-called weed-and-feed products, which combine fertilizer with a preemergent herbicide that keeps weed seeds from germinating. The best time to use these products is before the seeds germinate; many gardeners use the blooming of forsythias as the sign of proper timing. There is also an organic alternative called corn gluten, which, like the chemical herbicides, keeps crabgrass seeds from coming to life. As the gluten decomposes, it adds nitrogen to the soil. Whether synthetic or organic, never use a weed-and-feed in areas where you have recently planted grass seed, because the product will keep those seeds from germinating, too.

easier. For instance, design the lawn in a fairly symmetrical rectangle or oval, with few tight corners or narrow corridors. Locate benches and other fixed features outside the lawn so you won't have to mow around them. If it's difficult to mow beneath trees, either remove the low branches or use a groundcover there instead.

Take a third. Mow often enough so that you remove only the top third of the leaf blades each time you mow. If the recommended height for your type of grass is 2 inches (5 cm), mow when it reaches 3 inches (8 cm). If the lawn gets away from you, use a bagger or rake up excessive amounts of clippings. They make great mulch in other parts of the yard.

Double duty. If the grass gets too long—when you're away on vacation, for example, or during prolonged rainy periods—another option is to mow twice. Adjust the mower blade to the highest setting for the first pass, then cut again a few days later with the blade lowered.

When mowing a slope, always make cuts perpendicular to the incline. Straining to push a walk-behind mower uphill and restraining it as you go downhill is not only exhausting but dangerous. Explore alternatives, including planting groundcovers or spreading shrubs. If you have

established grass on a slope, consider leaving it unmowed. You may find that you like its billowy, windblown look.

Don't mow when grass is wet. The cuts will be uneven, and the clippings will clump up, forming clods that will smother the lawn. Wet grass can also clog the mower and makes a soggy mess around the mower blade. It's slippery underfoot, which makes mowing wet grass dangerous as well.

Mow grass higher when it's stressed, whether from heat or drought. Taller grass blades encourage deeper roots and keep plant crowns cool. Cutting too short weakens the plant's resistance to disease and allows weed seeds to germinate by letting more light penetrate to the soil. Also mow high late in the year, when the grasss growth slows down. Lawngrasses withstand winter better when they hold a bit of blade above their crowns.

Mow grass shorter in spring, when the weather is comfortably cool and grass is growing fast. Keep shaded grass a bit shorter to stimulate growth.

Prevent mower damage to trees by putting attractive stones over a layer of landscape fabric

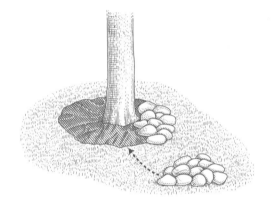

at their bases. You can also use mulch or a collar for low-growing groundcover plants.

Don't get stuck in a rut. Change the direction you travel with the mower each time you cut to prevent soil compaction and visible wear patterns. Alternate north to south and east to west with diagonal mowing patterns, which often look especially attractive.

☙ Watch Out!

To avoid the risk of cutting the cord on your electric mower, drape it over your shoulder or coil it around your elbow. Use a bright-colored extension cord so it's visible on the lawn.

Provide a strip. Lay a mowing strip of bricks at grade level along bed edges for the mower wheels to ride on. You can also make a strip with

stone, railroad ties, or other flat materials. This gives the lawn a clean edge and serves as a barrier to keep grass from creeping into flowerbeds.

Watch your feet. Never mow barefoot; wear heavy shoes or work boots to lessen the risk of accidents. And don't wear light-colored canvas shoes unless you like green footwear—grass can leave permanent stains in some fabrics.

Aerate your lawn. Wear golf shoes to aerate your lawn the next time you mow. They'll also help you get a firm grip on the ground if you have to push the mower up a hill.

For neater lawn edges after mowing, dig a furrow 2 inches (5 cm) wide around your lawn. Fill it with compost and plant with clump-forming lawngrass seed, such as perennial ryegrass or turf-type tall fescue. Even if the rest of your lawn is bluegrass or another creeping type, the thin edging of clump-forming grass will slow its spread.

CHOOSING THE RIGHT MOWER

How much mower do you need? The answer depends mostly on the size of your lawn and how often you like to mow. Some people love riding mowers, while others enjoy the ritual of walking behind a self-propelled gas or electric mower. If your lawn is tiny, an old-fashioned manual push reel mower may do quite nicely. When a bagger attachment is available, buy it. You may seldom use it to collect grass clippings, but a bagger is handy for doing a clean mowing just before an outdoor gathering or when you want to harvest shredded leaves to use as mulch in other parts of your landscape.

Walk-behind mowers

TYPE	FEATURES	LAWN SIZE	CUTTING PATH
Push reel mower	Blades on a revolving reel give a precise cut. Requires no energy—except your own—and is nonpolluting, low maintenance, quiet, and economical.	Lawns of a few square feet to ¼ acre (1,000 square meters). Good for fine-bladed grasses; hard to use in tall grass.	14 to 18 inches (35 to 45 cm)
Electric mower	Rotating blades give a good cut; runs quietly on regular household current or a rechargeable battery; folds for easy wall storage.	Small to midsize lawns of ¼ acre (1,000 square meters) or less; may clog when used on overgrown or wet grass.	16 to 20 inches (40 to 50 cm)
Self-propelled rotary mower	Motor drives two wheels as well as the blade for ease of operation; heavier than electric mowers but less costly and widely available.	Flat lawns of ½ to 1 acre (2,000 to 4,000 square meters) or smaller lawns that are hilly.	18 to 24 inches (45 to 60 cm)

Vehicular mowers

TYPE	FEATURES	LAWN SIZE	CUTTING PATH
Riding mower	Smallest type, with 6- to 12-horsepower mid- or rear-mounted engine; center or front mower deck with two or three rotary blades.	Lawns of ¾ acre (3,000 square meters) or more or smaller lawns if you want or need the convenience of riding.	25 to 36 inches (65 to 90 cm)
Lawn tractor	Front-mounted 12- to 15-horsepower engine and center mower deck; most run on regular gas, some on diesel.	Hilly lawns of more than 2 acres (8,100 square meters); hard to use on small lawns.	36 to 42 inches (90 to 110 cm)
Garden tractor	Front-mounted 15- to 30-horsepower engine, with mower towed at rear; attachments for tilling, aerating, and other tasks.	Estate-size lawns, farmsteads, or vast and varied terrain.	To 60 inches (150 cm)

Put on the finishing touch. Tidy the edges around flowerbeds, fences, walls, paths, and trees with a string trimmer, which can reach where mowers can't. Keep the cutting head level so you don't scalp the grass and be careful not to damage bark on trees and shrubs. Use an edger if you want an especially clean cut along edges that adjoin sidewalks or other hard surfaces.

All done mowing? Turn off the mower and clean the underside of the blade housing with a paint scraper or strong spray of water from the hose. Removing debris keeps the blade spinning freely and prevents rust. Also wipe the blade with a cloth dipped in undiluted white vinegar to kill any insects or grubs that the mower may have picked up.

Put safety first. Disconnect the sparkplug before doing maintenance work, cleaning the discharge chute, or turning the blades, which will cause some mowers to start. If you're removing the bagger to empty it, be especially careful when the mower is on.

Prevent clippings from sticking to your mower. The next time you give the underside of your lawnmower a thorough cleaning to remove stuck-on grass clippings, spray some nonstick cooking spray or rub some vegetable oil under the housing and on the blade. You will find that it will take a lot longer for the clippings to build up next time.

Split ends? Does your lawn look dull and gray after mowing? Examine the grass tips. If they've been shredded instead of neatly sliced, your mower blade needs sharpening. It's difficult to sharpen by hand because the blade must be perfectly balanced. Either have it done by a mower mechanic or simply buy a new blade.

POWERING DOWN YOUR MOWER

To make sure your mower's ready next spring, follow these steps at the end of the season.

- Change the oil and filter so you can start the next mowing season with fresh oil. Drain the old oil while the engine is still warm. It will flush out cleaner, and any contaminants won't settle back into the oil pan.

- Before storing your mower, drain the fuel tank completely or run the mower until the tank is empty.

- Thoroughly clean the mower, then tighten all nuts and bolts and check the belts, filters, and safety shields.

- Repair and treat any chipped or scratched metal surfaces with rust-retardant paint.

- Store your mower inside a dry building if possible. If you must store it outdoors, cover it with a waterproof tarp.

- Before starting the mower in spring, don't forget to add fresh oil. Start the engine and run it at low idle for a couple of minutes to distribute the oil throughout the engine.

GRASS CLIPPINGS CAN BE GOOD

Many gardeners believe that grass clippings left on the lawn create thatch—a dense mat that keeps nutrients from penetrating into the ground. It isn't true: Thatch is a layer of dead grass stems and roots that forms at the soil line. If you let the clippings decompose, they will release nitrogen into the soil almost continually, reducing the need for fertilizer by as much as 25 percent. "Grasscycling"—leaving grass clippings on the lawn instead of raking them up—is also environmentally prudent, helping to keep yard waste out of community landfills.

WATERING YOUR LAWN

How much water? The basic rule: Water heavily but infrequently. Your lawn needs about 1 inch (25 mm) of water per week during the growing season from either rain or a sprinkler. After 24 hours, an inch of water soaks the soil to a depth of 4 to 6 inches (10 to 15 cm) in heavy soil and about 1 foot (30 cm) in sandy soil. Water in the early morning so that the lawn can dry before sundown; grass that stays wet overnight is more prone to diseases. And never water in the heat of the afternoon, when moisture evaporates quickly.

Use the footprint test. If you walk over your lawn at midday and the footprints don't spring back within an hour, the grass is in need of water.

In cold climates, keep watering your lawn in late fall no matter how much snow you anticipate. Cold temperatures create desertlike conditions, with the freezing ground locking up water in ice and making it impossible for the grass roots to drink.

If a drought hits and you can't water, stop mowing, too. Long blades will help insulate the grass's crowns from hot sun. Limit foot traffic on a drought-stressed lawn, too, because it will be slow to recover from any injuries.

❧ Lawn Repair and Renovation

CATCHING PROBLEMS EARLY and fixing them is an important part of having a beautiful and lush lawn. Here are some things to keep in mind when you evaluate a troubled lawn.

EVALUATING A TROUBLED LAWN

Should you start over? Many landscaping pros evaluate a lawn based on this 50/50 rule of thumb: If more than half of your lawn is beset with weeds, invasive grasses, dead patches, or other problems, it's usually less work to completely renovate the lawn than to do spot repairs.

Reasons not to grow grass include the investment in maintenance—to look good and provide maximum benefits, grass needs regular mowing, food, and water. If a lawn would need daily watering, that's a good indication that you might want to try something very different in that area, such as a terrace or a small water feature.

Lawn alternatives. You may find it easier to substitute a groundcover for turfgrass, especially if your yard has steep slopes or areas of deep shade. Groundcovers don't need mowing or frequent weeding once they're established, and many require less sun than good-quality lawngrass.

A brown lawn may be caused by overzealous mowing rather than lack of water. Make sure you're removing only about a third of the blade when you cut.

Lawns beneath trees can suffer from fungal diseases encouraged by the shade and lack of air

circulation. Before taking drastic measures, prune off the tree's lower branches and watch your lawn improve.

REPAIRING A LAWN

Something old, nothing new. When you repair a lawn, stick with the same grasses you already have in place. It will look odd if you add a new, different variety to an established lawn to

GROW A MOSS LAWN

If part of your lawn seems determined to grow moss rather than grass, why not go with the flow? Over two to three seasons, you can turn a moist, shady spot into a moss lawn—relatively resilient, evergreen, velvety to the touch, and low maintenance. A bonus: Moss looks beautiful beneath the dappled shade of tall trees.

- Sour the soil to a pH of 5.5 to encourage moss growth. Use sulfur, aluminum sulfate, or ferrous sulfate on either bare soil or grass. These chemicals will kill grass, so just rake it up and add it to the compost pile.

- If moss is present in the area, gently pull any weeds or grasses—and be patient. It takes about three years for a moss "lawn" to fill in completely.

- If there are bare spots, fill them with moss taken from nearby areas. Press it firmly into the soil and water daily for the first two weeks after planting.

- Don't let leaves pile up on moss. Use a broom (not a rake) to sweep them up, or blow them off the moss with a leafblower.

Don't want moss? Correct conditions to make your yard less attractive to moss. Increase soil fertility with nitrogen and decrease acidity with lime. Aerate to combat soil compaction. Eliminate dampness by installing drainage tiles or dry wells and watering less. Remove or prune trees and shrubs that cast shade to admit more sunlight.

cover a dead spot, because the new grass is not likely to match the existing lawn's color and texture. If you've just moved in and aren't sure what variety grows in your lawn, dig up a clump and match it at the local nursery or home store.

Repair a small section of damaged turf by cutting out a section 1 or 2 feet (30 to 60 cm) square with the bare spot in one corner. Cut the roots with a spade, lift out the piece of sod, and

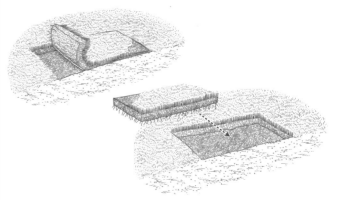

rotate it so the spot is in the opposite corner. Step on the patch to firm the roots in place. Keep moist until new grass fills the damaged section.

To patch larger bare spots, remove any dead grass and dig some compost into the soil. Rake smooth and at a level slightly higher than the surrounding lawn. Sow seed, or plant sod or sprigs. Tamp with the back of a rake to ensure that the seed or roots make good contact with the soil. Use clumps trimmed from the edge of your lawn to be assured of getting a good match.

Update an old bluegrass or fescue lawn by overseeding in spring or fall. Mow the grass very low, and rake vigorously to remove thatch and weeds while scoring the soil's surface. Spread a half-inch (13-mm) layer of weed-free compost, and sow seed at half the rate recommended for new lawns. Tamp to ensure soil contact, mulch, and water often to keep the seeds moist until they germinate. This is also a good way to introduce perennial ryegrass into a primarily bluegrass or fescue lawn, which improves its wear resistance during the winter months.

RESEEDING AND RESODDING

Read the label. Seed labels list the combined seed varieties. To ensure that you're getting good quality seed, check that the varieties are listed by trade name rather than generic name: 'Liberty' Kentucky bluegrass, for example, instead of Kentucky bluegrass. All of the better lawngrasses are sold as named varieties, and cool-season blends and other mixtures should also include variety names.

Seeds to avoid. Be wary of "bargain" seed mixtures, which often contain low-quality grasses like redtop *(Agrostis alba)* or rough bluegrass *(Poa trivialis)*. Such inferior lawngrasses can become weedy and quickly compromise the quality of your lawn.

Check and double-check. Seed labels also list the germination rate of each grass variety and the percentage of other ingredients, such as weed seeds and other seeds. Check that the germination rate is high—at least 75 percent for bluegrass and 85 percent for most other varieties. Then check

A COFFEE-CAN SPOT SEEDER

When it's time to reseed bare spots in your lawn, don't use a regular spreader. It wastes seed by throwing it everywhere, and only a small fraction will land on target. For precision seeding, you can fashion a spot seeder from an empty 1-pound (450-gram) coffee can and two plastic lids. In one lid, drill holes large enough to let grass seed pass through. Snap it in place when reseeding and keep the intact lid snapped over the can's bottom. When you're done reseeding, simply reverse the lids to seal in any unused seed for safe storage.

the amount of other seeds in the package; each type should be no more than 0.5 percent.

Don't make sod wait. Make advance arrangements to purchase sod so you'll know exactly when it will be delivered to your house or your

local nursery. Be ready to plant it as quickly as possible. If the sod is ready before you are, keep it in a shady place covered with a tarp to keep it from drying out.

Testing, testing. Get your new lawn off to a good start by determining what nutrients your soil needs. A soil test will also tell you whether you need to adjust your soil's pH.

Till the earth. Tilling to a depth of 4 to 6 inches (10 to 15 cm) not only lets you work fertilizers, amendments, and pH-adjusting materials into the soil but also aerates the ground so grass roots can take better hold.

Use the rake. After tilling, rake the soil well to remove any rocks and debris and create a smooth, level planting surface. Fill in any low spots before you begin planting.

Seed, sod, or sprigs? The answer depends on the type of grass you're planting, the season, and how much time you're willing to devote to the project. Sod gives instant results and requires

little follow-up care, and it's the best option in midsummer, when high soil temperatures may keep seed from germinating. The best times to start a new lawn from seed or sprigs are mid-spring or early fall.

Lay sod like bricks, using a staggered pattern so the end seams don't form a straight line; make sure the pieces butt together tightly. On a slope, run the strips lengthwise across the 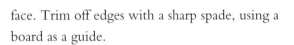 face. Trim off edges with a sharp spade, using a board as a guide.

How much to sow? The seeding rate depends on the grass species used—so make sure you have accurate measurements of the surface area to be planted and follow the recommendations on the seed package. Use a drop spreader to ensure even distribution over large areas. Sow half the seed in one direction, then sow the rest at right angles to the first.

Use a sprinkler to keep a newly planted lawn from drying out. Cover seeded areas with a thin layer of wheat straw to retain moisture and prevent erosion from heavy rains. The mulch will disappear as the grass grows, adding nutrients when it decays.

Wait to fertilize. Make the first application of fertilizer six to eight weeks after planting seed or sod. Unless a soil test determines a specific nutrient deficiency, use complete timed-release fertilizer—not fast green-up lawn food that's too high in nitrogen or a high-phosphorus winterizer fertilizer.

For a thick, lush lawn, begin mowing when the new grass begins to grow. To encourage newly sown grass to sprout and thicken, cut it when it reaches a height of 2 inches (5 cm) using a mower with the blade set to 1 inch (3 cm).

INSECTS AND YOUR LAWN

Avoid insecticides. A healthy lawn that receives good care seldom has problems with insect pests. Never treat a lawn with insecticides "just to be on the safe side." Doing so will kill beneficial insects and may also accidentally poison your favorite songbirds. Many lawn insecticides are harmful to humans, too, so they can be applied only by licensed pesticide applicators. Hiring a professional to cope with an insect problem is costly, but it may save you money in the long run. Many specialty insecticides are quite expensive and available only in large quantities. By working with a pro, you won't have to purchase 10 gallons (40 liters) of something when you need only a pint (500 ml). Your job is to keep a close eye on your lawn so any pest problems that do emerge can be caught early, before extensive damage is done.

Not all insects are pests. Don't assume that every insect is a pest, since lawns support a surprisingly huge zoo of unusual creatures. Harmless insects you're likely to see include earwigs, millipedes, centipedes, and grasshoppers. Thrips and fleas may use the lawn to launch themselves onto humans, but it's much easier to control fleas (and ticks) on pets than in a lawn. Spiders don't damage grass or other vegetation and in fact are generally beneficial because they eat large quantities of harmful insects.

LAWN-DAMAGING INSECTS

Ants in large numbers may not damage the grass, but tunneling in the soil and nest building can create problems.

Armyworms are the larval form of moths. When present in large numbers, they can chew turf down to the ground. Stressed southern lawns are easy prey for fall armyworms.

Billbugs are clay yellow to red-brown to jet black beetles with long snouts, and several species damage lawns by burrowing among grass stems near the soil surface and feeding on the leaves. The bluegrass billbug is a bluegrass pest, and the hunting billbug causes damage to zoysia.

Chinch bugs are about ¼ inch (6 mm) long and are black with white wings folded over their backs. They're often found on both warm-season and cold-tolerant grasses and can kill large areas of grass. Naturally occurring fungi often help keep chinch bugs in check.

Cutworms are the larvae of night-flying brown or grayish moths. Cutworms are present in most lawns, but they do serious damage only in newly seeded ones.

Grubs are the larval stage of many different beetles, including the Japanese beetle. They live underground, eating the roots of tender grass and eventually killing the plants. An organic treatment, beneficial fungus called milky spore disease makes lawns inhospitable to grubs.

Leafhoppers are infinitesimal—less than ⅕ inch (5 mm) long—and green, yellow, or brown-gray. Many species infest lawns, sucking sap from grass stems and leaves. They can badly damage a new lawn, and leafhopper damage in an established lawn often looks like a dry patch. Get expert advice before attempting to treat these invaders with insecticide.

Mites attack grass, sucking its sap and leaving behind blotched leaves. Only severe infestations of certain species will kill grass.

Spittlebug nymphs live inside frothy masses of spittle and suck juices from plants, but they are more a curiosity than a harmful pest. Chemical control is rarely warranted.

Sod webworm moths lay eggs on grass, and about two weeks later, the caterpillars begin to chew off blades close to the soil, leaving lots of brown stubble. Early August is the typical time for the heaviest damage, although June isn't unheard of. If the infestation is severe, an organic pesticide containing *Bacillus thuringiensis* (Bt) will quickly bring it under control.

TAKING CARE OF LEAVES

Do you have to rake? Yes, you do. Fallen leaves block light to grass, flowers, and even moss, so if you want a nice lawn or pretty flowerbeds, you need to rearrange nature's autumn fallout. Many gardeners regard fallen leaves as a blessing because they do such a good job of improving the soil when shredded and used as mulch or set aside to slowly ripen into compost. Save your raking chores for a clear, not-very-windy day, and perhaps you will even enjoy the job.

Design a leaf-eating landscape. Create beds near deciduous trees that can be filled with small shrubs and other plants that appreciate deep, natural mulch. When the leaves fall, simply rake them into the beds after running over them once with your mower.

Use a blower to remove leaves from decks, patios, and driveways. Wet leaves can be dangerously slippery underfoot.

Avoid back fatigue when you rake by moving your feet instead of standing in one spot and repeatedly bending and straightening. Instead of twisting the trunk of your body, rake leaves straight back and walk backward as you pull the rake with you.

Rake 'em wet or rake 'em dry. Wet leaves are heavier than dry ones, but they tend to stay put when raked into a pile. Wait to rake until the leaves are dry if you have allergies, because wet leaves can be a breeding ground for molds and mildews that make allergy sufferers miserable.

Got pines? Rake the needles as soon as they fall, before they get mixed with leaves, which usually fall later. Pack them into garbage bags and keep them in a dry place until you need more mulch for azaleas, blueberries, or other plants that like acidic soil conditions.

Mow over leaves on the lawn to collect them in the bagging attachment. High-nitrogen grass clippings combined with shredded, high-carbon leaves form a particularly good composting material. If you prepare planting space for spring flowers or vegetables in the fall, shredded leaves mixed with grass clippings make great winter mulch. When you rake back the mulch in spring, the soil will be ready to plant.

If you have a mulching mower, use it for grasscycling clippings back into the lawn, but don't expect the lawn to absorb a large supply of shredded leaves. Instead, rake or blow your leaves to a paved surface and mow over them several times to chop them up. They will then be ready to use as mulch, or you can put them in a separate pile to decompose.

COMPOST YOUR LEAVES

Before potting soils became widely available, gardeners hoarded their leaves until they decomposed into fluffy, crumbly leaf mold. Thin maple or dogwood leaves will rot into leaf mold in a matter of months, but thicker oak leaves may take two or even three years to fully decompose. You can speed the process by shredding the leaves first and then wetting them down well as you toss them into a pile. Moisture is essential, so locate your pile in a place where you can easily add water. You will still need to be patient, but after a year or so, the leaves are so fragile that they crumble in your hands, and you can start digging your black gold into your garden.

If you don't have a bagger on your mower, mow in square sections with the discharge chute pointed toward the middle of the square. It will toss the shredded leaves into a row so they will be easier to gather up and move.

Bundle them up. To save your back, don't pick up the leaves to put them in a wheelbarrow to transport them to the curb or leaf pile. Instead, rake them onto an old sheet or plastic tablecloth laid on the ground, gather up the four corners, and drag the bundle to the curb or leaf pile.

Set aside sticks and use them as fireplace kindling. If you have a large yard, a brush pile kept in an out-of-the-way place can become a shelter for chipmunks, birds, or other homeless wildlife.

PESTS, WEEDS, AND
EXPOSURE

It's much like the old saying "Into each life some rain must fall." No matter how much tender, loving care goes into your lovely garden, you will have to contend with outrageous insects, annoying pets, and wildlife that come from far and wide to nibble at your unintentional buffet. Every gardener must deal with weeds, and there's no avoiding other adversities presented by Mother Nature. Strong winds, anyone? How about an unexpected frost the day after you put out all your spring seedlings? Protecting plants is part of growing a garden, and doing it well is among the gardener's most useful skills.

Still, these problems are just stones in the road to the perfect garden, and they're certainly not reasons to give up altogether. You can't control the weather, but you can take steps to protect your plants. Most pests respond to some sort of organic concoction or maybe even get done in by a natural foe that you encourage to come around by growing beautiful flowers. And even if the pests cause a few casualties from time to time, they'll never get the best of you with these tried-and-true deterrents.

225

Control Techniques

PREVENTIVE MAINTENANCE is the best way to limit the trouble you'll have with pests and adverse weather conditions. Most important, begin with healthy plants that are well suited to your site and local weather conditions. Diversify the mix of plants in your garden to make sure that a single pest or other adversity can't cause serious damage.

From that healthy start, keep up with housekeeping. Deadhead spent flowers and clear away debris, which often denies pests a place to hide or nest. Monitor the garden often for evidence of pest damage so you can stop a small problem before it becomes a big one. Then use mechanical controls, such as barriers, traps, hand-picking, and floating row covers, and enlist allies such as chickens, frogs, birds, ducks, lizards, spiders, ladybugs, and bats—all predators that feast on unwanted garden pests.

BASIC SANITATION

Disease will strike plants from time to time, but you can reduce the odds with preventive measures and by purchasing plants that have been bred to resist diseases. One example is the 'Donald Wyman' crabapple—resistant to apple scab, fire blight, and rust. Plant catalogs often describe the disease resistance of their offerings, since most gardeners place a high priority on this valuable characteristic.

You can avoid damping-off disease by using sterilized potting media or seed-starting mix when you start seeds indoors. Damping off is caused by several strains of fungi that thrive in damp garden soil.

Keep leaves dry. Prune overgrown trees and shrubs to encourage better air circulation around and through plants. Plant annuals and perennials far enough apart and far enough from hedges and buildings to allow good air circulation. Most leafspot diseases and mildews are caused by fungi, which spread when leaves remain damp. Water your plants early in the day so the foliage dries completely before the dampness of evening returns.

Rotate each crop's location in the vegetable garden each year to stay one step ahead of any soilborne diseases, which usually require the presence of specific plants. Most of these diseases are caused by fungi that invade plant roots.

Rake up and dispose of all fallen leaves and fruit infected with fungi from around plants to reduce disease problems in the future.

Good sanitation keeps plant diseases from spreading. A solution of 2 tablespoons (30 ml) of bleach and 1 quart (1 liter) of water will disinfect several kinds of garden equipment, especially flowerpots and shears. Before reusing pots, wash them in the bleach solution, removing caked debris with a scrub brush or nail brush. Let the pots soak for an hour or more, then rinse and dry. You can sanitize garden pails in the same way.

Disinfect your pruning shears. Your shears can easily spread viral and fungal diseases as you move from branch to branch and plant to plant. When removing branches that show obvious signs of disease—or have suddenly wilted for no apparent reason—dip the shears' blades into a bucket of undiluted bleach after each cut.

BIOLOGICAL CONTROLS

What they are: Any biologically derived agents that help control garden pests. For example, some insects, called beneficials, feed on destructive bugs: Ladybugs eat aphids, green lacewings prey on a wide range of undesirable insects, and praying mantises eat just about anything they can catch. Critters from bats to toads are also exemplary bug zappers. Bees and wasps are helpful, too, as long as they're not nesting on your porch.

Ladybugs and other beneficials are drawn to nectar sources, such as Queen Anne's lace, lamb's quarters, goldenrod, and numerous other flowers. Other "attractive" flowers and herbs include members of the daisy family, such as yarrow, members of the carrot family (dill, parsley, and fennel), and both wild and tame cousins of familiar mint.

Supplement existing populations of beneficials with commercially available ones. You can mail-order ladybugs, lacewing eggs, and earthworms from suppliers around the country. Even beneficial nematodes, which kill caterpillars and grubs by invading their bodies, are available. Keep in mind that the right weather conditions—and a ready food source—are important if introduced beneficials are to remain active and thrive.

About toads. Toads are among the most efficient insect eaters, but be aware that they may consume as many beneficials as pests. Once you

attract them to your garden, they'll need water and shelter. Sink pans filled with rocks and water into the soil. For shelter, simply place a broken flowerpot upside down in a shady spot.

Put out a water dish. Be sure the beneficials visiting your garden have enough water to get them through a dry spell. Put out containers of water with rocks or sticks to act as perches. Change it often to keep mosquitoes from using it as a hatchery.

Pests, Weeds, and Exposure **227**

A natural insecticide called neem, derived from a common plant grown in India, *Azadirachta indica*, arrests the development of various insect pests. It's sold under various names, including Neemix and BioNeem.

Employ poultry. Bantam hens are better than pesticides at controlling insects. They're busy all day looking for caterpillars, snails, and beetles, and they don't dig big holes in the garden as larger chickens often do. Ducks and geese make great pest predators, too. If you use poultry, be sure to protect tender young plants with protective netting, because the fowl may peck up seeds and seedlings, too.

Welcome winter birds. After you clean up your garden in the fall, cultivate the soil in areas where you've had insect problems and let winter birds enjoy pecking up hidden pests and their larvae. You can do this in spring, too, when many birds need extra food for their young.

BEES

The great pollinators. Bees are essential in any garden. In their search for nectar and pollen, they carry pollen from flower to flower, facilitating fertilization in many edible and ornamental plants.

Which bees to attract? Bumblebees are more effective pollinators than honeybees, but for every plant there is a talented wild bee waiting to do its job. The shy, unobtrusive mason bee is among the finest pollinators because it works in

LOVELY LACEWINGS

Lacewing larvae are known as aphid wolves, and they have a voracious appetite not only for aphids but also for mealybugs, scale, and other insect plant pests. To attract them, just grow dill or sunflowers. To keep them in your garden, provide them with shelter, especially in winter, by filling a flowerpot with straw and hanging it in a tree. Many shrubs also provide a good habitat for overwintering lacewings.

weather too chilly and wet for other bees. Attract it with blocks of wood in which you've drilled holes 5 inches (13 cm) deep and ½ inch (13 mm) in diameter. Without help, mason bees nest in the holes in trees left behind by woodpeckers.

Attract a range of pollinators by growing flowers that secrete nectar and have a long blooming season. Good choices in a sunny border include bee balm, butterfly bush, cardinal flower, and goldenrod. Tuck in a few fragrant herbs, such as lavender and rosemary, and don't forget flowering vines, such as clematis, honeysuckle, and climbing roses. Tubular flowers attract butterflies and hummingbirds. Hummers often lap up tiny insects as they sip flower nectar.

Pesticide rules. When you treat plants for insect pests, protect bees in one of three ways. First, never use an insecticide on plants—whether fruit trees, flowering shrubs, or vegetables—while they are in bloom; wait until the petals have fallen. Alternatively, control insect pests with *Bacillus* *thuringiensis* (Bt) or insecticidal soap; neither will harm bees. When using more potent pesticides, cover plants with an old sheet for a day after you spray to exclude innocent pollinators.

On melons and cucumbers, blossoms are open for only one day. If an insecticide is needed, apply it in late afternoon, when most bees have returned to their nests. Pollinators are most active during the morning hours.

Avoid wearing perfume or cologne with a floral scent when you're working in the yard or garden. While it may attract bees, it also attracts wasps—especially the ubiquitous and annoying yellow jacket.

If you get stung, soothe the pain by applying a paste of baking soda mixed with water or rubbing alcohol to the sting. A folk remedy that may offer some relief is to gently rub the area with a freshly sliced white onion or potato.

LADYBUGS

A gift to gardeners. Ladybugs, also called lady beetles or ladybirds, dine heartily on pests in flowerbeds and vegetable gardens yet never damage the plants, and the larvae are hungrier than the adults. But don't expect them to be a cure-all: ladybug's appetites are limited primarily to aphids, mealybugs, spider mites, scale, thrips, and whiteflies.

Attract ladybugs to your flowerbeds with marigolds, angelica, butterfly weed, yarrow, roses, and goldenrod. In the vegetable garden,

HOW TO RECOGNIZE LADYBUGS

Among the 3,000 species of ladybugs, the type most familiar to gardeners is the one with a black-spotted orange back (**A**). But ladybugs can also be black or yellow, with or without white, red, or yellow spots. Two of the most common are the intriguingly named twice-stabbed ladybug (**B**) and the convergent ladybug (**C**). Convergent ladybugs often swarm in the fall, entering houses and buildings in great numbers. The easiest way

A   B   C   D

to make your house a ladybug-free zone is to vacuum up the intruders.

In the garden, ladybug larvae can consume up to 40 aphids in an hour; both adults and larvae (**D**) are predators. While ladybugs have a "flighty" reputation, they will stay put as long as they have a supply of food and water—including nectar- and pollen-rich plants and their favorite soft-bodied insects—and are not harmed by pesticides.

good lures include cucumbers, peppers, egg-plants, and tomatoes.

Buying ladybugs. Start with about 100 lady-bugs per 1,000 square feet (93 square meters); if they have enough food and water, they'll stay and lay eggs in a few weeks. Release them in your garden in the evening when it's calm and they have dew to drink. If it's dry, sprinkle your plants first. Place a handful of ladybugs around the base of a plant where you see pests and repeat every 20 feet (6 meters).

If purchased ladybugs arrive before there are insects for them to eat in the garden, you can store them for three weeks in the refrigerator.

Keep ladybugs at home by offering a hiber-nation site. Pile dead leaves, hay, straw, or other organic mulch at the base of a fence or around plants to serve as winter lodgings.

WASPS AND HORNETS

A hardworking family. Wasps comprise a large family of insects that includes hornets and yellow jackets. All are fierce predators of many common garden pests. Some members of the family, unfortunately, also damage fruit and deliver painful stings.

Bear with them. Yellow jackets and other wasps prey on fly larvae, beetle grubs, ants, and caterpillars. If you think their benefit to your garden outweighs the risk of getting stung, don't destroy their papery nests unless they're close to outdoor living areas or someone in the family is allergic to insect bites. Yellow jackets nest in the ground and can make mowing dangerous. Spray a wasp-killing aerosol pesticide into the nest at night, when the wasps are at rest.

Tiny helpers. Many beneficial wasps are so small—usually less than ¼ inch (6 mm) long—that you might not be able to see them. But you can sometimes find their handiwork. All benefi-cial wasps are parasitoids, meaning that they lay their eggs on an insect host, usually on eggs or larvae. The developing wasps then form cocoons on the host. If you see a grub or caterpillar with small, ricelike pouches on it, you have beneficial braconid wasps in your garden.

Where to buy them. You can buy beneficial wasp eggs from mail-order insectaries and garden catalogs. Follow directions for releasing them—some wasps should be set loose over a period of several weeks. Don't bother to buy them unless you're sure the pests they use as nurseries are in your garden.

Be a good host. Encourage beneficial wasps to stick around by growing the adults' favorite nectar sources, which include numerous flowers, such as goldenrod, clover, coreopsis, marguerite, sunflowers, yarrow, coriander, parsley, and tansy.

To avoid stings, don't use scented products when you work in the garden, including per-fume, scented sunscreen, or hairspray. Also avoid light blue or yellow clothing, and work outside in the evening, when wasps are less active.

To keep wasps off fruit, cover ripening fruits with muslin or pantyhose tied at both ends—right on the tree.

Build a bug trap. To get rid of yellow jackets that appear from unknown places, try this. Cut the top off a plastic bottle and invert it inside its base to make a funnel, securing the edges with tape if necessary. Pour sugared water into the bottle and hang it in a tree or simply set it where yellow jackets are active. The wasps will climb in to reach the liquid and will either drown or be unable to climb out.

INSECTICIDES

No garden is pest-free, but a well-tended garden contains a balance of beneficial predators and healthy, resistant plants—along with a tolerable number of undesirable insects and other pests. Use pesticides only if an infestation is causing damage and cannot be otherwise controlled. Start with the least toxic substance possible and gradually move to stronger measures as needed.

What they're made of. Insecticides are derived from a range of organic and synthetic sources and are available in liquid or dry form.

Many gardeners prefer organic types, which are made from bacteria, viruses, fungi, fatty acids, minerals, oils, and plants; they decompose quickly into nontoxic substances that won't harm the environment. All-purpose synthetic pesticides that contain carbaryl, permethrin, or malathion remain active for a few days and kill both harmful and helpful insects.

How they work. Insecticides are generally sprayed or dusted on plants or soil, where they suffocate, paralyze, or poison insects on contact or by ingestion. You must completely cover the affected plant or soil surface, including leaf undersides. Many organic pesticides must be ingested by insects, but soaps and oils kill through direct contact, as do most synthetic insecticides.

Systemic insecticides are absorbed by the plant and circulated by its sap; they can't be washed away by rain. Pests are killed when they feed on any part of the plant. Systemic insecticides should be used only on ornamental plants—never on edible ones.

Know your enemy. Be sure to identify the pest correctly and choose the appropriate pesticide. Find out about the pest's life cycle and habits so you can treat it effectively.

Be kind to bees. Many synthetic pesticides harm bees and other desirable insects. Try to use the most "specific" substance possible—one that targets the pest you want to destroy—and don't apply a bee-killing pesticide during bloom time, when bees are most active.

Horticultural oils, which include dormant oil and summer oil, are used to smother eggs and developing insects on trees and ornamentals. Use the heavier dormant oil in late winter or early spring, once temperatures are over 40°F (4°C) but before plants leaf out. Use the lighter summer oils any time the temperature is below 85°F (29°C).

Insecticidal soap is one of the best cures for soft-bodied pests, such as aphids, mites, and leaf miners. It's safe on most plants and nontoxic to beneficial insects and animals. But don't spray it in direct sun, in extreme heat, or during drought, because it can injure the leaves of some plants.

Brew your own insecticidal soap by mixing 2 teaspoons (10 ml) of dishwashing liquid with a few drops of vegetable oil and 1 gallon (4 liters) of water. Use a plastic spray bottle to apply it—but wash the bottle thoroughly if it previously held household cleansers.

Test first. Some pesticides—including natural ones—can scorch, discolor, or damage foliage. Always read the label and test the substance first on a small, inconspicuous part of the plant if you're not sure of its safety.

SPRAYING TECHNIQUES

Sprayers are not only useful for applying pesticides. You can use a sprayer to apply foliar

IF YOU MUST SPRAY...

- Always read pesticide labels carefully and follow the directions on handling, use, and storage to the letter.
- Apply pesticides on a dry, calm day with moderate temperatures and low humidity.
- Keep children and pets away from pesticides while they're being applied and until they have dried or settled completely.
- Cover as much of your skin as possible. Wear rubber gloves, a long-sleeved shirt and long pants, eye protection, and a dust mask. Avoid touching your face or eyes.
- Never eat, drink, or smoke while handling pesticides. Be careful to avoid inhaling powders or sprays.
- Don't allow pesticides to contaminate ponds, streams, or swimming pools.
- Never apply pesticides to food crops unless the labels state that it is safe to do so.
- Clean all equipment carefully after application. Wash your hands and face thoroughly with soap and launder clothing separately.
- Keep pesticides in their original packaging and store them in a secure, dry, cool place.
- Repeat applications only as needed and as indicated on the product label.

fertilizers to lawns or vegetables or to spray a herbicide on poison ivy that's run up a tree. The simplest sprayer is a handheld, trigger-type, pump spray bottle, which is fine for applying homemade pest repellents to plants. When using garden chemicals, reserve a sprayer exclusively for pesticides. Label it clearly with an indelible marker and clean it out thoroughly after each use.

No muss, no fuss. The easiest way to treat large areas is with a hose-end sprayer. You place a water-soluble fertilizer or chemical in a glass or plastic reservoir whose top attaches to a hose; when the hose is turned on, the water pressure draws up, dilutes, and disperses the solution. Be sure to use only concentrates specified for hose-end applicators and to adjust the sprayer settings for the proper dosage.

Sprayer styles. There are many styles of tank sprayers for home gardens, ranging in capacity from 1 to 5 gallons (4 to 19 liters). The most common type is the compression sprayer, which works with air pressure that's built up when you intermittently pump a plunger. Another type is the knapsack sprayer; you maintain the pressure needed to expel the contents by continuously pumping a lever.

Stainless steel or plastic? While both types of tanks resist corrosion, translucent plastic lets you see when to refill, and it's usually lighter than stainless steel.

Measure and mix. Use only the amount of chemicals recommended by the manufacturer for a specific application, and dilute with water in the proper proportion. To help chemicals stick to plant leaves, you can add three drops of dishwashing liquid or insecticidal soap per quart (1 liter) of prepared spray.

When filling a sprayer with manure tea or other solution that may contain solids, strain it through a doubled-up pair of pantyhose legs or a coffee filter inserted into a plastic or metal funnel. Filtering is necessary to keep any particles from clogging the nozzle of the sprayer.

A clogged nozzle? Clear it by inserting a thin nail or sewing pin or by spraying it from the outside with a strong stream of water.

FUNGICIDES

Think ahead. To work effectively, many fungicides must be applied before a disease starts to develop. Note which plants in your garden are attacked by fungus each year and use a protective fungicide before any trouble begins.

Homemade fungicide. Spraying leaves with a mixture of 1 teaspoon (5 ml) of baking soda and several drops of vegetable oil dissolved in 1 quart (1 liter) of water helps prevent powdery mildew on houseplants and cucurbit crops. On roses, it protects against both powdery mildew and black spot.

Know your enemy. To pick the proper fungicide, find out exactly what kind of fungal disease is attacking your plant. Among the most common culprits that cause diseases on leaves are powdery mildew and rusts. Your local garden center, nursery, or Cooperative Extension Service can help you to identify the disease and suggest both the safest and most effective method of control.

Treat plant diseases with vinegar. You can use vinegar to treat a host of diseases, including rust, black spot, and powdery mildew. At the first sign of trouble, mix 2 tablespoons (30 ml) of apple cider vinegar in 2 quarts (2 liters) of water and spray it on the plants in the morning or early evening.

Take two and call me in the morning. Aspirin is not only a first-aid provision for you, but for your garden as well. Some gardeners grind it up and mix it with water to treat fungus conditions in the soil (others use the ground aspirin as a rooting agent). But be careful when using aspirin around plants; too much of it can cause burns or other damage to your greenery. When treating soil, the typical dosage should be a half to one full aspirin tablet in 1 quart (1 liter) of water.

Is it really a fungus? Sometimes a problem you suspect is fungal disease is actually the result of overwatering, underwatering, or a nutritional imbalance in the soil. If so, a fungicide is of absolutely no benefit. Seek expert advice when you are in doubt.

How to spray. When using a chemical fungicide, treat all leaf surfaces thoroughly, even the undersides, and work your way carefully from the lower leaves to the top of the plant. Read the manufacturer's directions and follow them to the letter, because fungicides can injure plant leaves when applied in certain types of weather.

Problem Creatures

CRAWLING, FLYING, SWIMMING, and most definitely gnawing—there are literally thousands of types of leaf-eating bugs, beetles, and root-chewing grubs that may infest your yard, lawn, and garden. But with due diligence and some home remedies and natural repellents, you can usually take care of the problem. If you can't learn to live with the few that don't respond to environmentally friendly repellents, use chemicals only sparingly and always take precautions to protect yourself and beneficial insects that feed on other bugs.

BUG-FIGHTING BASICS

Easy insecticidal soap. Keep a bar of soap next to your outdoor water faucet. When you wash your hands, rinse them into your watering can. Then, when you water your plants, they'll get a nice dose of soap, which is a mild insecticide that kills soft-bodied bugs.

Rotate your veggies. It's the best way to make sure that surviving pests from last year's garden, which waited through winter in the soil, have a hard time finding the plants they most like to eat.

Attract apple and other fruit tree pests with this solution, placed in milk jugs and hung from the tree limbs.

Combine 1 cup (240 ml) each of water, vinegar, and sugar, and you'll collect lots of insects that mistake the mixture for ripening fruit.

Make a fly trap from the same mixture and put it in jars whose lids have punched holes just wide enough for the flies to get through. Place the traps on your deck or porch so the flies are caught before they come into your house.

Too many June bugs? Although they don't eat plants, their larvae damage the lawn, and they make spending evenings outdoors unpleasant. On a rainless night, fill a large tub with water and place a lamp or shop light over it. Turn the light on after dark, and many of the June bugs that fly toward it will accidentally drop into the tub.

Reflective mulch. Shiny silver mulch helps prevent thrips and other insects from finding your plants under this mulch because as they pass by, they're confused by the light and fly away. You can make your own reflective mulch by placing sheets of wide, heavy-duty aluminum foil around plants and anchoring them with stones.

Natural Foes of Problem Insects

Lots of beneficial bugs and birds eat problem insects. Attract the good guys, and you'll reduce problems with the bad ones.

• **Aphids:** Praying mantises (**A**), ladybugs (**B**), and aphid wolves (**C**) (the larvae of green lacewings) are natural foes of

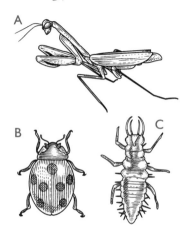

aphids. Hover flies and wasps kill aphids by injecting their eggs into aphids. Plant Queen Anne's lace to attract wasps and marigolds to attract hover flies. Birds, especially chickadees and house wrens, consume aphids by the thousands.

• **Caterpillars:** House wrens, mockingbirds, warblers, and catbirds devour harmful moth and butterfly caterpillars and the larvae of numerous other insect species. Install bird-houses in your garden or erect seed tables and plant fruit-bearing hedges.

• **Codling moths:** Woodpeckers pick out eggs of codling moths and many other insects that hide in tree bark. Attract woodpeckers to your yard in winter by hanging suet and seed feeders in affected trees.

• **Cutworms and moth larvae:** Trichogramma wasps are ben-eficial insects that parasitize many moth eggs, including those that hatch into army-worms and cutworms. Release wasp larvae in June when moths are laying eggs, or simply grow plenty of flowers.

• **Grubs:** Birds are hardworking grub eaters. Till your garden bed at least two days before you plan to sow or plant and let them pick it clean.

• **Japanese beetles:** Robins, starlings, and flickers, equipped with the long, pointed beaks needed for poking into soil, help control Japanese beetles by eating the larvae. Other birds, including cardinals and catbirds, eat the adult beetles. Make sure that fresh water is always available, but empty your bird feeders during Japanese beetle season to keep the birds hungry enough to snack on the beetles and grubs. Also invite birds into the garden by minimizing use of broad-spectrum pesticides.

• **Slugs and snails:** Blackbirds, ducks, frogs and toads, lizards, and snakes all consider slugs and brown snails a delicacy.

• **Whiteflies:** Lacewings and ladybugs are good whitefly predators.

A rhubarb insecticide. Soak 3 pounds (1 kg) of rhubarb leaves in 1 gallon (4 liters) of water for 24 hours. Bring the water to a boil and let it simmer for 30 minutes. Add 1 ounce (28 grams) of laundry soap flakes and let it cool before spraying it on bug-ridden plants.

Save your eggshells and use them to repel a wide range of garden pests. Crushed eggshells deter slugs and snails, and a layer of shells placed around onions and cabbage helps to discourage root maggots.

Use floating row covers to prevent damage by secretive critters that you rarely see, such as the moths whose larvae become squash vine borers, or flies, whose eggs hatch into beet leaf miners.

ANTS

Pros and cons. Gardeners usually consider ants to be pests, and it's true that ants can loosen the soil around young plants, causing them to die. Some species shelter and protect aphids so they can feed on the aphids' sweet honeydew. On the positive side, ants can improve air circulation in heavy soils, and their burrows improve water drainage.

Give ants an eviction notice. Mix equal parts of water and white vinegar and spray it into anthills and around areas where you see ants. They hate the smell of vinegar, and it won't take long for them to move on. Keep the spray bottle handy for outdoor trips and to keep ants away from picnic or play areas.

Scatter talcum powder liberally around house foundations and known points of ant entry. Other effective organic repellents include cream of tartar, borax, powdered sulfur, and oil of cloves.

Plant mint around the foundation of your house. Besides keeping ants away, the mint leaves can be brewed into delicious caffeine-free tea.

A mash of hot chiles and water will keep ants away. You can make another repellent by pureeing a few orange peels and a cup of warm water in the blender. Pour it directly into an anthill early in the morning.

Boric acid mixed with sugar is an effective ant poison—but only in gardens with no children or pets. Spread it on a piece of wood or stone near the nest, then cover it to protect it from rain. The foraging ants will love it and take some of the poison back to their nests.

To get rid of a colony, first plug the drainage hole of a large flowerpot with a cork or tightly wadded plastic wrap, then place the pot upside down over the anthill. Heat a teakettle of water to boiling and flood the surrounding soil. While you heat a second kettle of water, ants will seek shelter in the overturned pot. Quickly turn it upright and fill it with boiling water.

Create an ant barrier around plants, on front steps, and between garden rows with a sprinkling of agricultural lime, bonemeal, or powdered charcoal.

If ants are swarming your garden path, add 1 tablespoon (15 cc) of ground black pepper (or any other strong-smelling ground spice, such as cloves or dry mustard) to 1 cup (240 cc) of sifted white flour and sprinkle the mixture on and around the pests. They'll vanish within the hour. Sweep the dry mix into the garden or yard instead of trying to hose it off; water will just make it gooey.

Ant-free picnics. You watch helplessly as the ants march up the picnic table leg, onto the tabletop, and into the picnic meal. Here's a foolproof way to stop them in their tracks: Set the bottom of each table leg into a plastic container and fill the containers with water. The ants won't be able to crawl past the wet barrier.

Fire ants, better known in the South as red ants, are tenacious little creatures with vicious stings. They are especially partial to sun and sandy soil. If your yard is prone to infestation, provide shade with vine-covered trellises in a part of the garden where sun-loving plants won't be affected. And if you keep compost, store it in closed bins so fire ants can't use it to build their hills.

Inside the house, safely repel ants by sprinkling pennyroyal, camphor, clove oil, tansy, spearmint, or broken eggshells on a few dishes, then place them in closets and on shelves.

Wrap bands of paper coated with nondrying glue around the bases of fruit trees to prevent ants from reaching the fruit. An easy way is to fold a sheet of adhesive paper, such as the kind of liner used on shelving, in half with the sticky side exposed.

APHIDS

Don't waste time. Get rid of aphids the first time you see them; these pests reproduce rapidly. They not only suck the nutrients from plants but can also spread any number of plant viruses, including bean mosaic virus and cucumber mosaic virus. If hundreds of aphids cover stem tips, or they're clustered on the undersides of individual leaves, pinching off the infested plant part is easier than trying to kill the aphids.

To tackle aphids on rosebushes or other plants, bury dried or cut-up banana peels an inch or two (3 to 5 cm) deep around the base of the aphid-prone plants, and soon the little suckers will pack up and leave. Don't use whole peels or the bananas themselves, though; they tend to be viewed as tasty treats by raccoons, squirrels, gophers, rabbits, and other animals, who will damage plant roots as they dig up the fruit.

A simple and effective spray for aphids is 2 tablespoons (30 ml) of dishwashing liquid in 1 gallon (4 liters) of water. For another good spray, mix 1 tablespoon (15 ml) of liquid soap and 1 cup (237 ml) of vegetable oil, then add 2 teaspoons (10 ml) of the mixture to a gallon of water—but don't use it on squash, cauliflower, or cabbage, which can suffer leaf burn. When using either recipe, spray the plants with the mixture and follow with a spray of water. Wait about 15 minutes, then repeat.

Sprinkle wood ashes over bushes and low-lying plants; they are caustic and will dehydrate and suffocate aphids. Use a shaker with large holes, such as a grated-cheese container, or sprinkle them on by hand. After a day, wash away the ashes with a hose.

The smell of citrus pleases humans, but aphids don't like it. To make a pleasantly fragrant spray to use against aphids that have found plants on your porch or patio, blend the rind of a lemon with 1 quart (1 liter) of water and add a few drops of dishwashing liquid before spraying it on plants.

Spicy blender sprays. Use your blender to make organic aphid killers. Puree three or four jalapeño peppers and three cloves of garlic with 1 quart (1 liter) of water; strain and use as a spray. A mixture of mineral oil and garlic also works.

Concerned about using chemical sprays? Rotenone- and pyrethrum-based sprays are effective against aphids and harmless to humans, but using them is something of a tradeoff, since both kill earthworms and beneficial insects. Follow the directions on the container. Spray in the evening and be careful not to contaminate the adjacent soil.

CATERPILLARS

Caterpillars can wreak havoc in the garden. Treat the problem safely and effectively with a bacterial insecticide that specifically targets caterpillars, such as *Bacillus thuringiensis* (Bt). Harmless to animals, humans, and most other insects, Bt controls cabbage worms and loopers, hornworms, fruit-tree pests, and other crop-damaging caterpillars. It's also effective against cankerworms, fall webworms, tent caterpillars, and gypsy moths.

To keep cabbage loopers from damaging cabbages and their kin, poke branches of fresh arborvitae or broom into the ground between the plants. Or pinch tomato suckers off growing plants and spread them on the cabbages; tomato foliage emits a strong odor that will repel egg-laying white butterflies for a while.

❦ Watch Out!

Some caterpillars have stinging hairs, so never pick up a hairy caterpillar with your bare hands. Be especially careful if you encounter a caterpillar with a saddle-like marking on its back. The hairs of the saddleback caterpillar deliver a more painful sting than that of a bee.

Cedar shavings and chips—like those sold as bedding for small animals and dogs—make fragrant mulch that repels caterpillars, insects, snails, and slugs.

A caterpillar cocktail. If your cabbage loopers are chalky white and appear weak, they are infected with nuclear polyhedrosis virus (NPV). Process infected loopers in a blender with water, filter the solution through a coffee filter, and spray it on cabbage-family crops. The remaining pests will die within three or four days.

CUTWORMS

Frustrate cutworms with toothpicks. Cutworms kill your seedlings by encircling and severing the stems. Stick a toothpick in the soil about ¼ inch (6 mm) from each stem to prevent cutworms from encircling it.

Make vegetable garden collars. Use empty milk cartons to discourage grubs and cutworms from attacking your tomato and pepper plants. Just cut off the tops and bottoms of the containers and when the ground is soft, push them in around the plants.

Eliminate cutworms by tilling the soil as early in spring as possible to reduce weed seedlings—a favorite food. Cutworms are most numerous in new beds that were formerly occupied by grasses and weeds.

Protect young plants. Remove both ends of an aluminum can and push it into the earth to keep cutworms away from young garden plants. Use a soup can or a coffee can, depending on the size you need.

Foil those cutworms! Before setting out tomato, pepper, or eggplant seedlings, wrap

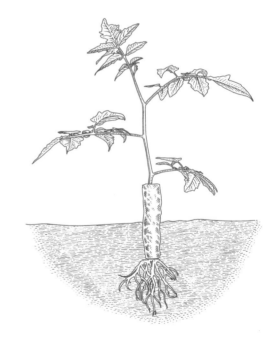

each stem with a 4-inch (10-cm) square of aluminum foil; leave it loose enough to allow the stem to expand as it grows. Plant the seedlings with 2 inches (5 cm) of foil above the soil and 2 inches below.

EARWIGS

Adios, earwigs. If your garden is under siege by earwigs—those creepy-looking insects with the sharp pincers on their hindquarters—get rid of them by making your own environmentally friendly traps. Tightly roll up a wet newspaper and put a rubber band around it to keep it from unraveling. Place it in the area where you've seen the earwigs and leave it overnight. By morning, it will be standing room only for the bugs. Place the newspaper in a plastic grocery bag, tie a knot at the top, and toss it in the trash. Repeat until your traps are free of earwigs.

Another way to capture earwigs: Cut a leaky garden hose into 1-foot (30-cm) lengths, making sure the inside is completely dry. Place the pieces where you've seen earwigs crawling around and leave them overnight. By morning, the traps should be filled with earwigs and ready for disposal.

Try a potato. Turn a potato into an earwig trap by cooking it, cutting it in half, and scooping out the middle to form two little bowls. Place them among your plants, and the earwigs will crawl inside to eat. Quickly gather them up and dump them into a pail of soapy water.

GRUBS, WIREWORMS, AND BORERS

What's a grub? Larvae of the Japanese beetle, June bug, rose chafer, and other beetles are fleshy, gray-white, wormlike creatures about 1 inch (3 cm) long, with six legs and brown heads. They curl into a circle when disturbed. Grubs live in the soil, feeding on grass and weed roots. Some species feed for one to three years before becoming adults.

Trap potato-eating wireworms, which are the larvae of click beetles, by scooping out small holes in the soil in several places. Toss in chunks of potato and cover with boards—the "nests" will attract swarms of wireworms. Every few days, collect the infested potatoes and drop them into a pail of soapy water.

GRUBS IN YOUR LAWN

If a patch of lawn is brown and spongy and can be rolled back like a carpet, it may be infested with grubs. To check for grubs, cut a square of sod about 4 inches (10 cm) wide and lift it up. If you see five or more grubs, that's enough to warrant treatment with milky spore disease, beneficial nematodes, or an insecticide containing imidicloprid (which won't kill beneficial earthworms). Another strategy is to water your lawn deeply but infrequently, letting it dry out between waterings. Beetles like to lay their eggs in moist soil; a dry lawn surface will discourage them and is inhospitable to any existing eggs.

You also can use beneficial nematodes (*Heterorhabditis* spp.), which are microscopic parasites, to combat grub infestation. After you spread them on the lawn, they will begin infecting and killing grubs within a few days. Both controls are generally available from garden centers and mail-order sources.

More solutions. Wireworms like moist soil, so you can deter them by improving drainage with organic matter or sand. Or plant mustard, buckwheat, or alfalfa in late summer and turn it under in spring. These green manures repel the pests and condition the soil.

Country gardeners may have a pest fighter: the chicken. Turn the soil, and chickens will eagerly scavenge for cutworms, wireworms, and grubs.

Squash the squash vine borer. Find the worm's entry hole in the vine and poke a piece of wire inside to kill it, or slit the stem open and remove the pest. Afterward, you can bury the wounded stem section of buttercup squash, and it will often develop new roots. Butternut squash are resistant to squash vine borers.

Band fruit-tree trunks with corrugated cardboard to trap codling moth larvae as they move down the trees to spin cocoons. Check for and destroy any pests weekly.

These pests aren't picky. Japanese beetles eat almost every part of more than 300 plants. They especially love members of the rose family (roses, raspberries, and apples), the hibiscus family (hollyhocks and hibiscus), sweet corn, and grapes.

Plant garlic among your roses, fruit trees, and berry bushes to deter Japanese beetles.

Check corn daily once the silk appears, because the beetles feast on the tender silks. Without the silk, no pollination can occur and no ears of corn will develop.

Cultivate the soil deeply in spring and fall to kill grubs and expose them to birds.

Handpicking can be effective for controlling adult beetles. Handpick in the early morning, when the beetles are sluggish and dew on their wings makes it harder for them to fly away. The easiest way to gather them is to knock them into a broad container filled with soapy water. The one thing Japanese beetles can't do is swim.

Try neem oil. This oil, which comes from the neem tree of India, is an effective botanical control for Japanese beetles. Applied to the soil, it keeps grubs from maturing into adult beetles. Applied to plants, it stops adult beetles from feeding. You can use neem on both ornamental and edible plants.

Pheromone traps give you a happy feeling because they nab hundreds of beetles, but they attract more beetles to your garden than would normally arrive. If you try the traps, set them at least 50 feet away from any of the beetles' favorite crops. Better yet, say nothing when you see your neighbors putting up the traps. Beetles from your yard will be drawn to their traps.

Mealybugs love houseplants, as well as certain fruits, vegetables, and shrubs. If you see small, pink or white cottony masses on leaf stems, you are seeing mealybugs. If you're a houseplant lover, always isolate newly purchased plants to ensure that they're free of these common pests.

Swab away mealybugs, dabbing them with cotton swabs dipped in full-strength white vinegar or rubbing alcohol. Or wipe down plant leaves with a sponge soaked in soapy water.

Outdoors, let the ladybug known as the mealybug destoyer (*Cryptolaemus montrouzieri*) prey on them. You can also spray plants with insecticidal soap or malathion.

Root mealybugs attack houseplant roots, so the plants appear thirsty and underfed. If you see cottony masses when you pull the plant from its pot, give the roots a thorough rinse and repot the plant in a clean pot filled with fresh soil.

MOSQUITOES

Their breeding ground. Mosquito eggs, larvae, and pupae all need water; only the adult is non-aquatic. If you eliminate all sources of still water near your house, you can reduce the number of young mosquitoes that develop into biting adults.

Repair, remove, or cover. Fix or get rid of any receptacle that holds stagnant water, such as a gutter that doesn't drain properly or a rain barrel you're no longer using. Also cover any receptacles that hold water permanently, including wells and cisterns.

Drain tree trunks. Remove water that pools in the holes of large tree trunks—a perfect mosquito breeding ground. An alternative is to coat the water's surface with a small amount of vegetable oil to smother any developing larvae.

Cover rain barrels and other water receptacles with custom lids. Attach a fine-mesh screen—with 14 to 18 wires per inch (3 cm)—to a removable frame sized to fit the container opening securely. Rainwater will pass through the screen easily, but mosquitoes won't be able to reach the surface to breed.

Get some dunks. A special strain of *Bacillus thuringiensis* (Bt) that's lethal to mosquito larvae is sold as little briquets or "dunks," which can be placed in any container of still water. Most stores that sell pond supplies have them. You can even place small pieces in a birdbath (don't worry—it won't hurt the birds).

Dump the eggs. Don't let water sit too long in the saucers under potted plants after rain or watering—adult mosquitoes may lay eggs there, and mosquito larvae need only a tablespoon or two (15 to 30 ml) of water to grow into adults.

Stock your pond. Goldfish can be the perfect allies in the war against mosquitoes. A yard that includes a garden pond stocked with goldfish often has fewer mosquitoes than yards with no water at all, because the pond works as a natural mosquito trap.

Use a fan when sitting on your deck or patio after dark. Mosquitoes are weak fliers and often can't make it to your skin if you're surrounded by fast-moving air.

ATTACK OF THE GYPSY MOTHS

In 1868, a professor returned to America from France clutching a package. Inside were a handful of gypsy moth caterpillars in a cage—the raw materials for the professor's dream of breeding a hybrid to make silk. Soon thereafter, wind blew open the cage, and the caterpillars escaped. Within a decade, they were chomping a swath through oaks, apples, birches, and other favorite hosts, infesting millions of acres. The larvae are so destructive that they can defoliate a tree in two weeks.

Numerous attempts have been made since the early 1900s to eradicate gypsy moths—with everything from DDT to beneficial insects—but they remain a serious pest.

You can often spot their brown egg clusters on tree bark or see—and hear—the caterpillars, which are spotted blue and red, feeding in early summer. Adults emerge in July; males are brown and females white. You can control larvae by wrapping burlap barriers around tree trunks or by spraying *Bacillius thuringiensis* (Bt) every 14 days from April to June. Scrape egg masses into a pail of kerosene.

Homemade repellents. To keep mosquitoes from biting you, try a mixture of essential oils diluted with baby oil. It's often effective for a short time, although it's not nearly as long lasting as a repellent that contains chemical DEET.

MOTHS

The adult moths that gather around lights on summer evenings are not gardeners' enemies, because they seldom feed on plants. It's the moth larvae that chew on, bore into, and roll themselves up in plants—whether leaves, fruits, stems, or roots. The larvae, which are called caterpillars or worms, represent the main feeding stage in a moth's life cycle. Caterpillars eat heartily to store energy for their development in the cocoon and eventual metamorphosis into winged adults.

Not all moths are harmful. Many moth species cause little damage and should be left alone. Also keep in mind that some caterpillars turn into beautiful, harmless butterflies.

The worst pests on garden plants? Gypsy moths, webworms, leaf miners, budworms, and bagworms. Watch for codling moths, cankerworms, and leaf rollers on fruit; cutworms, borers, tomato hornworms, and cabbage loopers prefer vegetables. You can control moths as eggs, larvae, or adults.

Pheromone traps, which lure adults with sexy scent, work in two ways. They capture moths in a sticky substance and alert you to when the pests are active; you can then time spraying to kill eggs or larvae. Just hang traps from trees that are likely to be infested.

Good bacteria. *Bacillus thuringiensis* (Bt) is effective against not only gypsy moth larvae but also bagworms, cabbage loopers, codling moths, and tent caterpillars.

Control larvae of codling moths, gypsy moths, and others by using barriers that trap caterpillars as they crawl down trees. Tie a 6-inch (15-cm) strip of burlap around a trunk tightly with twine. Check under the fabric regularly and destroy any pests you find.

Eliminate them. To control many moth larvae, pick them off plants and squash them or drop them in a pail of soapy water.

SLUGS AND SNAILS

Signs of snails and slugs. These little critters are the culprits if you find leaves filled with holes that have clean edges, often with a shiny trail of slime left behind.

Repel snails and slugs. Spread sawdust, wood ashes, crumbled eggshells, or diatomaceous earth around plants to keep them away. Strips of gritty sandpaper also work. To stop slugs and snails from getting into your potted plants, put used sanding disks under the bases of your pots. Just make sure the sandpaper is wider than the pot base.

Spray leftover coffee onto plants that are being bothered by slugs or snails. Mollusks are easily poisoned by caffeine, which enters their bodies as soon as the coffee touches them.

Make a trap by propping an upside-down flowerpot up on one side and putting a piece of orange or grapefruit rind inside in the evening. Next morning, you'll find the critters inside. Use upturned half-grapefruit rinds as lethal traps before discarding them. Slugs will use them as shelter, making them easy to gather up.

Trap them with beer. Set a margarine tub so the rim is at soil level and pour in an inch (3 cm) of stale beer. They'll crawl in and drown. Dump the container and add new beer every day.

Hair is horrible as far as slugs are concerned. Save hair from hairbrushes or pet combs and place it beneath plants being damaged by slugs.

Stalk them at night, because slugs and snails are nocturnal. After dark, hunt in their favorite feeding places, armed with a flashlight and a saltshaker or a bucket of salty water. Salted slugs and snails don't survive. Or spray them with a 50-50 solution of ammonia and water.

Snails and slugs won't crawl across copper; it gives them a slight electrical shock. Attach copper strips 3 inches (8 cm) wide to stakes to create a barrier around a flowerbed or glue them to the sides of a planter.

SPIDER MITES

These minuscule mites—called two-spotted spider mites, red mites, and simply spider

---

FIGHT SLUGS WITH VEGETATION

The one good thing about crabgrass is that it's poisonous to slugs. If you have a patch, gather some of the leaves (without seeds), chop them into pieces, and dry them for a few days. When you need slug bait, mix the dried leaves with some cornmeal and beer and place the "crabgrass cookies" where slugs will be sure to find them.

Plants that are reputed to repel snails include azaleas, apricots, basil, beans, California poppies, corn, chard, daffodils, fennel, fuchsias, grapes, ginger, holly, parsley, Peruvian lilies, pumpkins, plums, rhododendrons, rhubarb, sage, and Swedish ivy.

---

mites—attack fruit trees, shrubs, houseplants, and greenhouse plants. Although nearly invisible to the eye, they make themselves known by tiny webs on the undersides of leaves, as well as by leaves that are curled and grayish; the leaves usually become speckled with tiny yellow and brown dots. If the infestation is severe, leaves and buds will fall off, and the plant will die.

A spider mite test. Hold a sheet of white paper under a plant and tap the leaves gently. Any red spider mites will show up on the paper as little moving dots.

Favorite outdoor targets are cucumbers, beans, and strawberries. Hawthorns, rosebushes, and other shrubs are also affected, as well as many annual flowers.

Allow natural predators, such as ladybugs, green lacewings, or *Amblyseius californicus* (a predator mite) to control outdoor infestations. When impatiens or other temporary plants become infested, dispose of them before the mites spread to more long-lived plants.

Wet your plants. Spider mites thrive in dry, dusty conditions, which some mite predators dislike. Invite predators by misting plants early in the morning, every three days.

A buttermilk bath. Many gardeners swear by a buttermilk spray as a defense against mites. Mix ½ cup (120 ml) of buttermilk, 3½ cups (830 ml) of wheat flour, and 5 gallons (19 liters) of water and slather it on the undersides of infested leaves.

Don't handle clean plants after you've touched infested ones. And never use a feather duster to clean houseplants. Either can spread mites from plant to plant.

TICKS

What are they? Ticks are parasites related to mites and spiders. They need blood to complete their life cycle and feed on warm-blooded hosts.

Know their hangouts. Deer ticks favor shady, damp areas, especially at the edges of woods and fields. These are the ticks that transmit Lyme disease, and they are very small. Larger dog ticks live in fields and sunny, open areas near tree groves; they're active in warm weather.

TICKS ON HUMANS

When you're working around tall grass or densely planted trees, take precautions against ticks.

Protect yourself. Wear a hat, a long-sleeved shirt, lace-up shoes or boots, and long pants with the cuffs tucked into your socks. Spray your clothes with tick repellent and wear light colors to make detecting ticks easier.

Check yourself often. Look over your clothing frequently while gardening and check your body thoroughly once you finish. Deer ticks are tiny and hard to spot; dog ticks are larger—about the size of a match head. Both like to burrow in along your hairline or other moist places, such as under the waistband of your pants.

If you get bitten, remove the tick immediately—but don't bother trying to make it withdraw with oil, alcohol, salt, or a flame. Instead, use tweezers to grasp it as close to your skin as possible, then gently pull. Be careful not to squeeze its body, which could release fluids. Try to remove the tick with its mouthparts intact.

Treat a bite. Wash the bite with antibacterial soap and swab it with iodine or hydrogen peroxide; it may take weeks to heal. Keep any tick you remove in a tightly closed jar. If you develop any signs of a tickborne disease—a headache, a dark ring around the bite, or other unusual symptoms—see a doctor immediately. Lyme disease and other tick-transmitted illnesses are highly treatable when caught early.

Control measures. Use an approved insecticide recommended to treat tick infestations outdoors. Because ticks are carried by wild animals, however, no outdoor pesticide can provide complete control. Veterinarians can provide medications that keep ticks off dogs and cats.

Reduce wildlife activity. Clean up woodpiles, hedgerows, brush, leaves, and weed patches to discourage mice, the main carriers of Lyme disease. Clean up spilled seeds from bird feeders and stop feeding birds between April and late fall.

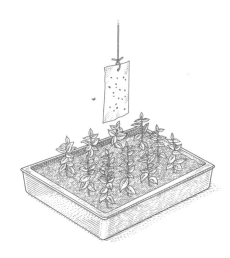

WHITEFLIES

Know your enemy. Tiny whitefly adults—about 1/16 inch (2 mm) long—resemble moths with white, powdery wings. Shake a suspect plant. If a white cloud rises, the plant has whiteflies.

Watch for whiteflies outdoors as soon as the weather warms; they attack many vegetables and flowers. Indoors, look for them in fall, when they come in from the cold; they particularly like chrysanthemums and poinsettias. Affected plants have yellowing, sticky foliage and may become covered with black mold that grows on the honeydew secreted by whiteflies.

Homemade sticky traps. Don't waste money buying yellow sticky traps to catch whiteflies. Instead, make your own by coating yellow construction paper with petroleum jelly. Place the traps on sticks on the ground a few inches from plant foliage or hang them over trays of seedlings or infested houseplants.

Attract and repel. Nicotiana or catnip (*Nepeta cataria*) lures whiteflies away from other plants, where you can destroy them. To repel whiteflies, plant some marigolds or nasturtiums among more susceptible plants, such as salvias.

Choose a cure. Control whiteflies on houseplants by wiping the leaves with cotton dipped in diluted rubbing alcohol. You can also spray with insecticidal soap, pyrethrum, or a solution made by mashing garlic cloves in water.

Suck them up. Use a small handheld vacuum to scour whiteflies off leaves—or even out of the air as they hover over plants.

❧ Problem Animals

MANY GARDENERS GO YEARS without enduring raids on their gardens by four-legged pests, but for others, deer or rabbits are daily challenges. Most of us enjoy seeing occasional glimpses of wildlife—as long as it's not ruining our plants. Whether animals are friends or foes depends in large part on how hungry they are. When animal populations are high and food is in short supply, animals overcome their instinctive fear of humans long enough to pilfer a good meal. Sometimes you can make a good guess at how close wild animals are to starvation by the persistence with which they go after your garden.

Animals that have plenty of other sources of food often can be deterred by insulting their senses of smell, using creative scare devices, or lacing their food with offensive flavors. For example, the noses of most mammals are offended by vinegar and ammonia. Many of the tips on the following pages capitalize on this fact, and you may dream up more ways to help animals decide that your garden isn't such a great place to have dinner after all.

ANIMAL-CONTROL BASICS

Keep stray animals out of your trash. Keep raccoons and other scavengers out of your garbage cans by spraying the outsides and lids with half-strength ammonia, or spray the garbage bags as you place them in the cans. Reapply the spray often, especially after a heavy rain.

Repel unwanted garden visitors. Put those old, deflated, shiny metallic balloons—the ones lying around your house from past birthday parties—to work in your garden. Cut them into vertical strips and hang them from poles around your vegetables and on fruit trees to scare off invading birds, rabbits, and squirrels.

Grow a garlic barrier. Protect a favorite stand of flowers or vegetables from hungry rabbits, moles, gophers, squirrels, shrews, and voles by encircling it with garlic plants.

Keep out four-legged creatures. Some animals—including cats, deer, dogs, rabbits, and raccoons—can't stand the scent of vinegar even after it has dried. Keep these unwanted visitors out of your garden by soaking several rags in white vinegar and placing them on stakes around your vegetable rows. Resoak the rags every 7 to 10 days.

Make a scent fence. This mixture doesn't smell so great to people, but if you won't be around and think wild animals will take advantage of your absence, it's worth a try. In a 3-quart (3-liter) jar, mix three raw eggs, shells and all, and a small bottle of hot sauce. Fill the jar three-quarters full with water, cap it tightly, and shake it. Let the mixture ferment for five days, then drizzle it around the perimeter of your garden.

Use a scent fence. Dig a shallow trench along the side of your garden that's often breached by wild visitors and fill it with the debris from your vacuum cleaner bag. To wild things, it will smell strongly of people, convincing them to stay away.

Thrift-shop row covers can protect all sorts of plants from rabbits, deer, and hungry birds. Collect sheer white or beige curtains and throw them over the plants at night. If you want to leave them on during the day, hold them aloft with pieces of PVC pipe stuck into the ground.

Whistling jars. Many old-time gardeners placed empty canning jars around the perimeter of the garden, and you can use glass bottles, too. The glass reflects light, and when the wind blows over the tops, the containers "sing." The sights and sounds discourage rabbits and many other unwanted visitors.

BIRDS

Birds like lots of the same foods we grow for ourselves—and they don't have the good manners to leave some for others! Tactics from row covers to scarecrows can thwart winged raiders, and you can also plant a few taste treats to lure them away from crops you want for yourself.

Cover berry bushes with ¾-inch (19-mm) mesh to keep birds from pecking the fruit. Build a framework to hold the netting 1 foot (30 cm) from the branch tips—so birds can't reach in—and staple the netting to the top and sides. Use netting to keep birds from nabbing ripe cherries, too. Dwarf trees aren't difficult to cover.

Protect row crops, such as strawberries from birds with ¾-inch (19-mm) mesh rigged over hoops. Tie the ends of the mesh around stakes and anchor the sides with bricks or stones. You can also use the hoops to support sheer cloth or floating row covers to protect crops against insects. Be sure to bury or securely weight the edges.

Keep birds off fruit trees. Nothing scares off those pesky intruders better than dangling aluminum pie pans. String them up in pairs (to make noise), and you won't have to worry about finding nibbled apples or peaches come harvest.

The straw man. Enlist the help of children to make an old-fashioned scarecrow stuffed with straw. It will be more effective if you hang streamers of shiny or reflective material from its arms. Keep birds wary by frequently changing the scarecrow's location, pose, and clothing.

Don't wait until crops are ripe before installing scarecrows. If you do, birds will already be familiar with your crops and will be more difficult to deter.

Rubber snakes and lizards tied among the branches of fruit trees will keep birds from coming close, and you can move them to the vegetable garden when the fruit harvest is over.

Make a snake. Cut a length of hose and lay it in your grass snake-style. Birds will steer clear.

Stuffed animals, which you can purchase for pocket change at garage sales, make good bird deterrents, and they look cute in the garden, too. Move them around from time to time so the birds don't figure out the game too quickly.

A wise move. A plastic or inflatable owl or falcon perched atop a roof or fence can deter many destructive birds, which mistake it for a real predator. Decoys are sold through specialty catalogs and at garden centers.

Beak busters. Paint a few dozen walnut shells bright red and scatter them through the strawberry patch before the berries ripen. By the time the fruit is ready for harvest, local birds will have learned to stay away from these unpalatable red globes.

CHIPMUNKS

While mostly harmless to the home gardener, chipmunks are known to feed on newly seeded garden beds. They can be a nuisance in rock gardens as well, where they burrow and disturb both rocks and your plants. The primary tactic for getting rid of Chips and Dales is to eliminate the places where they might take up residence, such as hollow logs and rock piles.

Keep chipmunks from burrowing in the garden by sprinkling dried bloodmeal on the soil surface; its odor is repellent to them. The blood also supplies the soil with nitrogen.

Bulb eaters. Chipmunks have an appetite for newly planted bulbs—especially crocuses, hyacinths, and tulips. For protection, plant bulbs in wire baskets or sprinkle moth crystals on top. You can even plant bulbs deeper than usual and cover them with coarse gravel, because the animals usually give up on digging when they get to the stones.

A harmless trap. If chipmunks become problematic, and it's not feasible to remove all of their potential homes, try trapping them and moving them to another site. Place a Havahart trap or small box trap baited with oats, corn, or peanut butter by the burrow entrance. Check with a wildlife official to ensure that moving wild animals is legal in your state or province.

DEER

Deer look shy and sweet, but they have proliferated in recent years and become a pest in many areas. They'll eat almost anything—flowers, leaves, fruits, and vegetables—so your garden offers an inviting menu. While they're eating your plants, deer will trample the garden and nibble bark from trees, and they may even harm lawn furniture—or themselves—while trying to satisfy their appetites.

Hit the hot sauce. Deer will find another place to dine if you spray your bushes with a very dilute mixture of cayenne pepper and water.

Protect individual shrubs by covering them with ½-inch (13-mm) wire or vinyl mesh. Secure it at the plant base with twine.

Protect planting beds by erecting an inconspicuous fence with black or dark green, 2-inch (5-cm) mesh netting. Fasten it to stakes or trees; it must be at least 8 feet (2 meters) tall and enclose the area completely. Otherwise, deer will be able to enter but won't have room to leap out. They will not only destroy your plants and the netting but may also injure themselves.

Stake chicken wire flat around the perimeter of your garden. Deer don't like to walk on it, and it's not an eyesore like an upright fence.

Discourage deer from nibbling on your tender young trees by tying white plastic bags to some of the branches. It works perhaps because the bags look like white tails—the deer's warning sign of danger. They're visible on moonlit nights, and they rustle in the breeze, which also helps spook deer.

Make bloodmeal sachets. To deter deer with the smell of bloodmeal, place about ¼ cup (60 cc) in a coffee filter, pull the edges together, and staple the packet shut. Push a wire through the top and tie the sachet to a plant you want to protect.

A "no trespassing" sign. To leave a scent deer don't take to, fill the foot sections of some old pantyhose with human hair collected from hairbrushes or your local barbershop. Even better, stuff the pantyhose with Rover's fur after a good brushing. Tie up the ends and hang the nylon sachets where deer tend to snack. They won't be back for seconds. The hair or fur loses its scent after a while, so replace it every four or five days.

GOPHERS

Gophers are bothersome rodents across North America and serious pests in the western two-thirds of the continent. They dig and live in a subterranean maze: a deep main tunnel contains the nest and food-storage areas, while extensive surface tunnels give them access to underground plant parts. To keep these destructive little diggers at bay, you can install barriers, catch them in traps, or try to repel them.

How to recognize them. Gopher tunnels often end in a distinctive fan-shaped mound of dirt. In contrast, moles push out soil from their holes in a circular pattern.

Effective barriers. Erect a barrier around your yard or garden beds with ½-inch (13-mm) mesh wire fencing. Be sure it's at least 2 feet (60 cm) high and is buried at least 2 feet deep; go 3 feet (1 meter) deep in light or sandy soil. Alternatively, line planting holes with chicken wire or the bulb cages sold at garden centers.

Protect tree bark with ½-inch (13-mm) galvanized hardware cloth. Sink the bottom edge underground and wrap the cloth completely around the tree.

The right trap. While rat traps will capture gophers, there are humane traps specifically designed for certain regions and certain species. Check with your local Cooperative Extension Service or wildlife management agency for their recommendations. Also ask about any laws regulating the trapping of wildlife.

GROUNDHOGS OR WOODCHUCKS?

Whether you call them groundhogs or woodchucks, these large rodents are the gardener's nemesis. They adore succulent vegetables from your garden, and they gnaw constantly—cucumbers, young tree trunks, you name it. These wily animals also leave behind ankle-wrenching potholes in the lawn.

Give peace a chance by planting a decoy crop of lettuce near the entrance to their tunnel. With luck, you'll keep them satisfied eating "their" lettuce instead of yours. If that doesn't work, the fumes of fox urine concentrate, which you can purchase at hunting stores, will discourage groundhogs from entering your garden. Be careful where you sprinkle this substance, however; the smell packs a punch.

Set up the trap in a shallow trench near the tunnel entrance and cover the trigger mechanism with a little soil. Sprinkle nuts, sunflower seeds, or grain over it, adding more bait inside the trap. Always wear rubber gloves when handling traps and bait so you don't leave your scent on them.

Encourage natural predators. If you want a real natural solution to your gopher problem and you live in a relatively rural area, make your yard and garden as safe and hospitable as possible for owls, hawks, gopher snakes, and king snakes, which are natural predators of gophers. Dogs, cats, and skunks will also pursue gophers, but dogs and skunks are diggers too—they may cause more damage to your garden than gophers do.

Vibrating soil. Many garden centers and specialty catalogs sell devices designed to repel gophers and moles. Wind-powered models that rattle when pushed by a breeze can double as lawn ornaments.

A homemade repellent. Soak rags in ammonia, drop them down a gopher hole, and seal all tunnel openings with dirt. The gophers will leave in a hurry. This tactic is most effective in spring, before gophers have made themselves thoroughly at home.

MICE

Mice may browse your ornamental plants for edibles or go straight for seed packets, bulbs, and birdseed stored in the shed. Whatever you do to keep them away, do it quickly—the little cuties multiply rapidly, and when there's a big, hungry pack of them, they'll eat just about anything.

Some don't like it hot. You can make ornamental plants too "hot" for hungry mice. Chop up a hot pepper and combine it with 1 tablespoon (15 ml) of ground cayenne pepper and ½ gallon (2 liters) of water. Boil the mixture for 15 to 20 minutes. then let it cool. Strain it through cheesecloth and add 1 tablespoon (15 ml) of dishwashing liquid. Pour it into an ordinary spray bottle and spray vulnerable plants.

(Continued on page 256)

Deterring Dogs and Cats

Pets may be members of the family, but the way they treat your garden may make you want to disown them! Since animal instinct makes it unlikely that they'll change their ways without your insistence, use these gentle tactics to show them what's acceptable and what's not. The same strategies work with strays and neighborhood ramblers, too.

DOGGIE, DON'T!

Keep dogs away from your most vulnerable garden plants by fortifying the area with thorny hedges and plants. Roses, barberry, pyracantha, holly, and gooseberry are all bothersome enough to deter the most determined canine intruders.

Fence off the vegetable garden with wire fencing or, even better, a picket fence. Border the barrier with colorful flowers for a decorative effect.

Use the sprinkler. If a neighborhood dog is an unwanted visitor in your yard, set up a sprinkler in the area it frequents and train it to stay away by regularly surprising it with a spray of cold water.

A natural repellent. Plant common rue (*Ruta graveolens*) anywhere that dogs are a problem. One rue plant beside each tomato plant will discourage dogs. A bonus: Pesky ants are also repelled by rue.
   Note: Rue is toxic to humans, especially to children.

KEEP AWAY, KITTY!

Felines are attracted to freshly dug earth. After you've been digging or cultivating, insert brambles or thorny prunings into the soil. The sharp branches will keep cats from getting too comfortable in your newly worked beds. If that doesn't work, try stretching some small-gauge chicken wire across the surface of the soil.

Save breakfast leftovers. Cats won't think of your garden as a latrine any more if you spread a pungent mixture of orange peels and coffee grounds around your plants. The mix is a great fertilizer, too.

Protect the birds. Keep their broods out of the reach of your cat's claws by planting a climbing rose on the sunny side of a tree where birds like

GROW A HAPPY CAT COMBO

Cats find the scents of certain plants irresistible. Indulge them by devoting a sunny corner of a flowerbed to growing feline favorites: mugwort, catmint, and catnip. Place cuttings of the plants where your cat likes to play or use dried leaves to stuff a cushion that she can nuzzle up to.

to nest. A collar of chicken wire will keep cats from climbing the tree, too.

Cover your seedbeds with holly branches or rose trimmings, which will discourage cats in search of a comfort station. It will also discourage neighborhood dogs looking for a cool, soft place to nap.

Keep cats out of your vegetable garden and add mulch to growing vegetables by placing conifer branches that you've trimmed off among garden rows. The needles serve as a prickly barrier that keeps animals from digging in the garden, while the dropped needles provide mulch.

Compost concern. Never add those dog or cat droppings to compost. They may carry disease organisms, roundworms, or tapeworms.

Store all insecticides well away from pets. Keep bonemeal and bloodmeal away, too, because dogs love them. Avoid using these fertilizers when setting out bulbs or other plants if you share your garden with a sharp-nosed dog.

Keep cats safe. Outdoor plants that can be poisonous to leaf-chewing cats include azaleas, delphiniums, daffodils, rhubarb, oleanders, foxgloves, and wisteria. Also, with their grooming habits and thin skin, cats can readily absorb garden poisons. Use the least toxic substance to control pests and weeds and let any sprays dry for at least 24 hours before letting your cat go near a treated area.!

PETS AND INDOOR PLANTS

Indoors, houseplants often need protection from cats and from playful puppies who may nibble on houseplant leaves. Many houseplants defend themselves with leaf and stem sap that causes a burning sensation, so smart animals learn to leave them alone. Try these tactics to support the learning process.

Prevent digging. Deter your cat from digging in large potted plants by placing inflated balloons on top of the soil. After popping a few balloons with its claws, the cat won't be tempted to return. Or cut pieces of bubble wrap to cover the soil, leaving slits for water to get through. Yet another tactic: Sprinkle rough gravel on the soil surface.

Toxic foliage. If your cat or dog is an inveterate leaf chewer, don't keep chrysanthemums, ivies, or philodendrons in the house.

Don't let mice spend their winter vacation in your garage or potting shed. They'll seek other quarters if you place a few mothballs in their favorite hiding places as well as near cracks where they're likely to squeeze their way inside.

A bulb screen. Use ½-inch (13-mm) wire mesh to keep mice away from your flowering bulbs. For individual bulbs, use wire-mesh baskets. In mass plantings, lay a sheet of wire mesh, with the edges turned down, over the planted bulbs before filling the bed with soil.

MOLES AND VOLES

Rarely seen aboveground, moles have tapered snouts and barely noticeable eyes. They don't eat vegetation, but their constant tunneling for insects and worms can mar your lawn and garden and heave roots and seedlings from the ground. Even more destructive, tiny voles sometimes move into mole tunnels and proceed to eat flower bulbs, girdle the stems of woody plants, and gnaw roots. Plants they don't kill outright may be invaded by diseases or die from water stress during periods of hot, dry weather.

Two repellent plants. Site mole plants (*Euphorbia lathyris*) near tunnels to deter moles. Castor bean plants (*Ricinus communis*) also work, but these plants are toxic. Never put them where they would be accessible to children.

Good vibrations. Moles are sensitive to sound. Repel them by using one of the commercial sound devices sold at garden centers. Or make your own by planting 5-foot (1.5-meter) metal stakes by the tunnels and attaching empty

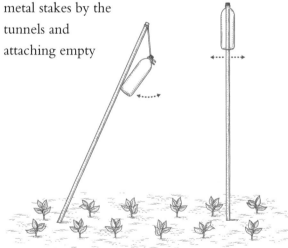

plastic bottles to the tops so they knock about in the wind. Or, insert a child's pinwheel every 10 feet (3 meters) or so into a mole run.

Repel moles. Moles may hate the smell of soiled cat litter even more than you do. Pour some down their tunnels. Or mix ½ cup (120 ml) of castor oil in 2 gallons (8 liters) of water and drench the molehills with it.

An organic vole repellent. If your vegetable garden or lawn shows signs of vole infestation, try a fertilizer that includes castor oil meal. This organic but poisonous product enriches the soil and discourages rodents of all sorts. Distribute several handfuls per square yard (square meter) and water it in; the effects of the repellent will last for several months.

Fortify a small garden plot against intruders by digging a trench 6 to 8 inches (15 to 20 cm) deep and 1 foot (30 cm) wide around the perimeter of the plot and filling it to the top with small pebbles or crushed gravel.

RABBITS

Peter Rabbit of storybook fame was typical—rabbits are dauntless and will eat just about anything that grows in the garden, including beans, carrots, lettuce, peas, the tender shoots of ornamentals, and even the bark of apple trees. Be aggressive early in the planting season because rabbits will quickly learn where the bounty grows, and they multiply quickly—as will your pest problem!

The right fence. To keep rabbits out of your planting beds, install a 2- to 3-foot (60-cm to 1-meter) fence of 1½-inch (4-cm) wire mesh on wood supports. Extend the

mesh 8 to 12 inches (20 to 30 cm) deep in the soil so that even the most determined diggers can't tunnel underneath it.

Pests, Weeds, and Exposure **257**

Repel with smells that rabbits dislike. One such odoriferous cure is bloodmeal, which is also an excellent fertilizer. You can even try leaving out an old pair of smelly sneakers, strategically placed. Be aware, however, that odor repellents are usually less effective than taste repellents.

Commercial taste repellents, including No Nib'l and Ropel, are available at some garden centers and hardware stores. Apply by dusting or spraying them on plants.

Plant borders. Plant a clover border around the vegetable garden; rabbits love clover and may prefer it to your edibles. Or border beds with plants rabbits don't like, such as marigolds, globe thistle, catmint, and black-eyed Susans—although if they're hungry enough, rabbits will eat these plants, too.

Use a blender to make a homemade repellent. Blend 1 quart (1 liter) of water, two to four hot peppers, and three to five cloves of garlic. Strain it into a sprayer and apply.

Save cabbages from hungry rabbits by planting shallots, onions, leeks, garlic, and other onion relatives between the rows.

Shelter strawberries, a favorite food of rabbits, by placing fine polypropylene bird netting over your strawberry patch. Use the ¾-inch (19-mm) size and double it over.

Protect young young trees. Wrap the bottom 1½ feet (45 cm) of the trunk with commercial tree wrap, burlap, or wire mesh. Wrap 1½ feet higher than your anticipated snowfall; rabbits will climb snow banks to reach the bark.

SQUIRRELS

Omnivorous and wily rodents, hungry squirrels are difficult to keep away from bulbs and tender shoots, and they will tear through a plastic bird feeder to get every last seed. You may have to employ several different strategies repeatedly, but start with the most important one: Never feed them. Well-fed squirrels have more babies, which makes a bad problem worse.

Nuts to nuts. Squirrels are so fond of nutmeats, especially filberts and walnuts, that they can empty a whole tree in short order. To make nuts less accessible, prune the lowest branches to at least 6 feet (2 meters) above the ground, then band the trunk with a piece of aluminum roof flashing 2 inches (5 cm) wide. Adjust the flashing as needed to allow for tree growth.

Make a walk-in tomato cage that's 6 feet (2 meters) tall and wide and 10 feet (3 meters) long using wooden supports and chicken wire. Be sure to bury the wire 6 inches (15 cm) deep to deter burrowers.

Spray tactics. Try using a scent repellent, such as one formulated for deer. Spray it around garden beds, trees, and bird feeders. You can also soak flower bulbs in a repellent before planting them.

🌿 Problem Plants

IF YOU LOVE TO GROW SHRUBS, flowers, and vegetables, it's a sad fact of life that you'll also be contending with their not-so-lovable relatives. Weeds, toxic plants, and even stumps and dead trees can be stubborn problems, but these tips will help you find solutions that work while protecting your beloved plants.

WEED-CONTROL BASICS

A weed is any plant—even an ornamental—that grows where you don't want it. Common weeds are fast-growing, resilient nuisances that not only make the garden look unsightly but also steal nutrients and light from other plants, and they may host pests and diseases. But don't automatically reach for the sprayer to treat lawn and garden weeds. A combination of the right tools, a little elbow grease, and some good old ingenuity will usually do the trick.

How do they grow? Weeds can be annual, biennial, or perennial. Annuals and biennials reproduce by shedding seeds—but a single plant of some weeds can yield more than 40,000 seeds. Perennials can spread by roots, stems, and seeds.

Shade them out. Weed seeds need light to germinate. Keep the soil around your plants covered with organic mulch, black plastic mulch, layers of wet newspaper, or fabric weed barrier.

Build a shield. Use edging materials like bricks or underground barriers of metal or plastic around garden beds to keep lawn grass and

THE 10 LEAST WANTED WEEDS

WEED	TYPE	DESCRIPTION
Bindweed	Perennial vine	Pointed leaves; twines on plants
Canada thistle	Perennial	Lobed, spiny leaves; wide-spreading roots
Chickweed	Annual	Floppy stems and leaves; blankets the ground
Crabgrass	Annual	Coarse-textured grass; invades lawns
Dandelion	Perennial	Toothed leaves; yellow blooms; in lawns
Ground ivy	Perennial	Lobed, mint-like leaves; creeping habit
Nutsedge	Perennial	Grass-like leaves; triangular stems
Plantain	Perennial	Broad, round leaves; hugs the ground
Poison ivy	Perennial vine	Three-lobed, glossy leaves
Purslane	Annual	Succulent leaves; purple stems; forms mat

perennial weeds from creeping into flowerbeds and vegetable plots.

Solarizing the soil means letting the sun do the weeding for you. Till the soil and water it. Lay a sheet of clear plastic over the area, anchor the edges with stones, and wait four to six weeks. The sun's heat will "cook" weed seeds, and maybe soilborne diseases as well. Don't dig the solarized plot before planting, because cultivating will bring buried weed seeds to the surface.

Get a head start. Cultivate your garden in the fall by working in plenty of compost. Rake beds or rows into the shapes you want, then mulch the surface with newspapers topped with straw, chopped leaves, or other organic mulch. In spring, there will be no weeds to pull, and your garden will be ready to plant.

Planning a new bed? Instead of digging out weeds and grass, smother them to death with a piece of old carpeting. This method works best during the hottest weeks of summer. Remove the cover in the fall, dig up the bed, and it will be ready to plant first thing in spring.

Be careful with compost. You can toss weeds into the pile if they're young and have not yet bloomed, because they have no seeds that will come back to haunt you next year. To kill weed seeds, compost needs to heat up to 160°F (71°C), and few heaps ever get that hot. One solution is to dispose of weeds in a special compost heap, then use the finished compost only when amending deep planting holes, where the weed seeds are buried at least 4 inches (10 cm) below the soil surface.

Keep soil covered. Don't let soil remain bare for any length of time, or weeds will move right in—they think that's their job. If you remove plants from a bed, blanket the openings with mulch or plant a cover crop or another plant.

HAND WEEDING

Few gardening projects are as satisfying as removing every last weed from a row of vegetables or a bed of flowers. If you schedule the job so you can do it in nice weather, weeding can even be enjoyable. Be sure to wear gloves to protect your hands, and have a roomy pail or wheelbarrow handy to carry away the pulled plants. If the weeds you pull aren't holding seeds, you can leave them on the soil surface as mulch.

Buy a dandelion digger, which has a sharp, notched end that will pry up stubborn weeds with taproots. You can also buy weeding tools with hoe-like blades and short handles, which are good for slicing weeds off below the surface.

Water before weeding. Weeds are easier to pull with their root systems intact if the soil is moist. Also, neighboring plants are less likely to be damaged when the soil is damp.

Take it all. Be sure to remove any part of the weed that can regenerate. Some weeds, such as quackgrass and bindweed, have buds on their roots that can grow into new plants.

Sprinkle salt on weeds that sprout in paved areas or wild patches. But don't use it around desirable plants, because it can injure their roots.

Pour it on. Drench weeds growing up through the cracks in paving stones or bricks with boiling water. Some old-time gardeners insist that water from boiled potatoes is even more effective. The safest way to carry boiling water is in a teakettle with a capped spout.

HOEING WEEDS

Every garden has weeds, so every gardener needs a hoe. Used wisely, a sharp, long-handled hoe makes quick work of young weeds, and you can use a hoe to mound up soil around the bases of

Grandpa's wisdom

One weed you should never hoe is common purslane, a ground-hugging annual pest. Its tiny seeds remain in the soil and germinate if exposed by cultivation, and its fleshy, water-retaining stems can form new roots even after the plants are hoed up. Pull out seedlings by hand and carry them out of the garden to dry.

your plants, too. For delicate work or tight spaces, many types of small hoes are available, including heart-shaped, rectangular, and three-pronged ones. These narrow tools penetrate everywhere and can be used between flowers and vegetables without the usual risk of bruising.

Hoeing know-how. Use a hoe with a handle at least 4½ feet (1.4 meter) long so you can work standing straight—not bent over, which can strain your back. Keep the blade sharp by filing it often with a steel file. Sever weeds by sliding the blade just below them, parallel to the surface.

Hoe when the soil is dry. You'll do a better job of chopping out weeds, and any leftover plant parts will be further damaged as they cook in the sun.

But not during a drought. While hoeing to uproot weeds, you expose more soil to the air, which lets more moisture evaporate. In very dry conditions, use pruning shears to clip off weeds at the soil surface and follow up with water-retentive organic mulch.

HERBICIDES

Weeds that can't be removed by hand or mulched into oblivion can be killed with herbicides. When weeds are young, a natural or low-toxicity product, such as organic herbicidal soap, will often do the trick. Save harsher chemicals for dangerous weeds such as poison ivy. Use them sparingly and pay close attention to safety precautions.

Kill weeds with vinegar. Vinegar is a completely nontoxic alternative to commercial weed killers. In both field and greenhouse studies, researchers at the Agricultural Research Service in Beltsville, Maryland, proved its effectiveness at killing five common weeds—including the all-too-common Canada thistle—within their first two weeks aboveground. The vinegar was hand-sprayed in concentrations varying between 5 and 10 percent.

Isolate weeds when spraying herbicides. To improve your odds of killing only the plant you want to be rid of, cut a 2-liter soda bottle in half and place the top half over the weed you need to spray. Then direct your pump's spraying wand through the opening in the bottle and blast away. After the spray settles down, pick up the bottle and move on to your next target.

Try undiluted apple cider vinegar to kill off everything from poison ivy to crabgrass. Use it on a windless, sunny day and protect any nearby plants from accidental exposure.

A toxin-free zone. Because a tree's roots are concentrated under the canopy, never use granulated herbicides to kill weeds there. Instead, remove them manually and cover the soil with organic mulch.

Don't risk runaways. Take care when applying herbicides on the top of a slope if desirable plants are located below. Water runoff could carry the poisons where you don't want them to go.

Keep cans separate. Reserve a single watering can, a sprayer, and measuring implements for use only with herbicides.

Be weather-wise. Herbicides work best when temperatures are mild—70° to 80°F (21° to 27°C)—and the soil is moist. Don't apply sprays before a rain, which will wash them away.

You've poisoned a plant by accident? If so, water it immediately and thoroughly to flush the chemicals. Continue watering daily for a week to limit the damage.

POISONOUS PLANTS

Hundreds of plants have toxic parts, which may be fruits, flowers, foliage, or roots. While some are infamous noxious weeds, like poison ivy, many others—from azaleas to tomatoes—are common ornamental and food plants. Learn to recognize and avoid all specimens that are toxic to touch or eat and be sure to keep children and pets away from them as well.

Leaves of three, let it be. One of the most common toxic plants east of the Rockies is poison ivy (*Rhus radicans*), recognized by its clusters of three leaflets that turn red in fall. The creeping vine bears small white flowers in spring and white, waxy berries through winter. A resin in the sap, called urushiol, causes an itchy rash on contact with any part of the plant. Even the smoke from burning the plants is an irritant.

INEBRIATED HOME BLEND WEED KILLER

For a quick and easy weed killer, mix at least 1 ounce (30 ml) of vodka, a few drops of dishwashing liquid, and 2 cups (473 ml) of water in a spray bottle (the exact proportions aren't critical). Apply the mixture to the leaves of weeds until it runs off. A couple of caveats: This will work only on plants growing in strong sun, and you should make applications at midday on a sunny day when the plant is actively growing. Why does it work? Alcohol can break down the waxy cuticle covering of leaves, leaving them susceptible to dehydration in sunlight.

The western cousin of poison ivy is Pacific poison oak (*R. diversiloba*). It also contains urushiol, has three toothed leaves, and causes skin irritation. This pest grows as a vine or, more commonly, as a shrub. A second type of poison oak (*R. toxicodendron*) is native to the southeastern United States.

A serious threat. Poison sumac (*R. vernix*), which grows in eastern and midwestern regions, can cause severe skin inflammation on contact. Usually found in freshwater swamps, the shrub has smooth, elliptical, pointy-tipped leaves that grow in clusters of up to 13.

There's no cure for the inflammation once you've come in contact with toxic plants. Try to limit an outbreak by washing your skin immediately after exposure with plenty of soap and hot water. Lather again, leaving a thick soap paste on your skin for 5 minutes, then rinse thoroughly. Treat any blisters with calamine or hydrocortisone, and try not to scratch.

Can't wash? Look for wild impatiens, commonly called jewelweed, crush the leaves, and rub them on the area that you think touched poison ivy. Leaves of plantain, another common weed, may soothe the rash.

Fido, too? Pets can also develop an allergic skin reaction, so don't let them romp near toxic plants. If they've been exposed, bathe them with soap and water. Wear rubber gloves, because even if the pup doesn't develop a rash, you might.

Don't try to pull up toxic plants—even with your skin protected. If you find a small patch, clip plants back to the ground with long-handled loppers, then smother the site with newspapers or black plastic. For large areas, eradicate with a systemic herbicide, such as glyphosate. Repeat applications for more than one season are often necessary.

COARSE UNDERGROWTH

When clearing overgrown ground to plant a new garden bed or lawn, extraordinary measures may be required to rid the area of stubborn weeds, brush, brambles, and vines. You may not be able to eliminate all woody plants at once, so settle for a slow approach—and be persistent.

A slow death. An easy way to clear undergrowth from a small area is by smothering it.

Cut down all the unwanted vegetation in spring. Cover the ground with black plastic and anchor the edges with boards or stones. At

summer's end, remove the plastic and dig up any remaining plants.

Mechanical means. You can rent heavy-duty tools designed specifically for cutting through undergrowth. A brush trimmer is similar to a string trimmer but has a toothed metal blade instead of a filament line. If you have a lot of woody growth with trunks under 2 inches (5 cm) thick, a brush trimmer can do the job. To cut down dense grass mixed with brambles, you'll need a "brush hog," which resembles a lawnmower with a large front cutting deck.

The last resort. Use herbicides to clear undergrowth that won't respond to cutting, pulling, or smothering—or those that shouldn't be touched, like poison ivy. Keep in mind that you'll still have to go through and cut down the woody plants, even if they are dead. If you do resort to herbicides, they're best used after the

site has been cleared, as a way to deter the little sprouts that will regrow from stumps left behind.

STUMPS AND DEAD WOOD

Stumps and dead trees present their own challenges. Before resorting to more drastic measures, consider using them to beautify the landscape. Stumps in particular take a long time to go away because they're attached to a huge base of roots underground. Short of hiring a bulldozer or digging yourself dizzy, here are some other ways to deal with a stump that has you stumped.

Disguise it. Unless you want to replant an area around a stump or the stump is in a prominent sightline, leave it in place. The easiest solution is to simply hide it with groundcover such as ajuga or periwinkle. Level the top of the stump and use it as a platform for a birdbath or decorative garden ornament.

A natural flowerpot. Another way to disguise a stump is to turn it into a flowerpot.

NUANCES OF NETTLES

Stinging nettle (*Urtica dioica*) is one of two plants that are called nettle. The other one, dead nettle, is an ornamental groundcover. Stinging nettle, on the other hand, is a weed that nonetheless has several uses.

Scots maintain that the linens their countrymen weave from nettle are more durable and beautiful than those made from flax. Folklore holds that stinging nettle promotes the growth of some vegetables and increases the quantity of the essential oils found in herbs.

Nettle also attracts beneficial insects and helps repel pests around fruit trees.

Here's how to reap the rewards and avoid the pitfalls of stinging nettle:

- Use it as an indicator of fertile soil. If nettle is growing wild on your land, plant there with confidence: the soil will be good for other plants.

- Stinging nettle is hailed as a soil builder because its nitrogen-rich foliage decomposes to form humus that's said to be as potent as manure. Before nettle develops seeds, place branches on a newly turned bed. Let them decompose and dig them in. You can also add nettle to the compost heap.

- Steep 1 pound (450 grams) of nettle leaves in 1 gallon (4 liters) of water for at least a week, then water plants with the solution, a rich fertilizer and natural pest repellent.

- Tiny hairs covering the foliage of nettle cause a burning and itching sensation that's as painful as a bee sting. Always wear leather or rubber gloves when touching the plant. To harvest leaves, pick from the bottom of the stem upward.

- If you're stung, rub your skin right away with an onion slice, sorrel leaves, or rhubarb.

Unless nature has already done it for you, hollow out the interior with an ax or auger until you've created a cavity. Coat the sides with a layer of clay and drill a downward-slanting drainage hole at the base. Fill the cavity with soil and plant with trailing specimens.

Snap any suckers. A freshly cut stump will periodically send up new growth from its roots. Pull off or cut back these sucker shoots at their base and daub the wound with an herbicide. Killing the stump with herbicide in drilled holes will also prevent suckers from forming.

Overlooked treasure. That's what a dead tree is, where nature is concerned. It attracts birds and provides a habitat for mice, squirrels, and other creatures, and it can stand like a sculpture in informal, natural landscapes. It can also become an imposing support for climbers, such as English ivy, Boston ivy, winter creeper, Virginia creeper, clematis, trumpet creeper, or climbing hydrangea. But don't cover trees close to public areas because they may disguise any weakness.

Effective, but smelly. If you're not in a hurry to remove a stump, a slow but easy way to destroy it is to drill a hole 2 inches (5 cm) in diameter in its center and fill it with 3½ ounces (99 grams) of saltpeter (potassium nitrate). Plug the hole with a cork and let the saltpeter penetrate for 10 to 12 months. Reopen the hole, pour in some kerosene, and set the stump on fire (the smell is unpleasant, so avoid inhaling the fumes). The flames spread slowly and turn the roots to ashes. After the embers have cooled, clean up any remains.

Note: Do this only on stumps that are well away from any structure. And check first to see if it is legal in your locality.

Can't burn? If local ordinances prohibit open burning, use any commercial solution with a bacterial or fungal inoculant, which will help the wood rot faster.

Is it safe? If you have a dead tree on your property, first evaluate the risks it would pose if allowed to stand. Could it topple on or drop a limb on a building, utility line, or a walkway or other place where people gather? Would removing some of its limbs or topping it back remove the danger? If not, it will need to come down.

Once a dead tree becomes a log, use it to line a rustic path or edge a naturalistic garden bed. Place it beside a pond as shelter for frogs and newts. Drill cavities in the trunk or use existing crevices as planting pockets for honeysuckle, ivy-leaf geranium, rose verbena, or cape plumbago.

MISTLETOE

Christmas wouldn't be complete without mistletoe, but this native plant is also an invasive parasite that sucks the sap from its host tree and adds extra weight to the branches. Most trees can tolerate small colonies of mistletoe, which seldom grows so well that it threatens the life of the tree. If you want to get rid of it, pull or cut out each colony, which is easier said than done.

If you actually want to cultivate mistletoe, select a host tree that's at least 20 years old. Collect ripe white berries from mistletoe already growing on another tree of the same variety. Smash the berries on the underside of a branch 5 feet (1.5 meters) off the ground and about 6 inches (15 cm) in diameter. The sticky pulp will harden and help seeds adhere to the bark. After seeds have germinated, they will sprout and eventually invade the host tree.

Even if you buy just a few sprigs of mistletoe, be careful. Its stems, leaves, and berries are poisonous and should be considered dangerous—keep it away from children by hanging it in a high place, such as from a doorjamb or ceiling.

❧ Adverse Conditions

IF EVERY DAY INCLUDED gentle, ample rainfall and plenty of sunshine, gardening would be a snap. But would it be as interesting? Here's how to cope with the adversity Mother Nature throws your way, from frost and wind to drought—as well as tips on pollution problems. Begin by becoming a skilled weather watcher, because no one else's weather is exactly like yours.

UNDERSTAND YOUR WEATHER

Collecting weather data specific to your yard will help you tailor your gardening chores, improve plant selection and placement, and reduce the risk that extreme conditions will injure beloved plants. You can easily construct home weather gauges to help you quantify wind and rain. Other important data collection is mostly a matter of knowing the best way to use what you already have.

Do it yourself. Always rely on your own temperature readings. Published reports may vary several degrees from the temperature in your locale, which makes a difference when temperatures are expected to be very high or very low.

Where to put a thermometer? For the most accurate reading, place it in a spot that receives no direct sun.

Frost warnings. Under certain conditions, a thermometer set 5 feet (1.5 meters) above the ground can show a temperature up to 15°F (27°C) higher than one at ground level. So, if the temperature reads 45°F (7°C) at that height, there can still be frost damage to tender, low-growing plants.

Use a rain gauge to measure precipitation levels accurately. Improvise with a simple home-made version. Cut off the top third of a large plastic bottle, slide the top upside down into the base to act as a funnel, and tape the edges

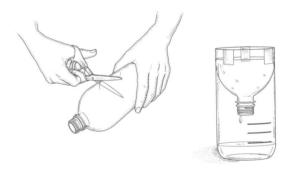

together. Mark off the measuring scale with narrow strips of waterproof tape or indelible ink, making the lines ¼ inch (6 mm) apart. If the bottle has the opaque plastic base common to many large soft-drink bottles, fill the base with water before setting the gauge outside. When it rains, check how far up the scale the water has risen. Note the amount, empty the gauge, and refill the base with water.

An ingenious tool. Use a maximum-minimum thermometer, available at most discount and home supply stores, to determine your garden's microclimates. With two separate gauges, it records the highest and lowest temperatures at a certain spot in a given time period. To see if a site for a new apple tree lies in a frost pocket, for example, place the thermometer there for two days. Compare the readings with those from a similar thermometer situated close to your house. A min-max thermometer is also handy in greenhouses or when checking the suitability of windowsills for houseplants.

Predict the weather with a trusty barometer, which gauges atmospheric pressure levels. Note that it's not the actual reading that matters but how the reading changes over time. A rapidly dropping barometer means you can expect unstable weather, and rising pressure usually accompanies clearing skies.

Use wild birds as barometers. When barometric pressure is very low, birds fly close to the ground, while high-flying birds indicate higher barometric pressure.

FROST AND FREEZES

Depending on your climate, frost can form on your plants from fall to spring. Hardy evergreens are immune from damage, but frost—which is basically frozen dew—can damage the tender young growth of even hardy plants, and it can kill plants with tropical temperaments. A true freeze, in which temperatures fall below 26°F (−3°C) for more than a few hours, is much more damaging to plants than a light frost. Signs of frost or freeze damage include puckered, distorted, or blackened foliage and blooms.

Alternate freezing and thawing harms plants just as much as the cold itself. Woody stems may split, and roots can heave out of the soil in a cycle of frost and defrost. The best defense for hardy plants is mulch. After cold weather arrives, spread 3 inches (8 cm) of shredded bark, leaves, or straw to help the soil maintain a constant temperature. Cover with netting, chicken wire, or tree branches to protect against wind.

Stop frost. When a light frost threatens your small plants, grab a bunch of plastic produce bags. Slip a bag over each plant and anchor the edges with small rocks. You can also use upside-down flowerpots or cardboard boxes. These covers will deprive plants of light, which does no harm for short periods of less than three days.

Another idea. Drape an old blanket over the plants before nightfall to trap soil heat and protect against light to moderate frosts. A thick quilt or comforter provides even more protection.

Pull and hang tomatoes. When the first frost is on the way, pull up your tomato plants, shake off the dirt, and hang them upside down from your garage rafters. The fruits will continue to ripen for several weeks.

Make a frost shade. Protect wall-trained vines, shrubs, and trees with a removable shade. To a piece of wood mounted at the top of the wall, attach a sheet of canvas large enough to cover the plants completely. Let the cloth hang down over the plants in very cold weather. Pull up the shade when it's warm and lower it in late afternoon to conserve heat for the night ahead.

PROTECT SPRING SEEDLINGS

There are lots of ways to protect spring seedlings from unpredictable late spring frosts.

- Cover each with an upside-down flower pot at night. Small cardboard boxes, held in place with a brick or stone, can be equally effective for rows of plants.

- You can protect cuttings and seedlings in pots with a plastic

bag or the top half of a plastic soda bottle placed over the plants. Remove the cap from the bottle for ventilation.

- Cut the bottoms from opaque plastic milk jugs and use the top portions as cloches. A stick pushed through a cut in the top of the handle and into the soil will help hold them steady in the wind.

- A light wood frame, two crossed hoops of wire, and a covering of clear plastic make a lightweight cover for seedlings. If built in several different sizes, the covers can be used for numerous plants and stacked for easy storage.

- Fill plastic milk jugs with water and place them in planting beds among your seedlings. The sun heats the jugs during the day; at night, these home-made heaters radiate warmth for delicate plants.

- In the vegetable garden, protect young spring sprouts with floating row covers. Lay the lightweight fabric right over the plants or hold it aloft with sticks or hoops made from heavy-gauge wire. Even lightweight row covers are

effective against frost down to 28°F (–2°C).

- Among the commercial devices designed to protect seedlings from frost are "hot-kaps." These inexpensive paper domes offer frost protection, but unlike plastic coverings, they're ventilated to keep plants cool in midday heat. The Wall-O-Water, a teepee-shaped contraption that encircles the plant, allows gardeners to plant weeks earlier than usual. Heat from the sun warms water in plastic protectors, which keep growing plants toasty on cold nights. This device works particularly well with tomatoes, squash, and roses.

An icy paradox. Let a sprinkler play over tender plants all night when a sudden freeze is predicted. Water gives off heat as it turns to ice and will keep the plants warmer than the air. This trick is often used to keep the blossoms on fruit trees from being ruined by late freezes.

Water and weed. Keep beds moist and free of weeds to head off frost damage in spring and fall. Soak beds in the daytime if frost is expected at night. This treatment helps heat rise from the soil on chilly nights and warm the plants.

A tailor-made muff. Wrap marginally hardy shrubs in insulated burlap screens. First, loosely stack oak leaves or straw around the plant (don't

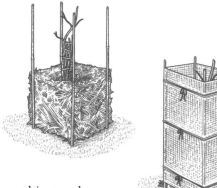

use thin maple or dogwood leaves because they'll become soggy and pack down). Then corral the insulation in a length of burlap supported by four corner stakes and tie it with cord. Leave the top open for air circulation.

Hill up roses. Pile mounds of soil 10 to 12 inches (25 to 30 cm) high around the bases of rosebushes to protect the roots, graft union, and lowest buds from cold injury. Remove the soil in early spring, but wait to prune until the tiny emerging buds indicate the extent of any injury.

Face facts. Once a tender plant has been injured by frost, little can help it—so don't bother blowing hot air or pouring warm water over it. Just lift it out and replace it. With hardy plants, simply wait until the weather warms in spring, then prune off branches that were killed by winter cold.

SNOW

Snow may seem like an annoyance when you're drooling over seed packets in the chill of winter, but it's often a gardener's best friend. Snow is not only gorgeous in the winter landscape, it also helps moisturize drought-stricken soil, insulates roots and dormant plants for extreme temperatures, and often cushions the weight of ice. Use these tips to maximize snow's benefits and minimize its drawbacks.

A useful signal. Areas of early-melting snow can indicate warm microclimates in your garden. Use them to grow tender plants or as a place to keep seedlings safe from sneaky late frosts.

No flattops. A hedge trimmed to a flat top may accumulate enough snow to cause branches to split or collapse under the weight. In heavy snowfall areas, protect hedges by cutting them to arched peaks, which naturally shed a heavy blanket of snow.

THE OLD-FASHIONED CLOCHE

Imagine a vast green field studded with shapely glass bell jars. A garden staple in turn-of-the-century France, glass cloches, or bell jars, were used to protect seedlings against frost. Use of these portable greenhouses has been recorded as far back as the 18th century, and French market farmers employed them by the thousands in fields outside Paris in the 1800s. Today, these devices are undergoing a revival in home gardens, where they double as handsome garden ornaments.

A slick trick for shoveling. Snow removal can be aggravating when snow sticks to the shovel. To make your job easier, coat your shovel with nonstick cooking spray before you start—the snow will slide right off!

Save snow for houseplants. Gather clean snow in a bucket and take it inside. When it has melted and the water reaches room temperature, use it to water your houseplants. Melted snow is as good as distilled water for plants that are sensitive to fluoride and the salts found in hard water. It often contains a few minor nutrients as well.

Snow mold is a fungal turfgrass disease that appears after snow has melted. To prevent it, cut back on nitrogen fertilizer in the fall, which encourages tender new growth that's easily damaged. Avoid piling up snow on your lawn, which delays spring melting.

Don't salt. Salty runoff can harm your plants. Instead of using road salt on walks and driveways, sprinkle on wood ashes, sand, gravel, sawdust, or fertilizer.

WIND

High winds can topple brittle trees and snap branches. Tall, stalked plants, from delphiniums and sunflowers to bush beans and tomatoes, can also take a beating in a windstorm. To minimize wind damage, plant tall plants in protected spaces or provide them with sturdy stakes. To reduce the effects of seasonal winds in late winter when you're trying to get a new garden started, create temporary windbreaks with shipping pallets or old doors. In climates where high wind is an ever-present threat, make plans for a permanent windbreak.

When the wind blows, protect young plants by hammering a few stakes around each plant and wrapping a barrier of burlap or a spun-bonded fabric around the stakes.

How much windbreak do you need? A windbreak can shelter a distance 10 times its height, so a wall only 3 feet (1 meter) high can provide some protection to plants up to 30 feet (9 meters) away. A stand of 5-foot (1.5-meter) evergreens will reduce wind velocity for a distance of about 50 feet (15 meters).

A temporary solution. To protect a small garden from wind damage, make a windbreak with plastic screening. You can buy it by the roll from a lumberyard or garden supply store. Install stakes or posts on the windward side of the garden and tie or staple the screening to them. A simple windbreak of this sort can reduce the force of the wind by as much as 60 percent.

Use deciduous trees to shield a garden from the drying effects of summer winds. When in full leaf, they provide summer wind protection for flowers, vegetables, and fruits. In winter, when the branches are bare, they allow the sun to shine through.

Save the trees. When landscaping a new yard, keep as many of the existing trees as you can for wind protection—especially those more than 30 feet (9 meters) from the house. If you decide to replace old trees with new ones, do it gradually over a period of several years. The existing trees will help buffer winds that might otherwise torture the new ones you plant.

Many plants won't tolerate deep planting that would provide extra support. Instead, plant at the recommended depth and support tall specimens with stakes or cages. As extra insurance, erect a barrier on the windward side.

For a permanent windbreak in a cold climate, plant trees and shrubs in two or more layers. To create a natural look, plant in a slightly curved row instead of a straight line. Space tall, dense evergreens, such as Douglas fir or spruce, as a background and fill in the front with flowering shrubs such as lilacs and viburnums. This living evergreen screen will protect downwind garden plants from winter cold and keep them from drying out, and it will reduce your heating bills, too. An evergreen windbreak on the side of the house that faces prevailing winds can reduce heating costs by as much as 20 percent.

Bundle baby trees. To minimize wind damage, cover the trunks of newly planted trees with commercial tree wrap, available at garden centers, or strips of burlap. You can remove the wrapping after the trees are established—usually within a year.

Let it through. In areas where high winds are common, prune deciduous trees so that strong winds can pass through their branches without doing damage. Remove the small interior branches to allow space for the wind. Carefully executed, such pruning can also enhance the appearance of the tree.

HEAT

Excessive heat from unrelieved sun exposure can be devastating to plants. This is true even in temperate zones during those terrible dog days of the summer, but it can also happen during the spring and fall in warmer zones. You have to especially careful with tender vegetables exposed to heat. Here are some tips for dealing with heat and exposure.

Heat-intolerant vegetables. Let cauliflower, cabbage, radishes, beets, spinach, and peas mature during cool weather by planting them as soon as the soil can be worked in spring. Plant a second crop in late summer. In hot regions they can be planted in late fall for a winter harvest.

Shade providers. Plant tall sun-worshipping plants like corn, sunflowers, or cosmos south of those that need a little shade each day, such as lettuce, spinach, and beets.

To create shade for plants that are heat and drought sensitive, construct a simple framework

of new or salvaged lumber over the planting bed. Cover the structure with wood slats, salvaged window screens, or even a piece of burlap.

Be careful with your lettuce. Choose a heat-tolerant butterhead lettuce so that you can grow it all season. Plant a succession of seedlings at two- to three-week intervals for a good supply.

Site heat-sensitive ornamentals on the shady side of buildings, next to taller shrubs, or beneath the overhanging branches of trees.

Don't plant under shallow-rooted trees, such as maple or beech.

Keep newly planted trees cool by painting their trunks up to the lower branches with white latex paint, which will reflect the sun's rays. Wrapping their trunks with burlap or crepe kraft paper will also help young trees escape the effects of heat.

Choose mulches wisely. Organic mulches like pine bark, wood chips, or shredded newspaper keep soil cool when spread 2 to 3 inches (5 to 7.5 cm) deep. Plastic mulches, unless covered with organic material, will merely make soil hotter. Any reflective materials, such as shiny pebbles, may contribute to foliage burn in hot or desert climates.

DROUGHT

Whether drought is a constant or an occasional fact of life in your region, compost, mulch, and deep watering are the best ways to prepare your plants and soil. A more permanent way to fight drought is by Xeriscaping—using only trees, shrubs, groundcovers, and other plants that are well adapted to the natural cycles of rainfall in your area. Don't worry that a Xeriscaped yard will appear drab and dry. If well designed, a naturally drought-resistant landscape can be full of color from flowers, foliage, and bark.

Get a jump on dry spells. Plants develop shallow root systems and become more vulnerable to drought if you water them frequently.

Instead, water less often—but slowly and deeply. This encourages deep root growth, which makes plants better able to search out scant moisture in the soil.

Using a bubbler, soaker hose, or drip-irrigation system, wet the soil to a depth of 1 foot (30 cm) for flowers and 1½ to 2 feet (45 to 60 cm) for trees and shrubs. Test how deep the water has penetrated by pounding an iron rod ½ inch (13 mm) thick into the soil. It will slide easily through wet soil but stop where the soil becomes dry.

Keep it cool. Stave off the effects of drought by mulching plants before hot weather strikes. The insulation provided by mulch makes plant roots less vulnerable to damage from surface heat and dryness. On a hot day, a 3-inch (8-cm) layer of shredded leaves will keep the soil as much as 18 degrees F cooler (10 degrees C) than any nearby beds that remain unprotected.

Compost goes a long way toward drought-proofing your garden. Use it as a soil amendment and as mulch to help the soil retain moisture, ensuring that your garden plants receive maximum benefit from watering and whatever precipitation you get. Spread a layer of compost about 2 inches (5 cm) deep over beds and dig it 1 to 1½ feet (30 to 45 cm) into the soil before planting; add another layer as mulch afterward.

Surviving water restrictions. When watering is restricted by law, use "gray water" from the kitchen sink, bathtub, or even your washing machine to irrigate your plants. Many ornamentals in particular thrive on the phosphates in detergents, which provide potash. The soap also acts as an insecticide. Just be sure that the detergent you use doesn't contain bleach, boron, or other toxic substances. Pour the soapy water gently over the plants, applying it to each spot no more than once a week. Alternate the applications with fresh water so that soaps won't build up in the soil.

No-no's for gray water include vegetables and other edible plants, ferns and similar shade-loving plants, and acid-loving plants, such as azaleas, rhododendrons, and violets.

Dormancy is grass's natural defense against drought. If it appears that a drought is going to drag on for a while, stop watering your lawn. Once the grass goes dormant—usually in one to two weeks—give it only ½ inch (13 mm) of water every two weeks. The roots and buds will stay alive without resuming growth.

Grow a clover lawn. Clover is more drought resistant than most turf grasses, and will stay green through the driest days of summer. Another reason to grow it: Because it absorbs nitrogen directly from the atmosphere, it also works as a fertilizer, amending soil that may later be bedded with plants.

Keep color in the yard by planting drought-tolerant flowers. Annuals that withstand dry conditions include gerbera daisies, sunflowers, portulacas, marigolds, and zinnias. Drought-tolerant perennials to consider include black-eyed Susans, penstemons, coreopsis, evening primroses, and yarrow.

POLLUTION

Polluted air and contaminated soil can harm plants, and gardeners can accidentally create pollution by using chemicals when they really aren't necessary. Preventing pollution is everyone's responsibility, and because plants often help remove chemicals from air, water, and soil, gardening can often help undo environmental damage.

Limit garden garbage. Reduce pollution by keeping garden debris out of the trash and composting it instead. Dispose of pesticide and other chemical containers properly.

Buy green. Use only garden products that don't pollute. Try organic fertilizers and pesticides, which won't harm the environment after they break down and don't pose disposal problems.

Prevent runoff. When using fertilizer, don't let it spill onto paved surfaces or into gutters; runoff washed by rain can end up polluting streams and lakes with phosphates. Properly applied fertilizer binds to the soil and seldom causes this kind of damage.

Stop the noise. Are you adding to noise pollution with your garden equipment? Use a manual mower or trimmer whenever practical. Make sure the mufflers on gas-powered tools are

POLLUTION-TOLERANT TREES AND SHRUBS

If you live on a busy street where automobile exhaust is present most of the day or in an area plagued with persistent air pollution problems, consider planting these pollution-tolerant plants.

Trees
- Crabapple (*Malus* hybrids)
- European birch (*Betula pendula*)
- Ginkgo (*Ginkgo biloba*)
- Golden raintree (*Koelreuteria paniculata*)
- Gray birch (*Betula populifolia*)
- Hawthorn (*Crataegus* spp.)
- Littleleaf linden (*Tilia cordata*)
- Maple (*Acer* spp.)
- Red oak (*Quercus rubra*)
- Pear (*Pyrus* spp.)
- Southern magnolia (*Magnolia grandiflora*)
- Sweet gum (*Liquidambar styraciflua*)
- Tulip tree (*Liriodendron tulipifera*)

Shrubs
- Arborvitae (*Thuja* spp.)
- Cotoneaster (*Cotoneaster* spp.)
- Forsythia (*Forsythia* spp.)
- Japanese kerria (*Kerria japonica*)
- Juniper (*Juniperus* spp.)
- Privet (*Ligustrum* spp.)
- Russian olive (*Elaeagnus angustifolia*)
- Spirea (*Spiraea* spp.)
- Tatarian dogwood (*Cornus alba*)
- Viburnum (*Viburnum* spp.)

working. Buy the quietest leaf blower available if you live in a neighborhood where there's a low tolerance for noise.

Stamp out fires. Don't burn leaves and other yard wastes—even if it's permitted in your area. Compost healthy plant debris, stockpile leaves to use as mulch, and chip or shred large branches.

Spray it away. If your plants are exposed to car emissions, soot, smoke, or other pollutants, give them a regular misting with the hose to clean their foliage. Avoid growing dark-colored flowers near dusty roadways, because they easily show dirt.

Plant a tree—especially if you live in an urban area. Tree leaves are natural air filters, absorbing chemical impurities that help create air pollution and releasing oxygen. They also trap dust, fumes, and odors. What's more, trees can reduce the temperatures of "heat islands," which contribute to smog buildup in cities.

SOIL IMPROVEMENT

The most fundamental element in the garden is soil—the very foundation for all plants. The gardener's job is to see to it that soil is healthy and in the best possible condition, which in turn leads to plants that grow vigorously and naturally resist challenges from pests, diseases, and stressful weather. But few gardeners are lucky enough to find great soil when they first push a spade into the ground. Instead, super soil for gardening must be created—a long-term process that is as interesting and rewarding as growing beautiful and productive plants.

Where to begin? Get to know your soil's texture and chemical nature, then begin improving it by adding organic matter. Dozens of materials are at your disposal, from grass clippings to yesterday's newspapers, and you can also make compost—perhaps the richest food you can feed your soil. Mulches should be part of your soil improvement practices, too, because they benefit both plants and soil.

Excellent-quality soil does a superior job of supplying nutrients and moisture, but many plants still need a bit of fertilizer to help them grow their best. Use the tips in this chapter to give your plants everything they need to prosper, from the ground up.

Understanding Soil

SOIL IS MADE UP OF inorganic particles—sand, silt, and clay—as well as organic matter, air, and water. It is very much alive, and it constantly changes as plants come and go, taking up nutrients and leaving behind their remains, which microorganisms break down into organic matter. Earthworms are powerful soil makers, too. They feed on dead plant material, and their continuous tunneling creates openings in the soil for air and water while enriching the soil with their nutrient-rich castings. Soil is also home to numerous insect larvae as well as beneficial fungi and bacteria. When you strive to improve your soil's quality, you become a part of this mysterious secret world.

The best garden soils have a mealy texture because their makeup includes large sand particles, small clay ones, and in-between–size ones called silt. Most important, excellent soil contains plenty of organic matter. When the balance is close to perfect, the soil is called fertile loam.

SOIL BASICS

To test your soil's texture, rub a pinch of moist soil between your thumb and forefinger. Soil that's too sandy feels gritty. Silty soil feels smooth and slick, while clay soil feels sticky and rolls up easily. Good garden loam feels mealy, and it may contain about 50 percent sand, 25 to 30 percent silt, up to 25 percent clay, and 5 to 10 percent organic matter.

Take the texture test. Lightly squeeze a handful of moist soil. If the clump crumbles, the soil is sandy. If it forms a sticky ball, it's clay. If it ends up as a spongy ball, you have loam.

How much organic matter does your soil have? To guess at the answer, drop a spadeful of moist soil on a hard surface: if it breaks into crumbs ½ inch (13 mm) in diameter, its organic matter content is close to ideal. If it breaks into large clods or shatters into a sandy pile, it needs substantial amending.

How rich is your soil? Rich soil teems with more than a dozen of the nutrients plants need for growth, including trace elements. Soils that are naturally rich (without improvement by gardeners) are usually limited to bottomland near rivers, which is enriched with organic matter each time floodwaters recede. Lean or infertile soils contain few plant nutrients. A soil test will tell you how your soil rates in terms of fertility, or you can watch your plants. Plants that grow slowly and never reach the size they should are a clear indication of low soil fertility.

Add organic matter. The single most important way to improve all soils is by adding organic matter. Work 1 to 4 inches (3 to 10 cm) of rotted manure, compost, chopped leaves, or other organic matter into the soil each year to turn any type of soil into fertile garden loam. Dig as deeply as possible, because digging or deep tilling aerates the soil. Beneficial soil microorganisms need oxygen to break down organic matter and release nutrients.

Tread lightly. To avoid compacting the soil by squeezing out the air pockets and pushing particles together, don't walk on, work in, or drive machinery over it when it's wet. Neither air nor water can move through tight, compacted soil.

Go for good resistance. Several common soilborne plant diseases and pests are permanent residents in gardens. If you're new to an area, talk with gardening neighbors or Master Gardeners to find out if fusarium, verticillium, or nematodes are prevalent in your area. If they are, choose plant varieties that offer genetic resistance to these diseases, because it's impossible to rid the soil of them entirely.

Water correctly. Some leafspot diseases overwinter in soil, so they can be spread to leaves when soil is splashed on foliage during heavy rains or routine watering. Use a soaker hose or drip irrigation and water only in the morning, so leaves can dry off quickly. Also use mulch, which forms a barrier between the soil and plant leaves.

Cook away problem critters. Heating soil with solarization (see page 263) can rid it of weeds and insect and disease problems as well as soil-dwelling nematodes—microscopic "eelworms" that swim through the spaces between soil particles and become parasites on plant roots.

CLAY SOIL

Clay soil is comprised of extremely tiny soil particles that stick together when wet and leave only a little space for air between the particles when the soil is dry. The density of clay soil makes it heavy to lift and slow to dry out after heavy rains. On the plus side, clay soil that is generously enriched with organic matter retains both nutrients and moisture for a long time. As a result, plants that are well rooted are able to tolerate periods of drought well.

Avoid drainage disasters. Clay soil drains slowly, and low spots where rainwater puddles for a long time are signs of particularly poor drainage. If you want to garden in such a spot, consider using raised beds. Or stick with nature's plan and turn the area into a bog garden.

Use a secret weapon. Many gardeners find that gypsum—a rock powder containing calcium sulfate—helps to loosen tight clay, improving soil structure and aiding air and water penetration. Spread and work in 10 pounds (4.5 kg) of gypsum per 100 square feet (9 square meters) for a new garden bed. Repeat every four or five years.

Easier digging? Use a digging fork to make punctures in tight clay before you begin cultivating it with a spade. Push the fork into the soil and wiggle the tines slightly as you pull it out.

Try double digging clay soil—a technique that improves drainage by breaking up compacted subsoil. First, dig a trench about 1 spade depth

deep and 2 feet (60 cm) wide; set the soil aside. Work a layer of compost or well-rotted manure into the base of the trench using a garden fork to its depth. Then dig another trench alongside the first, putting the soil from it into the first trench.

Continue digging side-by-side trenches, using the set-aside soil to fill the last one.

Crust-free sowing. Clay soil tends to form a hard crust over germinating seeds, which can prevent small seedlings from pushing through to the surface. Instead of covering seeds with soil, plant them in shallow furrows topped with compost or potting soil.

Prevent cracking. Large cracks often develop when clay soil dries in the summer, which can cause injury to plant roots. Prevent cracks by blanketing the soil with an organic mulch of shredded leaves, compost, or straw. As an extra edge against weeds, spread newspapers over the soil before piling on the mulch.

Keep off the clay. If you walk on or till clay soil while it's wet, you'll pack it even firmer. Instead, install permanent paths between garden beds to provide areas from which you can work. If you must venture into beds when the soil is moist, standing on a board will help distribute your weight, resulting in a little less compaction.

SANDY SOIL

Sandy soil is made up of very large, slick soil particles, so water passes through it quickly, often carrying away nutrients before plants have a chance to use them. To modify this tendency, enrich sandy soil with organic matter and plan to use a little more fertilizer when growing plants that are heavy feeders. Mulches are invaluable for keeping sandy soil moist in hot, dry weather. Weeds are often easy to pull from sandy soil, although they may surprise you with the size of their root systems.

Go green. You can fortify sandy soil with green manures—fast-growing plants that enrich the soil with nutrients and organic matter when they are turned under. Try buckwheat in warm weather or sow clover, oats, or vetch in the fall. Chop or mow down the plants three weeks before you plan to plant, then turn under the residue.

Water wisely. Because water soaks into sandy soil quickly, plants growing in these soils usually benefit from shorter, more frequent waterings than those in heavier clay soils. Soaker hoses and drip irrigation systems are the easiest and most water-thrifty forms of irrigation.

Grow sand lovers. Some plants prefer sandy soils to heavy soils. Among them are annual phlox, artemisia, California poppy, coreopsis, euphorbia, golden aster, Japanese anemone, lamb's ear, oregano, perennial flax, pinks, portulaca, purple loosestrife, red-hot poker, Rosemary, Russian sage, santolina, sea lavender, sedum, snow-in-summer, thyme, tulip, yarrow, and yucca.

Pining for food and water? If you have a ready source of surplus pine logs, you can slow water drainage and the leaching of nutrients from sandy soil with this trick. Bury the logs 3 feet (1 meter) deep under rows of moisture-loving plants like tomatoes or blueberries. As the soft wood decays, it will slow drainage and add nutrients.

Watch for nematodes. Especially in warm climates, sandy soils often become infested with nematodes. Organically enriched soil helps suppress these parasites, and you should use special soil amendments if they are prevalent in your area. Eggshells, crab shells, shrimp hulls, and other materials that are rich in chitin—the same material nematode eggs are made of—help bring nematodes under control by stimulating the activity of soil microorganisms that specialize in breaking down chitin.

SOIL CHEMISTRY

Two of the major chemical characteristics of any soil are its acidity and alkalinity, which are measured on the pH scale. The pH scale runs from 0 (pure acid) to 14 (pure alkaline); its neutral point is 7. Soil pH never runs toward the scale's extremes, but small numerical differences have big implications for plant growth. In very alkaline soil, with a pH above 7.5, many plants have trouble taking up nutrients, so they fail to thrive. The same thing happens in very acidic soils that have a pH below 5.0. Fortunately, the vast majority of garden plants are somewhat adaptable, growing nicely when the pH is between 5.5 and 7.0, and it's not difficult to alter any soil's pH by at least a point.

Start with a test. To determine your soil's pH, have a soil test done or use a soil test kit from a garden center. The procedure is simple: Crumble 1 tablespoon (15 cc) of soil taken from a depth of 4 inches (10 cm), add a measured amount of distilled water, stir, and let it settle. A short time later, you can dip litmus paper into the water and match its color to a guide sheet that comes with the kit.

Use the home advantage. Sending off for a detailed soil analysis is always a smart move, but learning to do your own pH tests has advantages, too. You can more easily track changes, and it's the best way to get to know differences in the soil in different parts of your yard.

Go beyond the numbers. Two minerals—lime and sulfur—are the main tools gardeners can use to lower or raise the soil's pH. However, other good soil-building strategies, such as adding organic matter and using mulches can help stabilize the soil's pH, too. Once you understand your soil's natural pH tendencies, you can fine-tune your gardening practices to prevent radical spikes or dips in pH levels.

ALKALINE SOIL

Alkaline soils can occur anywhere, but they are most common in warm, dry climates where low rainfall levels rarely rinse through the soil, thereby dissolving accumulated salts. Instead, scant soil moisture evaporates away, leaving behind salts and other chemicals. Having limited natural vegetation also contributes to alkaline soil conditions because little natural decomposition occurs. On the plus side, dry alkaline soils host fewer soil-borne diseases than rich, moist soils that have higher overall levels of biological soil activity.

SOIL PH ADJUSTMENT GUIDE

Use this guide as a starting point for adjusting the pH of 100 square feet (9 square meters) of average soil by 1 unit on the pH scale. Soils that are rich in organic matter or dense by nature usually need more lime or sulfur than porous, nutrient-poor soils.

Clay soil
- To raise 1 point: 8 pounds (3.6 kg) lime
- To lower 1 point: 6½ pounds (3 kg) garden sulfur

Sandy soil
- To raise 1 point: 3 to 4 pounds (1.4 to 1.8 kg) lime
- To lower 1 point: 2½ pounds (1.1 kg) garden sulfur

Fertile loam
- To raise 1 point: 6 pounds (2.7 kg) lime
- To lower 1 point: 5½ pounds (2.5 kg) garden sulfur

Test soil with cider vinegar. Add a few drops to a soil sample. If it fizzes, the soil is quite alkaline. For a more precise reading, pick up a home test kit or have a proper soil test done.

Reduce alkalinity by adding acidic materials such as peat moss, sulfur, or aluminum sulfate to your soil. See the "Soil pH Adjustment Guide" box above for general application rates for lime and sulfur. Sandy soils need less of each additive than heavier clay soils.

Go with the flow. Instead of struggling to acidify your soil, grow plants that prefer alkaline conditions. Desirable flowers in this category include Madonna lily, purple coneflower, phlox, candytuft, and numerous native wildflowers. Shrubs and trees suited to alkaline soil include lilac, juniper, apricot, and most species native to southwestern regions.

Improving drainage may help reduce alkalinity by allowing water to wash through the soil and carry away alkaline salts. Put plenty of shredded leaves, compost, or other organic matter into the bottom of planting holes.

Coffee grounds help reduce alkalinity, too. In addition to those from your kitchen, check to see if you can get a larger supply of grounds from a local coffee shop.

Mulch your way to neutral. Blanketing the ground with organic mulch such as straw or shredded leaves prevents evaporation of water, reducing the buildup of alkaline salts.

ACIDIC SOIL

In environments that would be thick forests if left in their natural state, the soil tends to be slightly to extremely acidic. Leaves, pine needles, and fallen trees are all acidic materials, which lead to the formation of acidic soil as they decompose. Much of eastern North America has slightly acidic soil, which is especially prevalent in areas with high rainfall because natural leaching by rain contributes to acidic soil conditions.

SHOPPING FOR LIME

Lime is available in several forms, with each having a different application in the garden. It's used to provide calcium, decrease soil acidity, and condition heavy clay soil.

- **Calcitic lime** (calcium carbonate) is the most common and least expensive. Typically sold in 50-pound (23-kg) bags, ordinary lime is made from finely ground limestone rock.

- **Dolomitic lime** is a mixture of calcium carbonate and magnesium carbonate. Its advantage over ordinary lime is that it adds both calcium and magnesium—two essential plant nutrients—to the soil. Dolomitic lime is available as a powder, or you can buy it in granular or pellet form.

- **Burnt lime or quicklime** is calcium oxide; it's lime that has been heated to release carbon dioxide. It was once used as a wash for tree trunks but is rarely used by modern gardeners.

- **Hydrated or slaked lime** (calcium hydroxide) is burnt lime that has been treated with water. It's a caustic pesticide and fungicide and can be dangerous to handle.

For a quick and easy soil test, wet a soil sample and add a pinch of baking soda. If the mix fizzes, the soil may be too acidic for most garden plants and vegetables. Have a proper soil test done to determine the extent of your soil's acidity. Meanwhile, you can go ahead and begin amending it with lime.

Baking soda is a quick fix. Plants that prefer neutral to slightly alkaline soil often respond to an occasional shower with a mild solution of 1 tablespoon (15 ml) baking soda in 2 quarts (2 liters) of water, which helps them take up nutrients in soil that's a little too acidic for them. Try it on clematis, delphinium, and dianthus. They'll show their appreciation with fuller, healthier blooms.

Follow nature's way. Many garden plants prefer slightly acidic soil, with a pH between 6 and 6.5, but woodland plants—both native and nonnative—thrive when the pH is even lower. Pine, oak, azalea, camellia, gardenia, strawberry, and blueberry are among the plants that grow best when the pH is below 6.0.

To lower acidity in garden soil, apply dolomitic limestone in small doses (see page 282). Heavy clay requires more lime than light sand.

WHAT ABOUT ASHES?

Your fireplace is a built-in source of garden fertilizer, and wood ashes can be used to repel pests, too. Like lime, ashes from a fireplace or wood-burning stove can raise the soil's pH, but they dissolve so quickly that they also can burn plant roots and injure earthworms and beneficial fungi. Spread no more than about 5 pounds (2 kg) per 100 square feet (9 square meters) of ashes at a time over your garden. In addition to raising the soil's pH, ashes provide potassium, one of the three major plant nutrients.

Give them time. To stay on the safe side, fertilize with ashes at least a week before you plant. When using ashes around actively growing plants, use a light hand.

Water the plants well or wait until rain is expected to add them. Rain leaches nutrients from ash and supplies it to the root systems of the plants.

Keep them dry. Store wood ashes in metal garbage cans with tight-fitting lids. Many of the nutrients in wood ashes—including potassium, phosphorus, and calcium—degrade rapidly when the ashes are moist.

Ward off slugs and snails by encircling your plants with a ring of ashes about 6 inches (15 cm) from the stem. The soft-bodied creatures will turn away.

Don't add briquet ashes to compost or your garden. Chemicals make ashes from your barbecue off-limits.

Heating economically. Shovel still-warm ashes into a covered metal container and place it in the center of a cold frame or in your greenhouse. The ashes will radiate heat for about 24 hours.

Good traction. Spread ashes on icy walkways to provide traction. Some of the ashes will stick to shoes, so be sure to use multiple doormats to keep them from being tracked into the house.

Rub it on. Birds flutter in ashes to get rid of parasites, and country gardeners who keep poultry can provide them with an ash bath. Put the ashes in a crate, and place it where it will stay dry. Make sure to change the ashes regularly.

Do you need to lime? Some gardeners lime their lawns and garden beds annually, which isn't always necessary. Test your soil's pH before deciding that you need to add lime. If the pH reading is below 6.0, liming is necessary to help plants take up all the nutrients they need.

Is it time to lime? Lime is basically ground rock, so it doesn't dissolve in soil quickly. For this reason, fall is the best season in which to lime since that allows time for the lime to work before spring planting season. You can add lime in winter, spring, or summer as well, but keep in mind that it takes two or three months to work.

Application is an art. If you are cultivating soil, dust or broadcast the lime over the surface,

☘ Watch Out!

All forms of lime are caustic, so wear gloves to protect your hands and wash it off your skin immediately. Wear a dust mask when handling powdered lime, and work on a still day. Pelleted or granulated lime is easier and safer to handle because it releases fewer airborne particles."

then mix it in. When liming your lawn, apply the lime to the surface and water it in thoroughly. If your soil is extremely acidic, and you need to raise the pH drastically, make several applications of lime over time, using no more than 5 pounds (2 kg) per 100 square feet (9 square meters) at once. Too much lime applied at once will burn plant roots and poison beneficial soil microorganisms.

❧ Enriching Soil Naturally

COMPOST HAS BEEN CALLED the universal cure for what ails your garden, and it is by far the chief way to enrich your soil naturally. Indeed, once you start using it, you'll discover that you never have enough of this black gold to work into the soil, use as top mulch, add to container plants, or even used to make into a disease-fighting tea (see page 290). But other organic aids—such as earthworms and peat moss—can also contribute a great deal to turning your soil into an inviting haven of rich, crumbly humus in which an enormous variety of plants can not only survive but thrive.

COMPOST

Turn kitchen scraps, yard waste, and garden trimmings into the rich organic matter known as compost. Packed with vital nutrients, compost is made by mixing a huge range of materials together, dampening them well, and letting them decompose in a pile or bin. Turn the mixture from time to time to add air, and after several weeks—or sometimes months—you'll have the finest soil amendment nature knows how to make. Fold crumbly compost into garden soil or use it as mulch around trees and shrubs. You can even sift it through a screen and scatter it on your lawn. Here are some of the fine points of turning garden trash into treasure.

Build a compost bin from new or salvaged building materials: chicken wire, wood pallets, or concrete blocks. A garbage can makes a compact, manageable compost container if you use a nail to fill it with holes to admit air and allow excess moisture to seep out. Whatever materials you use, be sure to build open slats or punch air holes to allow oxygen to enter and speed up the decomposition process.

Use shipping pallets to make an animal-proof bin. Assemble four pallets into a square and hold them together with bungee cords. Better yet, make two pallet bins side by side. That way, you can pile fresh materials into one side and use the other for almost-finished compost, which benefits from frequent turning and mixing.

Improvise. Make a lightweight compost container by reusing large plastic potting soil bags. Poke about 20 holes in the bag with scissors, fill it with moist material, and tie off the top. Leave the bag in the sun to allow heat to facilitate decomposition and shake or turn it occasionally to mix the contents. Take the finished compost to the garden in a wheelbarrow and use it right out of the bag.

Check your community resources. To help divert kitchen and yard wastes away from landfills, many cities have active composting programs.

Some will even provide you with a sturdy bin at little or no cost.

If your compost doesn't compost, add water until its consistency is similar to that of a wrung-out sponge. If the compost pile is too damp, insert a few thin layers of an absorbent material like sawdust, peat, or cut hay, until you reach the right consistency.

Shredded or chopped materials decompose faster than bulky ones. Before you put materials into the compost bin, cut up big broccoli stalks, break corncobs in half, and reduce the size of other large items, such as citrus or melon rinds. Break up sticks and run your mower over dry leaves a couple of times before putting them into your heap.

Cool compost is good. Compost piles that get hot have the advantage of killing some weed seeds and harmful microorganisms, but it can be difficult to run a hot heap if you're not using manure or lots of fresh green grass clippings. Cool compost, which decomposes slowly and never heats up, often retains more plant nutrients than hot heaps.

Be adventurous with raw compostables. While you should avoid composting all animal products except eggshells, many other throwaways are great for the compost pile. Among the materials you might try are shellfish hulls, wine-bottle corks, used matches, chewing gum, nutshells, shredded paper, and the cotton balls from medicine bottles.

BLACK GOLD FOR YOUR GARDEN

Riches abound in the kitchen garbage pail and lawn-clippings pile. Turn usable throwaways into invaluable organic matter that will enrich any soil with vital nutrients. You'll reap 1 pound (454 grams) of compost for every 10 pounds (4.5 kg) of trimmings.

Good things for your compost pile
- Chopped cornstalks
- Chopped leaves
- Fruit and vegetable scraps
- Grass clippings
- Hay or straw
- Immature grasses and weeds
- Manure from vegetarian animals
- Shrub trimmings

Noncompostables to discard in the garbage
- Diseased plants
- Invasive weeds
- Meats and sweet, fatty foods
- Pet wastes (rabbit manure is okay)
- Vegetation treated with chemicals

Compost likes strange soup. Pour vegetable cooking water; water from cut-flower arrangements; and leftover coffee, tea, or broth into the compost heap instead of down the drain.

Turn your heap into a garden. Take advantage of the rich soil around the base by sowing a few nasturtium seeds, which will scale the heap prettily and produce flowers for picking. Plant winter squash or pumpkins, which love growing around the edges of old compost piles. Sunflowers and tomatoes often pop up in old piles, too. If you like, you can lift the seedlings and transplant them to other parts of your garden.

Protect against flooding. To prevent your compost heap from getting too wet in rainy weather, place a layer of hay, dried grass, or a

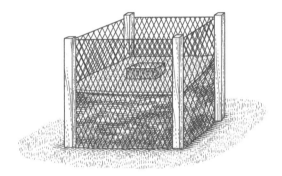

piece of old carpet atop the pile. When the compost is done, store it in a dry can or plastic bag until you're ready to use it in your garden.

Turn compost materials regularly to provide oxygen for the organisms that induce decomposition. A pitchfork makes a perfect turning tool. If you're adding a big load to an enclosed composter, use a broom or rake handle to poke air holes in the pile.

Can't mix? Layer the compost heap with a mix of materials to ensure rapid decomposition. Alternate layers of high-carbon matter, such as shredded leaves, straw, hay, or wood chips with layers of high-nitrogen grass clippings, garden trimmings, manure, and vegetable or fruit scraps from the kitchen. Add new matter to the hot

WELL-DONE SOIL FOR CONTAINERS

In the garden, beneficial soil microorganisms usually keep troublemakers in check, but this balance seldom exists in confined containers. Therefore, it's best to use sterilized soil for potted plants. Freshly opened bags of good-quality potting soil are fine, or you can sterilize homemade mixes in either of two ways.

- Put slightly moist mix in an ovenproof tray and cover it with aluminum foil, or use a roasting bag. Bake for 35 to 45 minutes at 180°F (82°C). Keep the kitchen windows open; the cooking soil can have an unpleasant smell.

- In hot summer weather, fill black plastic pots with soil, dampen well, and set them in full sun, covered with a sheet of clear plastic. Daytime temperatures beneath the plastic will rise to more than 150°F (66°C), and the soil will be ready to use in about a week.

center of the pile to speed breakdown and hide it from flies or other critters.

Take a sniff. A compost pile should give off no unpleasant odors. A bad-smelling pile is your clue that the compost isn't getting enough air or has too much water or fresh, wet materials. To remedy the problem, incorporate dry, carbon-rich materials, such as shredded leaves, sawdust, or old hay.

Sift for fine-textured compost. Make your own sifter by attaching wire mesh or fencing to a wooden frame and then shoveling compost through it. Or remove the bottom of a wooden crate and replace it with wire mesh, then sift by shaking. The finer the mesh, the finer your compost will be.

Store kitchen scraps on their way to the compost heap in the freezer—an easy way to reduce the number of trips you must make to the pile during inclement weather. In many cases (with lettuce and tomatoes, for example), freezing will even help speed up the decomposition process.

MANURE

Manure from vegetarian animals, such as cows, goats, horses, rabbits, and poultry is valuable as a soil builder and fertilizer, but it can have some unwanted side effects. Manure from animals that feed in open pastures often contains weed seeds, while manure from factory farms may contain residues of antibiotics and growth hormones. All manure can contain *E. coli* and other dangerous bacteria, so keep both your safety and that of your garden in mind if you decide to use manure.

Where to get it? Ask at local farms and stables and look at where the animals live and what they eat. Manure from grain-fed horses is usually quite rich, and manure from chicken houses is so packed with nitrogen that it must be composted before it's used in the garden.

Bagged manure has been composted and then processed to control weed seeds. It seldom has an unpleasant smell, and it can be used directly in the garden.

Compost and cover manure. The best way to handle manure is to put it in a pile,

water it, and cover it with a tarp to keep nutrients from leaching out when it rains. Turn the pile occasionally to speed decomposition, and mix some of the manure into your compost heap to provide needed nitrogen. As manure decays, it releases heat, which kills weed seeds. Compost with plenty of manure mixed in should release steam on chilly mornings. If it doesn't, turn it and mix in a little water.

Try a three-year rotation. Each year, enrich a third of your vegetable garden with composted manure. In the first year, use the space for heavy feeders, such as eggplant, cabbage or spinach, and squash. The next year, plant it with carrot, tomato, green bean, and other vegetables that need slightly less fertile soil. The third year, grow light feeders, such as garlic, turnip, onion, and radish.

Use this potent brew. Manure tea is a rich liquid fertilizer that gives plants a quick boost. To make it, put a shovelful of composted manure in a permeable bag, such as an old pillowcase, bind the top together with a big rubber band, and steep in a large tub of water for a week. Dilute the manure tea by half when using it to water plants.

PEAT MOSS

Peat moss is a popular soil amendment that's especially useful for working into planting holes for trees and shrubs. It does not contribute nutrients but loosens and aerates the soil and helps retain moisture. Derived from partly decayed sphagnum moss found in cold-climate bogs, peat moss has many garden uses. Here are some of the things you can do with a bale or two.

Up the organic matter in your lawn. A thin, ¼-inch (6-mm) layer of peat moss, spread onto the lawn, can improve its growth by boosting the organic matter content in the top inch (3 cm) of soil.

Start bulbs in the bag. Give dahlias and other summer-flowering bulbs a head start by planting them in a bag of peat moss outdoors. Cut open the bag, wet the peat well, and nestle the bulbs in it. If a cold spell threatens, cover the opening with a board. In spring, after you plant the bulbs, you'll still have the bag of peat for other uses.

Dig in. Peat moss is sold dried and pressed in plastic-covered bales and can be hard to scoop out. Loosen it with a hand cultivator before digging in with a shovel.

The peat paradox. Although peat moss is very moisture retentive, it's slow to absorb water when completely dry. Moisten it thoroughly before using it as a soil amendment.

Protect tender plants in a peat moss jacket. Ring the plant with a wire cage and line with plastic, then shovel in dry peat to cover the plant. Tent the top loosely with a plastic sheet to shed water but permit air flow.

Store tubers in peat. After lifting the tubers of tender plants for the winter, bury them in a tray of dry peat moss. It absorbs moisture without letting the tubers dry out and discourages the growth of fungi that contributes to rot problems.

Make a hit with heath. Because peat moss is acidic, it's ideal for heath, heather, and their other family members: rhododendrons, mountain laurel, and blueberries. Dig plenty of moist peat into planting holes and mix more in as you backfill around the plants' roots.

EARTHWORMS

A garden filled with earthworms is a healthy garden, and this is relatively recent news to gardeners. For thousands of years, people thought earthworms were little snakes and often poisoned them with salt. Charles Darwin deserves credit for noticing the important work done by earthworms as builders of good soil. We now know that earthworms spend their lives turning organic matter into nutrient-rich soil. The more earthworms you have, the less work you will need to do digging in organic matter, because the worms will do it for you.

Earthworms work best in soil that is above 45°F (7°C), and they're more numerous in warm climates than in cold ones. In fact, until worms were introduced by man, many of the soils in northern climates were wormless—a side effect of the slow movement of glaciers several hundred thousand years ago.

All earthworms are not alike. Of the thousands of species of earthworms, the gray-brown nightcrawler (*Lumbricus terrestris*) grows 4 to 8 inches (10 to 20 cm) long and is the most common type in North America. Another familiar species is the shorter redworm or red wiggler (*Eisenia foetida*), which is used for composting in worm bins. Many gardens host a half dozen species of earthworms.

Use natural cultivators. Earthworms are natural plows, burrowing tunnels that help aerate the soil and make it easier for water to penetrate.

HOMEGROWN EARTHWORMS

Composting with worms—called vermiculture—is a perfect solution for gardeners with limited space. A shallow plastic or wood box measuring 2 feet (60 cm) by 2 feet can comfortably handle the kitchen wastes of two people and can be placed in your kitchen or garage. The container should be free of any chemicals and well ventilated; leave the lid ajar to allow air to circulate and drill holes in the sides and bottom.

Place several hundred redworms in the box along with a bed of damp shredded newspapers or leaves lightly sprinkled with cornmeal. You can get redworms from bait shops. Begin feeding the worms 1 to 2 cups (240 to 475 cc) of vegetable scraps at a time, and keep them moist but not soggy.

If a fruit-fly infestation occurs, place a homemade trap in the worm box. Pour ½ inch (13 mm) of regular (not diet) cola into a fast-food takeout cup. Push the straw through the lid so that the bottom end is just above the surface of the liquid and cut the top of the straw back to 1 inch (25 mm) above the lid. Fruit flies will crawl down the straw to reach the sweet liquid but won't be able to get out.

Harvest worm castings every two to three months and fill the bin with a fresh supply of bedding. To save the worms while harvesting, dump the pile onto newspaper under a bright light; the worms will burrow toward the bottom. Scoop away worm castings until you reach the worms, then combine what's left with fresh materials.

The nightcrawler—so called for its evening feeding habits—operates at fewer than 6 inches (15 cm) under the surface but has been known to dig down to 6 feet (2 meters). In winter, it tunnels below the frozen section of the soil and helps break up the compacted layers.

Keep them fed. Earthworms need nitrogen in their diet and will appreciate a supply of compost as much as your plants do. Avoid using synthetic nitrogen fertilizers because the salts can be poisonous to earthworms. Mulches, compost heaps, and manure piles make ideal worm habitats.

Cultivate gently. To avoid cutting up worms with your tiller, work in the middle of the day, when they burrow deep into the ground. When digging and planting, use a garden fork, not a spade. If you gently fork up your soil one day, many of the worms will leave the area by the next day, and you can cultivate more vigorously without injuring as many worms.

Attract earthworms with mulch, which provides them with food and keeps soil from becoming either too hot and dry or too soggy and cold. Earthworms need even moisture

because they breathe through their skins. Those worms found struggling on pavement after heavy rains are trying to avoid suffocation.

FASCINATING EARTHWORM FACTS

More than 3,000 species of earthworms have been named and identified.

In the top several inches of organically enriched garden soil, there are approximately 50 earthworms per square foot (55 per 1,000 square cm), or 217,800 worms per acre (4,000 square meters). Earthworms are plentiful beneath lawns, too, where they dine regularly on dead grass roots.

Depending on the worm species, climate, and soil conditions, an acre's worth of worms can digest between 7 and 1,000 tons (6 and 900 metric tons) of organic matter per year.

Given an acre of soil in most parts of the United States, the amount of living matter represented by earthworms is outweighed only by that of the microorganisms and plants in the same acre. In other words, in an acre of meadow, the earthworms outweigh the cows!

✿ Using Fertilizer

PLANTS GROWING IN healthy, enriched soil continuously take up nutrients through their roots, which they use to grow leaves, stems, flowers, and fruits. Plants vary in their nutrient requirements, with some needing much more fertilizer than others. Spinach and broccoli, for example, are heavy feeders, while lettuce and most legumes require less fertilizer. Long-lived trees and shrubs often do a good job of foraging for nutrients with their huge root systems.

Keeping plants well fed isn't difficult, although choosing fertilizers can be confusing. Garden fertilizers have undergone big changes in the past

If you want the best fertilizer, look down at your shoes. The best fertilizer for a garden is the gardener's own footsteps—the care you give your plants.

few decades. Fifty years ago, gardeners relied on natural nutrient sources such as animal manures. Twenty years ago, chemical fertilizers became the top choices because they were inexpensive and easy to handle. While synthetic fertilizers are widely available, more gardeners prefer organic fertilizers, which provide nutrients to plants and then decompose into organic matter. All garden centers sell them, often in blends that are no more difficult to use than synthetic fertilizers. In the following pages, you'll find out how simple it is to buy and use the best natural fertilizers—as well as soil-friendly synthetic forms that are the next best choice.

FERTILIZER BASICS

Are your plants well fed? Learn to tell by looking at your plants' leaves. As the primary food factory for plants, leaves can indicate nutrient imbalances. Too little nitrogen, for example, turns leaves yellow, while excess potassium can cause stunted growth. Learn to recognize the look of healthy leaves so you can spot the onset of any problems.

Know the code. Fertilizer labels list nitrogen, phosphorus, and potassium by their chemical abbreviations—N, P, and K, always in that order. Labels also indicate the ratio of each element to the total mass. A 10-6-4 formulation, for example, contains 10 percent nitrogen, 6 percent phosphorus, and 4 percent potassium. All fertilizers have these three numbers listed on the label.

Don't forget about micronutrients. In addition to nitrogen, phosphorus, and potassium, plants need three other major nutrients—sulfur, calcium, and magnesium—as well as minute amounts of trace elements, including iron, manganese, zinc, iron, and copper.

When to feed. A good rule of thumb is to feed plants during their most active season of growth, keeping in mind that plants vary in their fertilizer requirements. Some, such as herbs, need fertilizer infrequently; others, such as roses, are hungry all the time. Withholding fertilizer in the fall helps new growth harden off before winter.

How to apply. For new beds, incorporate fertilizer when preparing the soil; simply broadcast it over the bed or row and dig it in thoroughly. For single specimens, such as a perennial, mix fertilizer into the planting hole or work it into the surface around plants. To fertilize established shrubs and trees, scratch fertilizer into the soil above the root zones. Always water thoroughly after fertilizing any plant.

Make a coffee-can spreader. Use a hammer and a large nail to punch holes in the bottom of a 2-pound (1-kg) coffee can to make a handy spreader for powdered or granular fertilizers.

SOIL-FRIENDLY FERTILIZERS

Garden center shelves are bursting with fertilizer choices, but depending on your gardening style, you probably need three or fewer products. Use them to supplement nutrients from compost or other soil amendments.

Blended organic fertilizers are dry powders, granules, or pellets made from plant or animal matter along with rock phosphate, granite dust, or other minerals. They persist in the soil for months, slowly releasing their nutrients. More nutrients are released when the soil is warm because soil microorganisms are most active in warm, moist soil.

Timed-release fertilizers are synthetic rather than organic, but many gardeners prefer them for fertilizing lawns, shrubs, and perennial flowers. Nutrients are released to plants slowly, and warm temperatures and repeated rainfall increases the speed of nutrient release.

Water-soluble liquids provide nutrients that are immediately available to plants, so they give fast results. Organic liquid fertilizers usually include fish byproducts, and synthetic forms are widely available, too. Use liquids to feed most container-grown plants and to treat nutritional deficiencies. When stressed by lack of nutrients, most plants can take up the nutrients present in liquid fertilizer through their roots and leaves.

Feeding a large tree? Mature trees have extensive root systems, so they often do a good job of foraging for nutrients. If you want to feed a large tree, here's how to make sure the fertilizer goes to the tree rather than to the grass or other plants growing beneath it. Use an electric or a manual auger with a long, large-diameter bit—at least 1 foot (30 cm) long and 1½ inches (4 cm) around—to bore deep holes. You can also use a crowbar or a stake pounded with a hammer. Space holes 2 feet (60 cm) apart around the drip line; make another ring of holes 2½ feet (75 cm) from the trunk. Fill the holes with organic or timed-release fertilizer and water well.

Mechanical spreaders, either drop or broadcast type, make short work of fertilizing lawns or other large areas. To avoid clogs, use only dry fertilizers. And keep the shut-off mechanism clean so that it can close completely.

With a drop spreader, apply fertilizer in a crisscross pattern for complete coverage, going over the same area both horizontally and vertically. Use half the recommended spread rate in each direction.

More is too much. When using any type of fertilizer, always follow the application rates recommended by the manufacturer. Using more won't boost or speed growth and may actually injure your plants.

Have an aquarium? If you have a freshwater aquarium, you can recycle the contents in the garden. When cleaning the tank, save the nutrient-rich water to pour over plants instead of just sending it down the drain.

Use liquid food for houseplants and patio plants grown in containers because it spreads easily through the soil and is immediately available to plants.

PRINCIPAL NUTRIENTS AT A GLANCE

Nitrogen (N)
- **What it does:** Helps new leaves, branches, and stems to form
- **Deficiency signs:** Slow growth; small, pale leaves; weak, easily bent stems
- **How to correct:** Feed with composted manure or liquid fish-based fertilizer

Phosphorus (P)
- **What it does:** Supports strong roots with numerous branches and root hairs; encourages flower formation
- **Deficiency signs:** Attacks by parasites on roots; poor flowering; reddish or purplish tint on leaves
- **How to correct:** Amend soil with rock phosphate, light application of wood ashes, or bonemeal

Potassium (K)
- **What it does:** Improves overall functioning of the plant
- **Deficiency signs:** Brown leaf edges; crinkled leaves, weak stems; fruit drop
- **How to correct:** Spray with liquid kelp; topdress soil with powdered kelp, greensand, or apply wood ashes lightly

NITROGEN

Nitrogen is one of the three primary plant nutrients. Airborne nitrogen can be used by nitrogen-fixing legumes, but most plants must take it up from the soil. Nitrogen is water soluble and is absorbed rapidly, so it must be replenished regularly.

The best organic sources of nitrogen are manure, bloodmeal, cottonseed meal, fish emulsion, and alfalfa or soybean meal. Good sources you can find in your own backyard are rich compost and fresh grass clippings.

Grandpa's wisdom

There's no need to dig nitrogen fertilizer into the soil around actively growing plants. Water it in or let the rain do it for you.

Grow green manure crops, such as clover, rye, or various vetches and peas, to add nitrogen to your soil. Sow seed wherever you want to enrich the soil and let the plants grow to 6 inches (15 cm) tall. Cut them to the soil line, then turn under. They will decay rapidly to release nitrogen, but wait at least a week before planting.

Feathery fertilizer. Poultry feathers make a nitrogen-rich fertilizer. Place them in a tub and top with a plastic screen and a few stones to hold them down. Cover with water and steep in a shady spot for two months, then strain the liquid and use it to fertilize plants.

Get a jump on spring by applying an organic nitrogen source in late fall. It will break down slowly and be available in the soil by planting time the following year.

How much is too much? You'll know you've applied excessive nitrogen if blossoms are sparse and foliage grows too fast and lush, which makes plants more vulnerable to pests, diseases, and environmental stress. There is no antidote; rain and frequent watering will eventually wash nitrogen away and hopefully let the plants recover.

PHOSPHORUS

The second major plant nutrient, phosphorus, energizes root growth and helps plants as they approach maturity and begin to flower. Unlike nitrogen, phosphorus persists in the soil and moves very little. When applied in liquid form, it remains in the top inch (3 cm) or so of soil; in dry fertilizers, it remains near the fertilizer particles. For this reason, make sure you mix phosphorus into the soil so its roots benefit.

Feeling blue? Plants suffering from lack of phosphorus sometimes develop a bluish cast. Leaves may also turn a dark, dull green on top and bronze-purple on the undersides. Stems remain thin and may turn purplish. For a quick boost, spray plants weekly as needed with fish emulsion; it has about 5 percent phosphorus which is immediately available to plants.

FEEDING YOUR GARDEN THE ORGANIC WAY

While organic fertilizers often supply secondary nutrients and trace elements, including calcium and zinc, their primary purpose is the same as that of synthetic fertilizers—to provide nitrogen, phosphorus, and potassium. Select an all-purpose fertilizer that contains all three elements or use one of these single-nutrient types to correct a specific deficiency.

Sources of nitrogen

MATERIAL	SOURCE	CONTENT	APPLICATION RATE
Alfalfa meal	Alfalfa by-products	5%	5 pounds (2.3 kg) per 100 square feet (9 square meters)
Bloodmeal	By-product of meat processing	15%	3 pounds (1.4 kg) per 100 square feet
Cottonseed meal	Dehulled cottonseed	6%	2–5 pounds (0.9–2.3 kg) per 100 square feet
Fish emulsion	By-product of fish processing	4%	1 part to 20 parts water
Fish meal	By-product of fish processing	10%	5 pounds per 100 square feet
Manure	Animal waste	2–13%	3–5 pounds (1.4–2.3 kg) per 100 square feet
Soybean meal	Soybean by-products	7%	5 pounds per 100 square feet

Sources of phosphorus

MATERIAL	SOURCE	CONTENT	APPLICATION RATE
Bird guano	Dried seabird manure	8%	3 pounds per 100 square feet
Bonemeal	By-product of meat processing	20%	3–5 pounds per 100 square feet
Fish emulsion	By-product of fish processing	5%	1 part to 20 parts water
Rock phosphate	Washed, crushed limestone	33%	10 pounds (4.5 kg) per 100 square feet

Sources of potassium

MATERIAL	SOURCE	CONTENT	APPLICATION RATE
Granite dust	By-product of quarrying	5–7%	10 pounds per 100 square feet
Greensand	Marine sediment	3–5%	10 pounds per 100 square feet
Kelp meal	Processed seaweed	12%	1 pound (450 grams) per 100 square feet
Liquid kelp	Extract of kelp meal	12%	2 tablespoons (30 ml) per gallon (4 liters) of water

Unfriendly soil? Phosphorus becomes less available to plants in acidic and cold, wet soils. This is critical in spring, when young roots are trying to get established. Watch for symptoms of deficiency and add phosphorus as needed. You can quickly sweeten acidic soil—and supply needed phosphorus—with a light sprinkling of wood ashes.

Bonemeal basics. Bonemeal is a slow-released source of phosphorus, remaining in the soil for up to a year. Buy steamed, crushed bonemeal that is finely ground so that soil microorganisms can break it down more readily. Bulbs always appreciate a bit of bonemeal mixed into the soil beneath them, where their roots are sure to find it.

Rock on. Rock phosphate is washed, crushed limestone and contains about 33 percent phosphorus. It releases the nutrient slowly and will work in acidic soil. Collodial phosphate is the

WHAT ABOUT MICRONUTRIENTS?

Trace elements, often called micronutrients, are required for plant health, but only in tiny amounts. They include boron, chlorine, copper, iron, manganese, molybdenum, zinc, and several others. Many organic fertilizers are rich in micronutrients; using them will guard against deficiencies. Kelp meal, kelp extract, granite dust, rock phosphate, manure, and greensand are all good sources of micronutrients. Many complete synthetic fertilizers also contain them, but it's important to check the level to make sure.

Two good clues. Micronutrient shortages often appear in leaves as chlorosis—yellowing of leaf tissue between the veins. Plants with a shortage of zinc show symptoms on the older, lower leaves. Those having a shortage of iron, manganese, or molybdenum show chlorosis on the young, upper leaves. Micronutrient shortages can also cause leaf veins to turn reddish; affected leaves often are smaller than normal, too.

Seaweed supplies boron. Corky spots in apples or hollow cores in broccoli stems indicate a shortage of this nutrient. To remedy the problem, mulch plants with seaweed or treat them to a seaweed spray every few weeks.

Get help from kelp. A type of seaweed, kelp contains trace elements and minerals that promote blossoming, help plants absorb water, and give them greater tolerance to cold. It also improves soil structure. Apply kelp supplements in conjunction with balanced fertilizer once or twice a month during the growing season.

All seaweed doesn't come in packages. If you live near the shore, you can collect your own. Seaweed fanciers will find the best pickings right after a storm, when most seaweed washes ashore. It's best to collect and use it as soon as possible. Wash off all the salt, chop the seaweed into small pieces, and dig it into the soil while the nutrients are still fresh.

Host a tea party for potted plants. Leave a used tea bag or tea dregs in water overnight and serve the brew to potted plants that may need micronutrients. Use only tea that hasn't been mixed with sugar or cream.

residue left from washing limestone and comes in small particles. It contains about 20 percent phosphorus, some of which is available immediately; it works best in neutral soil.

Fixing a phosphorus overdose. If you go overboard and end up with excess phosphorus, don't add any source of the nutrient for two years. Work in extra nitrogen and potassium to balance it out.

POTASSIUM

Potassium, also called potash, is listed on fertilizer labels by its chemical symbol, K. It's the third essential nutrient, indicated last in the N-P-K fertilizer analysis. Potassium is required for proper growth of fruits and flowers, ensuring good size, color, and number. It helps plants build proteins and sugars, aids them in taking in other nutrients, and helps them withstand cold weather and other types of environmental stress.

Warning signs. Plants need potassium when the leaves turn grayish, yellow, mottled, or brown and the edges curl; lower stems and leaves are often affected first. Symptoms usually occur late in the season, when potassium is in high demand by developing fruits.

Spray on a quick fix. For a fast solution, spray plants with fish emulsion or liquid kelp. Many gardeners use seaweed or kelp sprays monthly through the growing season to prevent possible potassium deficiencies. Potatoes and other root crops need abundant potassium.

Greensand and granite dust are good organic sources of potassium; both are slow acting and long lasting. Dig them into soil in fall so they'll be available when you plant in spring. One application often lasts for several years.

Using Mulch

MULCH BENEFITS THE GARDEN in so many ways that most of your plants will need some type of mulch. It insulates the soil from temperature extremes, keeping it warmer in winter and cooler in summer, and minimizes erosion, moisture loss, and weed growth. In winter, mulched plants won't be heaved out of the ground by alternate freezing and thawing, and they won't be tempted to emerge prematurely during a brief winter warmup. As organic mulches break down, they enrich the soil with humus. Earthworms are often happiest living beneath a thick blanket of mulch.

Many materials make suitable mulch, as long as they cover the soil well and are healthy—that is, have never been exposed to toxic chemicals, insect pests, or diseases. Organic mulches allow water, air, and fertilizer to pass through, and they decompose to add nutrients to the soil; inorganic mulches are generally impermeable and durable. While you can purchase mulch in bags, bulk, or rolls, don't forget about materials you may have on hand, such as chipped brush, pine needles, leaves, or newspaper.

MULCH BASICS

When to mulch. For perennials, trees, and shrubs, you can leave mulch in place year-round. For vegetables and annuals, wait until the soil warms. For hardy perennials that are overwintering in the ground, wait till the soil freezes to apply a new blanket of insulating mulch. Rake it back first thing in spring to help the soil warm up a little faster.

Two mulching don'ts. Don't pile mulch too close to trunks or stems. It can smother plants; promote rot; and let slugs, mice, and other pests hide near a food source. And don't use plastic mulch around shrubs and other hardy plants. Because it's not permeable, it cuts off air and water to roots and can cause soil to heat up excessively in summer.

How much is enough? Mulch that covers the soil 2 to 3 inches (5 to 8 cm) deep is usually sufficient during the summer months. If you find erosion or weeds are a persistent problem, or if you're overwintering tender plants, spread mulch 4 to 6 inches (10 to 15 cm) deep. For permanently mulched shrubs or beds, just refresh the top each year to maintain the proper depth.

Match your mulch to the plants. Acid lovers, including rhododendrons and camellias, appreciate acidic mulch. Try pine needles, oak-leaf mold, shredded oak leaves, or composted sawdust from cypress or oak. On plants that don't need acid, use neutral materials, such as straw,

Grandpa's wisdom

As long as they're healthy, use the leafy tops of root crops, such as carrots, beets, and radishes as mulch. As you pull up the plants, lay the foliage between the rows in your vegetable garden.

buckwheat hulls, or corncobs; if you're using acidic mulch, add a little lime.

Smother weeds or other undesirable plant growth with a newspaper mat. Wet several sheets of paper to help them cling together, then place the mat so that plants are completely covered and no light can reach them; anchor the edges with rocks or soil. Top with wood chips or other mulch as camouflage and remove it once the weeds are dead.

TYPES OF MULCH

What to use. Many gardeners prefer ornamental mulches for year-round use or for flowerbeds. Shredded bark, wood chips, and cocoa or walnut shells are attractive but expensive. For seasonal use in the vegetable patch, hay, straw, chopped leaves, ground corncobs, and even newspaper are inexpensive and effective—and you can turn them into the soil at summer's end.

Live near a brewery? Ask the brewmaster if you can haul away the spent hops. The fine-textured mash makes ideal mulch.

GOOD USES FOR LEAVES

Raking leaves is an inevitable fall ritual, and it's an opportunity to harvest mulch and soil amendments for your garden. If you don't use them yourself, your community probably uses special leaf pickup procedures so they can take them to a central leaf-composting site. Don't let yours go until you've used all you can in your own yard.

Make them into mulch. Run over your leaves with a mower twice before raking them into shrub beds or spreading them over unoccupied space in your vegetable garden. Shredded leaves don't blow away the way whole leaves tend to do, and they don't pack into a smelly mess, either.

Dig them in. If you have a tiller, you can turn shredded leaves right into the soil. By spring, they will have decomposed enough to provide a few nutrients for plants and lots of organic matter for your soil.

Compost them. Leaves take a long time to break down, but if you're patient, this year's leaves can be next year's compost. Let your leaf pile weather until spring, then use it as an addition to your compost pile.

Free for the asking. Arborists and utility companies that trim trees around power lines often have surplus wood chips ground from felled trees. Also check with your municipality; some have leaf-composting or brush-chipping sites and offer free mulch to the community.

Use them over something else. Wood mulches break down slowly and may tie up soil nitrogen while they're decaying. To keep this from happening, use them as part of a double mulch. Spread hay or newspapers over the soil, followed by a 2-inch (5-cm) layer of sawdust or wood chips.

Woodworking shops and cabinetmakers are good sources of sawdust. Be sure to find out which wood they've been using, however: Walnut, cedar, and chemically treated wood should not be spread around the garden. Untreated pine is fine, as is hardwood sawdust from lumber mills.

Strawberries like the acidity of sawdust mulch. It can also keep slugs away. Raise the foliage and apply several inches around the bases of the stems, but be careful not to cover the plants' crowns.

Don't go overboard using wood mulches close to your house. They may harbor termites, mice, or other invasive pests.

ROLLOUT MULCHES

Give a reflective mulch a try. Silver- and red-colored mulches help repel pests because insects passing by are confused by the light and fly away.

Black plastic mulch is useful in vegetable gardens when you want to warm up the soil,

and it keeps dirt from splashing onto plants. Lay it on the bed and make slits for transplants or seeds; fold it up at season's end and reuse it the following year. But take note: Since rain can't pass through plastic, you'll need to water underneath with a soaker hose or drip line.

Bar those weeds. Perforated geotextile weed barriers block light to weeds yet let water

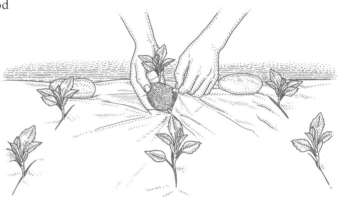

pass through freely, so they're good to use around shrubs and trees. Top them with shredded bark or wood chips.

Paper mulch comes in rolls that can be spread over the garden in spring and then tilled into the soil in the fall. These are great timesavers if you're growing pumpkins, watermelons, or other vining crops that need protection from weeds that spring up between wide rows.

GARDENING
TECHNIQUES

When you use the right tools and techniques in the garden, you'll save hours of work and still get great results. If you struggle through garden chores, you may not be using the best tools for the job. Cutting off a dead tree limb, for example, is a light job with a pruning saw, but it's a real challenge with pruning clippers.

The right techniques can unlock the secrets of seeds, too. Sprouting certain seeds can require special treatment to ready them for germination, such as exposure to cool weather or nicking and presoaking. Without these special keys, they'll remain locked in dormancy and just sit there without sprouting. In this chapter, you will find hundreds of tips on better ways to dig, weed, and water your garden, as well as ideas for working with seeds, propagating your favorite plants, and keeping up with other maintenance chores, such as staking and pruning. You won't have to wonder which tools will work best or when to do what. These are things that experienced gardeners learn over time, which is how they get great returns from only a few hours of light work in their gardens.

❧ The Organized Gardener

STAYING ORGANIZED is one of the most important ways to learn from your successes as well as to avoid making mistakes. Spend some time in winter sorting through seeds and supplies, tidying up your records after the frenzy of summer gardening, and making plans for the new season ahead.

RECORD KEEPING

Even if your memory is great, labels and notes are very important to the garden. You will want to refer back to names, planting times, and planting places.

Keep a binder-type notebook that has pockets for plant tags, seed packets, and receipts. When you want to make notes, you'll have the information you need.

Maintain a garden calendar to keep track of planting dates; things you want to do at certain times; as well as how much mulch, fertilizer, or other materials are required by various parts of your yard.

Use a card file divided into sections, such as lawns, shrubs, flowers, and vegetables. Make note cards for your favorite plant groups and write down varieties you try and how you care for

them. File seed packets in the appropriate sections until you get around to recording your notes.

Take pictures. Photos will help you remember where you planted what, and it's always fun to be reminded of your gardening adventures from past seasons.

LABELING

From seedlings to long-lived shrubs and trees, labels help you get to know your plants better. Don't count on your memory to recall variety or even species names. The more plants you grow, the easier it is to get confused. There are a number of options for plant labels and markers.

Thin, white plastic labels are inexpensive and good for marking seedlings and giveaway plants, but when you use them in a garden with many small plants, it can end up looking like a "mouse graveyard". Still, this basic type of stick-in-the-soil label is handy and versatile. You can write on them with a pencil (easier to erase; good for seedlings) or with an indelible pen (easier to see outdoors in the garden).

Metal labels are a more attractive and permanent option for labeling shrubs and trees. Writing on the labels in pencil embosses them.

They are attached with wire loops, which can be loosely tied to branches.

Ready-made ceramic labels embossed with plant names, such as Rosemary, look nice in an herb or vegetable garden, or you can make your own by painting or woodburning names onto wood stakes.

Try bamboo. For natural-looking labels that harmonize with the garden, use bamboo canes. Cut sections to the desired length, angling the ends to form a point that will go easily into the ground. Then use an indelible pen to write a plant name on each cane.

Raid the recycling bin. Cut plastic yogurt or cottage cheese containers into weatherproof labels and write on them with an indelible pen. If you prefer, cut up disposable aluminum pie pans and write on them with a marker or press hard with a pencil to make embossed aluminum labels.

Save your seed packets. For a vegetable garden, save empty seed packets to use as labels. Open the packets from the bottom so they'll be right side up in the garden and then, after you've planted the seeds, cover the packets with transparent plastic bags and display them on small sticks stuck in the ground.

Try laminated labels. Laminated labels look very trim and are easy to make. Print the plant names on a sheet of heavy paper, either from a computer or by hand. Laminate the sheet and cut the labels into any desired shape. Punch a hole in each one, loop a piece of twine through it, and tie it to a stem. You can either buy laminating paper or have the laminating done for you at a quick-printing shop.

Know where to look. Make it easier to find labels on trees and shrubs by always putting them in the same place—at head height on the north-facing side, for example.

Don't strangle the stems. If you use wire to attach labels to trees and shrubs, take care not to girdle the branches. Loop a length of wire loosely around a branch and twist near the ends to secure the label; loosen the wire periodically as the stem expands.

Label stored bulbs. After lifting bulbs for storage, you can write on them directly for later reference at planting time. Use a felt-tip marker to label them with the plant name, bloom color, and other information. You can also store the bulbs in labeled paper sacks.

✿ Basic Gardening Tools

EVERY GARDENER SHOULD HAVE a shed's worth of useful tools—many of them indispensable. When you purchase your own, always buy quality, even if it seems expensive. In the long run, you'll actually save money, since well-made tools have a longer life. Better design can also make high-quality tools easier to handle and more efficient to use.

HAND TOOLS

A big part of a gardener's life involves digging, moving, or reshaping soil. Are you using the best tools for the job? Here are some of the handiest tools for moving earth, whether you're digging a whole new garden from scratch or just making a small hole for a pumpkin seed.

Calling a spade a spade. A garden spade is a multipurpose tool with a broad, slightly curved blade. A spade's sharp edge and pointed end help it bite easily into rocky or heavy soil. Use a spade to dig holes, turn over soil, chop roots, and pry up rocks.

Shovels are a little different in that they have a flatter blade, so they're better for scooping materials from flat surfaces or cutting a clean edge around beds or lawns.

A digging fork has four flat or square tines, unlike the curved, narrow tines of a pitchfork.

It's used for turning and aerating soil or compost, mixing in soil amendments, lifting perennials and bulbs for division, and harvesting root crops.

TOOLS FROM YOUR KITCHEN

Some of the handiest small garden tools may be ready and waiting in your kitchen drawer. When big tools won't do, try these small ones.

A table fork is great for pulling weeds that have sprung up close to the base of little flowers and vegetables. Slip it under the weed's crown and twist, and the weed should come right out.

A serrated steak knife is perfect for getting beneath taprooted weeds, such as dandelions. You can also use it to cut through the large roots of hostas and daylilies when digging and dividing them.

An ice pick does a wonderful job of opening clogged drainage holes in containers, or you can use it to punch holes in an old piece of hose, turning it into a drip irrigation line.

A large serving spoon is useful for digging small seedlings that pop up in the wrong place and need to be moved. If you lift the seedlings from beneath, keeping the soil around their roots intact, they'll quickly become accustomed to their new location.

Pick a size. Spades and shovels come in many blade sizes and handle lengths. Before buying, try one for size to make sure that it feels comfortable. Handles on garden spades and forks range from about 27 to 39 inches (69 to 99 cm) long. Tall gardeners can spare their backs a lot of pain by using longer-handled tools, while shorter gardeners may find smaller styles with their shorter handles easier to work with.

Match your spade to your soil. Spades with narrow blades are easier to use in heavy clay, while wider regular blades are more efficient in sandy soil. Long, thin blades are good for careful thinning of crowded perennials.

Small garden? For working in tight spots, a small, short-handled spade called a border spade is easier to use than a full-size garden spade. Or use a spade intended for children.

Bang out dings. If a corner of the spade blade has been bent by hitting a rock, hammer it back into shape while holding it against a flat surface. File a new bevel on the dull edge.

Straighten a bent tine in a digging fork by driving a sturdy metal pipe—3 feet (1 meter) long and 1 inch (3 cm) in diameter—into the ground so it protrudes about 10 inches (25 cm) above the soil. Slide the damaged tine into the pipe and press slowly until it returns to its original position.

Keep a sharp edge. Use a steel file to sharpen the edge on your spade from time to time. It will make digging much easier and help your spade

TAKE-IT-EASY DIGGING TIPS

Get a head start on spring by spading the soil in autumn. Leave big clods in place throughout the winter and let rain, snow, and the alternate freezing and thawing of the soil will help break up any clumps by spring.

You can limit spading to every two to three years or so by digging deeply, incorporating plenty of organic matter, using mulch, and never walking directly on cultivated soil. Instead, lay down a plank path to keep the ground from becoming compacted.

Be kind to your back. Stand up straight when pushing a digging tool into the ground and as you draw the handle toward your body to loosen the soil. Bend your knees and lift the load with your upper body, supporting the handle shaft against your thigh for leverage. With heavy loads, don't twist at the hips when depositing soil to the side; instead, turn your body to face the pile.

When turning over large areas, use a tiller to do the heaviest work. Finish by hand, using a fork to break up any clods, remove stones, and dig up weed or tree roots.

do a much better job of slicing through roots and other obstructions. Use a flat file, drawing it smoothly along the original bevel from top to bottom; don't saw back and forth. File until the edge is evenly tapered and any nicks are removed. Make only a shallow bevel, since a blade that has been honed knife-sharp will chip. When you're finished, run the file along the back of the edge to remove the burr that has built up.

Clean your tools between uses. Rub off debris with a rag. Use steel wool or a wire brush to loosen encrusted dirt. Wipe metal surfaces lightly with oil. Before storing tools for the winter, wipe wood handles with boiled linseed oil to keep them from drying out.

POWER TOOLS

Most gardeners consider a lawnmower to be a necessity, but what about other power tools? Power tools that aren't used often tend to become undependable, so if you have a small task or one that you perform only once each season, a good-quality hand tool may do the job as well—at less expense and with much less noise. Or you may be able to rent power tools that you use only occasionally. When renting, reserve tools in advance; shredders, for example, are in great demand in fall.

Choose tools that can do multiple jobs. String trimmers often come with edging attachments, and they can help with leaf shredding, too. Place dry leaves in a garbage can and chop them with a string trimmer.

Go for less noise. Gas-powered tools tend to be the loudest, with electric motors noticeably quieter. Tools powered by rechargeable batteries are not especially powerful, but they're usually less noisy than other types.

Put safety first. Don't buy a tool whose on-off switch isn't well marked and easily reached. Check the amperage rating for any electric tool before connecting an extension cord (the rating will be listed on the tool). If you don't use an extension cord of sufficient gauge for the amperage, you risk having the tool's motor burn out. Disconnect the sparkplug cable on a gas-powered tool to prevent an accidental startup.

POWER TOOLS FOR GARDENERS

TOOL	PURPOSE	POWER OPTIONS	MANUAL ALTERNATIVE
Blower	Blows leaves into a pile for disposal. Cleans up grass after mowing or edging.	Gas or electric	Rake or broom
Edger	Cuts and trims lawn and border edges	Gas, electric, or battery	Flat-blade spade or half-moon edger
Hedge trimmer	Trimming shrubs and hedges; forming hedges into formal shapes or topiary	Electric, gas, or battery	Hedge clippers
Shredder	Chopping up leaves and other garden debris	Gas or electric	Pruning loppers or lawnmower
String trimmer	Trimming grass and weeds; edging	Gas, electric, or battery	Hedge clippers or half-moon edger

LADDERS

Few things are as easy as falling off a ladder, and it's true that ladder-related accidents are all too common. In addition to concentrating on keeping your balance, use these tips to keep from becoming a ladder casualty statistic.

Before climbing a ladder, check it for damaged rungs. You can lay a wood ladder flat on the ground and walk on the rungs—it's the safest way to find weak ones.

☙ Watch Out!

Keep aluminum ladders away from power lines to avoid danger of electrocution.

Extension ladders need a wide angle. Before climbing, position the base of an extension ladder so it's one-fourth of the ladder's length away from the vertical surface. For instance, if you lean a 12-foot (4 meters) ladder against a wall, the base should be at least 4 feet (1 meter) away from the edge of the wall.

Before carrying tools up a ladder, be sure you have a place to put them when you reach the top. It may be best to climb the ladder and have someone hand you the tools.

Never paint a wooden ladder, because paint hides rot and damage; protect the wood with varnish instead.

Keep your stance solid. Plant both feet on the same rung close to the uprights—not in the middle, especially on an old ladder. Lean in and keep your weight on the balls of your feet—not on the arch—so you can react quickly if you lose your balance.

MEASURING TOOLS

Use the handle for measuring. Mark the shaft of your spade every 4 inches (10 cm) with an indelible pen. When you need to figure spacing between plants, just lay it on the ground. Also mark the blade in 2-inch (5-cm) increments and use the marks as a ruler when you need to dig to a specific depth.

Measure fertilizers and soil amendments with a set of plastic measuring spoons and cups reserved for garden use. Confused by how much? If the label says 1 ounce, that's the same as 2 tablespoons; 4 tablespoons equal ¼ cup, or 2 ounces. There are 16 tablespoons in a cup, and 1 cup equals ½ pint. For the metrically inclined, 1 tablespoon is 15 ml (or 15 cc), and 1 cup is 240 ml—and there are still 16 tablespoons in a cup. A cup is just shy of being ¼ liter.

What's in the can? Depending on its size, a watering can holds between 2 and 3½ gallons (8 and 13 liters). Buy one with gradations marked on the side; it will make it easier to measure water when mixing soluble fertilizers. Or you can pour in measured amounts of water and add your own markings with an indelible pen.

1 square yard (1 square meter) of annuals needs about 1.2 gallons (4.5 liters) of water daily—and as much as 5 gallons (19 liters) in hot, dry weather. If you must carry water to your plants, save time and muscle by using plenty of mulch to hold moisture longer.

Simplify garden math by measuring the area of your lawns and beds, then write it down. You will then know how much fertilizer, mulch, or compost you need, because application rates are usually based on 100 square feet (9 square meters). For instance, if a bed is 5 feet by 5 feet (1.5 by 1.5 meters), its surface area is 25 square feet (2.25 square meters), so use one-quarter of the recommended quantity of fertilizer for 100 square feet.

❧ Watering Your Plants

PLANTS NEED MOISTURE for steady, healthy growth. Wise watering practices will save water and still deliver necessary moisture in a timely manner. Mulching will reduce watering chores by keeping moisture from evaporating. When growing plants with high water requirements, grouping them together saves time because you can water them all at once.

WATERING BASICS

Make a custom waterer for a specimen plant. Perforate a 1-gallon (4-liter) milk jug with several tiny holes on the bottom and sides and bury it near the plant with its spout right at the soil level. When the jug is filled, the water will seep out slowly and keep the roots moist.

Water in the morning. Less moisture evaporates in the cool of the morning, and there should be ample time for the water to soak in before the sun rises high in the sky. If you must water later in the day, do it early enough so that the leaves dry before nightfall, to discourage foliage diseases.

Keep leaves dry as you water, if possible, by watering only the soil around the plants. This is especially important for plants that are prone to fungal diseases, including roses, lilacs, phlox, and squash. Getting the leaves wet with overhead watering can encourage the spread of many mildew and leafspot diseases.

Plants often wilt in intense sun, but they may not need watering. To avoid possible overwatering, wait until the next morning. If the plants are still droopy, they definitely need water.

When watering mature plants, water deeply but infrequently to deliver moisture deep into the plants' root zones—usually between 6 and 18 inches (15 and 45 cm) deep. Deep watering also encourages deeper roots, which in turn need less water. After 24 hours, 1 inch (3 cm) of water penetrates 12 inches (30 cm) in sandy soil but only 4 inches (10 cm) in clay.

Young plants have shallow roots, so they need more frequent, light watering than mature, deeply rooted plants.

Water widely. Be sure to water trees and shrubs all the way out to the drip line, not just near the trunk or base. Most of the young roots are under the soil at the edges of the canopy.

During dry, dusty weather, water both the roots and foliage of evergreen shrubs and vines. The leaves will appreciate having dust and dirt washed away.

When potted plants wilt daily, they are probably potbound, so there's no room left in the containers for soil or water. Give them bigger pots and fresh potting soil into which you have incorporated water-holding gel crystals, and you'll find they stay happy far longer between waterings.

To water plants beyond the reach of your hose, make drip jugs or buckets. Use a nail or an ice pick to make two small holes 1 inch (3 cm) above the bottoms of plastic pails or milk jugs, then fill them with water. The water will slowly seep into the soil, but some will remain in the bottoms of the containers and provide enough weight to keep them from blowing away.

Too much water? In a site that has poor drainage, install a piece of perforated drainage pipe under the ground, making sure that it tilts

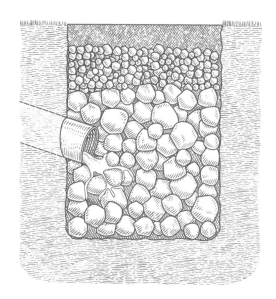

in the direction you want the water to go. If you need to provide a place for the water to go, create a dry well by digging a hole at least 3 feet (1 meter) deep and 2 feet (61 cm) across. Fill it two-thirds full with stones, top them with coarse gravel, and cover the top with soil.

WATERING TOOLS

Invest in good hoses. Look for three- or four-ply vinyl, nylon, or rubber hose that is reinforced with mesh and rated for high water pressure—up to 500 pounds per square inch (35 kg per square cm). Inexpensive hoses kink easily, so they're very frustrating to use.

Prevent kinking. Coil up your hose between uses, either over a hose hanger, around a hose reel, or inside a large tub or hose bowl. If you'll be using the hose again very soon, simply coil it into a figure eight on the ground.

Self-coiling hoses are ideal for watering plants on decks and patios. When not in use, they can be threaded over a stake like a Slinky.

A soaker hose for drip irrigation is made from perforated rubber so it seeps water along its entire length; it's useful for vegetables, trees, shrubs, and flowers. You can make your own soaker by punching small holes in a leaky old hose and clamping off the end.

Be sprinkler savvy. There are sprinklers for every purpose. Some have moving parts, and some are stationary, but all emit water through holes in tubing. Check the emitter holes from time to time to be sure they aren't clogged.

- **Ring-shaped stationary sprinklers** are inexpensive and can deliver water quickly to small areas, such as newly planted beds.

- **Spinning sprinklers** deliver water evenly to larger areas, so they're especially useful for large gardens or lawns.

- **Oscillating sprinklers** have water-powered gears that turn the sprinkler tubing for back-and-forth watering, which allows more time for the water to soak into the garden.

Avoid smashed plants by using hose guides. Instead of dragging a hose through the garden, run it around wood or metal stakes, a carefully placed rock, or manufactured guides with a lip that prevents the hose from slipping up over the top. There are even decorative hose guides that are disguised as garden art.

Get a splitter. Sometimes what you put on the end of your hose is as useful as the hose itself. When choosing any type of hose attachment, be sure there's a washer inside the large female end, which ensures a tight seal. One of the most useful attachments is a splitter. Also called a tap distributor, a splitter can turn a single outside faucet into two or even three outlets, so you can attach a hose to a distant sprinkler and still be able to wash your hands at the faucet. Having a splitter will save you many trips across the yard to change hoses.

Buy nifty nozzles. An all-purpose nozzle is adjustable and goes with a twist from a gentle spray to a strong jet of water. Some nozzles include an adjustable "rose," or emitter, that lets you change the pattern of the water from a gentle shower to a fine mist or a single strong stream.

A watering wand has a lightweight straight pipe and ends with a rose that breaks the force of the water and mimics gently falling rain, which is the kindest way to water tender flowers, stems, and leaves. Telescoping watering wands make it easy to reach hanging baskets and second-story window boxes.

Revival of the Rain Barrel

If you don't want your garden to wilt during the next bout of water restrictions, install a rain barrel; they were common fixtures in gardens in past centuries when water had to be pumped by hand and carried to thirsty plants. A rain barrel catches rainwater runoff from your roof or through your home's gutters. In addition to being free, the water from a rain barrel is soft water, untreated with chlorine, fluoride, or other chemicals, which have negative effects on some plants.

Keep a lid on it. To keep pets, kids, and mosquitoes out of your rain barrel, be sure it has a tight lid. If the water comes into the barrel via your gutters, use gutter guards to keep out debris.

A water diverter fitted between two sections of downspout channels water to the barrel as needed. When the barrel is full, flip up the diverter to make your gutters work as usual.

Get fishy. Stop by a pet shop and get a few inexpensive comets, which are plain goldfish, and let them live in your rain barrel in the summer. They will eat any mosquitoes or other insects that manage to sneak in.

Make your own. Wood rain barrels are attractive, but you can make a perfectly serviceable one from a plastic trash can or used plastic drum. If you choose a used container for your barrel, be sure to find out what was stored in it. Pickle barrels are nontoxic, while drums used to store pesticides, detergents, or other chemicals may contain unwanted residues. Clean the barrel, give it a top that can be secured tightly, fit it with connections to the downspout, and install a spigot near the bottom. Even without a spigot, it can be used for hand watering with a dipping bucket or watering can.

Give it feet. Raising a rain barrel by placing it on a platform will make it possible to use the force of gravity to move water from the barrel to your garden.

Pruning and Grooming

IF YOU PRUNE TREES AND SHRUBS when they are young, shaping them as they grow, they will need less pruning as they mature. Work with the natural shape of the plant whenever possible. While the tree is young and lower branches are small, nip them off so you won't have to remove them when they're large. This will prevent unsightly scarring. A second reason to prune is to relieve plants of dead or diseased parts. Good pruning and grooming practices will minimize how much damage your plants must endure from cold or diseases caused by too little sunshine and fresh air.

PRUNING BASICS

Unless you want a formal or exaggerated look, use a tree or shrub's natural framework and growth pattern. A plant that's allowed to develop with its natural architecture will be more structurally sound than if it were trained into an unnatural shape.

Conifers require specific pruning techniques. Don't cut back firs, spruces, pines, or other needle-leafed conifers, because they won't fill in below the pruning cut as other plants do. To help a conifer develop more bushy branches, just use your fingers to pinch off half of each "candle"—a new shoot with growth buds—

before it opens its needles in spring. Take care not to remove the entire candle, since doing so will stop further growth of the branch.

Renovate a leggy conifer by practicing Japanese "cloud" pruning to transform it into an

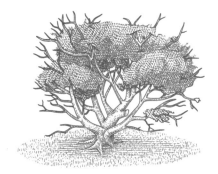

interesting specimen. Select a few well-placed branches with good foliage. Remove twigs and branches along with the lower stems and prune the tops into fluffy, elliptical shapes. The foliage will appear to be floating like clouds above the woody branches.

Forget about using wound paint. Instead, let the tree heal itself; it forms a natural protective layer inside cuts and wounds. Painting over pruning cuts can encourage decay.

The best time to prune most plants is at the end of their dormant season, just as new growth begins. One exception is flowering shrubs. Prune those that bloom in spring after they flower. Late-flowering shrubs that bloom on wood produced the same year can be pruned before growth starts in the spring. Another exception is mature fruit trees. You needn't wait until they are dormant to remove any weak, broken, or diseased branches.

A gentle approach to tree pruning is better than a heavy-handed one. Instead of severely pruning a tree all at once by topping back overgrown branches, shape the tree gradually over a

THE LANGUAGE OF PRUNING

There are many ways to prune, so pruning practices have their own vocabulary. Choosing the right approach will make a huge difference in the results you get when you prune your plants as well as in how often they need additional shaping.

Deadheading: Removing the spent blossoms of flowering plants to encourage continued blooming. Deadheading keeps plants from wasting their energy producing seeds and makes them look neater.

Heading back: Cutting back the main branches of a tree or shrub by at least half their length. This stimulates new growth, which emerges from the buds closest to the cut stubs' ends.

Limbing up: Removing the lower branches of a mature tree. Limbing up raises the shade canopy, which benefits grasses and groundcovers by increasing available light. It also opens up the space under the tree for recreation or relaxation.

Pinching: Removing the growing tip of a plant to encourage the formation of bushy growth and improved blooming. Late-blooming perennials such as chrysanthemums and asters benefit greatly from early-season pinching.

Pollarding: A specialized form of pruning used to create a formal shape or restrict the crown of a mature tree. Some weeping trees and shrubs are handled this way at a young age, as are those forced to grow into broad umbrella shapes.

Shearing: Cutting back numerous stem tips across as flat plane, as is done with hedges or shrubs that are pruned to formal shapes. Depending on the plant, shearing must be done two or more times during the growing season.

Thinning: Removing entire branches flush with the trunk or pruning out selected lateral branches. Sucker-producing shrubs also are pruned by thinning out old branches at the soil line. Thinning takes out older growth, often without stimulating new growth.

Topping: Drastic cutting back of large branches on a mature tree. This practice is no longer recommended, as it traumatizes the tree and leads to weak new growth.

three- to five-year period. This allows for the removal of only a few branches at a time, thereby retaining the tree's outline and its energy-producing leaves. In addition to stimulating the growth of numerous weak branches, topping back can expose the inner branches and trunk to sunscald.

🦌 Watch Out!

When pruning big trees, take care to prevent falling limbs. Before making the first cuts through a heavy branch, prevent damage to whatever lies below by making a safety sling. Loop a sturdy rope over a higher branch and tie it securely to the branch to be pruned. As you cut the successive sections away, a helper holding the rope below can gently lower the newly pruned pieces to the ground.

Developing new suckers is the way some shrubs grow. To prune forsythias, shrubby dogwoods, deutzia, kerria, and nandina, select entire stems for removal instead of cutting back the tips of long stems. Pruning older canes at the base allows the new growth more room to develop.

Pruning cuts on woody growth should be almost flush with the "branch collar"—the swollen or wrinkled area close to where the branch joins the trunk or a larger limb. Keeping the collar intact helps the plant produce a protective callus, which is how woody plants heal.

Look for promising buds. Whenever possible, prune to just above a bud that faces a direction in which you want the branch to grow. Usually, this is an outward-facing bud. The new branches will grow out and give the tree or shrub an open shape. Buds or branches facing inward will grow that way, blocking sun and fresh air and making pest control more difficult.

Newly planted hedges can tolerate a severe pruning after the first year of growth. The hedge will thicken out much more quickly as each shrub pushes out vigorous new shoots.

Sensible hedge shearing. When trimming the top edge of a hedge, drive a stake at each end and tie a string between the stakes at the desired height. Then simply follow the line to make an even cut.

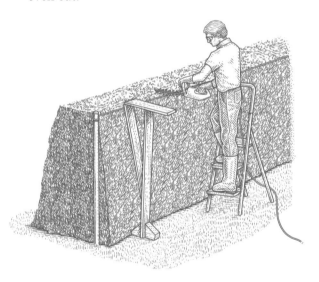

Keep a sheared hedge full at the bottom by pruning at a slight angle, with the base slightly wider than the top. This will allow sunlight to reach the bottom branches, resulting in a greener, fuller hedge.

Plan for fast cleanup. A tarp spread under the shrubbery when pruning will save you the trouble of finding and raking up all the clippings. Just bundle them up and take them to the compost pile.

PRUNING TOOLS

Use the right tool for the job, and pruning will be much easier. A good set of trimming tools includes hand pruners, a pair of loppers, and a pruning saw to handle large branches. Loppers are suited to jobs too large for shears and too small for saws. Manual or power hedge trimmers are also available for shearing dense plants that have smaller leaves and branches.

Curved bypass hand shears give the cleanest cut. Check to make sure they have a sturdy frame, a spiral-type spring between the handles, replaceable blades, and a nonslip grip. Those with a thumb-operated lock allow you to put the shears into your pocket between cuts. When protected from moisture, a good pair of pruning shears will last for years.

Avoid shears with lightweight folded metal frames that are likely to twist under heavy loads. Those shears with a forged metal blade instead of replaceable blades can be sharpened, but they will become useless if the blade is nicked or chipped.

Anvil shears have a cutting blade that is pushed against a metal sole, or anvil. On the plus side, they cost less than bypass shears and are less likely to twist when cutting larger branches. On the downside, they can crush the wood as they cut, and they leave a stub.

When pruning a branch, hold the shears so the upper blade faces toward the part of the branch that will remain on the plant. This way, any damage that might occur will be on the pruned branch instead of the one that's staying with the plant.

Wear oven mitts for pruning. Although oven mitts may be a bit too awkward to use for weeding or planting seedlings in your garden, they can come in awfully handy when it comes time to pruning trees, hedges, and bushes—particularly those thorny devils, such as holly, firethorn, and rose bushes.

If your hands are small, use short, lightweight shears. Lefthanders can find specially made shears with an inverted blade, counter blade, and locking clip.

Long-handled pole pruners, ranging from 6 to 12 feet (2 to 4 meters) long, free you from having to use a ladder, but they're useful only for branches about 1 inch (3 cm) thick. Some come in one piece, while others have interlocking pieces with a spring-operated blade that works like a giant pair of pruning shears.

Pruning loppers are used for cutting branches too large or tough for shears but not large enough for a saw. Avoid using an anvil model except for cutting dead wood. Investing in a sturdy bypass type with a forged, tempered steel blade will pay off if you care for a number of woody shrubs and trees.

Maintain your shears and loppers for long-term use. If properly cared for, they take less effort to use and make cleaner cuts. Regularly lubricate the pivot area with light machine oil or petroleum jelly to ensure smooth operation. Clean sap off blades with light oil and steel wool. Regularly sharpen the blades with a fine file or stone and replace them when they become worn.

Use a bow saw for heavy-duty cutting of wood more than ½ inch (13 mm) thick. The deep, pointed teeth cut on both push and pull strokes, so be careful when handling this tool. Many small pruning saws can be folded into their handles for safer carrying.

Size up your hedge trimmers. Manual hedge clippers are sufficient for small jobs, but you'll need an electric or battery-powered trimmer if you have a large or long hedge. When using a power hedge trimmer, wear snug clothing so nothing can get caught in the blade. When lowering the trimmer to your side, be careful not to hit your leg or catch your clothing.

Keep trimmer blades clean. Power trimmer blades must slide back and forth easily, so it's important to keep them clean and sharp. Clean the blades and eliminate sticky resin or sap with a brush dipped in gasoline or turpentine. After the blades dry, oil them with a cloth dipped in light machine oil. The oiled blades won't rust, and your trimmer will be ready to use when you need it.

Don't go overboard. It's easy to overprune with a hedge trimmer. Trim lightly at first and go over the hedge a second time only if needed. After pruning a hedge with a power trimmer, use hand-held pruning shears to do the fine detail work.

PINCHING

When the tip of a stem or branch is cut off, the plant releases hormones that energize the next buds on the stem, causing new branches to grow. Pinching makes use of this natural growth pattern by removing the terminal, or dominant, bud or growing tip. The terms *pinching, pinching back, pinching off,* and *pinching out* are interchangeable.

Blackberries and raspberries will produce more fruit if you pinch back the tips of new stems when they're about 5 feet (1.5 meters) long. Small lateral branches will then develop, which will bloom and bear fruit the following summer.

For big blooms on dahlias and chrysanthemums, pinch out the side shoots to train the plant to have a single upright stem. When buds appear, remove the lateral ones on the main cluster, leaving only the central bud.

For bushy dahlias and chrysanthemums with more, smaller blossoms, take the opposite approach. Start pinching out the main stem tips when the plants are 8 inches (20 cm) tall and continue until mid-July, just before the buds begin to form.

On rose standards, keep the trunk tidy and direct the energy to the topgrowth by pinching or cutting out little buds that form along the stem.

Pinch back excess flowers on fruits and vegetables for beautiful produce that's bigger and more plentiful. Eggplants and peppers often sprout many flowers that if left alone will make many small fruits.

Pinch to eliminate aphids. These small sucking insects cluster on tender new growth and are common on beans, roses, sweet peas, and many other flowers. Simply pinching off infested stem tips gets rid of hundreds of aphids while stimulating growth of new lateral branches.

DON'T FORGET TO DEADHEAD

When you remove spent flowers from annuals or long-blooming perennials, you are deadheading the plants. This makes the garden look much neater, and nicely groomed gardens are always more enjoyable places than those filled with drooping blooms. Deadheading is essential if you want to keep annuals in bloom, because they decline quickly once they've had the chance to produce mature seeds. When you cut flowers for bouquets, think of it as preemptive deadheading; plants respond to their loss by gearing up to produce replacements.

Pinch to preserve variegation. Variegated plants, with leaves marked in white, pink, or yellow, sometimes send out a stray branch with leaves of solid green. Pinch or cut these back to the main stem; otherwise, the entire plant may revert to green.

SCULPTED PLANTS

Many plants can be molded into distinctive shapes with the use of special pruning techniques. Perhaps you want to grow a tree-form standard, a wall-hugging espalier, or an interesting topiary. Before you get started, make sure the plant you want to use is willing to cooperate. If it's already growing in your garden, analyze it from every angle and study the structure of its leaves, stems, and flowers. Sculpted plants naturally draw attention, so it's often a good idea to grow companion plants that will help frame the finished specimen. When starting with a new plant, be sure to choose one that is the right size for the place and the project.

Try a template. Even if you have a good eye for plant form, a template can help you maintain a perfectly clipped shape when you're pruning. To trim a globe, for example, make an arch of stiff wire of the size you need and attach it to the plant's crown. Clip away growth that falls outside the template, rotating it around the plant as you work.

Work with weepers. To encourage a tree or shrub that has a weeping growth habit to spread out in an open fashion, each year trim branches just above a shoot that points away from the crown. Pinch off buds that face upward or toward the center of the crown.

Create comely columns. When pruning a plant to grow as an upright column, don't prune the top or pinch back vertical stems; doing so will encourage the growth of lateral stems. Instead, prune the oblique stems to maintain the natural silhouette.

Train tree-form standards. A standard is created by carefully pruning and training a shrub to grow into the shape of a small tree. Standards are often 3 to 4 feet (1 meter) tall, comprised of a single trunk with a knot of foliage and flowers at the top. They can be much smaller, however, and the little ones are effective in pots used as tabletop features. The top is often clipped into a sphere, cone, or weeping shape.

To make a standard, select a shrub with at least one straight vertical stem. Prune off all other low-growing stems and tie the selected one to a durable stake. When the plant is tall enough, pinch off the tip to make the top bushy. As the top grows, shape it into the desired form by more pinching and pruning. Carefully remove all unwanted buds that sprout along the main stem or trunk.

Good plants for standards include fuchsia, Rosemary, dwarf cherries, and roses. To create a standard rose with a full top, grafting is necessary to increase the number of stems.

Show them off. Because standards are unusual and eye-catching, they deserve a prominent place in the landscape. Use them to line a walkway or plant one on each side of a doorway, beside a gate, or at both ends of a garden bench.

Feature a fine-figured trunk. A standard can be made with a braided trunk. This interesting effect can easily be created with three flexible *Ficus benjamina* plants grown in the same pot. When they are 15 to 18 inches (38 to 46 cm) tall, cut off all lateral branches and carefully braid the three stripped stems. As they grow, the stems will thicken and wind together to form a sturdy, handsome standard with a single trunk. Allow a bushy top to grow above the triple trunk.

❦ Watch Out!

The tops of stakes can be dangerously sharp, so make eye protectors by covering them with pieces of sponge or cork, old tennis balls, small terra-cotta figurines, or even balls of modeling clay.

STAKING PLANTS

You know the old saying "As the twig is bent, so grows the tree." Stakes—whether temporary or permanent—get your plants growing in the right direction and give roots time to grow into steady anchors to keep the plants stable.

Plan ahead. Anticipate the need for stakes and set them in place before the plants grow too much or the flowers flop over and become

(Continued on page 324)

Want to Try Topiary?

Topiary is the traditional sculpting of plants into geometric figures, animals, and objects. You can train plants into desired forms by pruning, or you can grow plants over a wire frame and clip them to follow the shape of the frame. While some shapes, such as spirals and standards, are quite formal, others are fun and fanciful. Use topiary to frame an entry door, line a path, or create a garden centerpiece.

The best plants for topiary are evergreen trees, shrubs, and herbs that have strong, woody stems and small, dense leaves and are able to withstand regular pruning. In the North, try yew, privet, boxwood, ivy, Japanese holly, germander, and euonymus. In warm climates, use yaupon holly, myrtle, bay laurel, pittosporum, Rosemary, and fig.

Start with a simple shape. A good choice for beginners is a geometric figure, such as an oval or triangle. Make a framework by pounding wood or plastic stakes into the ground around a young shrub. Form wire mesh into the desired shape around the stakes. As the plant grows, clip any shoots that poke through the mesh. Once the shrub has filled the mold, remove the mesh. Shear the plant regularly to maintain its shape.

Trim lightly, trim often. During the early stages of training, prune back stems primarily to induce branching so the plants fill the form. Once the shrub begins filling in, trim lightly but regularly—especially in spring and after flowering—to maintain the plant's fullness and shape. The frequency depends on the plant's growth rate and the intricacy of the design. But don't prune late in the season, because pruning always stimulates new growth, which is easily damaged by cold.

Provide a winter cover. If you live in a climate where heavy snow or ice is common, protect topiary from snow and ice buildup by erecting a wire mesh shield over the plants. Cover the mesh with burlap and brush off any accumulation to keep it from becoming so heavy that it crushes your creation.

Use the right tools. Take small cuts with sharp pruning shears. Use guides, such as levels or stakes, even if you have a good eye. Trim from the top down and from the center out, working on all sides of the plant to keep your trimming symmetrical.

Grow a faux flowerpot
by planting a hedge around a shrub trained into a tree shape, called a standard. Create the standard by removing shoots along the stem and snipping the top into a globe, then stake the stem. For the "pot," plant low-growing, mounding

TRY TOPIARY WITH VINES

Ivy, jasmine, creeping fig, and other small-leafed climbers can be trained as container topiaries, which can be kept outdoors from spring through fall and brought indoors in the winter. You can use either of two methods: a freestanding wire frame shaped like a wreath or heart or a moss-filled frame to create a topiary in a geometric or animal shape.

Method 1. Choose a freestanding frame twice as tall as the plant's pot. Insert its base firmly in the soil around the plant. Wind one plant stem around one wire of the frame, then repeat with the remaining stems. If a stem is stiff, tie it in place with soft green twine until it conforms. Pinch or snip any stems that grow out of place.

Method 2. Fill a wire form with a mix of soil and sphagnum moss and mist with water to moisten. Plant ivy or creeping fig around the base of the form. The stems will climb up the wire and root in the stuffing. Peg stems into the mix with florists' pins or bobby pins and keep the soil and form moist.

shrubs in a ring around the standard. When they're about one third as tall as the standard's stem, clip them into a

flowerpot shape. Remove the stake from the standard and keep all the plants trimmed.

SINGLE-STAKE STRATEGIES

The easiest way to train young trees to grow upright—or to help a plant develop a long, lean trunk so you can train it to grow as a standard—is to attach it to a single sturdy stake. Good materials to use as ties include old stockings or pantyhose (**A**), which are nice and stretchy, and adjustable plastic ties (**B**) with

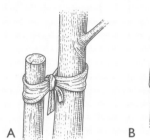

A   B   C

buckles. Old inner tubes (**C**), cut into strips and secured with twine or wire, also make good tie material.

soiled. Some plants grow surprisingly fast, and it can be difficult to put supports in place once the plants start to sprawl.

Naturally rot-resistant wood makes good stakes. Good choices include redwood, cypress, red cedar, chestnut, and hazelnut. You can also use bamboo or metal stakes. Stakes made from pruned-off branches blend beautifully into an informal garden. Set stripped branches, chosen for their appealing shapes, into the ground right next to the plants in need of support.

Make them disappear. Green ties, stakes, and netting are relatively invisible in the garden. Use a dark green shade of outdoor enamel to paint stakes before installing them near plants.

Staking newly planted trees. When given support, a freshly planted tree puts down new roots more quickly and grows faster. Place three stakes around the tree in a triangular pattern. Then use taut wire or twine to attach the tree to the stakes, using pieces of cloth, old garden hose, or cut-up rubber inner tubes to cushion the parts of the wire that are in direct contact with the tree. Don't tie too tightly, because slight movements caused by the wind help newly planted trees develop stronger, thicker trunks.

Cage in floppy flowers. Large, heavy flowers, such as irises, delphiniums, gladiolus, chrysanthemums, and peonies will hold their heads high if you make a low cage from several bamboo stakes tied together with hemp or jute twine. In addition to tying the stakes together around the outside of the plant, include crosswise strings to further support the plants' branches.

Elegant Espaliers

To practice the centuries-old art of espalier, start with the right plant and train it to lie flat against a wall or fence, with its branches forming a selected pattern. Pears and apples are easy to train in a variety of patterns, but other woody plants lend themselves to certain forms. Rockspray cotoneaster and yew work well as fans. Forsythia and mock orange are appropriate for arched and curving designs.

Before you begin, draw the design you want on paper so you can refer to it as you decide which stems to bend, tie, pinch, or prune.

Start with a frame. Use thin, solid stakes of bamboo, oak, or heavy-gauge, vinyl-coated wire to build the framework. You'll also need soft string, raffia, or thin cloth strips to tie the branches into place, making a loose loop to allow for growth. Never use wire loops, which can cut and injure the plant.

Choose a young plant. Select a plant with flexible young stems; it should be no more than 3 feet (1 meter) tall. Set the plant 6 to 12 inches (15 to

30 cm) from the wall to allow for air circulation. Spread the roots outward, away from the wall, and backfill with rich garden loam.

Prune large stems when the plant is dormant and note the plant's overall shape. You can pinch out buds and shoots through late spring, but stop pruning in early summer to give new growth time to harden off by winter.

Don't skip spring training. Train stems when they're young and flexible so they don't snap. If a shoot is stiff, tie it to a length of wire and gently bend it a little at a time over the course of a few weeks. Remove the wire once the stem has matured in the desired shape, which may take as long as a year.

GOOD PLANTS FOR ESPALIER

- **Deciduous trees and shrubs** that perform well include dogwood, forsythia, laburnum, mock orange, cherry, redbud, rose, and viburnum.
- **Good evergreens** for espalier include camellia, holly, lilac, pyracantha, dwarf southern magnolia, winter jasmine, and yew.
- **Fruits** for espalier are apple, blackberry, fig, grape, and lemon.
- **Vines** to try as espalier include bougainvillea, clematis, and wisteria.

✤ Seeds and Seedlings

GARDENERS ARE ALWAYS on the prowl for new plants, and growing them from seed is great, affordable fun. Seeds can range from dust-like specks to the size of coconuts, and they also vary in the speed with which they grow. Some leafy greens race from seed to bloom in six or eight weeks, while trees often need decades to reach maturity. Why not enjoy being part of this intriguing natural process? When winter has you in its grip, it's gratifying to see some seeds sprouting in pots on a windowsill or under lights in the basement.

STARTING SEEDS

Indoors or outdoors? Indoor sowing is the preferred method for starting tiny seeds that are easily disturbed by weather and pests, and since certain plants don't like to be transplanted, they're best sown where they will grow. Starting seeds indoors also gives you a jump on the planting season. Outdoor sowing is most practical for vegetables and fast-growing annual flowers.

Warm them up. Plant varieties have individual preferences for germination conditions, especially with regard to temperature and light. Many seeds, such as nasturtiums, lettuce, and peas, like a temperature around 75°F (24°C), which can often be found on top of a refrigerator or near a stove.

Testing leftover seeds. Leftover seeds from previous years may still be good, but why take a chance? One simple way to see if old seeds are still viable is to place them in a glass of water. Seeds that fall to the bottom have a good chance of growing; discard those that float to the top. Another test is to place 20 or so seeds from the old packet between two moist paper towels and tuck it into a plastic sandwich bag for a few days, then look inside to check for germination. Use the percentage of germinated seeds as a guide for how much to sow, or go ahead and plant the sprouted test seeds.

Plastic cake, cookie, and salad containers with clear domed lids—like those you get from supermarkets or fast-food restaurants—make great containers in which to start flowers and herbs from seed. The clear cover admits light and helps the seeds stay moist.

To help seedlings develop stiffer stems, place them near a gentle fan for a half hour daily. When you move them outdoors, they'll be better prepared for strong gusts of wind.

Too many seedlings? It's easy to sow too many seeds when you're working with small seeds, such as petunias or pansies. Thin them when the seed-starting medium is moist by pulling out the extras with a pair of tweezers.

Snip doubles down to singles. Beets, chard, and a few other plants have two seeds within each seed capsule. If both of them germinate, use small cuticle scissors to nip out the extra seedling.

Grandpa's wisdom

Wait for cloudy weather to set out seedlings. Transplant on a cool, overcast, or drizzly day or late in the afternoon, so that plants don't suffer in the heat and light.

An old aquarium is a great place for starting seedlings in small containers. The glass case retains moisture and humidity, and the light helps the seedlings green up quickly. Move them to a brighter place soon after they germinate.

Provide small sips of water. Use a clean dishwashing liquid bottle or a turkey baster to gently dribble water on germinating seeds. Overwatering can lead to problems with damping off, a fungal infection that causes seedling stems to fall over and rot.

Plan ahead for moving day. A week or more before setting seeds out, feed them with liquid fertilizer and set them outdoors for a few hours each day. Plants adjust to the outdoors best if they gradually become accustomed to sun and wind.

Hands off the stems. Gently lift seedlings out of their containers by pushing from the bottom while sliding them onto a table knife. Support the roots in one hand and position the plant by holding a side leaf. Set most seedlings slightly deeper than they grew in their containers. Tomatoes can be planted much deeper because they will develop roots along the buried section of the stem.

Shade tender seedlings for two to three days after setting them out by covering them with a flowerpot. Instead of struggling to cope with strong sun, the plants can concentrate on developing new roots. Try this trick with purchased bedding plants as well as homegrown seedlings.

Should you save your own seeds? You may have better luck saving seeds from nonhybrid varieties than from hybrids, whose offspring won't breed true to their parents' traits.

To harvest seed, remove the entire seedhead or pod from a plant and store it in a dry place. To prepare the seeds for planting, shatter the flower or open the dried pods and gather the heavy seeds on a piece of paper.

Keep stored seeds dry. Use film canisters or baby food jars for individual seed types. Other useful containers are sealed paper envelopes or bags, drawstring muslin sacks, and self-sealing plastic storage bags.

Make knee pads from mouse pads. Your old computer mouse pads are just the right size to cushion your knees when you're setting out seedlings or do other work in the garden. Kneel on them loose or attach them directly to your pant legs with duct tape.

SOWING SEEDS

Once the soil warms in spring, you can sow what you want to grow by planting seeds directly in the ground. If your soil tends to form a crust as it dries, cover the seeds with potting soil instead of regular garden soil.

Can't tell seedlings from weeds? If you sow seeds in a pattern, such as a straight or zigzag line, it's easier to eliminate weeds by finding look-alike seedlings.

Space the seeds in your garden with ease, using an empty soda bottle as your measuring tool. Find the recommended distance between seeds and then cut off the tapered top of the bottle so its diameter equals that distance. When you start planting, firmly press the bottle, cut edge down, into the soil and place a seed in the center of the circle it makes. Line up the bottle so its edge touches the curve of the first impression, press down again, and plant a seed in the center. Repeat until you've filled your rows.

Overseed a little, but don't get carried away. Planting two seeds instead of one guards against skips in the row, but if you plant far too many seeds, you'll have a lot of thinning to do. If the seeds are small and difficult to sow at the desired

WORKING WITH DIFFICULT SEEDS

Most seeds are eager to germinate soon after they come in contact with warm, moist soil, but some need extra help. Seeds with very hard seedcoats sprout faster when the seedcoats are nicked or filed to help them take up water—a practice called scarification. Other seeds must be tricked into thinking they have waited in moist soil through winter. This trick is called stratification.

Scarify hard-coated seeds, such as morning glories, moon-flowers, gourds, and sweet peas, by nicking them with a sharp knife, rubbing them with a file or sandpaper, or clipping them along one edge with a nail clipper. If you've had trouble getting any type of seed to sprout, scarifying often solves the problem.

Stratify seeds of hardy shrubs, such as cotoneaster and holly, by soaking them in water overnight, then combine them with a mixture of moist peat and sand in a plastic bag. Place the mixture in the refrigerator and keep it at 34° to 41°F (1° to 5°C) for 4 to 12 weeks, depending on the type of seed. Then plant the seeds when the weather warms in spring. Seeds that are sown one year but don't come up until the next have helped themselves to natural stratification. This often happens with larkspur, lupine, and vetch seeds.

spacing, mix them with dry sand before sowing. You can also buy seeds encased in easy-to-handle clay pellets or attached to biodegradable tape.

Make your own seed tape by placing seeds on strips of toilet tissue. Position the seeds at the proper spacing, fold the tissue in half lengthwise, and lightly moisten it with a pump spray bottle. Press it flat, let it dry, and then simply cover it with soil when you're ready to plant.

Thin to win. Unless you've spaced your seeds widely as you planted them, you will need to thin the seedlings, whether they've been grown indoors or outdoors. If they are too close together, they don't have room to grow properly. Removing small, deformed, or overcrowded seedlings helps healthy specimens perform better.

When to thin? Thin most seedlings when the first set of true leaves appears. Before thinning, dampen the soil and let it sit for an hour to limit damage to roots when you separate the plantlets. After thinning, water the remaining plants to settle the soil that was disturbed around their roots.

DIRECT SEED THESE FAVORITES

Many beloved garden plants are difficult or impossible to transplant without causing serious damage—or death—to the seedlings. Practice your direct-sowing skills on carrots, corn poppies, lupine, and larkspur, which are rarely sold as bedding plants because they're such terrible transplanters.

Thin leafy greens gradually. You can enjoy eating baby lettuce when the plants are only 1 inch (3 cm) tall. If you pull plants a few at a time, you'll have a longer harvest season, and each time you thin the plants, the remaining ones will have more room to grow.

Save volunteers. Sometimes when you're weeding, you'll encounter volunteer plants that you'll want to transplant. Be ready for this by having a small bucket with a few inches of water handy to carry them in. Lift the misplaced plants from beneath and get them settled in a new home as quickly as you can.

Propagating Plants

EXPANDING YOUR COLLECTION OF plants with seeds is interesting and inexpensive, but vegetative propagation methods, such as division and rooting cuttings, will help you increase the supply of plants you already have. Many plants are surprisingly simple to propagate, although some are challenging or impossible to coax into producing new roots. Learning a few basic propagation skills can help you turn a specimen into a lush bed or provide a way to share your riches with fellow gardeners.

PLANT DIVISION

Perennials grow into bushy clumps that need occasional thinning and separation. This is a task mainly for spring, but you can divide plants in fall if you live where winters are mild. Perennials can best withstand some handling and breakage when their strong spring growth is ready to begin. When handled properly, divided plants quickly settle in and make new growth.

Examine what you have. Is the crowded clump made up of many plants, or crowns, with individual root systems? If so, your job is to dig, then pull or cut the individual plants free from the greater mass. Discard old, woody crowns or those that lose their roots as you divide the clumps.

Have new planting places ready. Small divisions often have few roots, so they can't tolerate stress from dry conditions. Keep divided plants in a shady spot or cover them with a damp cloth. Replant them into a new bed or into containers of moist soil as quickly as possible.

Take a little off the edge. You don't have to dig up a big clump of daylilies in order to get a few new plants. Instead, take a division or two from the outside of the clump by cutting straight down through the roots. This is a great way to share plants with friends without disturbing the parent clump.

Share the wealth. If you end up with more plants than you can use, give them to your friends, offer them to neighbors, or donate them to plant sales.

Recruit great divisions by letting the plants know your plans ahead of time. Place a bucketful of compost over the base of the plant from which you plan to take a division. After a couple of weeks, the stems beneath the compost may have already begun to grow roots, which will help supplement the below-ground roots that will be lost as the plants are dug and moved. This method works especially well with groundcover plants, such as pachysandra and lamb's ear.

Divide crowded bulbs. Dig crowded clumps when the bulbs are dormant—usually late summer or early fall. Many bulbs form smaller offspring—tiny versions of themselves called bulblets. With narcissus and tulips, break off the bulblets by hand and replant them in a special nursery bed. They will grow to blooming size in two to three years.

Clean smelly hands with toothpaste. When you're through doing dirty, stinky work, such as dividing up plants, wash your hands with toothpaste and they'll smell great. The ingredients in toothpaste that deodorize your mouth will work on your hands as well.

ROOTING CUTTINGS

As plants develop new stems, they prepare for possible disaster by stowing away special cells in their nodes—the places where leaves join the stem. If you pinch off the stem's tip, the nodes will morph into new stems or leaves. But if you leave the tip intact, nodes buried in moist soil—or sometimes in plain water—will mobilize and grow new roots. It's not magic; there are some essential things to know to make your stem rooting projects successful.

The perfect combination of conditions includes high humidity paired with limited indirect light. Give cuttings only enough light to keep them alive, and cover them with a plastic tent so the leaves don't have to replenish lost moisture. Until the cuttings grow roots, they

have no way to gather enough water to keep unprotected leaves provided with the water they need. Try to keep humidity close to 100 percent.

Start with what's easy. Mint is so easy to root from stem-tip cuttings that you can grow a plant from a stem purchased at the supermarket.

Gardening Techniques **331**

Other easy rooters include coleus, chrysanthemum, and any type of sedum. Among shrubs, forsythias, hydrangeas, and roses often root in only a few weeks.

Cuttings need a few leaves to nourish the developing roots, but too much foliage demands more moisture than a rootless stem can provide. Pinch off the lower leaves as well as any buds. You will know new roots have begun to develop when new leaves appear.

Cleanliness is crucial. A severed stem is actually a gaping wound through which fungi can enter. Root cuttings in sterile seed-starting mix, vermiculite, or a 50-50 mixture of peat moss and sand, and make sure containers are clean.

Clay pots work well for rooting cuttings when covered with a loose, clear plastic bag, such as a produce bag, held above the cuttings with wood skewers or a wire hoop.

Speed counts, which is the main reason to use rooting powder, which contains hormones that encourage the cutting to form roots quickly. Very fast rooters don't need rooting powder, but for woody, slow-rooting plants, it can mean the difference between rooting and rotting.

Use a natural solution. Willows and black locusts give off indolebutyric acid, a natural rooting hormone. Soak pieces of willow or black locust stems in rainwater for two days and water cuttings with the solution. Or simply

SET UP A HOME NURSERY

Having your own home nursery is an economical, enjoyable way to fill your garden or grow extra plants to swap with fellow gardeners. You can use it to grow annuals, perennials, and woody plants, and it can be a good place to grow rooted cuttings. A home nursery need not be elaborate; you can do a lot in a sheltered, out-of-the-way spot. Any area that gets sun and has access to water will do. Set aside a shady corner of your nursery for sun-shy or fragile plants.

• Grow plants in containers in your home nursery. This makes them easy to move around, and keeps their root systems compact. You can use the same plastic pots that commercial nurseries use, although many types of containers will do.

• Fill a framed bed with a half-and-half mixture of peat moss and sand and use it to grow rooted cuttings or perennials that have been divided into small clumps.

Kept moist, they will quickly grow roots and will be easy to lift and transplant.

• Very young trees, shrubs, and perennials bought from a commercial or mail-order nursery are usually inexpensive, but they may be too small to plant out right away in the garden. Raise these "babies" in your home nursery for a season or two until they're large enough to take their place in your garden.

include a willow stem in a container in which you're rooting stems in water.

Slip in a seed. A third way to supplement the root-inducing hormones in a cutting is to slit a notch in the base of the cutting, then wedge a wheat or corn seed in the notch before setting the cutting to root. As the seed germinates, it releases hormones that help keep the cutting in a root-growing mood.

Go beyond the tip. Stem-tip cuttings are often the first choice for rooting, but you can also use other sections of the stem. As long as there is a pair of leaves at the top of the cutting, nodes near the tip will quickly replace the lost ones at the tip, and you'll have a new plant that's branched at the base, too.

Root rhododendrons. Certain large-leafed species of rhododendron, including *Rhododendron minus* 'Scintillation', are fairly difficult to propagate; roots form in the stem and are then stopped by the bark layer, which is sensitive to hormones. To remedy this, make a vertical wound on one side of the cutting with a grafting knife, lift or remove the flap of bark, and treat only the exposed stem with hormone powder. Roots will grow from the callus tissue around the wound.

Try rooting roses. Heirloom, English, miniature, and many modern roses are good candidates for cuttings because they grow well on their own roots and don't necessarily need grafting. Between bloom cycles, take 3-inch

ROOTING CUTTINGS, STEP BY STEP

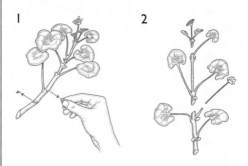

1. Take a healthy stem and remove large, older leaves.

2. Cut the stem into 3-inch (8-cm) sections, making sure that each section has a leaf joint (node) and two or three leaves. Remove any flowers or buds.

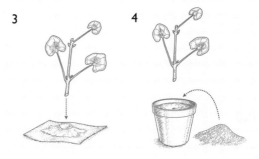

3. Dip the base of each cutting into rooting powder and shake off the excess.

4. Plant in moist seed-starting mix or other medium, pressing gently to make sure there are no air pockets around the stem.

(8 cm) cuttings from new growth, keeping four leaflets intact. They will root in a few weeks when kept warm and moist.

Three Ways to Layer

One of the most fascinating—and easy—ways to propagate plants is by layering. Layering involves burying a stem in soil to induce it to root while it's still attached to the parent plant. Layering is usually slower than rooting stem cuttings, but it's much more dependable.

The three ways to layer—simple layering, mound layering, and air layering—have in common one crucial step. To get a stem to develop roots where you want them, you must distress it, which activates the plant's survival instincts. It's a good idea to dust a little rooting powder on the wounded section of the stem before covering it up.

Simple layering: All you have to do is bend down a long stem so that a section can be buried 2 inches (5 cm) below the ground. First, pinch off leaves in the buried section of stem and distress it near a node. Hold the buried section of stem in place with a stone or wire pin. Stems set to layer in spring are usually ready to dig and move by late summer, or you can wait until the following spring. It works especially well with vines; raspberries; forsythias; climbing or rambling roses; and herbs, including Rosemary, tarragon, and thyme.

Mound layering: This method is particularly effective with groundcovers, shrubs, and scented geraniums. Before growth begins in spring, cut down all stems to a few inches above the ground to force out new basal shoots. When the shoots reach 6 inches (15 cm) tall, cover them 3 inches (8 cm) deep with a mound of damp compost or peat moss so the base of the plant senses that it is underground. After six weeks or so, remove the mound and clip off the stems you want to root near the soil line. Then handle them like rooted cuttings, because they will have root buds.

Air layering: If you can't bring the stem to the soil, bring soil to the stem with air layering. This method is often used to propagate sheffleras, philodendrons, and other upright houseplants, but you also can use it with outdoor plants. Make a slit on a branch between 6 and 18 inches (15 and 46 cm) from the tip and insert a matchstick to hold it open. Wrap a wad of moist sphagnum moss around the wound and cover with aluminum foil. Cover that with a plastic sleeve and tie the ends tightly. Check occasionally to see if the moss is still moist and whether roots have formed, which can take several months. Once roots are visible, cut the stem and treat it like a halfway-rooted cutting.

Root shrubs in shade. Cuttings from some shrubs, such as buddleias and roses, can be rooted in the shade of larger plants that get regular irrigation. Protect the cuttings with upturned glass jars, removing the jars when watering.

Include a little heel. Cuttings that include a small heel from where the stem attached to a larger stem often root better than those taken from the tips—especially with woody plants, such as lavender or evergreen shrubs.

Propagate in water. The stems of some houseplants and even tomatoes will root in a glass of water. Cover the filled glass or a narrow-necked bottle with a piece of aluminum foil and push the cuttings gently through, making sure that any leaves remain above the foil. Keep the water topped up and replace it completely if it turns green. When roots are more than 1 inch (3 cm) long, pot the cuttings in moist potting mix. Cuttings left in water too long can be slow to adapt to soil.

Need to travel with cuttings? If you must transport unrooted cuttings, enclose them in a plastic bag with a bit of moist paper towel or newspaper. Better still, keep them fresh in an ice chest or a Thermos with a few ice cubes. If you have access to a refrigerator when you stop for the night, place the cuttings inside—but don't forget them!

Make your own container to transport cuttings. Cut off the top of a plastic jug or soft-drink bottle and place moist sphagnum moss or florist's oasis inside, then insert the cuttings into the damp material.

✿ Buying Plants

WITH TENS OF THOUSANDS OF PLANTS to choose from, finding the best new plants for your garden can be a challenge. Instead of using the trial-and-error method, use the strategies here to become a smart plant shopper.

NURSERIES AND GARDEN CENTERS

Shop locally. Make friends with a local nursery, because local growers are invaluable sources of information on plants and problems specific to your area. The best nurseries provide not only plants but also sound advice from experts, whose livelihoods depend on raising quality plants that thrive in local conditions.

Be an early bird. Find out what day the nursery receives new plants from wholesale growers; it's often Thursday or Friday, in preparation for the weekend rush. Shop on these days to get a better choice of plants.

Buy in bulk. Discounts are often available on quantities of the same plant. If you're planning a large installation, such as a hedge, buy the plants all at once instead of over time. You may get a discount, and you'll be assured that all the plants will match.

Seek out specialists. Besides large-scale general nurseries that stock everything from marigolds to magnolias, shop at specialty growers who restrict their business to a few types of plants, such as daylilies, roses, or fruit trees. They're more likely to grow outstanding, rare varieties that you won't find elsewhere.

Purchase special services. Many nurseries offer landscape services as well as plants. You may want to buy a large specimen tree, for example, but need help getting it into the ground. Many nurseries have the special equipment needed to make big planting projects a success.

Check guarantees. Policies on replacing failed plants vary among nurseries, so ask before you buy. Some growers will replace a plant for free, while others charge a percentage of the plant's cost; there's usually a time limit—perhaps six months or a year. Always retain receipts to validate your purchases, especially when buying costly plants. And be prepared to explain why your plant died; if you didn't care for it properly, the nursery isn't responsible.

Inspect plants and ask questions. Examine plants carefully for any signs of pests, disease, or weakness. Ask growers how the specimens were propagated and raised and what conditions they will require. If the height and spread isn't given on a plant tag, ask about the plant's mature size.

A pretty little shrub pruned back in a nursery display may grow into a monster.

Buy flowers before they bloom. Potted lilies covered with flowers are beautiful, but they will finish blooming in a few weeks, and you'll have to wait a year for more flowers. Perennials, flowering shrubs, and even orchids are best purchased in bud, before they bloom. However, if you want a special color in an azalea or crepe myrtle, purchasing a blooming plant is the only way that you can be certain you're getting what you want.

Check the roots. A plant's roots are a good guide to the plant's health and age. Pull the plant gently from the pot and inspect the roots; they should be healthy, vigorous, and evenly distributed through the soil. If they're thickly coiled in the bottom of the pot or are poking out of the drainage hole, the plant is potbound and has been in the container too long. Such roots usually have difficulty growing out when transplanted into garden soil.

Set them free. Once you return home with your new purchases, unpack the plants promptly and make them comfortable. Place them in the shade and let them get air; water them if necessary. If you can't plant them right away, place them in a sheltered spot and keep them moist. Sink larger container-grown plants into the soil, pot and all. The roots will stay cool, and the plants will need less water. On cool nights, set tender plants in a warm cellar or garage.

BOTANICAL NAMES

Common names for trees, shrubs, and flowers vary from region to region. Only the botanical or variety name ensures that you're getting exactly the plant you're looking for.

Demystify plant names. Because they're a combination of Greek, Latin, and other

LATIN TRANSLATIONS

The words found in plant names often describe a plant trait. Knowing what these terms mean helps you understand botanical nomenclature and makes it easier to visualize a particular plant.

WORD	MEANING
alba	white
aurea	golden foliage
contorta	twisted
edulis	edible
elata	tall
grandiflora	large-flowered
grandifolia	large-leafed
japonica	from Japan
lutea	yellow
maculata	spotted
nana	dwarf
occidentalis	from the West
odorata	scented
orientalis	from the East
pendula	weeping
purpurea	purple
repens	creeping
rugosa	wrinkled
scandens	climbing
sempervirens	evergreen
spicata	flowers in spikes
stricta	upright
sylvestris	from the woods
tomentosa	downy

languages, botanical names may take some getting used to, but they are the best means of precisely identifying plants. A plant's scientific name has several main parts.

- **Genus** name is first, indicating the plant group. It is written with an initial capital letter and is often in italic type, as in *Primula*.

- **Species** name is next. It is the name of a specific plant within a genus group and doesn't begin with a capital letter, as in *Primula japonica*.

- **Cultivar** name may follow the genus and species names. This name starts with a capital letter and is usually in Roman type and single quotation marks. For example, the full name of the white-crested iris is *Iris cristata* 'Alba', while the pyramidal Chinese juniper is *Juniperus chinensis* 'Pyramidalis'.

- **x** in the middle of a name means the plant is the result of a cross between species.

The surname of the person who discovered a plant is often used for the species name and given a Latin suffix indicating possession: *-ii* or *-i* for a man and *-ae* for a woman. For example, *Prunus sargentii*, or Sargent's cherry, was named for dendrologist C. S. Sargent. *Phlox henryae*, or Henry phlox, was named for botanist Mary Gibson Henry.

Plants' special characteristics can also become part of their names. The endings *-issimus, -issima,* and *-issimum* indicate the superlative degree and are used in species names to describe a particular attribute. *Lonicera fragrantissima* (winter honeysuckle), for example, is exceptionally fragrant, while *Salix* x *elegantissima* (Thurlow weeping willow) is one of the most graceful specimens.

The names of places are often part of a plant's botanical name. The China rose, for instance, is *Rosa chinensis*, while the Siberian iris is *Iris sibirica*.

GARDEN
STRUCTURES

Plants make the garden, but manmade structures of all kinds make a garden more livable and enjoyable. From flower-covered garden walls to cool, shaded patios with romantic lighting, the things you build in a garden help define the space and open up new ways to enjoy it. To decide what kinds of structures your garden needs, simply imagine the ways you want to use your outdoor space. If you're a passionate plant person at heart, a sturdy cold frame will serve you better than a nicely outfitted barbecue area that serves as an outdoor kitchen. Yet the latter—along with comfortable outdoor furniture—is a reasonable priority if you love to entertain. Gardeners who long for more privacy can have their desires fulfilled with the help of a fence or wall.

Easy access is important in any landscape, and some plants will not flourish without good support, so we'll begin with fences, walkways, and other must-haves that often turn up on gardeners' wish lists. Throughout this section, you'll find hundreds of tips that will help you start off on the right foot with every garden construction project you undertake, whether it's a cold frame for seedlings or a soothing fountain for an out-of-the-way corner.

❧ Trellises and Arbors

WHEN VINES and other flexible plants are trained to grow on trellises and arbors, they gain a great deal in stature and add to the subtle complexity of your garden.

TRELLISES

A light trellis or lattice can provide a framework for climbing plants and reduce the effects of wind. Or try transforming a blank wall into a vertical garden with a trellis covered by climbers. You can select traditional latticework panels, a fan shape, or a sculptural trellis, or you can just use your own imagination to make an original, one-of-a-kind plant support.

Choose wisely. Redwood, cypress, and cedar trellises are rot resistant, will age to gray, and don't require painting. Iron and steel trellises that have a rustproof finish are good for heavy plants. For low maintenance, try plastic, fiberglass, or enameled aluminum trellises in white, green, or brown. In the vegetable garden, use a net or wire trellis to support pole beans and other climbers.

One size fits all. An expandable plastic trellis with riveted joints can be contracted or stretched, like an accordion, to fit any space. If you have an old baby gate in the attic, get it out and use it as a trellis.

Not just for walls. A freestanding trellis can be erected anywhere as long as it's attached to sturdy legs that extend 1 to 1½ feet (30 to 45 cm) into the ground. At home supply stores, plastic lattice panels are available with matching grooved molding that makes them easy to frame and attach to posts.

Create a curtain of bamboo. Use bamboo poles as a lightweight but sturdy trellis; this looks especially nice in a Japanese-style garden. Secure the poles by crisscrossing waterproof nylon cord over the joints.

Air space. Attach 1×2 (19×38 mm) pine furring strips vertically to a wall before hanging a trellis, which creates a gap between the trellis and the wall. This will give stems some room to grow behind the trellis, let water evaporate from the wall, and increase air circulation around the plants. Attach a trellis to mounting boards with hooks and eyes instead of screws so that if you need to paint or repair the wall, you can easily lift it off.

The right trellis. Make sure your trellis meets the needs of the plants you want to grow. Clinging vines, such as ivy and trumpet vine, don't need a trellis—their stems can adhere to any surface. "Grabbers," such as clematis, have tendrils that need to coil around thin supports. Twining vines like to encircle round poles, and roses need to be tethered to their trellis with strips of soft cloth.

ARBORS AND PERGOLAS

Gardeners have used arches, arbors, and pergolas to add interest and height to gardens since the time of the Romans, whose artwork depicts arches adorned with vines and roses. Now available in either modern materials or traditional wood, these practical ornaments may enhance gardens of any size or design and serve every type of climbing plant. A pergola is an arbor that you walk through or sit beneath. It can be a simple, open frame or a series of arches that create a tunnel effect. A pergola should have a focus—it can be a destination, showcase a view, or create a stopping point along a garden path.

Placement is key. Tucked away in a secluded nook and sheltered by fragrant flowering vines, an arbor becomes a romantic hideaway. It can accent a garden, offer an inviting destination, or command an imposing view. Arbors provide shade in summer and year-round screens to hide garden work areas.

Consider perspective. The arch of a pergola, inviting you to pass underneath, has the effect of dividing a garden in two. If you have a small garden, a pergola may make it seem larger, particularly if you position it so that it hints at wider vistas beyond. On the other hand, a pergola will make a long garden appear shorter.

Choose the right color. In a small garden, choose an arbor pergola with a slim framework or one that's painted green to blend in with the background. In a large garden, you can afford to draw attention to the pergola's structure or color.

Design in proportion to the plantings your arbor will support. Anticipate the size of mature vines and climbers. Delicate latticework can't support mature wisteria, while heavy timbers will dwarf fragile clematis.

Check with a building inspector to make sure you'll be complying with local zoning codes and building regulations before you invest your time and money building any large structure for your plants, whether it's an arbor or a greenhouse.

The best woods for arbors and pergolas are redwood, cedar, cypress, teak, oak, and locust. Pressure-treated lumber is an inexpensive alternative that's useful when lumber must be in contact with soil. It tends to bow and split, however, and doesn't take stain well.

Use rust-resistant fasteners made of brass, bronze, hot-dipped galvanized steel, or stainless steel. If your local hardware store doesn't stock these, try a marine supply store. Always predrill holes for nails, bolts, and screws to avoid splitting the wood.

Use waterproof glue on joints where extra strength is required. Epoxy glues are extremely strong and will accept stain well; they're available at woodworking and marine supply stores.

Paint problems. After a few seasons, paint chips, blisters, and peels, so the structure will need to be scraped, sanded, primed, and repainted. White or green is traditional for arbors, but you may choose to duplicate the color of the trim on your house to create a unifying link between the house and garden. Stains are easier to apply than paint, they protect the wood, and they never blister or peel. For color, pigmented stains are a good substitute for paint and come in a wide assortment of tints.

Pave the area beneath your arbor with brick, flagstone, or gravel if the arbor casts dense shade. Grass can't survive without sunlight.

Add lattice panels to your arbor to serve as trellis screens. Traditional arbor plants include clematis, jasmine, wisteria, climbing roses, ivy, and, of course, grapes—a favorite since the time of ancient Rome. Or hang baskets of flowering plants that add fragrance and splashes of color.

✿ Greenhouses

GARDENERS HAVE USED glass houses to propagate and grow tender plants since the 19th century. These days, a sunroom or attached greenhouse can be a relaxing haven when it's too cold outside to garden. Or, if you just want to grow more plants in your garden, a small greenhouse—or even a cold frame—will provide ideal conditions for starting plants and extending their lives.

PLANNING A GREENHOUSE

A greenhouse is a substantial investment, but to serious gardeners, its benefits are incalculable—including a much longer growing season and the opportunity to raise exotic flowers. A good greenhouse will also soothe your gardening spirit because you will have a vibrantly alive place to work (or play) while you're waiting for spring to come. If you have your heart set on a greenhouse, here are some tips for turning your dream into a reality.

Consider the cost. When designing a greenhouse, take into account not only the price of the structure but also the long-term cost of operation, especially providing heat. A "warm" greenhouse should be kept above 60°F (16°C), while a "cool" greenhouse must always be kept above 45°F (7°C).

Location is key. Site the greenhouse to receive as much sunlight as possible during the winter months. Attached greenhouses should have southern exposure, while a freestanding house's long axis should be oriented north to south. Protect the greenhouse from prevailing winds with a hedge or berm. Also plan for easy access to water.

For winter warmth, instead of heating the entire greenhouse, create an alcove in one corner for your most tender plants. Block off the space by hanging sheets of plastic and keep the area warm with a small, thermostatically controlled electric heater.

Go with the flow. A greenhouse needs ventilation to let stale air escape and fresh air circulate. To provide proper airflow, install at least one vent in each side of the roof and each side wall. Open the vents in the morning when the temperature is rising and then close them in the afternoon to conserve heat. Crack the vents even on windy or cold days.

Eliminate guesswork in regulating airflow by installing automatic vent openers. Activated by a thermostat, they constantly adjust the ventilation when cloud cover or other factors cause temperature fluctuations.

Summer shade. To keep a greenhouse from becoming unbearable in hot months, block the sunlight with blinds or fabric shades, which can be rolled into place with pulleys. You can also shade a greenhouse by planting deciduous trees nearby. Locate them on the south side, far enough away that falling leaves and branches won't land on the greenhouse. Or train vines, such as clematis or morning glory, to climb tall trellises that will cool the greenhouse with their shade.

For maximum convenience, use tables, or "benches," about 30 inches (75 cm) high and 3 feet (1 meter) wide, so you can work without bending over and comfortably reach to the far side of the tabletop. Store pots, soil, tools, hoses, and similar items underneath the benches to keep walkways uncluttered.

Organize your plants according to their needs. Keep plants with fuzzy foliage, which

BUILD A SEASON-STRETCHING COLD FRAME

Often nothing more than a simple wooden box with the bottom removed and a translucent top, a cold frame is an invaluable tool for starting seedlings or hardening off young plants. You can often construct a cold frame from salvaged materials, such as old bricks or scrap boards for the frame and a discarded window frame for the top.

A slanted lid or roof made of glass, fiberglass, or plastic will keep seedlings warm, and rain and snow will slide off. In winter, top a cold frame with an old blanket on chilly nights to keep out cold. On warm spring days, open the top to vent hot air.

Place the frame flat on the ground on well-drained soil. If you want to plant directly into it, layer coarse sand or gravel on the bottom and top this with at least 6 inches (15 cm) of good planting soil. Container-grown plants can be nestled down into the soil, too.

In summer, substitute a shade cover for the clear or opaque top and use your cold frame as a propagation bed. Light fabric, such as sheer curtains, draped over the top will filter out hot sun. For a neat look, glue a triangular piece of Velcro to each corner of the frame and sew matching pieces onto the fabric so that the covering fits snugly.

should be kept dry, away from those that like to be misted. Place sun lovers on the south side of the greenhouse and shade lovers on the north. Make sure no leaves are touching the sides of the greenhouse in winter.

Summer cleaning. The greenhouse is often sparsely populated in summertime, so that's the best time to give it a thorough cleaning. Wash all surfaces with detergent and disinfectant to combat insects and diseases. (Keep these chemicals away from plants.) Use an algicide if slime has accumulated on the floor and benches.

Good housekeeping in the summer includes routine greenhouse maintenance. Check the glass for damage; you can repair cracks temporarily with glazing tape, but broken panes should be replaced as soon as possible. Clean out gutters and downspouts. Repair any rusted metal or flaking paint on the frame.

Prepare plants for overwintering in a greenhouse about six weeks before you move them in. Clean up damaged stems and foliage, pot up transplants, and treat the plants for pests and diseases, which can spread rapidly in the confines of a greenhouse.

Keep it clean. To head off an epidemic, follow strict sanitary procedures. Use sterilized soil; containers made of plastic, metal, or glass; and tools reserved just for the greenhouse. Inspect plants regularly for pests and diseases, and isolate any problem specimens.

Walkways and Steps

PATHS AND STEPS make your garden more accessible, and they can enrich your landscape with their texture and lines. But to be effective, they need to be thoughtfully sited and well constructed. Consider how a path will be used when selecting your materials. A high-traffic connection between the house and driveway, for example, calls for a stone or brick path. A little-used woodland walk might be covered with pine needles or moss.

PLANNING A PATH

Straight or sinuous? A linear path looks formal and is best used in structured gardens, perhaps running between double borders or raised beds. A curved path works well in naturalistic settings, such as cottage or woodland gardens.

Plant Dutch white clover between the rows in a vegetable garden to create resilient paths. When the clover is tilled under at season's end, it will add valuable nitrogen to the soil.

Grass paths are elegant, if high-maintenance, choices in regions with sufficient rainfall. They can make a small yard appear larger by extending the lawn into the garden.

Beautify with blooms. Soften the edges of paths by lining them with colorful borders of flowers. Select low-maintenance, mounding or sprawling plants of medium height. Good choices include lavender, cranesbill, aubrieta, baby's breath, candytuft, coral bells, fringed bleeding heart, and astilbe.

No artificial lighting? Line a path with large white stones, which will seem to glow at twilight or in moonlight. During the growing season, plant edgings of white or pastel flowers.

Old bricks may look charming, but don't count on them for solid support or durable paving. They may be susceptible to splitting, chipping, and cracking. If you're lucky enough to find a trove of attractive old bricks, use them purely for decorative rather than structural purposes.

CREATING A PAVED PATHWAY

You can install paving stones or brick pavers on a bed of mortar or sand. Mortar is best for holding small, light, or irregularly shaped materials. It's also good if you have clay or sticky soil or live in a climate where frost heaves are common. Sand is a good choice in mild climates and for holding large, heavy materials.

Is it on the level? Don't just "eyeball" the installation of paving stones—mark off straight

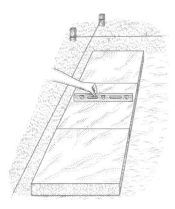

edges with stakes and string, and begin on a straight edge. Always use a level when preparing the base and setting the stones.

Make a base. Prepare the site properly before setting paving materials in place. Excavate about 6 inches (15 cm) into the soil and tamp the ground absolutely flat; be sure to slant the surface slightly away from any buildings to allow for water runoff. Then lay down 3 to 4 inches (8 to 10 cm) of gravel or crushed rock and top this with a 2-inch (5-cm) layer of sand.

To set stones in sand, either butt them together or space them ½ inch (13 mm) apart on all sides. Pour sand on top and work it well into the cracks with a broom; apply water to the joints to settle the sand. Once the stones are dry, add more sand and sweep until the cracks are filled, then apply water again. The more sand is packed into the joints, the tighter the hold will be. Interlocking pavers should be tapped together to ensure tight, uniform spacing.

To set stones in mortar, spread strips of mortar over the base where the stones will sit. Place the stones, leaving ½ inch (13 mm) of space between them; use premade spacers to ensure evenness. Tamp the stones into the mortar and check for levelness, then fill the joints with more mortar, removing the spacers

PAVING YOUR WAY

A simple walkway of paving stones is a garden staple. Here are some tips to ensure that your path is as durable as it is attractive. Paving materials include brick, flagstone, cobblestone, concrete or clay pavers, and more costly, cut granite. Select a surface that harmonizes with your garden while providing the durability you need.

The wet test. Spray a paving stone with water before buying. You can test its slipperiness and see how it looks when wet.

Uneven surfaces, like those formed with cobblestones, are attractively rustic but hard on the feet. For high-traffic areas, choose a smooth, level surface, such as brick, pavers, or flagstone.

Consider drainage. Rainwater sheets off a mortared walkway, and it needs somewhere to go. Open paving, in which the crevices between pavers are filled with sand, is usually self-draining.

COMMONSENSE STEPPING STONES

Reduce wear and tear in heavily trafficked areas of your lawn, grass path, or garden by laying a few flat paving stones at one-step intervals. Set them deep enough that a mower can pass over them easily.

Plan a stepping-stone path by walking along the path with normal strides and marking your footfalls with sand or sticks. Lay the stones in place and walk across them to double-check the spacing, before setting them permanently.

Lay a stone carpet. Place stepping stones in flowerbeds to keep your feet clean and dry and minimize soil compaction when you're working in the garden.

Tuck plants in among the stones and turn a stepping-stone or gravel path into a miniature flowerbed. Use ground-hugging specimens that will appreciate the radiant heat and fill in quickly, such as aubrieta, alyssum, thyme, bellflower, creeping phlox, and ajuga.

before it hardens. Smooth and recess the joints slightly by running the rounded end of a stick or paintbrush over them. Remove any excess mortar from the stone surface.

A green alternative. Instead of using sand or mortar, fill the spaces between the stones with a one-to-one mix of sand and compost. Plant with pearlwort, moss, mother-of-thyme, or other low-growing groundcovers for an attractive "joint" that won't need mowing.

SAFE, ATTRACTIVE STEPS

Steps connect the levels of your garden and yard and can be beautiful design elements of their own—yet safety should always be a primary concern. From choosing materials that feel safe underfoot to using the proper dimensions, good steps deserve careful planning.

Rock solid. Stone steps with naturally rough surfaces offer maximum traction. If your garden receives full sunlight all winter, make your steps of dark stone, which will absorb heat to melt ice or snow. Keep in mind, though, that these stones will be hot in summer.

Buying brick? Bricks come in different sizes and shapes and offer a wide choice of step designs. Arrange bricks on firm ground on a bed of coarse sand.

Easy risers. Railroad ties or landscape timbers made from rot-resistant or treated wood make excellent risers for steps. They can be sawed into two or three pieces as needed.

Economical steps can be cut directly into the soil. Pack the earth thoroughly and face the risers with stone or sawn log disks to stabilize the soil. Cover the treads with crushed gravel.

Slippery when wet. Logs, smooth stones, and slates are poor choices for steps because they can become slick in rain or snow.

Make the grade. On steep slopes, lay out steps so they zigzag up the hill; steps can be tiring and even dangerous if they're too steep.

The right height. The proper proportion of tread (flat surface) to riser (the vertical) is simply stated: Twice the height of the riser plus the width of the tread should equal 26 inches (66 cm). Using this formula, a 4-inch (10-cm) riser calls for an 18-inch (46-cm) tread; a 5-inch (13-cm) riser needs a 16-inch (40-cm) tread; and a 6-inch (15-cm) riser needs a 14-inch (36-cm) tread. The steepest practical step is an 8-inch (20-cm) riser with a 10-inch (26-cm) tread.

Grow a green staircase. Use honeycombed concrete paving stones on the treads and fill in the spaces with soil. Then plant creeping thyme, bentgrass, creeping phlox, or moss to add beauty and stability to the steps. Maintain the plants by hand trimming. You can find or create pockets of earth on other types of steps, allowing you to plant perennial flowers, such as periwinkles, saxifrage, cranesbills, or lavender for a unique, multilevel rock garden.

Start at the bottom when you are building steps, so each tread can rest upon the riser of the step beneath it.

Soften the edges of stairways that appear too wide by planting fast-growing, sprawling plants along the edges. Ivy, lavender, nasturtiums, and other plants with attractive foliage and blossoms are good choices. Blooming vines, such as clematis, wisteria, and honeysuckle can be trained to grow along treads and handrails.

Gentle landings. If your slope is gradual, plan for landings every seven or eight steps. They should be at least three times the width of the treads.

Build a handy ramp. Lay a 2×10 (38×235 mm) piece of lumber along the tops of shallow steps to create a ramp for a wheelbarrow.

USING SPECIMEN STONES

Unusual, eye-catching stones make lovely natural ornaments. Select a few for their unique size, shape, or color and place them among plants or alongside a bench or path.

- A row of fieldstones makes attractive—and effective—bed edging.
- Install flat stones in beds to stand on when watering, weeding, or spraying.
- Instead of trying to move big stones, use them as natural centerpieces for creeping, sprawling, or trailing plants.
- Create a standing stone by digging a shallow hole and planting the bottom third of a large upright stone. Fill in around it with plants.
- Prevent weeds and mower damage by putting attractive stones on top of a layer of landscape cloth around the base of a favorite tree.

🌿 Garden Enclosures

THERE ARE MANY REASONS to enclose a garden—and many ways to do it. Fences and walls can block an unsightly view, create shelter from the prevailing winds, or simply preserve your privacy. Whichever method or materials you choose, you can find an attractive way to protect your garden sanctuary from the outside world.

The most popular choice is a fence, or you can build a wall or plant a hedge. Use the information in "Fences, Walls, or Hedges: Weighing Your Options" opposite and the tips that follow to help you decide.

FENCES

In addition to defining a boundary, a fence can buffer wind and provide support for climbing plants. Because a fence is permanent, choose materials and a style that harmonize with your garden and house. Consider the initial and lifetime repair costs as well as maintenance requirements.

Work with a helper. Erecting a fence takes two people. It's not that fence panels are particularly heavy, but they have to be held upright while they're fixed in place, and one of you needs to keep checking the level. Choose a calm day to work, since solid panels are difficult to handle in the wind.

The right look. Informal gardens are the right settings for rustic styles, such as a post-and-rail, picket, or split-rail fence. Formal gardens look better with board, post-and-board, or iron fences.

A handmade border. Make a low waffle fence to separate different beds in your landscape, or make a higher version as a privacy

panel. Insert sturdy wood stakes every 6 to 12 inches (15 to 30 cm) and interlace the uprights with pliable vines or willow stems to create a lattice. The result is a charming, handmade fence.

Sloping ground? A fence that follows the terrain will complement a naturalistic garden. Fencing in a stair-step style creates a more formal look. If you decide on a stairstep-style fence, you'll need to level the grade between posts and fill in the open spaces between the bottom rails and the ground.

Go for quality. A fence is a long-term investment. Select durable, rot-resistant wood that will weather the elements—especially for the posts. Wise choices include cypress, red or white cedar, redwood, and pressure-treated pine. For other components, you can use a less durable wood, such as spruce, hemlock, or fir. You can buy ready-made fencing panels, but beware of using thin panels that are likely to blow over in the first gust of wind. In addition to wood, vinyl fence panels that look like wood are widely available.

Easy digging. Use a posthole digger to scoop out deep, narrow holes without disturbing the surrounding soil. Or use a soil auger, which bores neat holes with little effort. Set posts 1½ to 2 feet (45 to 60 cm) deep. In cold climates, dig 3 feet (1 meter) deep to get below the frost line.

Anchor the posts. Use metal spear connectors, available at home supply stores, to solidify fence posts. These spears can be easily driven into the ground with a sledgehammer before the post is attached. However, they'll be sturdier if sunk in concrete.

Cutting your own pickets? Clamp several pickets together in a bench vise and saw through them all at once to save time and assure consistent length. But before going to the trouble of cutting your own, check out precut pickets—

FENCES, WALLS, OR HEDGES: WEIGHING YOUR OPTIONS

Open Fence

MATERIALS	EXPENSE	SPACE NEEDED	ADVANTAGES	DISADVANTAGES
Wood or wire	Moderate	Little ground space needed	Easy to erect, lets in air and sunlight; simple designs won't compete with other garden features; can be decorated with climbers or other plantings	Requires some maintenance

Solid Wall

MATERIALS	EXPENSE	SPACE NEEDED	ADVANTAGES	DISADVANTAGES
Brick, stone or cement	Moderate to expensive	Takes up ground space	Adds structure and presence in the landscape; provides permanent backdrop for self-clinging climbers and other plantings; retains heat well for plants that need warmth.	Relatively difficult and time-consuming to erect

Hedge

MATERIALS	EXPENSE	SPACE NEEDED	ADVANTAGES	DISADVANTAGES
Perennial shrubs	Fairly inexpensive	Takes up ground space	Creates an attractive, all-natural "living fence," especially if flowering plants are used; provides shelter for wildlife	Takes time for plantings to establish, requires pruning and regular maintenance

and preassembled panels—which are widely available at home supply stores.

Rotted board ends? Saw off the damaged portions and attach a 2×4 (38×89 mm) horizontally at the base of the posts. To prevent future problems, set the replacement 1 inch (25 mm) above ground level so air can circulate freely.

Properly space your fence by using a spare picket as a spacer to ensure consistent gaps when you're assembling a picket fence.

Trim post tops to a point, slant, or dome to shed water, or buy protective post caps, sold at hardware and home stores.

Prevent rot by coating individual wood pieces with a preservative, stain, or paint before assembling the fence, so all the surfaces will be covered. Check the fence at least once a year to see if it needs touchups, repair, or recoating, which should be done before the bare wood is exposed to the elements.

Don't go cheap on chain link. Select sturdy iron or heavy-gauge galvanized chain link. Plastic coating increases a metal fence's longevity; choose green to help it blend with the surroundings or black if the fence will be located in a shady area.

Make a fence disappear. Let a hedge or climbers grow through a chain-link fence to help it fade into the landscape. To reduce weed-trimming chores, plant daylilies or other vigorous perennials at the base.

GARDEN ON A WALL

The face and top of a dry stone wall are perfect spots to site trailing or climbing specimens, such as sweet peas or creeping phlox, which will cascade prettily down the sides. Be aware of the microclimate around a wall when selecting plants. The leeward side receives less rain than the windward side and is subject to downdrafts as wind is forced over the solid wall surface. A sunny, south-facing wall is good for heat-loving plants, while the north side is better for those that prefer a cool environment.

Start from seed. Enclose a seed inside a small ball of moist soil and pack it into a crevice between the stones. Add more soil if possible and keep the seed moist by spritzing it with water until it germinates and establishes roots. Spray the seedling with liquid fertilizer diluted by half, but don't force growth too quickly.

Transplant into pockets. Add some soil to pockets or gaps in a stone wall, then use a chopstick to tuck in a plant's roots, dividing them as needed for fit. Cover the roots with more soil mixed with sphagnum moss.

Use the heat. In cooler northern regions or at higher altitudes, plant vegetables on a south-facing slope in front of a wide, low wall and spread the vines and stems over the wall. Plants that appreciate this extra warmth include tomatoes, zucchini, melons, and pumpkins.

Avoid rust. Use galvanized or brass nails or screws as fasteners for your fence to prevent rust that will stain the wood.

Coat costly cast-iron fencing with rust-inhibiting paint before setting it up, then repaint every three years. Watch for chipping or flaking that will leave metal exposed.

GARDEN WALLS

Whether you need to mark a boundary, highlight a border, or hold back a slope, a wall adds structure and texture to the garden. Select a material that fits your style and budget. While you can build a wall yourself, hire a professional if you want a wall over 3 feet (1 meter) high or if you don't want to deal with mortar. Also, check with your local building inspector to see if there are restrictions on wall size and location in your area.

Shop locally for stone. When building a wall, look for a type of stone you like that is locally available in good supply. Chances are good that once the wall is built, you will want to add other stone features to your landscape. They should match the type of stone in your wall.

Buy faced stone, which is flat on two sides for easy stacking. You won't need to cut or shape the stone—simply sort through the pile to locate the best stone for each place in your wall.

Prepare a good foundation. Stacked stone requires a nearly level foundation that tilts slightly backward toward the slope. A foundation

CHOOSING WALL MATERIALS

• **Dry stone** is the most popular type of wall-building material. All you need is stone, a few tools, patience, and a strong back to build this mortarless wall.

• **Concrete blocks** are relatively inexpensive and easy to work with, but they're heavy and look utilitarian. You can dress up the sides of a concrete block wall with paint or stucco and cap the top with terra-cotta roof tiles.

• **Landscaping blocks** are as easy to lay as concrete blocks, but they're much more attractive and much more suitable if you want to build a wall that curves.

• **Bricks** are available in numerous colors, shapes, and textures and offer a tidy, formal look. Use ordinary bricks where they won't be seen and "facing" bricks for visible surfaces.

• **Landscape (railroad) ties** are a good, economical choice for low retaining walls and raised beds. Two strong people can easily position them; secure them in place with rebar stakes.

for a brick wall must be absolutely level. Cut the foundation into the soil with a spade, then use a thin layer of crushed stone to sculpt the foundation into perfect condition.

Bricklaying is an art. If you want to tackle a brick wall yourself, be sure to keep it level and plumb—check often with a string guide, level, and bob. If you set a brick too high, tap it into the mortar with the trowel handle. If a brick isn't plumb, remove it, scrape it off, and reset it—don't wiggle it around in the mortar.

For a professional finish, use a pointing trowel to bevel the mortar on a brick wall while it's still moist. Give horizontal joints a slight downward slope so they shed water.

Help water drain from a retaining wall built of landscape ties by drilling "weep holes" into the ties with an extension bit. Or lay a piece of perforated drainage pipe behind the wall before backfilling with soil, and position the pipe's outlet where the water can do no harm.

Tone it down. If you cover a cement-block wall with white masonry paint, keep in mind that it will radiate heat and cause intense glare. Cool it down by planting a climbing vine at the base. English ivy and climbing hydrangea will adhere to the wall; install a trellis for twining vines, such as clematis.

Batter up. The slight backward slope of a wall, called the batter, helps the wall withstand pressure from the earth behind it. Slant the wall 1 inch (3 cm) for every 1 foot (30 cm) of height. Check the angle with a wooden "batter frame" and a plumb bob.

Clever cover-up. Conceal an unsightly wall by turning it into a shelter for stacks of firewood. Add a small lean-to with a tile roof to protect the logs from rain.

❧ Decks, Patios, and Porches

FOR READING, GRILLING, summer socializing, and long afternoon naps, a deck, patio, or porch is the place to be. Here are some tips to help you fashion a beautiful and functional hub for outdoor living. A deck or patio creates an exterior living space that links your house and garden. Select a uniform style for the floor, furniture, planting containers, and plants that will harmonize with the overall look of your property. The main difference between a deck, a patio, and a porch is that a porch has a protective roof. Porches, therefore, can be furnished more elaborately (and comfortably) than decks or patios.

PLANNING A PATIO OR DECK

The right place. Build your deck or patio on the quiet side of the house and out of your neighbors' view. Site it for convenient access from the house; you don't want guests marching through the bedroom on their way to the barbecue.

Check local building codes. In some cities or neighborhoods, you may need a permit to attach a deck to your house.

Build around a tree to create a deck or patio with cool shade during the summer months. Shady patios are much more pleasant to use on hot summer days, and the tree can offer shelter from sudden downpours.

Can't decide? One of the reasons decks are so popular is that they're simple to build. Also, wood is much more forgiving than concrete and asphalt and remains relatively cool for bare feet through the hot months. Composite decking planks, made from plastic and sawdust, cost more than regular wood, but they resist weather and never need painting or staining.

Stain, don't paint! Paints blister and peel over time and need scraping, priming, and repainting. Stains require less maintenance, and they penetrate the wood to create a soft patina that enhances the natural grain. Many have an acrylic latex base that allows for easy cleanup with soap and water.

Plan for lighting. Make your patio or deck livable after sunset by installing general and accent lighting. Use brighter lights for dining and seating areas and dimmer ones to outline patio edges and adjoining paths. You may wish to install sound speakers as well.

South-facing patios may need shade for comfort in high summer. Install a living umbrella by planting a pretty shade tree just outside the south or west edge of your patio. Select a variety that has a tall trunk, high branches, and deep roots that won't eventually raise the paving materials. In hot climates, consider installing a pergola over part of the patio.

Consider the wind. A trellis around the deck will help block harsh winds. Fill it with an attractive climber, such as morning glory, clematis, or jasmine.

Eliminate weeds. If weeds pop up between patio pavers, stones, or bricks, kill them with boiling water instead of herbicide. The scalding heat will get rid of dandelions, crabgrass, clover, plantain, and other unwelcome visitors.

Built-in seating space. On small patios with little room for freestanding furniture, build a low wall around the perimeter. Top it with flat, smooth stones or bricks, and removable cushions.

Light the grill. Most patios and decks would be incomplete without a barbecue. Be sure to locate the grill on a level surface and far enough from your house so that flying embers won't cause damage.

DECK AND PATIO PLANTINGS

Plant in levels. Place some pots and planting boxes on the floor and plant them with low-growing, mounding plants that look good when viewed from above. Use mounting brackets to secure window boxes to deck railings. Hang baskets at standing eye level so the entire area has a strong sense of height.

Grow a natural screen. If you need privacy or shelter from the wind, edge the patio or deck with tall shrubs or use tall ornamental grasses, which remain attractive through winter. For privacy on a busy street, use lattice panels planted with quick-growing vines.

Soften the edges. Surround your deck or patio with small shrubs to minimize hard edges while preserving the view. Fragrant plants are especially welcome, but avoid those that have prickly leaves or thorns.

Create a garden amphitheater. If your patio is sunken or at the bottom of a slope, surround it with a terraced garden. Use complementary materials for stairs, paths, and retaining walls, and plant the beds with a variety of trees, shrubs, flowers, and groundcovers.

Minimize mess. Keep plants that drop fruits or seedpods far from a patio or deck. Cherry, mulberry, crabapple, and other fruit will stain the surface and furniture, and nuts, catkins, and other debris will need to be swept up. Limit spills by keeping containers and plants out of high-traffic areas.

Clean stains from your patio. If you do get plant or even nasty rust stains on your concrete patio, here's how to get rid of them. Mix unsweetened lemonade Kool-Aid with hot water. Scrub and the stain should come right out.

PLANTS ON THE PORCH

Whether screened, glassed in, or open to the elements, a porch is the perfect place to sit and enjoy a cool evening, or sip your morning coffee. Coordinating your porch furniture and plants will create a more inviting environment. If you move tropical houseplants outdoors onto your porch in summer, rattan or wicker furniture will create a tropical mood. Sleek contemporary furnishings look more at home with flowerpots filled with brightly colored summer annuals. A partially enclosed porch is usually safe for painted wood furniture.

Allow for air. Both you and your plants will be more comfortable if the porch is well ventilated. Make sure a breeze can move through it, or install an overhead fan to keep the air circulating. Gently moving air from a fan will also discourage mosquitoes because they are weak fliers.

Year-round residents. A few plants that may have trouble in an open garden may grow happily in pots kept on open porches. Try sempervivums and small hardy evergreen shrubs.

Watering the plants on your porch is easy if you take the time to install a spigot nearby. Make sure any rugs and mats on the porch are water resistant.

Give plants a lift. Use tables, tiered plant stands, hanging baskets, and cradle or trough planters to raise plants off the ground. This makes small pots more visible, and many plants appreciate the improved air circulation, especially begonias, African violets, and other humidity-sensitive specimens. Plants raised off concrete surfaces are also less likely to be discovered by slugs.

A vacation for houseplants. A porch affords more protection for houseplants than they would have in the yard. Place small plants on shelves and large ones on the floor, in areas where they will get bright indirect light but little if any direct sun.

PATIO FURNITURE

Nothing beats relaxing on the patio or under a shady tree in a comfortable chair, but your favorite furniture won't be attractive for long if you don't take care of it. Follow these tips for years of service from your outdoor furniture.

Spruce up metal chairs and tables by scraping off rust or chipped paint with sandpaper or a wire brush and smooth the metal with steel wool. Rinse well and let dry before painting. To

BUYING GARDEN FURNITURE

Garden furniture is made from a variety of materials, from bent twigs to wrought iron. Consider the pros and cons of each before making a selection.

Wicker and rattan furniture has a traditional look and modest cost, but it's susceptible to mildew and requires protection from weather and indoor storage in the winter.

Metal is durable but cold to the touch and usually needs cushions. Steel and iron are expensive and can rust; aluminum is rust-free, and cheaper.

Resin is used for inexpensive, lightweight, often stackable furniture. It's casual, available in many colors, and easily cleaned with soap and water.

Wood furniture comes in numerous styles. Weather-resistant hardwood can be left untreated; it's low maintenance and durable but costly. Regular and pressure-treated wood are inexpensive but need regular painting or staining. Tropical hardwoods are another option, if you can be sure the wood is plantation grown and not cut from old-growth forests. Let rot-resistant hardwoods weather to a silvery gray or apply oil or stain annually to maintain their original appearance.

save time, choose a metal paint that doesn't require a primer.

Sponge, don't brush. Painting an intricate metal design can take hours. Speed the process by dabbing on paint with a clean kitchen sponge instead of painting with a brush.

For a perfect match, paint wood furniture with leftover paint from your house. This way, even a ragtag assortment of Adirondack chairs will look like a matched set.

The best fabric for cushions is vinyl-coated polyester, which resists stains, dries quickly, and is easy to clean with soap and water. Treat mildew with a solution of 1 cup (240 ml) each of laundry detergent and bleach mixed with 3 gallons (11 liters) of water. Rinse well and let the cushions dry in the sun.

Maintain the luster of aluminum furniture by applying a coat of liquid wax at the beginning of the season. Wipe it down with soapy water occasionally and remove any stains with a light liquid abrasive.

Revive wicker. If your wicker furniture begins to dry out, refresh it with water. Spray it with a garden hose or moisten towels with warm water, wring them out, and lay them over the pieces for an hour or so.

🌺 Garden Amenities

IT'S THE LITTLE TOUCHES that make a garden distinctive: a lamp placed just so, a fountain burbling in the corner, a sculpture beside a turn in a path. Make the most of your outdoor space by adding a few carefully chosen upgrades.

GARDEN ORNAMENTS

Accessorize your garden as you would your home—the possibilities are limited only by your imagination. In addition to traditional ornaments, such as pots, statuary, birdbaths, and sundials, you might use mirrored globes, wind chimes, abstract sculpture, baskets, whirligigs, grapevine wreaths, or decorative wall plaques.

HIDE YOUR CANS

Don't fret about unsightly garbage cans. Instead, build a handy potting table that doubles as a can enclosure. The sides can be brick, masonry, or treated wood; the top should be weather resistant and big enough to work on—3X5 feet (1X1.5 meters) or so. Use the tabletop to prepare soil mixes and repot plants. The space below provides storage not only for garbage cans but also for pails, peat moss, and other gardening supplies.

Consider style. Match the ornament to the style of your garden. Classical statuary, for example, looks best in a formal garden, while a folk-art whirligig or whimsical birdhouse suits a cottage garden.

A skep—a straw hive once used for bee-keeping—makes an ideal ornament in an herb garden. Make sure it has no opening for bees to enter, or you may find a bee colony living in your garden.

Make an ornament stand out by placing it in front of an evergreen backdrop. Good choices are yew or boxwood hedges, bamboo, small conifers, and ferns.

Pot within a pot. Ornamental urns seldom have drainage holes. To ensure proper drainage for a potted plant inside the urn, put it on an overturned pot or bricks.

GARDEN BENCHES

A bench is the perfect place to sit for a moment and contemplate the beauty of your garden—or just to take a load off your feet. And it needn't be new to deserve a place in the garden: A well-weathered seat that has aged gracefully over the years adds charm to any outdoor space.

Build a bench from a durable material, such as concrete, stone, or iron or from long-lasting and attractive wood, such as cedar, cypress, teak, or oak.

Go for quality in a store-bought bench. Opt for solid joinery (mortise-and-tenon joints pinned with dowels) and brass or bronze fasteners.

Stain for color. If you want to color a wood bench, use high-quality pigmented stain instead of paint. A penetrating stain won't blister and peel the way paint does when exposed to the elements.

Make a rustic bench from half of a fallen tree trunk, a large stump, or slabs of secondhand stone purchased from a demolition company.

For firm footing, place a bench with legs on four flat, secure stones or blocks; this will keep it level and prevent the legs from rotting. Install

pavers, stepping stones, or a swath of gravel in the heavily trodden area just in front of the bench to prevent muddy messes.

Give it flair. Position your bench inside a bower of blooming roses, under an overgrown arched trellis, or beneath an arbor covered with fragrant flowers. Build a bench around a favorite tree to use as a reading spot. Perch a bench on a knoll with a view or tuck it into a quiet niche on your property as a haven for solitude and privacy.

A storage bench with a hinged seat cover that, when lifted, reveals a handy storage bin for small tools, gloves, potting soil, pots, and seed is always a helpful addition.

Sew a fitted cover of heavy canvas or use a large waterproof tarp to protect your bench from ultraviolet rays, harsh weather, falling debris, and tree sap.

LANDSCAPE LIGHTS

Lighting adds drama to a landscape. Illuminating a favorite tree or shrub from below gives a whole new perspective to the garden at night. Small uplights also draw attention to statuary or a fountain, as if your garden were the courtyard of a famous museum.

Low-voltage lighting systems are available at many lighting and home stores. Use 25- to 75-watt bulbs to mark paths, steps, driveways, patio edges, and garden beds. A standard 12-volt system is powered through a transformer plugged into the household current; it's economical, safe, and easy to install. Simply sink the spike ends of the fixtures into the soil and clip the fixture wires to the 12-volt line; you can bury the wires or hide them behind plants.

Go solar. If lighting part of your garden would require the costly installation of special wiring, look for solar-powered kits at home supply stores. Their light output is modest, but they're ideal for remote areas of the yard.

Designing a new garden? Consider full-voltage lighting. The cables can be buried at a safe depth during construction, and you can use outlets for other purposes, such as powering tools or stereo equipment. Make a plan first, then let an electrician handle installation. Take photographs as the work progresses so you'll be able to find the cables if you need to make repairs.

Don't overdo it. While light is needed for safety and beauty, it's nice to leave some areas in shadow for contrast and an air of mystery.

Select inconspicuous fixtures. You want to see the light, not the lamps. Make sure the fixtures have a durable finish to withstand water, fertilizer, cold, and sun.

Match the light to the task. Floods and spots cast strong beams—good for uplighting and silhouetting. Spread lights cast diffuse pools to illuminate walkways or highlight a surface. Motion-activated security lights deter intrusions by people and by raccoons and other nocturnal animals.

Beware the bulb color. The blue undertone in white light attracts insects, while yellow light is less attractive to bugs. Bulbs with a red or pink tone make green plants look dull and lifeless; use a warm gold light instead.

FOUNTAINS

Fountains are cooling and soothing, and in arid climates, they lower the temperature of the surrounding air—a bonus for overheated plants and people. The trickle of a fountain also creates calming background music that can deaden the rumble of traffic and other undesirable noises. Easy-to-assemble kits make it possible to have a fountain in almost any size, from a half barrel to a column of water rising high above a pond.

Fountain types. A fountain can be a free-standing structure, a jet of spray shooting up from a pool, or a wall-mounted spout that runs into a reservoir. In all cases, a pump is necessary to keep water circulating. Kits sold at home stores and garden centers contain all the required equipment, including the fountain nozzle and power cord.

Consider style. For a formal garden, you may want a classic standing fountain. In a naturalistic garden, a small pool with a softly dancing water jet might be best. You can even find nozzles that spray water in various shapes, including tulip, daisy, and mushroom forms.

What kind of pump? Submersible pumps are made for safe, quiet operation underwater. Surface pumps sit aboveground and must be concealed. Choose a pump with a capacity slightly greater than the amount of water flow your fountain requires.

Power safely. Plug an electric pump into a ground-fault circuit interrupter, which may need to be installed by a licensed electrician. The device will shut down power from the outlet to the pump when it senses any problems.

Fountain placement. Make your freestanding fountain a centerpiece by situating it prominently at the intersection of two paths. A wall fountain is less conspicuous; the element of surprise is part of its charm. Place it at the end of a walk or at the side of a patio or courtyard garden.

Simple and soothing. Build your own small Japanese-style fountain in a quiet corner of the garden. Submerge a pump in a stone bowl and use a hidden tube to connect it to a hollow bamboo pole. Add a second bamboo cane that will fill with water and tip to spill its contents gently into the basin. Adjust the pump so the bamboo emits a light trickle.

Keep kids safe. A safety solution for fountains with pool reservoirs is to sink the pool into the ground a few inches below grade level and place a grill over the pool. Conceal it with pretty stones.

Do not disturb. If you add water lilies or other aquatic plants to your fountain basin, keep them away from a submersible pump. Many aquatics have delicate roots that can't tolerate much movement.

BARBECUE GRILLS

Grilling meals for friends is a favorite summertime ritual—the perfect way to show off your garden. Whether you use a portable grill on the deck or patio or build a permanent barbecue from brick or stone, follow these tips for the best experience.

START CHARCOAL WITHOUT LIGHTER FLUID

Punch ½- to ¾-inch (13- to 19-mm) holes around the lower rim of a 2-pound (1 kg) coffee can, then remove both ends of the can. Set the resulting sleeve in the center of the grill and place a layer of crumpled newspaper inside. Fill the rest of the can with charcoal and light the paper through the punched holes. The can will act as a flue to draw flame up through the charcoal. When the coals are aglow, lift the sleeve with tongs and spread the hot coals for grilling.

Choose the right location. Don't put the barbecue so close to the house that smoke wafts through the doors or windows. Set the grill in a quiet corner of the landscape and make it accessible to the kitchen by a level, paved path—that way, it will be easy to transport food and supplies on a butler's table or cart.

Stone gives a rustic look to a barbecue. Sandstone is an excellent choice because it withstands heat well. If you use limestone, basalt, shale, or granite, line the firebox with bricks to protect these vulnerable stones from excess heat.

Don't be stingy when you buy a portable barbecue, but don't buy more than you need. Gas grills with electric ignitions are fast and easy to use, but they are vulnerable to moisture and should be kept in a sheltered spot or protected with a waterproof cover when not in use.

If you use bricks to build a barbecue, make sure they have been fired at a high temperature. Well-fired bricks make a ringing sound when tapped with a hammer.

Add real wood-smoke flavor to food cooked on your gas grill with a handful of green twigs from garden trees or herbs. Toss them onto the fire just before you start barbecuing. Apple, cherry, and hickory twigs work well, and rosemary, sage, tarragon, bay, and thyme clippings add a special flavor.

Keep smoke out of your eyes. Place the grill so it's protected from the prevailing wind, but choose a semipermeable hedge as a windbreak. (A solid fence or wall actually increases air turbulence on the downwind side.) Be sure to keep the grill at a safe distance from anything flammable.

Keep the grate dry. When rainwater mixes with charcoal ashes, it forms lye, a powerful corrosive solution. Keep a charcoal grill covered between uses and dump out ashes every few times you use it. Don't put them in the garden, because they will kill nearby plants.

FIREWOOD

If you're lucky enough to have a woodlot, or even a few isolated hardwoods, on your property, you may be able to gather your own firewood. Downed branches and old trees may provide a steady supply of usable wood for a decorative outdoor fireplace.

Gathering wood. Pick diseased or damaged specimens first when cutting trees for firewood. By removing sick trees, you allow more space for the healthy ones to thrive.

The best firewood comes from hickory, oak, beech, maple, apple, walnut, elm, poplar, and pine. Cut firewood to size between November 1 and Easter. To burn well, the wood should age for at least a year.

Avoid rot. Don't pile firewood against a wall or directly on the ground. Instead, stack it on shipping pallets so air can circulate underneath. Stabilize the pile with a 4×4 (89×89 mm) post driven at least 2 feet (60 cm) into the ground on either end of the stack. Place the largest logs on the bottom and stop stacking at 5 or 6 feet (1.5 or 2 meters). Don't fill the spaces between logs with kindling.

Keep it dry. Cover the woodpile with a weatherproof canvas or plastic tarp. Anchor the tarp on top with a few logs or stones.

Direct deposit it. If you store firewood in the basement of your house, let gravity do the work for you. Instead of lugging it down piece by piece, make a simple ramp or chute for sliding the wood through a ground-level window. Be sure to check logs thoroughly for insects before moving any wood into the house.

Bag it. Store hard-to-stack kindling in paper shopping bags, putting just the number of twigs needed to start a fire into each bag. When it's time to get a blaze going, put the whole bag in the fireplace, top it with well-seasoned split logs, and ignite for a great fire-starter.

SWIMMING POOLS

A pool is a wonderful backyard amenity, but few additions to a home require as high a level of planning and maintenance. Minimize the headaches by researching pool designs carefully and adding the right comfort and safety features. You can complement—or contrast—the style of the pool with that of your house and landscape. A strongly angular pool adds formality, while a freeform, curvilinear pool offers a more relaxed look.

Here to stay. Because a swimming pool is a dominant, permanent feature of your landscape, choose its location with utmost care. For example, in cold climates, you may want to separate the pool from the rest of the yard behind a fence or screen so it won't seem desolate when it's not in use.

Block the wind. Protect a pool from prevailing winds by planting an evergreen screen. Avoid plants that will shed leaves during the season when the pool is in use.

Add amenities. Allow space for lounging furniture as well as a storage area for pool supplies. Shade a sitting area, but not the water, with small trees or an umbrella.

Play it safe. Cover the pool with a tarp or net when it's not being used. The cover should be sturdy enough to support a person without sinking, yet easy to install and remove. Tarps also help prevent water evaporation and heat loss and keep out debris.

Handle a hot spot. Because the water and pool apron radiate heat and light, choose plants that can withstand intense conditions.

No slipping. To prevent accidents, choose a nonskid surface—such as textured concrete—for the apron around the pool. It should be sloped away from the pool so runoff from the surrounding area won't contaminate the water.

Scrub the surface with a stiff brush if it becomes slippery from algae.

Blend poolside plants. Key poolside gardens to the rest of the landscape. For formal settings, arrange stately plants in well-trimmed borders, perhaps with a manicured lawn and straight paths. For an informal look, create a naturalistic garden with native plants in curving beds.

Choose clean companions. Select plant materials that won't drop too many leaves, fruit, or other litter that can get into the pool. Ornamental grasses and evergreen shrubs are good choices. If you insist on "messy" specimens, plant them in containers that can be moved away from the pool when they're ready to shed.

No bees, please. If you don't want to get stung, avoid flowers attractive to bees, such as lamb's ears, cleome, anise hyssop, loosestrife, New England aster, butterfly weed, and baptisia. Also avoid plants with thorns, bristles, or spines, all of which are unfriendly to exposed skin.

Plant Index

General Index